DICHO Y HECHO
SECOND EDITION

DICHO Y HECHO

BEGINNING SPANISH

SECOND EDITION

ALBERT C. DAWSON
University of Richmond

LAILA M. DAWSON
University of Richmond

JOHN WILEY & SONS
New York · Chichester · Brisbane · Toronto · Singapore

ILLUSTRATIONS BY SONIA BENCIVENGA
AND MARY JANE STOKES

Library of Congress Cataloging in Publication Data:

Dawson, Albert C., 1939-
  Dicho y hecho.

  Includes index.
  Summary: An introductory textbook of Spanish emphasiz-
ing four basic skills; speaking, listening, writing,
and reading.
  1. Spanish language—Text-books for foreign speakers—
English. 2. Spanish language—Grammar—1950-
[1. Spanish language—Grammar] I. Dawson, Laila M.,
1943- . II. Bencivenga, Sonia. III. Stokes, Mary
Jane. IV. Title.
PC4112.D35 1985   468.2'421   84-15394
ISBN 0-471-87901-0

Printed in the United States of America

10 9 8 7 6 5 4 3

PREFACE

Why Dicho y Hecho?

Because in order to learn more and learn better,

- first-year language students need to relate visually and actively in the classroom, laboratory, and text with the material they are studying.
- first-year language students need material that is carefully organized around key topics and concepts that provide a strongly unified, integrated, and progressive approach to learning.
- first-year students need material that is synthesized and reinforced in a straightforward, direct manner that allows ample opportunity for in-class practice and consequent internalizing through student-to-teacher, and student-to-student interplay.
- first-year students need to gain confidence in their individual linguistic abilities through (1) active classroom reinforcement of practical, conversational vocabulary that is applicable first and foremost to their own identities and lives; (2) basic syntax that is not confused by the presentation of extensive rules covering the totality of grammatical complexities and exceptions; and (3) exercises that aid the students as they grow from control of form and structure to situational and conversational application to creative usage.
- first-year students need (1) a clear, uncomplicated introduction to the Hispanic world—its geography, its history, its cultural distinctiveness, its people; and (2) a clear establishment of their relationship to the Hispanic world and to what they have learned through the potential contact of travel.

■ PROGRAM

Dicho y Hecho is a *complete* first-year language program composed of:

— the main textbook of fourteen chapters (including laboratory and visual components entitled *Integración*);

— accompanying tapes;

— Workbook (exercises designed to practice writing and translation skills, and to reinforce classroom activity);

— Instructor's Manual (including visuals for transparencies, tapescript, suggested methodology, prospective syllabus, sample tests, and an Intensive Component with cultural micrologues and additional exercises for oral reinforcement).

■ CONTENTS

Pronunciation: The basic sound system is presented in a preliminary section (*La Pronunciación:* The Sounds of Spanish), the contents of which are recorded on a

v

separate tape. This tape affords opportunity for the student to continue practicing special problems of pronunciation throughout the year.

Vocabulario: In each chapter a drawing introduces the unit of vocabulary. These word units, topically organized to facilitate presentation and learning through word association, are based on realistic situations and experiences. Introductory exercises practice vocabulary through use of the illustration and application of the vocabulary to areas of personal and general reference. Vocabulary is also practiced and reinforced through contextual usage in the *Conversación*, through exercises based on grammar presented in each chapter, through creative-application activities and ultimately through the oral-aural-visual component (*Integración*).

Conversación: The purpose of the *Conversaciones* is to provide a concise, practical context for application of the vocabulary and introduction to the grammar. These short situational dialogs, designed for oral practice, follow the same topical themes as the accompanying vocabulary units.

Estructura: Each grammatical structure is presented in its simplest and most commonly used form without complex ramifications. Related grammatical structures are progressively presented. Grammar is uniquely combined with carefully designed graphic illustrations to make the language come alive in both classroom and laboratory.

Ejercicios: Each segment of grammar is followed by a variety of precise, fast-moving exercises which progress from simple practice of form to conversational and situational to creative, open-ended expression.

Perspectiva Original: Creative application activities provide opportunities to practice and apply thematically the vocabulary and grammar of each chapter. Activities include mini-dramas, compositions, oral-presentations, and games.

Panorama Cultural: Reading selections are divided into two groups. The first group (Chapters 1 to 11) is composed of brief historical-geographical-cultural synopses of the major Spanish-speaking areas of the world. The second group (Chapters 12 to 14) of readings is travel-oriented, involving the student imaginatively in travel experiences to and in a foreign country.

Integración: This unique oral-aural-visual component, at the end of each chapter, is an integral part of both the classroom and laboratory experience. The illustrations and oral and written exercises that appear in the *Integración* not only provide a format for the tape program but also offer to the student and teacher multiple, creative possibilities for enjoyable and challenging classroom application. *Integración* provides practice and reinforcement of vocabulary, grammar, and auditory comprehension.

Graphic Illustrations: The illustration that introduces each chapter and those that appear in the *Integración* constitute a unique and innovative classroom and laboratory tool. In classroom and laboratory use they offer easily recognized, visual stimuli for quick, accurate student responses. Used in the classroom in the form of transparencies, they encourage an open, communicative atmosphere between student and teacher. All illustrations are specifically designed to enhance the learning, practice, and reinforcement of the vocabulary and grammar of each chapter and offer an alternative to the traditional mode of teaching, learning, and testing.

Repaso de Vocabulario Activo: At the end of each chapter the active vocabulary (without translations) is presented in a check list alphabetized by parts of speech.

Ejercicios de Repaso: Review exercises at the end of each chapter may be used in the classroom or by students individually as a study aid for tests and a means of evaluating progress. An Answer Key for the review exercises is in Appendix IV.

Reference Tools: Appearing at the end of the text are the following helpful reference tools: Spanish names of punctuation marks; definitions of grammatical terms used in the text; paradigms of regular, stem-changing, orthographic-changing, and irregular verbs; answers to review exercises; recipes from the Spanish-speaking world; Spanish-English, English-Spanish vocabularies (active vocabulary labeled by chapter); and the index.

■ METHODOLOGY

Regardless of methodologies used, the controlling principle for successful acquisition of a target language in a classroom setting is that the student grasp meaning, structures, and concepts quickly and easily for application. The text material must be presented in a concise and clear manner so that valuable class time, drill sessions, and laboratory work can be devoted to practice in the target language. With this principle in mind we present a blending of methodologies that allow (1) for maximum flexibility, (2) for the establishment of an "affective" learning atmosphere, and consequently (3) for providing opportunity to make the teaching/learning experience an enjoyable one.

It is for the reasons of teaching flexibility and rapid student comprehension that we present Spanish vocabulary with English equivalents, grammar with English explanations, and grammatical nomenclature in both languages. The classroom/application exercises, however, are almost exclusively rendered in the target language and are designed for maximum student oral expression. Writing skills are developed through the exercises in the student Workbook, the translation section of the *Ejercicios de Repaso*, and the composition sections of *Perspectiva Original*.

The variety of components and supplementary materials of *Dicho y Hecho* offer ample opportunity for first-year language programs to adapt this program to their particular system of language instruction, ranging from more traditional and cognitive methodologies to intensive and direct method.

"¡ . . . que sea para ustedes una buena experiencia!"

ALBERT C. DAWSON
LAILA M. DAWSON

ACKNOWLEDGMENTS

The authors are indebted first and foremost to the artists Sonia Bencivenga (first edition) and Mary Jane Stokes (additions to the second edition), who have brought a uniquely personal flavor and touch of life to the text through the illustrations.

We wish to express our sincere appreciation to our colleagues and friends from several colleges and universities, and most especially from the Department of Modern Foreign Languages of the University of Richmond and the Department of Foreign Languages of Virginia Union University.

For their invaluable assistance provided in the final stages of manuscript preparation, we would like to recognize Ron Nelson, Foreign Language Editor of John Wiley and Sons; Elizabeth Hovinen; Dr. Umberto Cardounel, University of Richmond. We also wish to thank the following reviewers: Jerold Anderson, Montgomery College; David Bost, Furman University; Richard A. Clark, Butte College; James J. Davis, Howard University; Jackie L. Jarest; Mary A. Kingsley, Augsburg College; Kathleen Kulp-Hill, Eastern Kentucky University; José Palomo, Santa Ana College; Camille M. C. Qualtere, State University of New York at Albany; Shirley Sullivan, Orange County Community College; Mirtha Toledo-Smith, Valparaiso University.

We wish also to express a special note of acknowledgment to our two children, Eric and Sheila, who remained so loving and supportive throughout all stages of our work.

LMD
ACD

CONTENTS

CAPÍTULO TRES   57

CAPÍTULO CUATRO   81

TO THE STUDENT

Dicho y Hecho has been designed specifically with you in mind, as all material is presented with the purpose of making your study of the Spanish language a practical, enjoyable, and personal experience.

Dicho y Hecho offers a total and thorough program of language study through textbook, workbook, tapes, and a unique section called *Integración*, which can be used in both classroom and laboratory.

The objectives of *Dicho y Hecho* are:

1. To simplify the approach to studying first-year Spanish by concentrating on essentials and avoiding idiomatic variables.
2. To present thematic units of vocabulary that stress practical words essential for self-description, self-expression, and the satisfaction of daily needs in a Spanish-speaking environment.
3. To provide stimulating graphic illustrations that help you comprehend, practice, and review grammar and vocabulary. (Illustrations focus on a core of interesting characters with whom you can relate.)
4. To offer a wide variety of creative activities that help you use Spanish more readily and enjoyably.
5. To offer numerous review exercises with answer keys as a convenient tool for testing your own progress.

Here are our suggestions for effective use of the program:

1. Study and practice the grammar and vocabulary of each chapter through the exercises in the text.
2. Use the graphic illustrations as a visual and creative review and reinforcement of the material studied.
3. Use the *Integración* in the text with the tape program as additional oral and written reinforcement and application.
4. Improve your writing skills and reinforce classroom activity by completing the workbook exercises for each chapter (answer keys are provided).

PRONUNCIATION

■ LA PRONUNCIACIÓN *The sounds of Spanish*

NOTE: The contents of this section are recorded on a separate tape labeled **La pronunciación**.

I. *A sampling of Spanish you already know*

Can you give the Spanish pronunciation of these Spanish/English words?

patio	burro	fiesta	siesta	frito	bandido	amigo	taco
adiós	loco	marihuana	matador	tequila	hacienda		
adobe	vista	rodeo	Vega	Pinto	El Dorado	Del Monte	
Fresca	Toro	Colorado	Nevada	California	Florida		
Arizona	San Francisco	Los Ángeles	Amarillo	San Antonio			
Las Vegas	Río Grande	Linda	Teresa	María	Dolores		
Margarita							

II. *Cognates: a sampling of words identical or similar in Spanish and in English*

Practice the pronunciation of the following cognates.

hospital	hotel	teléfono	rancho	chocolate	dentista
doctor	general	presidente	millonario	piano	tractor
animal	mosquito	elefante	inteligente	estúpido	
ignorante	famoso	honesto	popular	importante	inferior
superior	extraordinario	interesante	romántico	fantástico	

1

ridículo	sentimental	terrible	responsable	pesimista
optimista	idealista	realista	generoso	independiente
tímido	dinámico	invitar	visitar	comunicar	preferir

III. Vocales *Vowels*

Unlike English vowels, each Spanish vowel has only one basic sound, even though there may be slight variations created by its position within a word or phrase. Spanish vowels are short and clipped, never drawn out.

Listen carefully and repeat each sound as it is pronounced. (The English equivalents in italics are only approximations.)

a	*bah*	ama, fama, lana, mapa, lata
e	*Betty, let*	nene, bebe, leche, fe, ese
i	*bikini*	mi, si, sin, fin, Fifi
o	*more*	loco, coco, toco, foco, mono
u	*flu*	tu, su, Tulum, Lulú

EJERCICIO 1

Memorize the following verse, focusing on the vowel sounds.

a   e   i   o   u
Arbolito del Perú
Yo me llamo _____.
¿Cómo te llamas tú?

EJERCICIO 2

Repeat the following sounds, and then pronounce them on your own, gradually increasing your speed.

ama	eme	imi	omo	umu
aba	ebe	ibi	obo	ubu
ala	ele	ili	olo	ulu
afa	efe	ifi	ofo	ufu

EJERCICIO 3

Pronounce the following words, concentrating on the vowel emphasized.

a	patio	taco	fantástico
e	Teresa	teléfono	médico
i	Linda	ridículo	disco
o	famoso	Dolores	rosa
u	estúpido	pluma	uno

IV. Diptongos *Diphthongs*

DEFINITION: In Spanish, a diphthong is a combination of two vowels, at least one of
which is an unaccented **i** or **u**.

Diphthongs are pronounced as a single syllable.

b**ie**n   **cui**dado   ag**ua**

EJERCICIO 4

Pronounce the vowel combinations as found in the following sounds and words.

ai	aire	baile
au	auto	Laura
ei	seis	veinte
eu	Europa	seudo
ia	piano	Diana
ie	fiesta	diez
io	adiós	idiota
iu	triunfo	viuda
oi	oigo	heróico
ua	cuatro	Guatemala
ue	bueno	Venezuela
ui	Luisa	ruina
uo	cuota	mutuo

V. Consonantes Problemáticas *Problem consonants*

b   The consonants **b** and **v** are identical in pronunciation. Initial **b** and **v** (and after **m** and **n**) are pronounced like the English *b* in *boy*.
      bueno   bien   vista   violeta   sombrero
      In other positions they are pronounced less explosively.
      lobo   favor   jueves   adobe

c   In Spanish America, **c** before **e** or **i** has the English *s* sound as in *sister*.
      cero   cinco   gracias   centro
      In most regions of Spain **c** before **e** or **i** is pronounced with a *th* sound as in *thanks*.
      cero   cinco   gracias   centro
      Before **a**, **o**, **u**, or consonants **c** has the English *k* sound as in *cat*.
      como   cama   clase   criminal

d   At the beginning of a word or after **n** or **l**, **d** is hard as in *dog*.
      día   dos   cuando   caldo
      In other positions, particularly between vowels and at the end of a word, **d** has a slight *th* sound as in *this*.
      médico   todo   madre   sed

g   Before **e** or **i**, **g** has the English *h* sound as in *help*.
      generoso   inteligente   gitano   mágico

In other positions (except between vowels where it is slightly softened) it is hard as in *goat*.

gracias   gusto   tango   amigo

In the combinations **gue** and **gui**, **u** is silent as in *guest*.

guitarra   guerra   guía

h   Silent as in *honest*.

ħotel   ħospital   ħonor   alcoħol

j   Approximates the pronounced *h* sound of English as in *help*.

jueves   jardín   junio   ejercicio

ll   Approximates the English *y* sound as in *yes*.

llamar   calle   silla   llevar

ñ   Has the sound of *ny* as in *canyon*.

señor   niño   mañana   año

q   Occurs only in the combinations **que** and **qui**, which have a silent **u.**

que   chiquita   queso   quince

r   If not initial, **r** approximates the sound of *tt* as in *Betty likes butter better* or *dd* as in *Eddy*.

tres   tarea   escriba   oración

rr   Has a trilled sound as in mimicking a motorcycle; initial **r** has the same sound.

perro   pizarra   roto   Rodolfo

Try the following verse:

Erre con erre cigarro
erre con erre barril.
Rápido corren los carros
carros del ferrocarril.

x   Before most consonants **x** has an *s* sound.

extra   sexto   experiencia

Between two vowels **x** has a *ks* sound.

examen   existir   taxi

z   In Spanish America **z** is pronounced the same as *s*.

zapato   Arizona   paz   lápiz

In most regions of Spain **z** is pronounced with a *th* sound as in *thanks*.

zapato   Arizona   paz   lápiz

EJERCICIO 5

Practice the following consonants.

ca	que	qui	co	cu		lla	lle	lli	llo	llu
ca	ce	ci	co	cu		ña	ñe	ñi	ño	ñu
ga	gue	gui	go	gu		va	ve	vi	vo	vu
ga	ge	gi	go	gu		ba	be	bi	bo	bu
ha	he	hi	ho	hu		za	ze	zi	zo	zu
ja	je	ji	jo	ju		sa	se	si	so	su

VI. El alfabeto *The alphabet*

The letters and their names in Spanish are:

a (a)	**j** (jota)	**r** (ere)
b (be)	**k** (ka)	**rr** (erre)
c (ce)	**l** (ele)	**s** (ese)
ch (che)	**ll** (elle)	**t** (te)
d (de)	**m** (eme)	**u** (u)
e (e)	**n** (ene)	**v** (ve) (uve)
f (efe)	**ñ** (eñe)	**w** (ve doble) (uve doble)
g (ge)	**o** (o)	**x** (equis)
h (hache)	**p** (pe)	**y** (i griega)
i (i)	**q** (cu)	**z** (zeta)

EJERCICIO 6

Spell the following words using the Spanish alphabet.

1. rancho
2. general
3. hotel
4. señorita
5. ejercicio
6. yo
7. Amarillo
8. quince
9. terrible
10. examen
11. voz
12. gusto

VII. Acentuación *Accents and stress*

A. In Spanish if a word has a written accent mark (called in Spanish **acento**), the accented syllable is stressed.

   t<u>í</u>mido   din<u>á</u>mico   rid<u>í</u>culo

B. In words without a written accent the following rules apply.

   1. The next to the last syllable is stressed if the word ends in a vowel or **n** or **s**.

   <u>pa</u>tio   a<u>do</u>be   re<u>pi</u>tan   <u>lu</u>nes

   2. The last syllable is stressed if the word ends in a consonant other than **n** or **s**.

   ani<u>mal</u>   doc<u>tor</u>   liber<u>tad</u>

EJERCICIO 7

Pronounce the following words, stressing the correct syllable.

1. pro/fe/sor
2. den/tis/ta
3. es/tú/pi/do
4. ge/ne/ral
5. pre/si/den/te
6. u/ni/ver/si/dad
7. vi/si/tar
8. per/so/nal
9. te/lé/fo/no
10. lla/mo
11. ro/mán/ti/co
12. cla/se

CAPÍTULO 1

■ SALUDOS Y EXPRESIONES COMUNES
Greetings and common expressions

Greetings

Buenos días, señorita.	*Good morning, miss.*
señora.	*ma'am. (Mrs.)*
señor.	*sir. (Mr.)*
Buenas tardes.	*Good afternoon.*
Buenas noches.	*Good evening (night).*
Hola.	*Hello.*

Well-being

¿Cómo está usted?	*How are you? (formal)*
¿Cómo estás?	*How are you? (informal)*
¿Qué tal?	*How are you? (How's it going?)*
Muy bien, gracias.	*Very well, thanks.*
Regular. Así, así.	*Fair. So, so.*
¿Y usted?	*And you? (formal)*
¿Y tú?	*And you? (informal)*

Getting acquainted

¿Cómo se llama usted?	*What's your name? (formal)*
¿Cómo te llamas?	*What's your name? (informal)*
Me llamo . . . (name).	*My name is . . . (name).*
Permítame presentar a (name).	*Allow me to introduce (name).*
Mucho gusto.	*Very pleased to meet you.*
El gusto es mío.	*The pleasure is mine.*

7

Expressions of courtesy

Muchas gracias.	*Thank you very much.*
No, gracias.	*No, thank you.*
De nada.	*You are welcome.*
(Sí,) por favor.	*(Yes,) please.*
Perdón.	*Pardon me, excuse me.* (to get someone's attention or to seek forgiveness)
Con permiso.	*Pardon me, excuse me.* (to seek permission to pass by someone)

Departure

Adiós.	*Goodbye.*
Hasta luego.	*See you later.*
Hasta mañana.	*See you tomorrow.*

NOTE: In Spanish there are two different forms of address depending upon the degree of formality or informality which exists between the persons speaking.

¿Cómo está usted?
¿Y usted?
¿Cómo se llama usted?

Used in formal situations.
Last-name basis relationships.

¿Cómo estás?
¿Qué tal?
¿Y tú?
¿Cómo te llamas?

Used in informal situations.
First-name basis relationships.
(classmates, peers, children, and the like)

¡Saludos!
Madrid, España

EJERCICIO 1   Saludos

Greet the following people according to the time of day, and ask how they are (formally or informally as appropriate).

Modelos   Anita—9:00 A.M.   **Buenos días, Anita. ¿Qué tal?** (or) **¿Cómo estás?**

Mr. García—2:00 P.M.   **Buenas tardes, señor García. ¿Cómo está usted?**

1. Mrs. Gómez—4:00 P.M.
2. Miss Ramos—11:00 P.M.
3. Susana—8:00 A.M.
4. Mr. López—1:00 P.M.
5. Pepe—11:00 A.M.

EJERCICIO 2   ¿Cómo se llama usted?

Get acquainted with your classmates and instructor by first getting their attention and second by learning their name.

Modelos   **Perdón, ¿Cómo se llama usted? (Me llamo . . .)**
Perdón, ¿Cómo te llamas? (Me llamo . . .)

EJERCICIO 3   Las presentaciones

Take turns introducing classmates to each other or to the instructor. Each party should respond to the introduction accordingly.

Modelo   (Introduction) **Permítame presentar a _____.**
(Response to introduction) **Mucho gusto.**
(Follow-up to response) **El gusto es mío.**

EJERCICIO 4   Las cortesías

Give an expression appropriate to the following situations.

Modelo   Someone asks if you would like some cake.
Your response: **Sí, por favor.**

1. Someone has given you a gift.
2. Someone asks if you would like an appetizer of squid.
3. Someone asks if you would like a bowl of ice cream.
4. Someone thanks you for your help.
5. You wish to pass by or through a group.
6. You are leaving a party.

EJERCICIO 5   Saludos y expresiones

Give a logical response to each greeting, question, or expression.

1. Buenos días.
2. ¿Cómo está usted?

3. ¿Qué tal?
4. ¿Cómo se llama usted?
5. Permítame presentar a María Santos.
6. Muchas gracias.
7. Adiós.
8. Mucho gusto.

EJERCICIO 6   ¡Vamos a conversar! (*Let's converse.*)

You and a classmate create a dialog which might take place on the first day of classes. Use as many greetings and expressions as possible.

■ VOCABULARIO *En la clase de español*

la **clase de español**	*Spanish class*	el **papel**	*paper*
el **cuaderno**	*notebook*	la **pizarra**	*blackboard*
el **ejercicio**	*exercise*	la **pluma**	*pen*
el **escritorio**	*desk*	la **pregunta**	*question*
el **estudiante, alumno**	*student* (m.)	el **profesor**	*professor, teacher* (m.)
la **estudiante, alumna**	*student* (f.)	la **profesora**	*professor, teacher* (f.)
el **lápiz**	*pencil*	la **puerta**	*door*
la **lección**	*lesson*	la **respuesta**	*answer, reply*
el **libro**	*book*	la **silla**	*chair*
la **mesa**	*table*	la **tarea**	*assignment*
la **oración**	*sentence*	la **tiza**	*chalk*
la **palabra**	*word*	la **ventana**	*window*

Instrucciones

abra	*open* (singular command—to one person)
abran	*open* (plural command—to more than one person)
cierre(n)	*close*
conteste(n)	*answer*
escriba(n)	*write*
estudie(n)	*study*
lea(n) en voz alta	*read aloud*
repita(n)	*repeat*
siénte(n)se	*sit down*
traduzca(n)	*translate*
vaya(n) a	*go to*

EJERCICIO 7   Las instrucciones

Complete each classroom direction with as many vocabulary items as possible.

Modelo   Vaya a . . . **la pizarra**
la mesa
la ventana

1. Abra . . .
4. Repita . . .
7. Escriba con (*with*) . . .

2. Estudie . . .
5. Cierre . . .
8. Conteste . . .

3. Traduzca . . .
6. Lea . . .
9. Siéntese en (*in*) . . .

EJERCICIO 8   En la clase de español

You and a classmate practice (1) naming as many classroom items as you can; (2) giving classroom instructions to each other.

■ CONVERSACIÓN

Hoy es el primer día de clases en la universidad. Susana y Pepe son estudiantes.

SUSANA	**¡Hola, Pepe! ¿Vas a la clase de historia?**
PEPE	**Sí. ¿Sabes quién es el profesor?**
SUSANA	**Es la¹ señora Gómez.**
PEPE	**¡Qué bueno! ¡Es una profesora magnífica!**
SUSANA	**Oye, ¿qué hora es?**
PEPE	**¡Ay! Son las diez. ¡Vámonos!**

NOTE 1:   In Spanish, the definite article (**el**—masculine or **la**—feminine) is used with titles when the person is not addressed directly.

Today is the first day of classes at the university. Susan and Pepe are students.

SUSAN	*Hi, Pepe! Are you going to history class?*
PEPE	*Yes. Do you know who the professor is?*
SUSAN	*It's Mrs. Gómez.*
PEPE	*Great! She's a marvelous teacher.*
SUSAN	*Listen, what time is it?*
PEPE	*Oh! It's ten o'clock. Let's go!*

Los estudiantes van (*go*) a clase en la Universidad de Puerto Rico. San Juan, Puerto Rico

■ ESTRUCTURA

I. Articulos y sustantivos *Articles and nouns*

A. Los articulos en el singular

Definite and indefinite articles in Spanish are either masculine or feminine, depending on the noun with which they are used.

> **Artículos determinados en el singular: el** (masculino),
> **la** (femenino)

el alumno   *the student* (m.)
la alumna   *the student* (f.)

> **Artículos indeterminados en el singular: un** (m.), **una** (f.)

un alumno   *student* or *one student* (m.)
una alumna   *student* or *one student* (f.)

B. Los sustantivos en el singular

All nouns in Spanish, even those referring to nonliving things, are either masculine or feminine.

> **Most nouns that end in <u>o</u> and nouns referring to male beings are masculine.**

el patio   *the patio*
un cuaderno   *a notebook*
el padre   *the father*
un hombre   *a man*

> **Most nouns that end in <u>a</u> and nouns referring to female beings are feminine.**

la mesa   *the table*
una familia   *a family*
la madre   *the mother*
una mujer   *a woman*

All other nouns must be memorized as masculine or feminine. Always study vocabulary by saying the article with the noun.

masculine: **el papel**   *the paper*
             un hospital   *a hospital*
feminine: **la noche**   *the night*
             una clase   *a class*

EJERCICIO 9   ¿El o (*or*) la?

Lea las palabras con (*with*) el artículo determinado.

Modelo   fiesta   **la fiesta**

1. burro
2. oración
3. tiza
4. respuesta
5. lápiz
6. taco
7. papel
8. clase
9. ejercicio
10. profesora

EJERCICIO 10   ¿Un o una?

Cambie (*change*) el artículo determinado al indeterminado.

Modelo   el hombre   **un hombre**

1. la pregunta
2. el libro
3. la ventana
4. el estudiante
5. la puerta
6. el rancho
7. la alumna
8. la lección
9. el hotel
10. el escritorio

C. Los artículos determinados en el plural: los (m.), las (f.)

los alumnos   *the students* (m.)
las alumnas   *the students* (f.)

D. Los sustantivos en el plural

Nouns ending in a vowel add **-s** to form the plural.

el libro   **los libros**
la mesa   **las mesas**
la clase   **las clases**

Nouns ending in a consonant add **-es** to form the plural.

el profesor   **los profesores**
la oración   **las oraciones**
el lápiz   **los lápices** (note spelling change)

EJERCICIO 11   Del singular al plural

Cambie (*change*) los artículos y los sustantivos al plural.

Modelo   la ventana   **las ventanas**

1. el cuaderno
2. la pluma
3. la silla
4. el papel
5. la pizarra
6. el profesor
7. la puerta
8. la lección
9. el lápiz
10. la palabra

II. Los adjetivos *Adjectives*

Adjectives in Spanish agree in gender (masculine or feminine) and number (singular or plural) with the nouns they modify.

A. Los adjetivos en el singular

Adjectives ending in **-o** change **-o** to **-a** to agree with a feminine singular noun.

Carlos es (*is*) **honesto**.
Teresa es **honesta**.
Carlos es un alumno **extraordinario**.
Teresa es una alumna **extraordinaria**.

Adjectives ending in **-e** or a consonant, except those of nationality, remain unchanged in gender (masculine or feminine).

Carlos es **inteligente**.
Teresa es **inteligente**.
Carlos es un alumno **superior**.
Teresa es una alumna **superior**.

Adjectives of nationality that end in a consonant add an **-a** for the feminine singular form. Adjectives of nationality are not capitalized in Spanish.

Roberto es **español**.
Lolita es **española**.

B. Los adjetivos en el plural

To form the plural, adjectives ending in a vowel add **-s** and those ending in a consonant add **-es**.

Pepe es **romántico**.   Pepe y Pancho son (*are*) **románticos**.
La respuesta es **importante**.   Las respuestas son **importantes**.
El libro es **popular**.   Los libros son **populares**.
El profesor es **espãnol**.   Los profesores son **españoles**.

C. Posición de los adjetivos

Descriptive adjectives most commonly *follow* the noun.

Felipe es un alumno **responsable**.
Lupe es una persona **dinámica**.

EJERCICIO 12   Descripción

Complete las oraciones según (*according to*) los modelos.

Modelos
 a) Jorge es (is) *italiano*.
    Mónica es **italiana**.
 b) Marta es *una estudiante chilena*.
    José es **un estudiante chileno**.
 c) La clase es *importante*.
    Las clases son (*are*) **importantes**.

1. Carlos es *argentino*.
   Teresa es _____.
2. Tomás es *inteligente*.
   Elena es _____.
3. El profesor es *español*.
   La profesora es _____.
4. La señora Gómez es *una profesora magnífica*.
   El señor Pinto es _____.
5. Diego es *un alumno excelente*.
   Mónica es _____.

6. Susana es *generosa*.
   Susana y Linda son _____.
7. La señorita es *americana*.
   Las señoritas son _____.
8. Juan es *popular*.
   Juan y Felipe son _____.
9. Eduardo es *sentimental*.
   Eduardo y Raúl son _____.
10. La clase es *interesante*.
   Las clases son _____.

Después de (*after*) las clases los estudiantes
de la universidad conversan. Madrid, España

III. Puntuación y posición de palabras *Punctuation and word order*

A. Puntuación*

In questions and exclamations, written Spanish uses an inverted question mark at the beginning of questions and an inverted exclamation point at the beginning of exclamations, as well as the expected punctuation at the end.

¿Cómo se llama usted?
¡Magnífico!

B. Posición de palabras en preguntas

In questions the subject most commonly follows the verb.

¿Cómo está **usted**?
¿Es **Carlos** inteligente?

C. Posición de palabras en oraciones negativas

In negative statements, **no** is placed before the verb.

Carlos **no** es inteligente.

NOTE: In answering a question with a negative statement, the **no** is repeated.

¿Es Carlos generoso?   **No**, Carlos **no** es generoso.

EJERCICIO 13   Sí y no

Conteste las preguntas según el modelo.

Modelos   ¿Es Lucy sentimental?
          Sí, Lucy es sentimental.
          No, Lucy no es sentimental.

1.   ¿Es Drácula cruel? Sí, . . .
                    No, . . .
2.   ¿Es Snoopy ridículo? Sí, . . .
                      No, . . .
3.   ¿Es King Kong romántico? Sí, . . .
                        No, . . .
4.   ¿Es Superman inteligente? Sí, . . .
                      No, . . .
5.   ¿Es Charlie Brown popular? Sí, . . .
                        No, . . .

*For a list of the Spanish names of punctuation marks see Appendix I.

La semana tiene 5 vuelos a EUROPA por Aeroméxico

Lunes, Martes, Miércoles, Jueves y Viernes a las 12:00 horas en punto.

IV. Dias de la semana   *Days of the week*

¿Qué día es hoy?   *What day is it today?*

lunes	*Monday*	**viernes**	*Friday*
martes	*Tuesday*	**sábado**	*Saturday*
miércoles	*Wednesday*	**domingo**	*Sunday*
jueves	*Thursday*		

NOTE 1:   The days of the week are not capitalized in Spanish.

NOTE 2:   The definite article **el** or **los** is used with the day of the week to indicate *on.*

el lunes   *on Monday*   **los miércoles**   *on Wednesdays*

EJERCICIO 14   ¿Qué día es?

Conteste las preguntas según el modelo.

Modelo   Si (*if*) hoy es lunes, ¿qué día es mañana?
Mañana es martes.

1. Si hoy es miércoles, ¿qué día es mañana?
2. Si hoy es viernes, ¿qué día es mañana?
3. Si hoy es domingo, ¿qué día es mañana?
4. Si hoy es martes, ¿qué día es mañana?
5. Si hoy es jueves, ¿qué día es mañana?
6. Si hoy es sábado, ¿qué día es mañana?

V. Números *Numbers (0-29)*

cero	0	**quince**	15
uno	1	**diez y seis (dieciséis)**	16
dos	2	**diez y siete (diecisiete)**	17
tres	3	**diez y ocho (dieciocho)**	18
cuatro	4	**diez y nueve (diecinueve)**	19
cinco	5	**veinte**	20
seis	6	**veinte y uno (veintiuno)**	21
siete	7	**veinte y dos (veintidós)**	22
ocho	8	**veinte y tres (veintitrés)**	23
nueve	9	**veinte y cuatro (veinticuatro)**	24
diez	10	**veinte y cinco (veinticinco)**	25
once	11	**veinte y seis (veintiséis)**	26
doce	12	**veinte y siete (veintisiete)**	27
trece	13	**veinte y ocho (veintiocho)**	28
catorce	14	**veinte y nueve (veintinueve)**	29

NOTE: In mathematics *plus* is **y** or **más**
minus is **menos**
equals is **son**

EJERCICIO 15   De uno a veinte y nueve

1. Vamos a contar (*Let's count*):
    a.   de cero a veinte y ocho—0, 2, 4, 6, . . .
    b.   de uno a veinte y nueve—1, 3, 5, . . .
2. Mi número de teléfono es . . .
3. Matemáticas:

3	6	7	8	10	20	28	21	26	18
+4	+6	+4	+5	+9	−5	−2	−5	−12	−17

Las estudiantes charlan (*chat*)
en camino a (*on the way to*) las clases.
Universidad de Granada,
España

VI. La hora *Telling time*

la hora	*the hour, the time*	**de la mañana**	A.M. *(in the morning)*
		de la tarde	P.M. *(in the afternoon)*
¿Qué hora es?	*What time is it?*	**de la noche**	P.M. *(in the evening, at night)*
¿A qué hora?	*At what time?*		
cuarto	*a quarter*	**Es el mediodía.**	*It's noon.*
media	*half*	**Es la medianoche.**	*It's midnight.*

¿Qué hora es?

$$\textbf{Son (es) + las (la) + } \textit{(hour)} \begin{array}{c} \textbf{y} \\ \textbf{menos} \end{array} \textit{(minutes)}$$

During the first thirty minutes after the hour, give the hour just past plus (**y**) the number of minutes. After thirty minutes, give the next hour less (**menos**) the number of minutes to go before the coming hour.

Es la una.

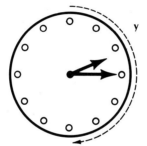

Son las dos y cuarto.

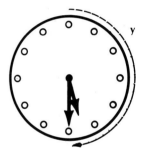

Son las cinco y media.

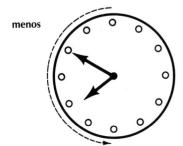

Son las ocho menos diez.

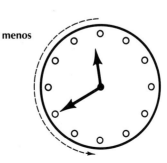

Son las doce menos veinte.

EJERCICIO 16   ¿Qué hora es?

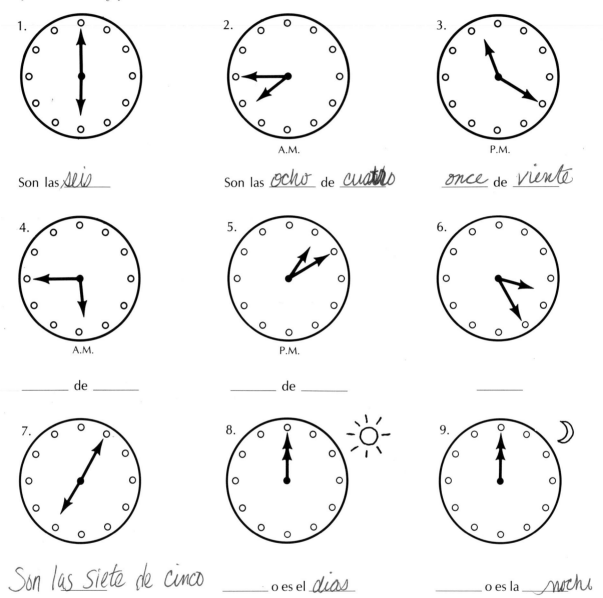

1.

Son las *seis*

2.

A.M.

Son las *ocho* de *cuatro*

3.

P.M.

once de *viente*

4.

A.M.

_____ de _____

5.

P.M.

_____ de _____

6.

_____

7.

Son las siete de cinco

8.

_____ o es el *dias*

9.

_____ o es la *noche*

EJERCICIO 17   ¿A qué hora?

Pregúntele a un(a) estudiante a qué hora es el programa, la clase, etc.; escuche la respuesta. (*Ask a student at what time the program, the class, etc. is; listen to the response.*)

Modelo   el programa / 9:00. (pregunta) **¿A qué hora es el programa?**
(respuesta) **A las nueve.**

1. la clase / 10:00   2. el concierto / 7:00   3. la excursión / 2:30   4. el examen
/ 10:15   5. la fiesta / 8:45

■ PANORAMA CULTURAL

Nación	Población (1983) (aproximada)	Nacionalidad
México	77,000,000 millones	mexicano
Guatemala	8,000,000	guatemalteco
El Salvador	5,200,000	salvadoreño
Honduras	4,100,000	hondureño
Nicaragua	3,000,000	nicaragüense
Costa Rica	2,400,000	costarricense
Panamá	2,100,000	panameño
Cuba	10,300,000	cubano
La República Dominicana	5,800,000	dominicano
Puerto Rico	3,700,000	puertorriqueño
Colombia	28,600,000	colombiano
Venezuela	14,900,000	venezolano
El Ecuador	9,000,000	ecuatoriano
El Perú	18,800,000	peruano
Chile	11,500,000	chileno
Bolivia	5,800,000	boliviano
El Paraguay	3,300,000	paraguayo
La Argentina	27,800,000	argentino
El Uruguay	3,000,000	uruguayo
España	35,000,000	español
	279,300,000	

La *lengua* española

* El *mundo* español es extenso y diverso.
* *De todas* las lenguas del mundo el español es una de las cinco lenguas más importantes.
* El español es la lengua nacional de *unos* veinte países y es de mucha importancia en los *Estados Unidos.*
* *Como* el *inglés* de *Inglaterra* es un *poco* diferente del inglés de los Estados Unidos, el español *tiene*, de *país* a país, variaciones de pronunciación y de vocabulario.
* El origen del español *como* el francés, el italiano, el portugués y *otras* lenguas, es el latín. Es una lengua romance.

language
world
of all

some
United States
As/English/England/little
has/country
like/other

■ INTEGRACIÓN

A. ORAL EXERCISE: GREETINGS AND COMMON EXPRESSIONS
    Listen and repeat.

B. ORAL EXERCISE: GREETINGS AND COMMON EXPRESSIONS
    Give a logical response to each greeting, question or expression.

	Example	(tape)	Muchas gracias.
		(your response)	**De nada.**
		(tape confirmation)	De nada.
		(your repetition)	**De nada.**

C. ORAL EXERCISE: VOCABULARY AND DIRECTIONS FOR THE CLASS
    Complete each classroom direction using the vocabulary item given in each
    drawing.

Example	(tape)	Lea _____
	(your response)	**Lea el libro.**
	(tape confirmation)	Lea el libro.
	(your repetition)	**Lea el libro.**

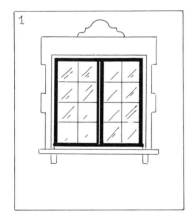

1

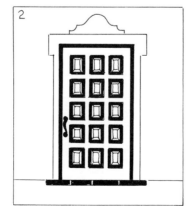

2

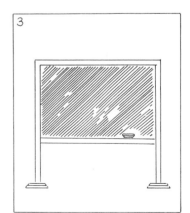

3

4

5

6

7

8

9

10
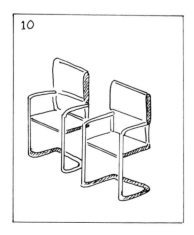

11
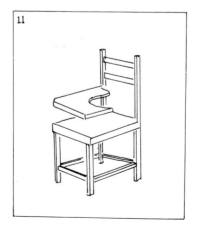

D. ORAL EXERCISE: **Conversación**
    1. The dialog will be read twice. Listen the first time; the second time pauses will be provided for you to repeat each phrase.
    2. Listen to the statements related to the dialog, then indicate if the statements are true or false.

    (**cierto**—true, **falso**—false)

Example	(tape)	Susana y Pepe son profesores.
	(your response)	**Falso**
	(tape confirmation)	Falso

E. ORAL EXERCISE: DEFINITE AND INDEFINITE ARTICLES
    Give the definite and indefinite articles that correspond to each noun provided.

Example	(tape)	mesa
	(your response)	**la mesa, una mesa**
	(tape confirmation)	la mesa, una mesa
	(your repetition)	**la mesa, una mesa**

F. ORAL EXERCISE: THE PLURAL OF ARTICLES AND NOUNS
    Change each singular article and noun to its plural form.

Example	(tape)	el alumno
	(your response)	**los alumnos**
	(tape confirmation)	los alumnos
	(your repetition)	**los alumnos**

G. ORAL EXERCISE: ADJECTIVES
    Complete the sentences making the necessary changes in adjective agreement.

Example	(tape)	Alberto es americano.
	(tape)	Carmen es . . .
	(your response)	**Carmen es americana.**
	(tape confirmation)	Carmen es americana.
	(your repetition)	**Carmen es americana.**

H. WRITTEN EXERCISE: THE PLURAL OF ARTICLES, NOUNS, AND ADJECTIVES
    A sentence containing a singular (masculine or feminine) article, noun and adjective will be given twice. Rewrite the sentence in the plural.

Example	(tape)	La señora es cubana.
	(tape repeat)	La señora es cubana.
	(your written response)	**Las señoras son cubanas.**

I. ORAL EXERCISE: NEGATIVE STATEMENTS
    Change each affirmative statement to the negative by placing **no** before the verb.

Example	(tape)	Charlie Brown es cruel.
	(your response)	**Charlie Brown no es cruel.**
	(tape confirmation)	Charlie Brown no es cruel.
	(your repetition)	**Charlie Brown no es cruel.**

J.   ORAL EXERCISE: DAYS OF THE WEEK
      Listen and repeat.

K.   ORAL EXERCISE: DAYS OF THE WEEK
      The tape will name a day of the week. Give the day that follows, and listen
      for the tape confirmation.

L.   ORAL EXERCISE: NUMBERS 0–29
      Listen and repeat.
      0, 1, 2, 3, 4, 5, 6, 7, 8, 9, 10, 11, 12, 13, 14, 15, 16, 17, 18, 19, 20, 21, 22,
      23, 24, 25, 26, 27, 28, 29.

M.   ORAL EXERCISE: NUMBERS 0–29
      Answer the following math problems and listen for the tape confirmation.

N.   ORAL EXERCISE: TELLING TIME
      Tell the time on each clock, and listen for the tape confirmation.

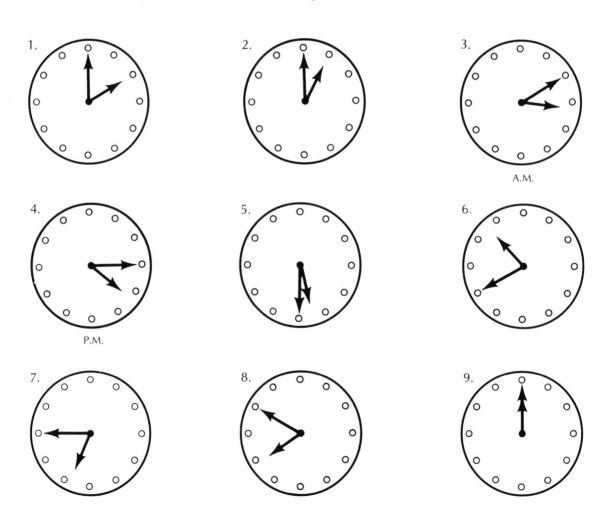

1.

2.

3.
A.M.

4.
P.M.

5.

6.

7.

8.

9.

O.   DICTATION: **El mundo hispánico**
Write the three sentences you hear. Each sentence will be read three times:
the first time at normal speed, the second time with pauses for writing, and
the third time at normal speed for correction.

■ REPASO DE VOCABULARIO ACTIVO

Saludos y expresiones comunes

Buenos días, señorita (señora, señor).
Buenas tardes.
Buenas noches.
Hola.
¿Cómo está usted?
¿Cómo estás?
¿Qué tal?
Muy bien, gracias.
Regular. Así, Así.
¿Y usted?
¿Y tú?
¿Cómo se llama usted?
¿Cómo te llamas?
Me llamo . . . (*name***).**
Permítame presentar a (*name***).**
Mucho gusto.
El gusto es mío.
Muchas gracias.
No, gracias.
De nada.
(Sí,) por favor.
Perdón.
Con permiso.
Adiós.
Hasta luego.
Hasta mañana.

En la clase de español

la **alumna**	el **escritorio**	la **mesa**	la **pluma**	la **respuesta**
el **alumno**	el (la) **estudiante**	la **oración**	la **pregunta**	la **silla**
la **clase de español**	el **lápiz**	la **palabra**	el **profesor**	la **tarea**
el **cuaderno**	la **lección**	el **papel**	la **profesora**	la **tiza**
el **ejercicio**	el **libro**	la **pizarra**	la **puerta**	la **ventana**

abra(n)	conteste(n)	estudie(n)	traduzca(n)	siénte(n)se
cierre(n)	escriba(n)	lea(n) en voz alta	repita(n)	vaya(n) a

Días de la semana

¿Qué día es hoy?	martes	jueves	sábado
lunes	miércoles	viernes	domingo

Números

cero	ocho	diez y seis
uno	nueve	diez y siete
dos	diez	diez y ocho
tres	once	diez y nueve
cuatro	doce	veinte
cinco	trece	veinte y uno . . .
seis	catorce	
siete	quince	

La hora

¿Qué hora es?	media	de la noche
¿A qué hora?	de la mañana	Es el mediodía.
cuarto	de la tarde	Es la medianoche.

Artículos

el	los	un
la	las	una

■ EJERCICIOS DE REPASO

I. Saludos y expresiones comunes

Indique el saludo, pregunta o expresión que corresponde a cada respuesta. (*Give the greeting, question, or expression that corresponds to each reply.*)

Modelo   Buenas noches.
Buenas noches, señor (señora, señorita).

1. Me llamo Jorge.
2. Muy bien, gracias.
3. Mucho gusto.
4. De nada.
5. El gusto es mío.
6. Hasta luego.

II. Vocabulario e instrucciones

A. Traduzca al español. (*Translate into Spanish.*)

1. the pencil
2. the pen
3. the notebook
4. the paper
5. the exercise

6. Open the book. (plural command)
7. Close the door, please. (singular command)
8. Repeat the answer. (sing. com.)
9. Study the lesson. (pl. com.)
10. Write the word. (sing. com.)

B. Traduzca al inglés. (*Translate into English.*)

1. la tarea
2. la tiza
3. el escritorio
4. la silla
5. la ventana

6. Conteste la pregunta.
7. Vaya a la pizarra.
8. Lea en voz alta.
9. Siéntese.
10. Traduzca la oración.

III. Artículos

Indique los artículos determinados e indeterminados según el modelo. (*Indicate the definite and indefinite articles according to the model.*)

Modelo   patio   **el patio   un patio**

1. mesa
2. profesor
3. libro
4. lección
5. clase

IV. Artículos, sustantivos y adjetivos

A. Cambie a la forma femenina. (*Change to the feminine.*)

Modelo   *El profesor* es magnífico. (La profesora . . .)
          La profesora es magnífica.

1. *La alumna* es americana. (El alumno)
2. *El señor Lunares* es español. (La señora Lunares)
3. *Diego* es inteligente. (Marta)
4. *Mónica* es una alumna superior. (Andrés)

B. Cambie al plural. (*Change to the plural.*)

Modelo   *Juan* es popular. (Juan y Felipe)
          Juan y Felipe son populares.

1. *La profesora* es mexicana. (Las profesoras)
2. *El estudiante* es peruano. (Los estudiantes)
3. *Ana* es sentimental. (Ana y Lupe)
4. *La clase* es interesante. (Las clases)

V. Posición de palabras en oraciones negativas.

Cambie a la forma negativa. (*Change to the negative.*)

1.   Los libros son interesantes.
2.   El profesor es ridículo.
3.   La pregunta es importante.
4.   Andrés es un alumno extraordinario.

VI. Números; días de la semana

Complete.

1.   dos, cuatro, seis, _____, _____, _____, _____, _____, _____,
     _____, _____, _____, _____, veinte y ocho.
2.   uno, tres, cinco, _____, _____, _____, _____, _____, _____,
     _____, _____, _____, _____, _____, veinte y nueve.
3.   lunes, _____, _____, _____, _____, _____, domingo.

VII. La hora

A. ¿Qué hora es?

1.

P.M.

2.
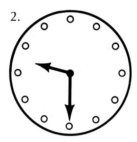
P.M.

3.
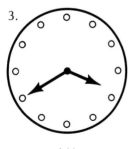
A.M.

4.
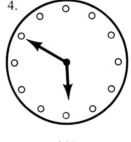
A.M.

B. ¿A qué hora?
Conteste según el modelo. (*Answer according to the model.*)

Modelo   ¿A qué hora es la clase? (11:00)
          La clase es a las once.

1. ¿A qué hora es el programa? (12:15)
2. ¿A qué hora es el drama? (8:00)
3. ¿A qué hora es el examen? (11:00)
4. ¿A qué hora es la excursión? (6:45)

NOTE: The Answer Key to the **Ejercicios de Repaso** can be found in Appendix IV.

CAPÍTULO 2

■ VOCABULARIO *La familia*

el **abuelo**	*grandfather*		el **amigo**	*friend* (m.)
la **abuela**	*grandmother*		la **amiga**	*friend* (f.)
el **esposo**	*husband*		el **hombre**	*man*
la **esposa**	*wife*		la **mujer**	*woman*
la **familia**	*family*		el **muchacho, chico**	*boy*
el **hermano**	*brother*		la **muchacha, chica**	*girl*
la **hermana**	*sister*		el **niño**	*child* (m.)
el **hijo**	*son*		la **niña**	*child* (f.)
la **hija**	*daughter*		el **novio**	*boyfriend*
la **madre**	*mother*		la **novia**	*girlfriend*
el **nieto**	*grandson*			
la **nieta**	*granddaughter*		el **abogado**	*lawyer* (m.)
el **padre**	*father*		la **abogada**	*lawyer* (f.)
los **padres**	*parents*		el **médico**	*doctor* (m.)
el **pariente**	*relative*		la **médica**	*doctor* (f.)
el **primo**	*cousin* (m.)		el **hombre de negocios**	*businessman*
la **prima**	*cousin* (f.)		la **mujer de negocios**	*businesswoman*
el **sobrino**	*nephew*			
la **sobrina**	*niece*		la **casa**	*house*
el **tío**	*uncle*		el **coche, carro, auto**	*car*
la **tía**	*aunt*			

NOTE: In a group comprised of males and females the masculine form predominates.

los hermanos   *the brothers and sisters*
los hijos   *the sons and daughters*

EJERCICIO 1 La familia

Conteste en español en oraciones completas según el dibujo (*according to the drawing*) de la familia.

1. ¿Cómo se llama el padre? **El padre se llama** . . .
2. ¿Cómo se llama la madre?
3. ¿Cómo se llama el hijo?
4. ¿Cómo se llama la hija?
5. ¿Cómo se llama el tío?
6. ¿Cómo se llama la tía?
7. ¿Cómo se llama el abuelo?
8. ¿Cómo se llama la abuela?
9. ¿Es la casa colonial o (*or*) contemporánea?
10. ¿Es el coche un Mercedes o un Volkswagen?

EJERCICIO 2 Los parientes

Exprese la relación entre (*between*) las dos personas según el dibujo.

> Modelo   Elena/Pepito
> **Elena es la hermana de** (*of*) **Pepito.**

1. Sonia/Elena
2. Felipe/Sonia
3. el señor Torres/Pepito
4. Elena/la señora Torres
5. Elisa/Pepito
6. Pepito/Sonia
7. Felipe/Elena
8. Pepito/Elena

EJERCICIO 3 Identificación

Dé tres sustantivos que identifican más a la persona. (*Give three nouns that further identify the person.*)

1. el abuelo: el hombre, el esposo, el padre.
2. la abuela: _____, _____, _____.
3. el tío   _____, _____, _____.
4. la tía   _____, _____, _____.
5. el padre: _____, _____, _____.
6. la madre: _____, _____, _____.
7. el hijo: _____, _____, _____.
8. la hija: _____, _____, _____.

> refrán (*saying*): **De tal padre, tal hijo**

■ CONVERSACIÓN

Juan Hidalgo es un estudiante mexicano.[1] Es de Monterrey, una ciudad grande y moderna que está en el norte de México. Juan está visitando una clase de español en los Estados Unidos.

LINDA	**¿Dónde está tu familia, Juan?**
JUAN	**En este momento están de vacaciones en Acapulco.**
TERESA	**¿Cómo es tu padre?**
JUAN	**Pues, es un hombre alto, muy simpático y de profesión, es médico.**
DANIEL	**¿Y tu madre?**
JUAN	**Mi madre es bonita, morena y muy inteligente. Es una profesora de arqueología.**
MARÍA	**¿Tienes hermanos?**
JUAN	**Sí. Tengo dos hermanos y tres hermanas.**

NOTE 1:   The words *mexicano* and *México*, although written with an **x**, are pronounced with a Spanish **j**.

Juan Hidalgo is a Mexican student. He is from Monterrey, a large, modern city which is in the north of Mexico. Juan is visiting a Spanish class in the United States.

LINDA	*Where is your family, Juan?*
JUAN	*At this moment they are vacationing in Acapulco.*
TERESA	*What is your father like?*
JUAN	*Well, he is a tall, very nice man, and he is a doctor by profession.*
DANIEL	*And your mother?*
JUAN	*My mother is pretty, dark complected, and very intelligent. She is an archeology professor.*
MARÍA	*Do you have brothers and sisters?*
JUAN	*Yes. I have two brothers and three sisters.*

■ ESTRUCTURA

I. Los pronombres personales *Subject pronouns*

yo	*I*	**nosotros (as)**	*we*
tú	*you (familiar, first-name basis)*	**vosotros (as)**	*you (plural, familiar)*
usted	*you (formal, last-name basis)*	**ustedes**	*you (plural, formal)*
él	*he*	**ellos**	*they (m.)*
ella	*she*	**ellas**	*they (f.)*

NOTE 1:   Subject pronouns are often omitted in Spanish when the reference is clear.

NOTE 2: The **vosotros** form, commonly used in Spain, is rarely heard in Spanish America, where **ustedes** is used instead.

NOTE 3: **Usted** is often abbreviated to **Ud.** or **Vd. Ustedes** is often abbreviated to **Uds.** or **Vds.**

NOTE 4: Spanish does not have a subject pronoun equivalent to *it*.

Es mi coche.   *It's my car.*

EJERCICIO 4   Los pronombres

Sustituya según el modelo. (*Substitute according to the model*).

Modelo   *Juan* es mexicano.   **Él es mexicano.**

1. *María* es alta.   *Ella es alta*
2. *María y Elena* son amigas.   *Ellas son amigas.*
3. *Carlos y yo* somos (are) estudiantes.   *Nosotros son estudiantes*
4. *Carlos y Felipe* son hermanos.   *Ellos son hermanos*
5. *Pepe* es sincero.   *Él es sincero*

II. El verbo irregular <u>ser</u> en el presente *The irregular verb <u>ser</u> (to be) in the present tense*

You may have observed in Chapter 1 that Spanish has two verbs meaning *to be*.

Los alumnos **son** inteligentes.   *The students are intelligent.*
¿Cómo **está** usted?   *How are you?*

These verbs (**ser** and **estar**) are not interchangeable. Each verb will be presented and practiced individually. Then their contrasting uses will be explained.

Ser is an irregular verb (it does not follow a set pattern of conjugation), and thus must be learned separately.

ser—to be

yo **soy**	*I am*	nosotros(as) **somos**	*we are*
tú **eres**	*you are*	vosotros(as) **sois**	*you are*
usted **es**	*you are*	ustedes **son**	*you are*
él **es**	*he is*	ellos **son**	*they are*
ella **es**	*she is*	ellas **son**	*they are*

Ejemplos   Juan Hidalgo **es** un estudiante mexicano.
¿**Eres** tú sincero?
Yo **soy** religioso.
Carmen y Linda **son** famosas.

EJERCICIO 5   ¡Vamos a practicar! (*Let's practice.*)

Complete las oraciones con la forma correcta del verbo **ser** y el adjetivo.

1. Yo soy americano(a).
   Tú **eres americano(a).**
   Usted _es_ _____.
   Él _es_ _____.
   Ella _es_ _____.
   Nosotros _somos_ _____.
   Vosotros _sois_ _____.
   Ustedes _son_ _____.
   Ellos _son_ _____.
   Ellas _son_ _____.

2. Él es inteligente
   Ustedes _son_ _____.
   Yo _soy_ _____.
   Ellas _son_ _____.
   Juan y Felipe _son_ _____.
   Nosotros _somos_ _____.
   Vosotros _sois_ _____.
   Usted _son_ _____.
   Tú _eres_ _____.
   Juanita _es_ _____.

VOCABULARIO   Adjectives commonly used with **ser**—*to be.*

gordo(a)	*fat*	**viejo(a)**	*old*
flaco(a)	*skinny*	**joven**	*young*
delgado(a)	*slender*	**nuevo(a)**	*new*
feo(a)	*ugly*	**fuerte**	*strong*
guapo(a)	*handsome, good-looking*	**débil**	*weak*
		simpático(a)	*nice (persons)*
bonito(a)	*pretty*	**difícil**	*difficult, hard*
hermoso(a)	*beautiful*	**fácil**	*easy*
alto(a)	*tall, high*		
bajo(a)	*short, low*	**alemán(a)**	*German*
moreno(a)	*brunette*	**americano(a)**	*American*
rubio(a)	*blonde*	**chino(a)**	*Chinese*
rico(a)	*rich*	**español(a)**	*Spanish*
pobre	*poor*	**francés(a)**	*French*
grande	*large, big*	**inglés(a)**	*English*
pequeño(a)	*small, little*	**japonés(a)**	*Japanese*
bueno(a)	*good*	**ruso(a)**	*Russian*
malo(a)	*bad*		
tonto(a)	*dumb, silly*	**muy**	*very (adverb)*
inteligente	*intelligent*	**y**	*and (conjunction)*

NOTE 1:   **Alemán, chino, español, francés, inglés, japonés**, and **ruso** in the masculine form also function as the name of the language. Note that they are not capitalized.

NOTE 2:   **Bueno** and **malo** may be placed before a noun. If the noun is masculine singular the **o** is dropped.

Es un **buen** muchacho.
No es un **mal** abogado.

NOTE: **Y** changes to **e** when followed by **i** or **hi**.

Carlos es guapo **e** inteligente.

EJERCICIO 6   Descripción

Complete con adjetivos apropiados según los modelos.

A. Descripción

> Modelo   Nosotros somos . . .
> Nosotros somos **inteligentes y jóvenes**.

1. Yo soy . . .
2. Mi (*my*) padre es . . .
3. Mi madre es . . .
4. Mi hermano(a) es . . .
5. Mi novio(a) es . . .
6. Mis (*my*) clases son . . .
7. Mis amigos son . . .

[handwritten: o > u   y > e]

B. Nacionalidades

> Modelo   La princesa Diana es . . .
> La princesa Diana es **inglesa.**

1. La cámara Yashica es . . .
2. El coche VW es . . .
3. Los Beatles son . . .
4. Los coches Peugeot y Renault son . . .
5. Los autores Pushkin y Dostoyevski son . . .

EJERCICIO 7   ¡Al contrario! (*To the contrary!*)

Lea la descripción y haga una oración afirmativa usando el adjetivo de significado contrario. (*Read the description and make an affirmative sentence using the adjective of opposite meaning.*)

> Modelo   Jane Fonda no es *fea*. **Es bonita**.

1. Fat Albert no es *flaco*.
2. Richard Gere no es *viejo*.
3. Ralph Sampson no es *bajo*.
4. Liza Minelli y Liz Taylor no son *rubias*.
5. Muhammed Ali no es *débil*.
6. John Travolta y Robert Redford no son *pobres*.
7. Richard Chamberlain no es *tonto*.
8. El libro no es *difícil*.
9. Los carros no son *nuevos*.
10. La casa no es *pequeña*.

EJERCICIO 8   ¿Cómo es?

Conteste en español en oraciones completas usando la forma correcta del verbo **ser**.

Modelos   ¿Es usted americano(a)?
Sí, soy americano(a). (o) No, no soy americano(a).
¿Son ustedes jóvenes?
Sí, somos jóvenes. (o) No, no somos jóvenes.

1. ¿Es usted simpático(a)? *Soy simpático.*
2. ¿Son ustedes fuertes? *Somos fuertes.*
3. ¿Es usted guapo(a)? *Soy guapa*
4. ¿Son ustedes alumnos buenos? *Somos alumnos buenos*
5. ¿Es usted rico(a)? *Sí, soy rica*
6. ¿Son ustedes inteligentes? *Somos inteligentes*
7. ¿Es el profesor (la profesora) de español joven? *El profesores de español joven.*
8. ¿Es la clase de español difícil? *La clase es de español difícil.*

¡Qué (how) magnífico es ser jóvenes y novios! Teotihuacán, México

III. El verbo irregular <u>estar</u> en el presente *The irregular verb estar (to be) in the present tense*

estar—*to be*

yo **estoy**	*I am*	nosotros(as) **estamos**	*we are*
tú **estás**	*you are*	vosotros(as) **estáis**	*you are*
usted **está**	*you are*	ustedes **están**	*you are*
él **está**	*he is*	ellos **están**	*they are*
ella **está**	*she is*	ellas **están**	*they are*

Ejemplos   Yo **estoy** en la clase de español.
La señora Hidalgo **está** en Acapulco.
Nosotros **estamos** muy bien.

EJERCICIO 9   ¡Vamos a practicar!

Complete las oraciones con la forma correcta del verbo **estar**.

1. Yo estoy muy contento.
   Tú *estas contento*
   Usted *esta contento*
   Él *está contento*
   Ella *está contento*
   Nosotros *estamos contento*
   Vosotros *estais contento*
   Ustedes *están contento*
   Ellos *están contento*
   Ellas *están contento*

2. Ella está en la clase.
   Tú *estas en la clase*
   Ellos *están en la clase*
   Usted *esta en la clase*
   Yo *estoy en la clase*
   Roberto y yo *estamos en la clase*
   Ustedes *están en la clase*
   Él *está en la clase*
   Carmen y Linda *están en la clase*
   Vosotros *estais en la clase*

VOCABULARIO   Words and phrases commonly used with **estar**—*to be*

bien	*well*	**allí**	*there*
mal	*bad, badly*	**aquí**	*here*
enfermo(a)	*sick*	**en el campo**	*in the country, field*
cansado(a)	*tired*		
contento(a)	*happy*	**en la ciudad**	*in the city*
triste	*sad*	**en la escuela**	*at school*
aburrido(a)	*bored*	**en las montañas**	*in the mountains*
cerrado(a)	*closed*	**en la playa**	*at the beach*
abierto(a)	*open*	**en la universidad**	*at the university*

NOTE: **Bien**, **mal**, **allí**, and **aquí** are adverbs and therefore do not change to agree with the subject.

EJERCICIO 10   ¿En qué condición están?

Complete con la forma correcta del verbo **estar** y el adverbio o adjetivo.

    Modelo   cerrado—el libro, las ventanas
                  El libro está cerrado.
                  Las ventanas están cerradas.

1. abierto—el cuarderno, la puerta
2. bien—el profesor, la profesora
3. mal—los niños, las niñas
4. enfermo—mi hermano, mi hermana
5. cansado—tú, vosotros
6. contento—usted, ustedes
7. triste—ellos, ellas
8. aburrido—nosotros, nosotras

EJERCICIO 11   ¿Cómo está? o ¿Dónde (*where*) está?

Conteste en español en oraciones completas usando la forma correcta del verbo **estar**.

1. ¿Está usted cansado(a)? ¿enfermo(a)? ¿aburrido(a)? ¿triste?
2. ¿Está usted bien o mal?
3. ¿Está el libro cerrado o abierto?
4. ¿Están ustedes en la playa o en la escuela?
5. ¿Están ustedes en el campo o en la ciudad?
6. ¿Está el presidente aquí?

IV. Ser versus estar

A. Ser is used:

1. To indicate characteristics native or natural to the person or thing described; it denotes identity. Use **ser** to tell who or what the person or thing is.

Él es profesor.[1]   *He is a professor.*
Ella es abuela.[1]   *She is a grandmother.*
Yo soy católico.[1]   *I am a Catholic.*

Use **ser** to tell nationality or origin.

Yo soy mexicano.[1]   *I am a Mexican.*
Yo soy de México.   *I am from Mexico.*

NOTE 1:   After **ser**, the indefinite article is omitted before unmodified nouns of vocation, religion, and nationality.

Use **ser** to tell what the subject is like.

¿Cómo es usted?   *What are you like?*
Ella es alta.   *She is tall.*
Él es fuerte.   *He is strong.*
Ellos son inteligentes.   *They are intelligent.*

2. To tell time.

¿Qué hora es?   *What time is it?*
Son las dos.   *It's two o'clock.*

3. To show possession (you will study this in Chapter 5).

El coche es de Juan.   *The car is John's*
Es mi coche.   *It is my car.*

B. Estar is used:

1. To show conditions not native or natural to the person or thing described; it tells in what state the subject is at a given time.

¿Cómo está usted?   *How are you?*
Estoy enfermo.   *I am sick.*
Pepe está cansado.   *Pepe is tired.*
Estamos tristes.   *We are sad.*
Estamos contentos.   *We are happy.*
Las ventanas están abiertas.   *The windows are open.*
La puerta está cerrada.   *The door is closed.*

2. To show location; to tell where the subject is.

La casa está en el campo.   *The house is in the country.*
Estamos en la clase.   *We are in clase.*

EJERCICIO 12   Ser y **estar**.

Conteste en español en oraciones completas.

A. The verb **ser** + characteristics.

1. ¿Cómo es usted? (*What are you like?*)
2. ¿Cómo es su (*your*) casa?
3. ¿Cómo es su profesor(a)?
4. ¿Cómo es el presidente?
5. ¿Cómo son los médicos?

B. The verb **estar** + conditions and locations.

1. ¿Cómo está usted?
2. ¿Cómo está el profesor?
3. ¿Cómo está su madre?
4. ¿Dónde (*where*) está usted?
5. ¿Dónde está su padre?
6. ¿Dónde están los estudiantes?

EJERCICIO 13   ¿Ser o **estar**?

Haga una oración con la forma correcta de **ser** o **estar** según las indicaciones. (*Make a sentence with the correct form of **ser** or **estar** according to the cues.*)

>   Modelos   católico/el abogado
>   **El abogado es católico.**
>   contento/el esposo
>   **El esposo está contento.**

1. gorda/la profesora
2. enfermos/los niños
3. en la ciudad/el hombre
4. altas/las montañas
5. en la playa/los chicos
6. de Francia/el médico
7. grande/la familia
8. vieja/la casa
9. abierta/la puerta
10. joven/María
11. aquí/el lápiz y la pluma
12. morena/la sobrina
13. en la mesa/el cuaderno
14. triste/el hijo
15. aburrido/yo
16. cansados/nosotros

EJERCICIO 14   Una breve (*brief*) presentación

Describa para (*for*) la clase un miembro (*member*) de la familia, indicando:
¿Cómo se llama?
¿Cómo es?
¿Cómo está?
¿Dónde está?

Frecuentemente en la familia hispánica los abuelos, los padres y los hijos viven (*live*) en la misma (*same*) casa. Sevilla, España

V. El verbo irregular ir en el presente   *The irregular verb ir (to go) in the present tense*

ir—*to go*

yo **voy**	*I go, do go, am going*
tú **vas**	*you go, do go, are going*
usted **va**	*you go, do go, are going*
él **va**	*he goes, does go, is going*
ella **va**	*she goes, does go, is going*
nosotros **vamos**	*we go, do go, are going*
vosotros **vais**	*you go, do go, are going*
ustedes **van**	*you go, do go, are going*
ellos **van**	*they go, do go, are going*
ellas **van**	*they go, do go, are going*

Ejemplos   Yo **voy** a (*to*) la clase los lunes.   *I go to class on Mondays.*
Ellos **van** a Nicaragua.   *They are going to Nicaragua.*
¿**Vas** a la oficina los miércoles?   *Do you go to the office on Wednesdays?*

NOTE 1:   **Ir a** + infinitive means *to be going to . . .*, indicating an action yet to occur.

Voy a visitar Monterrey.
I am going to visit Monterrey.

NOTE 2:   **Vamos a** + infinitive, used affirmatively, can also mean *let's.*

¡Vamos a conversar!   *Let's converse!*
¡Vamos a practicar!   *Let's practice!*

EJERCICIO 15   ¿Quién va? (*Who is going*)

Conteste en español según el modelo.

Modelo   ¿Quién va a Acapulco? (Yo)
    Yo voy a Acapulco.

1.   ¿Quién va a Monterrey? (Alberto, José y yo, mis tías, Carmen).
2.   ¿Quién va a la universidad? (Yo, vosotros, tú, ustedes).

va a Monterrey
Vamos a Monterrey
van a Monterrey
va a Monterrey

Yo voy a la universidad.

EJERCICIO 16   ¡Vamos a viajar! (*Let's travel.*)

Haga dos oraciones según el modelo.

Modelo   Yo (Puerto Rico/San Juan)
    Voy a Puerto Rico.   (I am going to Puerto Rico.)
    Voy a visitar San Juan.   (I am going to visit San Juan.)

1.   Elena (San Antonio/El Alamo)
2.   Nosotros (Panamá/El Canal)
3.   Rita y Sandra (España/El Museo del Prado)
4.   Yo (México/las pirámides)

VI. Las contracciones *Contractions*

Only two contractions exist in Spanish.

$$a + el = al$$
$$de + el = del$$

The word **a** (preposition meaning *to*) combined with the masculine singular article **el** becomes **al.**

    Voy **al** campo.   *I am going to the country.*
(but) Voy **a la** ciudad.   *I am going to the city.*

The preposition **de** (meaning *from*, *about*, or *of*) combined with the masculine singular article **el** becomes **del.**

    Soy **del** campo.   *I am from the country.*
(but) Soy **de la** ciudad.   *I am from the city.*

EJERCICIO 17   ¿Con (*with*) o sin (*without*) contracción?

1. Voy a (el hotel, el museo, la playa, las montañas, el patio).
2. Permítame presentar a (el profesor Díaz, la señora Gómez, el señor Hernández).
3. Son de (el Perú, la Argentina, el campo, la ciudad, el Paraguay).
4. Es el hijo de (la señora Torres, el señor Torres, la profesora).

PERSPECTIVA ORIGINAL

1. **Mi familia.**
   Bring to class a photo, or draw a picture, of your immediate family. Be prepared to give a brief description of each member.
2. **Conversación.**
   Following the format of the **conversación** (see p. 35), create a dialog about your family.

■ PANORAMA CULTURAL

La familia hispánica

La familia hispánica es generalmente *más grande* que la familia norteamericana. Es *costumbre* que en la familia los abuelos y *algunas veces* otros parientes *vivan* en la *misma* casa. En la familia tradicional el esposo es el *jefe* de la familia y *trabaja* en el mundo de los *negocios*. La esposa, *corazón* de la familia, es jefa de la casa y *cuida de* los niños. *También* la familia frecuentemente tiene una *criada*. Pero *hoy día* muchas mujeres deciden *por* más educación y la oportunidad de entrar en el mundo profesional.

larger
custom/sometimes
live/same/head
works/business/
  heart/takes care
  of/Also/maid/
  nowadays/for

Como (*like*) la médica bonita, muchas mujeres entran en el mundo profesional. Puerto Vallarta, México

¿Cómo se llama?

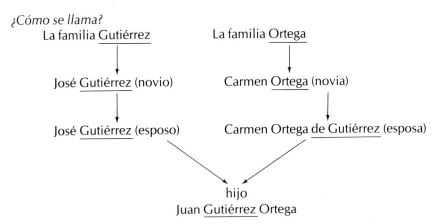

La familia <u>Gutiérrez</u>   La familia <u>Ortega</u>

José <u>Gutiérrez</u> (novio)   Carmen <u>Ortega</u> (novia)

José <u>Gutiérrez</u> (esposo)   Carmen Ortega <u>de Gutiérrez</u> (esposa)

hijo
Juan <u>Gutiérrez</u> Ortega

En los *países* hispánicos la esposa *conserva* su *nombre* y *también toma* el nombre del esposo. Carmen Ortega es de la familia Gutiérrez. El hijo *puede tener* el nombre de su padre y *el de* su madre. *En esta manera* el hijo se identifica con las familias de los dos padres, *pero* es el nombre del padre que continúa *por* las generaciones.

countries/keeps/
name/also/
takes/can/have/
that of/this
way/but/through

■ INTEGRACIÓN

A.   ORAL EXERCISE: **Conversación**
1.   The dialog will be read twice. Listen the first time; the second time pauses will be provided for you to repeat each phrase.
2.   Listen to the statements related to the dialog; indicate if the statements are true or false. (**cierto** = *true*, **falso** = *false*)

B.   ORAL EXERCISE: THE VERB **ser** IN THE PRESENT TENSE
Listen and repeat.

C.   ORAL EXERCISE: THE VERB **ser**
Repeat the sentence substituting the correct form of the verb **ser**. Do not forget adjective agreement.

Example	(tape)	Yo soy joven.
	(tape)	Él _____.
	(your response)	**Él es joven.**
	(tape confirmation)	Él es joven.
	(your repetition)	**Él es joven.**

D.   ORAL EXERCISE: THE VERB **ser** + CHARACTERISTICS (WHO OR WHAT)
Link each subject pronoun to all the *who* or *what* characteristics portrayed in the drawings. Use the correct form of **ser**.

Example	(tape)	Usted _____.
	(your response)	**Usted es profesora.**
	(tape confirmation)	Usted es profesora.
	(your repetition)	**Usted es profesora.**

ser

usted

1. Alicia

2. él

3. nosotros

4. yo   Carlos

5. Daniel   Enrique

6. tú   él

7 Carlota — Luisa

8 Juanita — Ana

9 Alberto — Pepe

10 el abuelo — Pepito

11 el elefante — el mosquito

E. ORAL EXERCISE: THE VERB **estar** IN THE PRESENT TENSE
    Listen and repeat.

F. ORAL EXERCISE: THE VERB **estar**
    Repeat the sentence substituting the correct form of the verb **estar**.

Example	(tape)	Yo estoy aquí.
	(tape)	Él _____.
	(your response)	**Él está aquí.**
	(tape confirmation)	Él está aquí.
	(your repetition)	**Él está aquí.**

G. ORAL EXERCISE: THE VERB **estar** + LOCATIONS OR CONDITIONS
    Link each subject pronoun to the locations or conditions portrayed in the drawings.
    Use the correct form of **estar**.

yo

Example	(tape)	Yo _____.
	(your response)	**Yo estoy en el campo.**
	(tape confirmation)	Yo estoy en el campo.
	(your repetition)	**Yo estoy en el campo.**

tú

yo

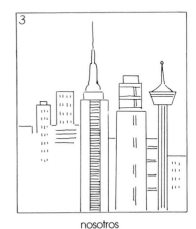

nosotros

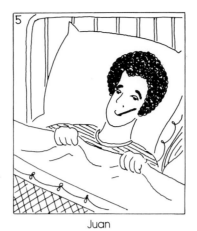

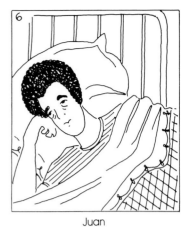

ustedes

Juan

Juan

Juan

Juan

H. ORAL EXERCISE: **Ser** OR **estar**?
    Describe Cecilia by completing the sentences according to the cue, using **es**
    or **está** as appropriate.

    Examples (tape)   joven
              (your response)   **Cecilia es joven.**
              (tape confirmation)   Cecilia es joven.

              (tape)   enferma
              (your response)   **Cecilia está enferma.**
              (tape confirmation)   Cecilia está enferma.

I. WRITTEN EXERCISE: **Ser** AND **estar**
    Write the answers to the eight questions on the tape. Each question will be
    given twice.

    Example   (tape)   ¿Está usted en la ciudad o en el
                                             campo?

	(tape repeat)	¿Está usted en la ciudad o en el campo?
	(your possible response)	**Estoy en la ciudad.**

J. ORAL EXERCISE: THE VERB **ir** IN THE PRESENT TENSE
Listen and repeat.

K. ORAL EXERCISE: THE VERB **ir** IN THE PRESENT TENSE
Repeat the sentence substituting the correct form of the verb **ir**.

	Example	(tape)	Yo voy a la playa. Tú . . .
		(your response)	**Tú vas a la playa.**
		(tape confirmation)	Tú vas a la playa.
		(your repetition)	**Tú vas a la playa.**

L. ORAL EXERCISE: CONTRACTIONS (**a** + **el** = **al**; **de** + **el** = **del**)
Complete the sentences using contractions as necessary.

	Example	(tape)	el rancho . . . Vamos a . . .
		(your response)	**Vamos al rancho.**
		(tape confirmation)	Vamos al rancho.
		(your repetition)	**Vamos al rancho.**

M. DICTATION: **La familia hispánica**
Write the three sentences you hear. Each sentence will be read three times: the first time at normal speed, the second time with pauses for writing, and the third time at normal speed for correction.

■ REPASO DE VOCABULARIO ACTIVO

Adjetivos

abierto(a)	**contento(a)**	**gordo(a)**	**pequeño(a)**
aburrido(a)	**débil**	**grande**	**pobre**
alemán(a)	**delgado(a)**	**guapo(a)**	**rico(a)**
alto(a)	**difícil**	**hermoso(a)**	**rubio(a)**
americano(a)	**enfermo(a)**	**inglés(a)**	**ruso(a)**
bajo(a)	**español(a)**	**inteligente**	**simpático(a)**
bonito(a)	**fácil**	**japonés(a)**	**tonto(a)**
bueno(a)	**feo(a)**	**joven**	**triste**
cansado(a)	**flaco(a)**	**malo(a)**	**viejo(a)**
cerrado(a)	**francés(a)**	**moreno(a)**	
chino(a)	**fuerte**	**nuevo(a)**	

Adverbios

allí	**mal**
aquí	**muy**
bien	

Conjunción

y

Preposiciones

a
de

Pronombres personales

yo	**nosotros(as)**
tú	**vosotros(as)**
usted	**ustedes**
él	**ellos**
ella	**ellas**

Sustantivos

la **abogada**	el **carro**	el **inglés**	la **novia**
el **abogado**	el **coche**	el **japonés**	el **novio**
la **abuela**	la **escuela**	la **madre**	el **padre**
el **abuelo**	el **español**	la **médica**	los **padres**
el **alemán**	la **esposa**	el **médico**	el **pariente**
la **amiga**	el **esposo**	las **montañas**	la **playa**
el **amigo**	la **familia**	la **muchacha**	la **prima**
el **auto**	el **francés**	el **muchacho**	el **primo**
el **campo**	la **hermana**	la **mujer**	el **ruso**
la **casa**	el **hermano**	la **mujer de negocios**	la **sobrina**
la **chica**	la **hija**	la **nieta**	el **sobrino**
el **chico**	el **hijo**	el **nieto**	la **tía**
el **chino**	el **hombre**	la **niña**	el **tío**
la **ciudad**	el **hombre de negocios**	el **niño**	la **universidad**

Verbos

estar
ser
ir

■ EJERCICIOS DE REPASO

I. Vocabulario

Indique la persona que corresponde a la definición. (*Indicate the person that corresponds to the definition.*)

	A	B
1.	La madre de mi madre.	nieta

abuela

2. El hijo de mi hermano. *sobrino*   tío
3. La hija de mi tía.   *prima*   novio
4. El hermano de mi padre. *tío*   abuela
5. La hija de mi hija.   *nieta*   sobrino
6. El amigo íntimo de una señorita.   prima

nivio

II. El verbo ser

Haga una oración con la forma correcta del verbo **ser**.

Modelo   inteligente/yo
Yo soy inteligente.

1. Nosotros somos simpáticos   2. Ella es abogada   3. Tú eres bonita
4. Ustedes son jovenes
5. yo soy fuerte
6. Vosotros sois american

1. simpáticos/nosotros   4. jóvenes/ustedes
2. abogada/ella   5. fuerte/yo
3. bonita/tú   6. americanos/vosotros

III. El verbo estar

Haga una oración con la forma correcta del verbo **estar**.

Modelo   contento(a)/usted
Usted está contento(a).

Nosotros estamos en la playa   2. Tú estás enfermo
3. Yo estoy aburrido
4. Las ventanas estan abiert
5. Ella esta triste
6. Vosotros estais cansado

1. en la playa/nosotros   4. abiertas/las ventanas
2. enfermo(a)/tú   5. triste/ella
3. aburrido(a)/yo   6. cansados/vosotros

IV. Ser versus estar

Haga una oración con la forma correcta de **ser** o **estar** según las indicaciones (*according to the cues*).

1. japonesa/ella   6. jóvenes/nosotros
2. grande/la casa   7. aquí/Cecilia
3. cansado(a)/yo   8. rico(a)/tú
4. médicos/ellos   9. viejo/el carro
5. muy mal/nosotros   10. en la clase/ustedes

V. El verbo ir

Haga una oración con la forma correcta del verbo **ir** + **a**.

Modelo   la playa/yo
Yo voy a la playa.

1. la escuela/Roberto y Pablo   4. Caracas/el señor Martínez
2. las montañas/nosotros   5. Los Ángeles/yo
3. la clase/tú   6. Sevilla/vosotros

VI. Repaso general

A. Conteste en oraciones completas.

1. ¿Cómo es usted?   *estoy bien*

2. ¿Cómo es su madre? *Su madre es bien*
3. ¿Cómo es el presidente? *El presidente es contento*
4. ¿Cómo son sus amigos? *Sus amigos son consado*
5. ¿Cómo está usted?
6. ¿Está usted en la playa? *No. estoy en la ferrocarril*
7. ¿Están ustedes en la universidad? *Si ustedes están en la universidad.*
8. ¿Va usted al hospital? *No usted va escuela*
9. ¿Van ustedes al campo?
10. ¿Va el profesor a la clase los domingos?

B. Traduzca al español.

1. I am tired.
2. The students are not here.
3. The grandmother is old.
4. The brothers are tall. *El hermano son alto*
5. The door is closed.
6. We are American; she is German.
7. He is not a doctor.
8. She is the daughter of the professor (m).
9. She is rich, intelligent, and beautiful.
10. Are you (familiar, singular) going to the country?

NOTE: The Answer Key to the **Ejercicios de Repaso** can be found in Appendix IV.

CAPÍTULO 3

■ VOCABULARIO *El mercado*

el **mercado**	market	el **maíz**	corn
		la **patata**	potato
el **bistec**	steak	el **tomate**	tomato
el **camarón**	shrimp	el **arroz**	rice
la **carne**	meat		
la **chuleta de cerdo**	pork chop	el **huevo**	egg
el **jamón**	ham	el **pan**	bread
la **langosta**	lobster	el **queso**	cheese
el **marisco**	shellfish, seafood		
el **pescado**	fish	la **banana**	banana
el **pollo**	chicken	el **durazno**	peach
la **salchicha**	sausage	la **fresa**	strawberry
el **tocino**	bacon	la **fruta**	fruit
		la **manzana**	apple
la **cebolla**	onion	la **naranja**	orange
los **frijoles**	beans	la **pera**	pear
los **guisantes**	peas	la **piña**	pineapple
las **habichuelas**	green beans	la **sandía**	watermelon
la **legumbre**	vegetable	la **uva**	grape
la **lechuga**	lettuce		

EJERCICIO 1   Vamos al mercado

Conteste en español según el dibujo. (*Answer in Spanish according to the drawing.*)

1.   ¿Qué frutas vende la señora? **La señora vende** . . . (*What fruit does the woman sell? The woman sells . . .*)

57

2.   ¿Qué legumbres vende la señora?
3.   ¿Qué carnes vende el hombre?
4.   ¿Qué más (*what else*) venden en el mercado?

EJERCICIO 2   Mi comida (*food*) favorita.

Conteste según el modelo.

> Modelo   ¿Cuál es su carne favorita?
> (*Which is your favorite meat?*)
> **Mi carne favorita es el* jamón.**
> (*My favorite meat is ham.*)

1.   ¿Cuál es su fruta favorita?
2.   ¿Cuál es su marisco favorito?
3.   ¿Cuál es su legumbre favorita?
4.   ¿Cuál es su carne favorita?
5.   ¿Cuál es su sandwich (o bocadillo) favorito? (**Mi sandwich favorito es de . . .**)
6.   ¿Cuál es su sopa (*soup*) favorita? (**Mi sopa favorita es de . . .**)

■ CONVERSACIÓN

Doña Rosa está en el mercado público y habla con doña María, vendedora de frutas.

DOÑA ROSA	**Buenos días, doña María. Hoy necesito frutas.**
DOÑA MARÍA	**Pues, tenemos naranjas, piñas y bananas.**
DOÑA ROSA	**A ver . . . Deme un kilo¹ de bananas y una piña, por favor.**
DOÑA MARÍA	**Muy bien. Aquí están . . . y mañana llegan fresas del campo.**
DOÑA ROSA	**¡Magnífico! Bueno, doña María, ¿cuánto es?**
DOÑA MARÍA	**Noventa pesos² en total, señora.**
DOÑA ROSA	**Muchas gracias. Hasta mañana.**

NOTE 1:   1.00 kilo (kilogram) = 2.20 pounds.
NOTE 2: $1.00 U.S.A. = approximately 165 Mexican pesos (1984).

Doña Rosa is at the public market and is talking with Doña María, a fruit vendor.

DOÑA ROSA	*Good morning, doña María. Today I need fruit.*
DOÑA MARÍA	*Well, we have oranges, pineapples, and bananas.*
DOÑA ROSA	*Let's see. . . . Give me a kilo of bananas and a pineapple, please.*
DOÑA MARÍA	*Very well, Here they are . . . and tomorrow strawberries are arriving from the country.*
DOÑA ROSA	*Wonderful! Well, doña María, how much is it?*
DOÑA MARÍA	*Ninety pesos total.*
DOÑA ROSA	*Thank you very much. See you tomorrow.*

*In Spanish the definite article is placed before nouns used in an abstract or general sense.

Las mujeres venden muchas legumbres frescas (*fresh*)
en el mercado público. Oaxaca, México

En los supermercados grandes y modernos venden
todo tipo de productos. Méxcio, D. F.

■ ESTRUCTURA

I. El presente de los verbos regulares -ar *The present tense of regular -ar verbs*

Spanish infinitives end in **-ar**, **-er**, or **-ir**. For example: visit**ar** (to visit), vend**er** (to sell), escrib**ir** (to write).

A. Ejemplos de los verbos -ar

caminar	to walk	**llegar**	to arrive
comprar	to buy	**necesitar**	to need
estudiar	to study	**tomar**	to take, drink, eat
hablar	to speak, talk	**trabajar**	to work

B. La conjugación de los verbos -ar en el presente

Present-tense conjugations of regular **-ar** verbs drop the **-ar** from the infinitive and to the remaining stem add the endings indicated.

endings (**-ar**) Modelo   **hablar** *to speak, talk*

-o	yo **hablo**	*I speak, do speak, am speaking*
-as	tú **hablas**	*You speak, do speak, are speaking*
-a	usted **habla**	*You speak, do speak, are speaking*
-a	él **habla**	*He speaks, does speak, is speaking*
-a	ella **habla**	*She speaks, does speak, is speaking*
-amos	nosotros **hablamos**	*We speak, do speak, are speaking*
-áis	vosotros **habláis**	*You speak, do speak, are speaking*
-an	ustedes **hablan**	*You speak, do speak, are speaking*
-an	ellos **hablan**	*They speak, do speak, are speaking*
-an	ellas **hablan**	*They speak, do speak, are speaking*

Ejemplos	Yo no **hablo** italiano.	*I don't speak Italian.*
	¿**Hablas** español?	*Do you speak Spanish?*
	Hablamos del profesor.	*We are talking about the profesor.*

EJERCICIO 3   ¡Vamos a practicar!

Conjugue los verbos en el presente. (*Conjugate the verbs in the present tense.*)
1. caminar   2. tomar   3. llegar   4. estudiar

EJERCICIO 4   Necesitamos información

Conteste según el modelo.

   Modelo   ¿Quién *estudia* el vocabulario? (Yo)
            Yo estudio el vocabulario.

1. ¿Quién *habla* español? (Yo, tú, él)
2. ¿Quién *compra* los lápices? (Nosotros, vosotros, ustedes)
3. ¿Quién *trabaja* en el mercado? (Yo, tú y yo, Fernando)
4. ¿Quién *necesita* estudiar la lección? (Esteban y Carlos, tú, usted)

VOCABULARIO

mucho	*much, a lot*	**a tiempo**	*on time*
poco	*little* (quantity)	**esta noche**	*tonight*
hoy	*today*	**todo el día**	*all day*
mañana	*tomorrow*	**toda la noche**	*all night*
ahora	*now*	**todos los días**	*every day*
temprano	*early*	**por la mañana**	*in the morning*
tarde	*late*	**por la tarde**	*in the afternoon*
más tarde	*later*	**por la noche**	*in the evening, at night*

EJERCICIO 5   Tú y yo

Hágale preguntas a un(a) estudiante según el modelo; escuche la respuesta. (*Ask a student questions according to the model; listen to the response.*)

Modelo   *trabajar*/todo el día
           (pregunta)   **¿Trabajas todo el día?**
           (respuesta)   **(Sí,) (No, no) trabajo todo el día.**

1. *trabajar*/por la noche
2. *llegar* a clase/a tiempo
3. *estudiar*/poco
4. *hablar*/mucho español
5. *llegar* a clase/tarde
6. *estudiar*/todos los días

EJERCICIO 6   ¡Más preguntas!

Conteste en español en oraciones completas.

1. ¿Llega el profesor (la profesora) a clase temprano?
2. ¿Toman los mexicanos mucha tequila?
3. ¿Caminan ustedes en la ciudad por la tarde?
4. ¿Necesitan ustedes trabajar mañana?
5. ¿Necesitan ustedes estudiar ahora? ¿más tarde? ¿esta noche?
6. ¿Necesitan ustedes ir al mercado hoy?

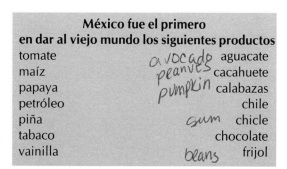

México fue el primero	
en dar al viejo mundo los siguientes productos	
tomate	
maíz	*avocado* aguacate
papaya	*peanuts* cacahuete
petróleo	*pumpkin* calabazas
piña	chile
tabaco	*gum* chicle
vainilla	chocolate
	beans frijol

II. El presente de los verbos regulares -er, -ir *The present tense of regular -er, -ir verbs*

A. Ejemplos de los verbos -er, -ir:

aprender	*to learn*	**abrir**	*to open*
beber	*to drink*	**escribir**	*to write*
comer	*to eat*	**vivir**	*to live*
vender	*to sell*		

B. La conjugación de los verbos -er, -ir en el presente

Present-tense conjugations of regular **-er** and **-ir** verbs drop the **-er** and **-ir** from the infinitive and to the remaining stem add the endings indicated. The **-er** and **-ir** verbs have the same endings except in the **nosotros** (we) and **vosotros** (you, familiar plural) forms.

endings (**-er**)   Modelo   **comer** *to eat*

-o	yo **como**	*I eat, do eat, am eating*
-es	tú **comes**	*You eat, do eat, are eating*
-e	usted **come**	*You eat, do eat, are eating*
-e	él **come**	*He eats, does eat, is eating*
-e	ella **come**	*She eats, does eat, is eating*
-emos	nosotros **comemos**	*We eat, do eat, are eating*
-éis	vosotros **coméis**	*You eat, do eat, are eating*
-en	ustedes **comen**	*You eat, do eat, are eating*
-en	ellos **comen**	*They eat, do eat, are eating*
-en	ellas **comen**	*They eat, do eat, are eating*

endings (**-ir**)   Modelo   **vivir** *to live*

-o	yo **vivo**	*I live, do live, am living*
-es	tú **vives**	*You live, do live, are living*
-e	usted **vive**	*You live, do live, are living*
-e	él **vive**	*He lives, does live, is living*
-e	ella **vive**	*She lives, does live, is living*
-imos	nosotros **vivimos**	*We live, do live, are living*
-ís	vosotros **vivís**	*You live, do live, are living*
-en	ustedes **viven**	*You live, do live, are living*
-en	ellos **viven**	*They live, do live, are living*
-en	ellas **viven**	*They live, do live, are living*

Ejemplos	**¿Comen** ustedes en la cafetería?	*Do you eat in the cafeteria?*
	Comemos mucho pescado.	*We eat a lot of fish.*
	¿Vives en San Diego?	*Do you live in San Diego?*
	No, **vivimos** aquí.	*No, we live here.*

EJERCICIO 7   ¡Vamos a practicar!

Conjugue los verbos en el presente.

1. aprender   2. vender   3. escribir   4. abrir

EJERCICIO 8   Necesitamos más información

Conteste según el modelo.

> Modelo   ¿Quién *escribe* los ejercicios? (Nosotros)
> **Nosotros escribimos los ejercicios.**

1. ¿Quién *bebe* Coca-Cola? (tú, usted, Lupe y Linda)
2. ¿Quién *come* en la cafetería? (Ana, vosotros, el profesor)
3. ¿Quién *abre* la ventana por la noche? (nosotros, yo, Pepito y Elena)
4. ¿Quién *vive aquí? (nosotros, tú, mi primo)*

EJERCICIO 9   Preguntas generales

Conteste en español en oraciones completas.

1. ¿Aprende usted español o chino?
2. ¿Aprenden ustedes ruso?
3. ¿Vive usted en el dormitorio?
4. ¿Viven ustedes en la ciudad?
5. ¿Escribe usted con (*with*) lápiz o con pluma?
6. ¿Escriben ustedes en la pizarra?
7. ¿Come usted muchas legumbres?
8. ¿Comen los profesores langosta y bistec todos los días?
9. ¿Va usted a comer en la cafetería hoy?
10. ¿Van ustedes a escribir todos los ejercicios?

EJERCICIO 10   Repaso (*review*) de verbos

Sustituya el verbo.

1. Yo *hablo* mucho en la clase.
   (estudiar) estudio
   (aprender) aprendo
   (escribir) escribo
2. Tú *necesitas* una Pepsi.
   (comprar) compras
   (beber) bebes
   (tomar) tomas
3. Ellos *caminan* en la ciudad.
   (vivir) vivan
   (trabajar) trabajan
   (estudiar) estudian

4. María y yo *trabajamos* por la tarde.
   (comer)
   (caminar)
   (llegar)
5. Ella *estudia* español.
   (hablar)
   (aprender)

■ VOCABULARIO

el **desayuno**	*breakfast*		la **galleta**	*cookie*
el **almuerzo**	*lunch*		el **helado**	*ice cream*
la **cena**	*supper, dinner*		el **pastel**	*pie, pastry*
la **comida**	*food, main meal*		el **postre**	*dessert*
			la **torta**	*cake*
la **ensalada**	*salad*			
la **sopa**	*soup*		el **azúcar**	*sugar*
			la **crema**	*cream*
el **agua**¹	*water* (f.)		el **hielo**	*ice*
la **bebida**	*drink, beverage*		la **mantequilla**	*butter*
el **café**	*coffee*		la **mermelada**	*jam*
la **cerveza**	*beer*		la **pimienta**	*pepper*
el **jugo**	*juice*		la **sal**	*salt*
la **leche**	*milk*			
el **té**	*tea*		**caliente**	*hot* (things)
el **vino**	*wine*		**frío**	*cold*

NOTE 1:   **Agua** is feminine even though it has the article **el**, for example, **el agua fría**. The plural form is **las aguas**.

NOTE 2:   Spanish uses the preposition **de** (of) to join two nouns for the purpose of description.

helado de vainilla	*vanilla ice cream*
torta de chocolate	*chocolate cake*
jugo de naranja	*orange juice*

EJERCICIO 11   Tú y yo

Hágale preguntas a un(a) estudiante según el modelo; escuche la respuesta.

Modelo   tomar/crema en el café
      (pregunta)   **¿Tomas crema en el café?**
      (respuesta)   **(Sí,) (No, no) tomo crema en el café.**

1. tomar/azúcar en el té
2. tomar/mantequilla en las patatas
3. necesitar/sal en la sopa
4. necesitar/pimienta en la ensalada
5. necesitar/hielo en la Coca-Cola
6. beber/cerveza
7. beber/vino
8. beber/mucha agua
9. comer/helado de chocolate
10. comer/mucho postre

La familia celebra el cumpleaños (*birthday*) del padre con una paella
deliciosa, ensalada, pan, vino y una torta especial. México, D. F.

EJERCICIO 12   ¡Vamos a comer!

¿Asocia usted las siguientes comidas con el desayuno, el almuerzo o la cena? (*Do you associate the following foods with breakfast, lunch, or dinner?*)

> Modelo   huevos fritos (*fried*)
> **el desayuno**

1. pan y mermelada
2. sopa y ensalada
3. pastel de manzana
4. huevos y tocino
5. arroz con (*with*) pollo
6. jugo de naranja
7. un sandwich de jamón y queso
8. un coctel de camarones

EJERCICIO 13   Una comida especial

1. Tú y tu novio(a) van a tomar el desayuno (un buffet) en el restaurante Casa Gallardo. ¿Qué (*what*) comen ustedes? ¿Y qué beben?

    Comida:

    Bebidas:

2. Una persona muy importante llega a la casa esta noche. ¿Qué vamos a preparar?

    Comida:

    Bebidas:

    Postre:

En el desayuno reciba a la familia con esta bebida. Tang es de riquísimo sabor a naranja. Se prepara en pocos segundos... Sólo tiene que servir dos cucharadas de Tang en un vaso de agua bien fría ¡ y ya tiene sus buenos días con Tang!

III. Palabras interrogativas *Interrogatives*

¿qué?	what	**¿cuál? ¿cuáles?**	which one? which ones?
¿cómo?	how?	**¿cuánto? ¿cuánta?**	how much?
¿cuándo?	when?	**¿cuántos? ¿cuántas?**	how many?
¿por qué?	why?	**¿dónde?**	where?
¿quién? ¿quiénes?	who?	**¿adónde?**	(to) where?
		¿de dónde?	from where?

NOTE: Some interrogatives, without written accents, become or are used to form conjunctions and relative pronouns introducing dependent clauses. The most common are:

que   *that, which, who*

¿Qué mercado es?	*What (which) market is it?*
Es el mercado **que** está en la plaza.	*It is the market that is on the plaza.*

lo que   *what, that which*

¿Qué compra él?	What does he buy?
Compra **lo que** necesita.	He buys what he needs.

cuando   *when*

¿Cuándo aprende usted?	When do you learn?
Aprendo **cuando** estudio.	I learn when I study.

porque   *because* (written as one word)

¿Por qué estudia usted?	Why do you study?
Estudio **porque** necesito aprender.	I study because I need to learn.

EJERCICIO 14   Interrogación

Conteste en español en oraciones completas.

1. ¿Quiénes son ustedes?
2. ¿Quién es usted?
3. ¿Cómo está usted hoy?
4. ¿Qué hora es?
5. ¿Cuándo estudia usted?
6. ¿Cuántos huevos toma usted en el desayuno (*for breakfast*)?
7. ¿Cuántas horas trabaja usted por (*per*) semana?
8. ¿Dónde vive usted?
9. ¿De dónde es usted?
10. ¿Adónde va usted?
11. ¿Cuál es su postre favorito?
12. ¿Cuáles son los días de la semana?

EJERCICIO 15   ¿Quién es usted?

Usted habla con su nuevo compañero de cuarto (*roommate*). Déle (*give him/her*) información y hágale preguntas según el modelo; escuche la respuesta.

> Modelo   Mi padre trabaja en Nueva York.
> (pregunta)   **¿Dónde trabaja su padre?**
> (respuesta)   **Mi padre trabaja en Chicago**, etc.

1. Soy de San Antonio.
2. Estoy muy contento(a) hoy.
3. Soy el (la) hijo(a) de la señora Gómez.
4. Mi bebida favorita es Coca-Cola.
5. Necesito un libro de español.
6. Necesito cinco cuadernos.
7. Trabajo por la noche.
8. Estoy en la universidad porque necesito aprender.
9. Voy a la cafetería ahora.

IV. Números *(30–100)*

treinta	*30*		**sesenta**	*60*
treinta y uno	*31*		**setenta**	*70*
treinta y dos	*32*		**ochenta**	*80*
cuarenta	*40*		**noventa**	*90*
cincuenta	*50*		**cien**	*100*

NOTE: **Uno**, even when part of a higher number becomes **un** or **una** to agree with a masculine or feminine noun.

veinti**ún** libros   *21 books*
setenta y **una** mujeres   *71 women*

EJERCICIO 16   ¡Los números hasta (*up to*) cien!

1. Vamos a contar.
   a) de treinta a cien—30, 32, 34, . . .
   b) de cinco a cien—5, 10, 15, . . .
   c) de diez a cien—10, 20, 30, . . .
2. Matemáticas

70	22	38	69	91	86	100
+10	+12	+15	+ 8	−45	−18	− 7

EJERCICIO 17   ¿Cuánto cuesta? (*How much does it cost?*) **dólares** = *dollars*

1. La cena para (*for*) dos en un restaurante elegante
2. Una radio pequeña
3. Los libros de texto para dos cursos

4. Una noche en el hotel—una persona
5. Una bicicleta para niños

PERSPECTIVA ORIGINAL

1. Mini-drama: **en el mercado público**.
   Following the format of the **conversación** (see p. 58) you and a classmate create a dialog that takes place between a buyer and a vendor at the open-air market.
2. **La entrevista**. (*The interview*).
   In Spanish ask a classmate a series of questions; for example:
   What is your name?
   Where are you from?
   Where do you live?
   What is your family like?
     (mother, father, brothers, sisters, etc.)
   What is your favorite food?

   Be prepared to report the information back to the class.

■ PANORAMA CULTURAL

La comida hispánica

La comida hispánica es rica, interesante y muy variada porque representa los muchos países situados en tres continentes y *también* las influencias de varias culturas: la india, la negra, la blanca. Muchas personas *piensan* que la comida española es *picante* y están *sorprendidas* al *descubrir* que es más típica de México que de otras partes del mundo hispánico. *Vemos* la variedad de comida comparando las tortillas, frijoles, chiles jalapeños o enchiladas de México con el famoso *asado* o bistec de la Argentina o los churros[1] con chocolate, la paella,[1] el *flan* y las *aceitunas* de España.

also
think
hot/surprised/dis-
covering/We
see
grilled roast/cus-
tard/olives

El joven prepara
los churros típicos de España.
Galicia, España

En contraste con la comida, las horas de comer son *casi* idénticas en muchas   *almost*
partes del mundo hispánico. El desayuno se come temprano por la mañana, a las
seis o a las siete, y en general se come poco—pan, mermelada y café con leche.

El almuerzo, la comida principal, se come a las dos o a las tres de la tarde y la
cena a las nueve o a las diez de la noche. *Después de* comer muchas familias, *so-*   *After*
bre todo los jóvenes, van al *cine*, a la plaza o al parque para conversar con amigos.   *above all/movies*

NOTE 1:   **Churros** are a donut-like pastry; **paella** is a dish of rice and assorted sea-
foods and meats.

NOTE 2:   For recipes of dishes from the Spanish-speaking world, see Appendix V.

Las tiendas de especialidades

En el mundo hispánico, *además de* los mercados públicos y los supermercados, *se*   *besides/are seen*
ven frecuentemente *tiendas* pequeñas donde se vende un artículo o producto   *shops*
especial. *Por ejemplo*, una tienda donde venden leche o productos de la leche   *For example*
se llama una lechería, o donde venden pan, una panadería. ¿Cómo se llaman las
tiendas en que venden pasteles? ¿carne? ¿tortillas?—Son pastelería, carnicería, tor-
tillería.

¿Cuántos kilos de tortillas
necesitas hoy? Oaxaca, México

■ INTEGRACIÓN

A. ORAL EXERCISE: **Conversación**
   1. The dialog will be read twice. Listen the first time; the second time pauses will be provided for you to repeat each phrase.
   2. Listen to the statements related to the dialog; indicate if the statements are true or false.

B. ORAL EXERCISE: VOCABULARY, **el mercado**
   Answer the questions on the tape according to the drawings, naming the items in each picture; listen to the tape confirmation.

las carnes

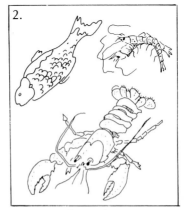

los mariscos

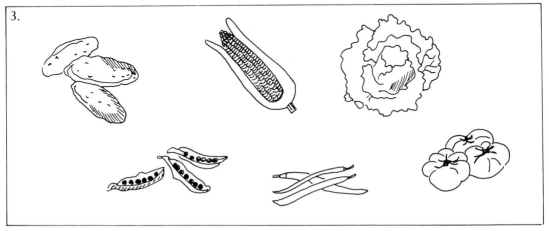

las legumbres

4.

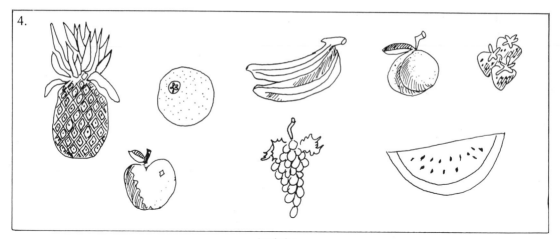

las frutas

C.   ORAL EXERCISE: **-ar** VERBS
Repeat each sentence substituting the correct form of the verb.
Example	(tape)	Ella camina todos los días. Nosotros . . .
	(your response)	**Nosotros caminamos todos los días.**
	(tape confirmation)	Nosotros caminamos todos los días.
	(your repetition)	**Nosotros caminamos todos los días.**

D.   WRITTEN EXERCISE: **-ar** VERBS
Write answers to the ten questions on the tape. Each question will be given twice.
Example	(tape)	¿Habla usted mucho?
	(tape repeat)	¿Habla usted mucho?
	(your possible response)	**Sí, hablo mucho.**

E.   ORAL EXERCISE: **-er** AND **-ir** VERBS
Repeat each sentence substituting the correct form of the verb.
Example	(tape)	Yo como en la cafetería. Él . . .
	(your response)	**Él come en la cafetería.**
	(tape confirmation)	Él come en la cafetería.
	(your repetition)	**Él come en la cafetería.**

F.   WRITTEN EXERCISE: **-er** AND **-ir** VERBS
Write answers to the eight questions on the tape. Each question will be given twice.
Example	(tape)	¿Come usted mucho?
	(tape repeat)	¿Come usted mucho?
	(your possible response)	**Sí, como mucho.**

G.   ORAL EXERCISE: VOCABULARY, **la comida**
Answer the questions on the tape according to the drawings; listen for the tape confirmation.

1.

el desayuno

2.

el almuerzo

3.

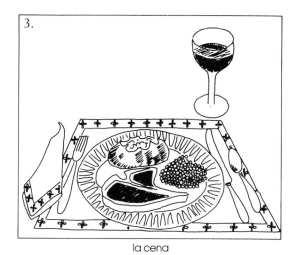

la cena

4.

el postre

H.   ORAL EXERCISE: INTERROGATIVES
Answer the questions on the tape according to the drawings.

¿Qué . . .?

Example
(tape)   ¿Qué es?
(your response)   **Es la mermelada.**
(tape confirmation)   Es la mermelada.
(your repetition)   **Es la mermelada.**

1.

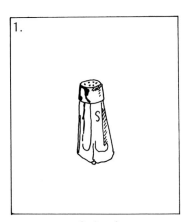

¿Qué . . .?

2.

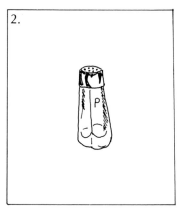

¿Qué . . .?

3.

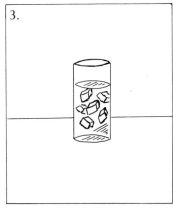

¿Cómo . . .?

4.

¿Cómo . . .?

5.

¿Quién . . .?

6.

¿Quiénes . . .?

7.

¿Cuántos . . .?

8.

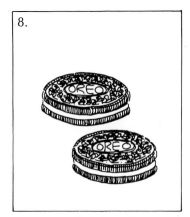

¿Cuántas . . .?

9.

¿Dónde . . .?

10.

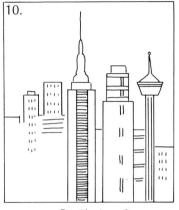

¿De dónde . . .?

¿Adónde . . .?

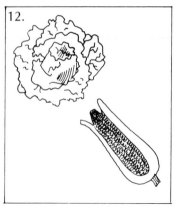

¿Cuál . . .?

I.   WRITTEN EXERCISE: INTERROGATIVES
      Write the answers to the eight questions on the tape. Each question will be given twice.

Example (tape)	¿Cómo está su madre?
(tape repeat)	¿Cómo está su madre?
(your possible response)	**Mi madre está muy bien.**

J.   ORAL EXERCISE: NUMBERS 30–100
      Listen and repeat:
      30, 31, 32, 33, 34, 35, 36, 37, 38, 39, 40, 45, 50, 55, 60, 65, 70, 75, 80, 85, 90, 95, 100

K.   ORAL EXERCISE: NUMBERS
      Supply the answers for the math problems you hear and listen for the tape confirmation.

L.   DICTATION: **La comida hispánica**
      Write the three sentences you hear. Each sentence will be read three times: the first time at normal speed, the second time with pauses for writing, and the third time at normal speed for correction.

■ REPASO DE VOCABULARIO ACTIVO

Adjetivos

caliente   frío

Adverbios y expresiones adverbiales

ahora	**poco**	**esta noche**	**por la tarde**
hoy	**tarde**	**más tarde**	**todo el día**
mañana	**temprano**	**por la mañana**	**todos los días**
mucho	**a tiempo**	**por la noche**	**toda la noche**

Palabras interrogativas

¿adónde?	¿cuándo?	¿de dónde?	¿qué?
¿cómo?	¿cuánto(a)?	¿dónde?	¿quién(es)?
¿cuál(es)?	¿cuántos(as)?	¿por qué?	

Conjunciones y pronombres relativos

cuando   lo que   porque   que

Sustantivos

el **agua**	la **fruta**	el **pastel**
el **almuerzo**	la **galleta**	la **patata**
el **arroz**	los **guisantes**	la **pera**
el **azúcar**	las **habichuelas**	el **pescado**
la **banana**	el **helado**	la **pimienta**
la **bebida**	el **hielo**	la **piña**
el **bistec**	el **huevo**	el **pollo**
el **café**	el **jamón**	el **postre**
el **camarón**	el **jugo**	el **queso**
la **carne**	la **langosta**	la **sal**
la **cebolla**	la **leche**	la **salchicha**
la **cena**	la **lechuga**	la **sandía**
la **cerveza**	la **legumbre**	la **sopa**
la **chuleta de cerdo**	el **maíz**	el **té**
la **comida**	la **mantequilla**	el **tocino**
la **crema**	la **manzana**	el **tomate**
el **desayuno**	el **marisco**	la **torta**
el **durazno**	el **mercado**	la **uva**
la **ensalada**	la **mermelada**	el **vino**
la **fresa**	la **naranja**	
los **frijoles**	el **pan**	

Verbos

abrir	comprar	necesitar
aprender	escribir	tomar
beber	estudiar	trabajar
caminar	hablar	vender
comer	llegar	vivir

Números

treinta	setenta
cuarenta	ochenta
cincuenta	noventa
sesenta	cien

■ EJERCICIOS DE REPASO

I. Los verbos -ar, -er, -ir
Sustituya el verbo.

1. Mi abuela no *toma* cerveza.
    (beber, comprar, necesitar)
2. ¿*Trabajas* en el dormitorio?
    (vivir, comer, estudiar)
3. Yo *como* temprano por la mañana.
    (llegar, trabajar, caminar)
4. Los profesores *escriben* los libros.
    (abrir, vender, estudiar)
5. Nosotros *estudiamos* mucho en la clase.
    (hablar, aprender, escribir)

II. Palabras interrogativas
Haga una pregunta pidiendo (*asking for*) la información correcta según el modelo.

Modelo   El señor Fulano no es el profesor.
          ¿Quién es?

1. Felipe no bebe vino.
2. Ana no vive en Madrid.
3. Roberto no es de Buenos Aires.
4. Alberto no trabaja por la mañana.
5. Elena no va al mercado.
6. Eduardo no necesita tres carros.
7. ¡No me llamo Lucinda!
8. La clase de matemáticas no es mi clase favorita.

III. Los números (30–100)
Diga (*say*) el número.

1.	33	5.	77
2.	44	6.	88
3.	55	7.	99
4.	66	8.	100

IV. Repaso General
A. Conteste en oraciones completas.

1. ¿Qué come usted en el desayuno (*for breakfast*)?
2. ¿Qué come usted en la cena?
3. ¿Cuál es su bebida favorita?
4. ¿Cuál es su postre favorito?
5. ¿Cuál es su fruta favorita?
6. ¿Cuándo estudia usted?

7. ¿Aprenden ustedes el español?
8. ¿Escriben ustedes todos los ejercicios?
9. ¿Dónde vive usted?
10. ¿Llega usted a clase a tiempo todos los días?

B. Traduzca al español.

1. I need cream and sugar in my coffee.
2. Does the soup need salt and pepper?
3. We drink wine every day.
4. Do you (formal, plural) sell ice?
5. We are buying beans, sausage, and watermelon.
6. Where are you (familiar, singular) going now?
7. Why are we writing the exercises?
8. When are they arriving?
9. Who (singular) works in the city?
10. He is going to live here.

CAPÍTULO 4

■ VOCABULARIO *El cuerpo y las actividades*

la **boca**	mouth		**abrazar**	to hug
el **brazo**	arm		**amar**	to love
la **cabeza**	head		**bailar**	to dance
la **cara**	face		**besar**	to kiss
el **cuerpo**	body		**buscar**	to look (for)
el **dedo**	finger		**cantar**	to sing
el **diente**	tooth		**cocinar**	to cook
la **espalda**	back		**correr**	to run
el **estómago**	stomach		**deber**	must, ought to,
la **garganta**	throat			should, to owe
el **hombro**	shoulder		**descansar**	to rest
el **labio**	lip		**escuchar**	to listen (to)
la **lengua**	tongue		**fumar**	to smoke
la **mano**	hand		**llamar**	to call
la **nariz**	nose		**leer**	to read
el **ojo**	eye		**limpiar**	to clean
la **oreja**	ear		**manejar**	to drive
el **pecho**	chest, breast		**mirar**	to look (at)
el **pelo**	hair		**nadar**	to swim
el **pie**	foot		**pintar**	to paint
la **pierna**	leg		**tocar**	to touch, to play
				(instruments)
el **resfriado**	cold (illness)		**usar**	to use
el **dolor**	ache, pain			
la **mentira**	lie			
la **verdad**	truth			

81

EJERCICIO 1   El cuerpo y las actividades

Haga (*make*) una oración según el modelo.

> Modelo   tocar el piano
> **Para** (*in order to*) **tocar el piano uso las manos y los dedos.**

1. nadar   6. besar
2. correr   7. leer
3. mirar   8. bailar
4. pintar   9. escuchar
5. abrazar   10. manejar

EJERCICIO 2   Usted y sus actividades

Conteste en español en oraciones completas.

1. ¿Nada usted mucho?
2. ¿Canta usted bien o mal?
3. ¿Con (*with*) quién baila usted?
4. ¿Quién cocina en su familia?
5. ¿Cuándo descansa usted?
6. ¿Debe usted limpiar el cuarto (*room*) hoy?
7. ¿Toca usted el piano? ¿el violín? ¿la guitarra? ¿la trompeta?
8. ¿Cuándo mira usted la televisión?

■ CONVERSACIÓN

Alicia visita la oficina del Dr. García.

DOCTOR	**Buenas tardes, Alicia.**
ALICIA	**Buenas tardes, Dr. García. No estoy muy bien hoy.**
DOCTOR	**¿Qué tienes, Alicia?**
ALICIA	**No sé, doctor, pero tengo un dolor de garganta horrible.**
DOCTOR	**¿Tienes dolor de cabeza también?**
ALICIA	**Sí, y estoy muy cansada; no puedo dormir.**
DOCTOR	**Parece que tienes un resfriado muy serio. Lo que necesitas es beber jugo de naranja, tomar estas pastillas y descansar.**
ALICIA	**Está bien, doctor. Muchas gracias por su atención. Llamo por teléfono si tengo más problemas.**

Alice visits Dr. García's office.

DOCTOR	*Good afternoon, Alice.*
ALICIA	*Good afternoon, Dr. García. I'm not very well today.*
DOCTOR	*What's the matter Alice?*

ALICIA	I don't know, doctor, but I have a horrible sore throat.
DOCTOR	Do you have a headache also?
ALICIA	Yes, and I'm very tired; I cannot sleep.
DOCTOR	It seems that you have a very bad cold. What you need is to drink orange juice, take these pills, and rest.
ALICIA	All right, doctor. Thank you for your attention. I'll call if I have more problems.

■ ESTRUCTURA

I. La a personal   *The personal a*

The Spanish personal **a** precedes a direct object that is a noun referring to a person or persons. The personal **a** has no English equivalent or translation.

> **Subject + verb + personal a + direct object (person)**

María espera **a** los muchachos.
Nosotros buscamos **a** María.

but

María espera el taxi.
Nosotros buscamos los libros.

NOTE: The personal **a**, like the preposition **a**, contracts with the masculine singular article **el** to form **al**.

Ellos llaman **al** médico.

EJERCICIO 3   ¿Con o sin **a**?

1. Miro . . . (María, el libro, la pizarra, la profesora, mi madre)
2. Buscamos . . . (mi hermano, el médico, los lápices, los niños, el abogado)

EJERCICIO 4   Preguntas muy personales

Conteste en español en oraciones completas, usando la **a** personal.

1. ¿A quién (*whom*) besas?
2. ¿A quién abrazas?
3. ¿A quién llamas por teléfono?
4. ¿A quién amas?
5. ¿A quién escuchas?
6. ¿Esperas a los profesores cuando llegan tarde a la clase?
7. ¿Buscas a la secretaria?
8. ¿Miras a las chicas bonitas (a los chicos guapos)?

II. Verbos con yo irregular en el presente *Verbs with irregular yo form in the present tense*

hacer *to do, make*   **poner** *to put, place*   **salir** *to leave, go out*

hago	hacemos	pongo	ponemos	salgo	salimos
haces	hacéis	pones	ponéis	sales	salís
hace	hacen	pone	ponen	sale	salen

ver *to see*   **traer** *to bring*   **dar** *to give*

veo	vemos	traigo	traemos	doy	damos
ves	veis	traes	traéis	das	dais
ve	ven	trae	traen	da	dan

traducir *to translate*   **oír** *to hear*

traduzco	traducimos	oigo	oímos
traduces	traducís	oyes	oís
traduce	traducen	oye	oyen (note addition of **y**)

EJERCICO 5   Una fiesta de sorpresa (*surprise*)

Usted y sus (*your*) amigos preparan para (*for*) una fiesta especial. Es el cumpleaños (*birthday*) de Carmen. Indique lo que las personas hacen según el modelo.

Modelo   *poner* las galletas en la mesa (Luisa)
Luisa pone las galletas en la mesa.

1. *salir* de la escuela temprano (yo, nosotros)
2. *hacer* las decoraciones (yo, Lupe y Linda)
3. *dar* las decoraciones a Luisa (yo, tú)
4. *poner* una torta en la mesa (yo, Luisa)
5. *traer* las bebidas (yo, ustedes)
6. ¡*oír* el coche de Carmen! (yo, nosotros)
7. ¡*ver* a Carmen! (yo, vosotros) ¡Sorpresa!

Spanish has two verbs meaning *to know*. Note the differences in the way they are used, and note their conjugations.

conocer   *to know, to be acquainted with persons or places, to meet*

conozco	conocemos
conoces	conocéis
conoce	conocen

Conozco al profesor.   *I know the teacher.*
Conocemos la ciudad de Madrid.   *We know (are acquainted with) the city of Madrid.*

saber *to know facts, skills, how to*

sé	sabemos
sabes	sabéis
sabe	saben

Sé el número.   *I know the number.*
Sabemos traducir la oración.   *We know how to translate the sentence.*

EJERCICIO 6   Personas famosas

A. Identifique a las personas famosas según el modelo.

Modelo   ¿Barbra Streisand?—cantar
Conozco a Barbra Streisand.
Ella sabe cantar.

1. ¿John Travolta?—bailar
2. ¿Olivia Newton-John?—cantar
3. ¿Michael Jackson?—tocar la guitarra
4. ¿Kareem Abdul Jabbar?—jugar al básquetbol
5. ¿Salvador Dalí?—pintar

B. Identifique las ciudades según el modelo.

Modelo   ¿Sacramento?—California
Conozco Sacramento.
Sé que es la capital de California.

1. ¿Lima?—el Perú
2. ¿Madrid?—España
3. ¿Buenos Aires?—la Argentina
4. ¿Caracas?—Venezuela
5. ¿Santiago?—Chile

EJERCICIO 7   Preguntas generales

Conteste en español en oraciones completas.

1. ¿Qué hacen ustedes en la universidad?
2. ¿Hace usted la tarea todos los días?
3. ¿Pone usted mucho azúcar en el café?
4. ¿Da usted dinero (*money*) a la universidad?
5. ¿Qué frutas ve usted en el mercado?
6. ¿Sale usted por la tarde o por la noche?
7. ¿Conoce usted al presidente de los Estados Unidos?
8. ¿Sabe usted el número de teléfono del profesor?
9. ¿Qué trae usted a la clase?
10. ¿Oye usted a los estudiantes en el corredor (*hallway*)?
11. ¿Traduce usted las lecturas (*readings*)?

El fútbol (*soccer*) es un deporte (*sport*) muy popular
en el mundo hispánico. Sevilla, España

III. Verbos con cambios en la raíz en el presente *Stem-changing verbs in the present tense*

Stem-changing verbs in the present tense change **o→ue**, **e→ie**, and **e→i** in all persons except **nosotros** and **vosotros**.

Modelos

o→ue		**e→ie**		**e→i**	
dormir *to sleep*		**querer** *to want, wish, love*		**pedir** *to ask for*	
du<u>e</u>rmo	dormimos	qu<u>i</u>ero	queremos	p<u>i</u>do	pedimos
du<u>e</u>rmes	dormís	qu<u>i</u>eres	queréis	p<u>i</u>des	pedís
du<u>e</u>rme	du<u>e</u>rmen	qu<u>i</u>ere	qu<u>i</u>eren	p<u>i</u>de	p<u>i</u>den

jugar (ue)[1]	*to play (sports)*	**c<u>e</u>rrar** (ie)	*to close*
poder (ue)	*to be able, can*	**prefe<u>r</u>ir** (ie)	*to prefer*
volver (ue)	*to return*	**rep<u>e</u>tir** (i)	*to repeat*
entender (ie)	*to understand*		

NOTE 1:   The verb **jugar** (*to play*) is unique because **u** changes to **ue**. The preposition **a**, plus the definite article, follows **jugar** when a sport is named.

Juego al béisbol.   *I play baseball.*

EJERCICIO 8   ¡Vamos a practicar!

Conjugue los verbos en el presente.
1. poder   2. cerrar   3. repetir   *pod*

EJERCICIO 9   Un día sin clases

Indique lo que usted y sus amigos hacen en un día sin clases.

> Modelo   *jugar* al tenis por la mañana (yo)
> **Juego al tenis por la mañana.**

1. *dormir* hasta (*until*) las diez de la mañana (nosotros, yo)
2. *poder* tomar un desayuno muy grande (Carlos y José, tú)
3. *jugar* al volibol por la tarde (nosotros, Teresa)
4. *querer* ir a un restaurante por la noche (vosotros, yo)
5. *pedir* una comida especial (tú, ellos)
6. *volver* a casa muy tarde (Teresa y yo, yo)
7. *preferir* no ir a las clases mañana (mis amigos, usted)

EJERCICIO 10   Ustedes y nosotros

Hágales preguntas a dos amigos según el modelo; escuche la respuesta negativa.

> Modelo   *entender* el ejercicio
> (pregunta)   **¿Entienden (ustedes) el ejercicio?**
> (respuesta)   **No, no entendemos el ejercicio.**

1. *dormir* en la clase de español
2. *querer* estudiar
3. *preferir* trabajar
4. *repetir* el vocabulario
5. *poder* hablar ruso

EJERCICIO 11   Preguntas personales

Conteste en español en oraciones completas.

1. ¿Prefieres manejar un Ford o un Mercedes?
2. ¿Prefieres pastel de manzana o pastel de limón?
3. ¿Quieres arroz o patatas con el pollo?
4. ¿Quieres estudiar o ir a la fiesta?
5. ¿Pides huevos revueltos (*scrambled*) o huevos fritos?
6. ¿Qué bebida pides con los camarones?
7. ¿Juegas al fútbol? ¿al tenis? ¿al básquetbol?
8. ¿Puedes cantar bien? ¿bailar? ¿pintar? ¿tocar un instrumento musical?
9. ¿Cuántas horas duermes?
10. ¿Entiendes al profesor (a la profesora)?
11. ¿A qué hora cierran las puertas de la cafetería? Cuando llegas tarde, ¿dónde puedes comer?

**Fray Felipe*, Fray Felipe
duermes tú, duermes tú
suena la campana, suena la campana
Din, don, dan, din, don, dan.**

La música de la guitarra
refleja (*reflects*) el espíritu del
mundo hispánico. Madrid, España

IV. Verbos con cambios en la raíz y con yo irregular en el presente *Stem-changing verbs with irregular yo form in the present tense*

venir (ie) *to come*		**decir (i)** *to say, tell*		**tener (ie)** *to have*	
vengo	venimos	digo	decimos	tengo	tenemos
vienes	venís	dices	decís	tienes	tenéis
viene	vienen	dice	dicen	tiene	tienen

*Sung to the tune of ''Frère Jacques.''

EJERCICIO 12   ¡Vamos a practicar!

Conteste según el modelo.

Modelo   ¿Quién no *tiene* un coche nuevo? (la profesora)
La profesora no tiene un coche nuevo.

1.   ¿Quién *viene* a clase tarde? (el profesor, yo)
2.   ¿Quién *dice* que el (la) profesor(a) es viejo(a)? (los estudiantes, yo)
3.   ¿Quién *tiene* una madre simpática? (nosotros, yo)

EJERCICIO 13   Preguntas generales.

Conteste en español en oraciones completas.

1.   ¿Viene usted del dormitorio?
2.   ¿Vienen ustedes de la cafetería?
3.   ¿Viene usted a clase a tiempo?
4.   ¿Dice usted mucho en la clase?
5.   ¿Dicen ustedes la verdad?
6.   ¿Dice usted mentiras?
7.   ¿Tiene usted dolor de cabeza? ¿de estómago? ¿de garganta?
8.   ¿Tienen ustedes muchos o pocos problemas?
9.   ¿Tiene usted un cuerpo fuerte o débil?
10.   ¿Tiene su profesor(a) una nariz grande o pequeña?

refranes: **Quien tiene dinero tiene compañeros.**
Quien mucho tiene más quiere.
Decir y hacer son dos cosas y la segunda es la dificultosa.

V. Expresiones con tener *Expressions with tener*

tener (mucha) hambre	*to be (very) hungry*
tener (mucha) sed	*to be (very) thirsty*
tener (mucho) frío	*to be (very) cold (persons)*
tener (mucho) calor	*to be (very) hot (persons)*
tener (mucho) sueño	*to be (very) sleepy*
tener (mucho) miedo	*to be (very) afraid*
tener razón	*to be right*
no tener razón	*to be wrong*
tener (número) años	*to be (number) years old*
tener que + infinitive	*to have to*
tener ganas de + infinitive	*to feel like*

Ejemplos	**¿Tienes hambre?**		*Are you hungry?*
	Sí, tengo mucha hambre.		*Yes, I am very hungry.*
	¿Cuántos años tiene usted?		*How old are you?*
	Tengo diez y nueve años.		*I am nineteen years old.*
	¿Qué tienes que hacer hoy?		*What do you have to do today?*
	Tengo que estudiar.		*I have to study.*

EJERCICIO 14   ¿Qué tiene?

Indique la expresión con **tener** que corresponde a cada (*each*) situación.

1. Carlos quiere comer un bistec con cebollas, patatas, pan y ensalada.
2. Carlos dice, "¡Ay! ¡Es una serpiente!"
3. Lo que dice Carlos es la verdad.
4. Lo que dice Pancho no es la verdad.
5. ¡Brrr! ¡Necesito cerrar la ventana!
6. ¡La temperatura está a treinta y siete grados (*100° Fahrenheit*)! ¡Necesito abrir la ventana!
7. Queremos beber una cerveza, una limonada, y una Coca-Cola con hielo.
8. ¡Necesitamos dormir!

EJERCICIO 15   ¡Es necesario!

Cambie las oraciones según los modelos.

> Modelo   *Debo* estudiar
> **Tengo que estudiar.**

1. *Debo* trabajar.
2. Juan *debe* limpiar la casa.
3. *Debemos* decir la verdad.
4. Los profesores *deben* leer muchos libros.

> Modelo   *Quiero* besar a mi novio(a).
> **Tengo ganas de besar a mi novio(a).**

5. *Quiero* abrazar a mi padre.
6. Ella *quiere* tocar la guitarra.
7. *Queremos* escuchar la radio.
8. Los niños *quieren* jugar al fútbol.

SQUIRT: Quita la sed

EJERCICIO 16   ¿Qué tiene usted?

1. ¿Tiene usted mucha hambre? ¿mucha sed? ¿mucho sueño?
2. ¿Tiene usted frío ahora? ¿calor?
3. ¿Tiene usted miedo de los elefantes? ¿de los tigres? ¿de los profesores?
4. ¿Siempre (*always*) tienen razón los profesores?
5. ¿Cuántos años tiene usted? ¿y su madre? ¿y su abuela? ¿y su profesor(a)?
6. ¿Qué tiene usted que hacer hoy?

7. ¿Qué tiene usted ganas de hacer hoy?
8. ¿Tienen ustedes ganas de salir de la clase temprano?

EJERCICIO 17   Vamos a repasar (*review*).

Haga una oración según el modelo. Use la forma **yo** del verbo y un infinitivo apropiado. (No repita los infinitivos.)

Modelo   Preferir (ie)
Prefiero descansar.

1. necesitar
2. deber
3. tener que
4. querer (ie)
5. poder (ue)
6. tener ganas de
7. ir a

La corrida de toros es una combinación de drama, expresión artística, espectáculo y deporte. Guadalajara, México

■ PERSPECTIVA ORIGINAL

1. Mini-drama: **en la oficina del médico**. Following the format of the **conversación** (see p. 82) you and a classmate create a dialog that takes place between the doctor and a patient at the doctor's office.

SUPPLEMENTARY VOCABULARY

problemas digestivos	*digestive problems*
problemas psicológicos	*psychological problems*
ataque cardíaco	*heart attack*
fractura del brazo, etc.	*broken arm*, etc.
embarazada, encinta	*pregnant*

2. Composición: **Un problema**
   You have been lost in the desert for several days!
   a) What are your problems?
      (thirsty? . . . etc.)
   b) What should you do?
      (look for water? . . . etc.)
   c) What do you feel like doing?
      (drinking a cold beer? . . . etc.)

■ PANORAMA CULTURAL

Los pasatiempos   *pastimes*

La conversación

Para la *gente* hispánica el *charlar* es un pasatiempo que es parte íntegra de la   *people/talking*
vida. Durante la semana la gente frecuentemente *se encuentra* en los bares o en   *life/during/meet/*
una plaza para hablar. *También* las horas de la comida son *largas* con las conver-   *Also/long/after*
saciones de *sombremesa*.   *dinner*

Los domingos los miembros de la familia *se pasean por* las calles o las plazas y   *stroll/through*
los hombres viejos se reúnen en los parques para *discutir* la política o los deportes.   *discuss*
La conversación es un arte—una *manera* de expresar la individualidad e identidad,   *way*
de *encontrar* unos momentos de tranquilidad y de continuar una tradición cul-   *finding*
tural.

El arte

El arte también es una parte inseparable de la vida. En el teatro o en las plazas,
como observadores o como participantes, los españoles son muy *aficionados* al   *fond*
drama, al baile (el ballet o danzas folklóricas y regionales) y a la música (la guitarra
de España, la música de mariachi de México, la *flauta* india del Perú, etc.).   *flute*

Los hombres viejos pasan muchas horas conversando y mirando (*watching*)
a la gente (*people*). San Sebastián, España

Los indios celebran una fiesta especial con danzas regionales
y la música de flautas. Tubala, Panamá

Los deportes   sports
    En la vida hispánica los deportes no son *tan* importantes *como* en los Estados   *as/as*
Unidos. Sin *embargo, casi* todas las naciones tienen *equipos* de fútbol (soccer), el   *Nevertheless/al-*
deporte más popular, y la *competencia entre* las naciones hispánicas es increíble-   *most/teams/*
mente intensa por el *sentido* de nacionalismo y patriotismo.   *competition/be-*
                                                                                          tween/feeling/only/
    ¡Pero el fútbol no es el *único* deporte! Todas las naciones participan en los de-   *swimming*
portes tradicionales y modernos como el básquetbol, la *natación*, la gimnasia, etc.

La corrida de toros   *bullfight*
    Muchos norteamericanos *piensan* que la corrida de toros es un deporte, pero   *think*
para los españoles es una combinación de drama, deporte, espectáculo e interpre-   *for*
tación filosófica del conflicto *entre* la vida y la *muerte*.   *between/death*

■ INTEGRACIÓN

A.   ORAL EXERCISE: **Conversación**
      1. The dialog will be read twice. Listen the first time; the second time pauses
          will be provided for you to repeat each phrase.

      2. Listen to the statements related to the dialog; indicate if the statements are
          true or false.

NOTE: From here on ''tape confirmation'' and ''your repetition'' are omitted in the
        examples in order to avoid redundancy. The tape, however, will continue
        to give the confirmation, and you should continue to repeat the confirma-
        tion to establish clearly the correct response.

B.   ORAL EXERCISE: VOCABULARY, **el cuerpo**
      Identify the parts of the body according to the drawings.

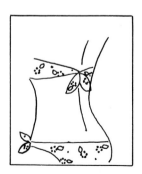

Example   (tape)   ¿Qué es?
             (your response)   **Es la espalda.**

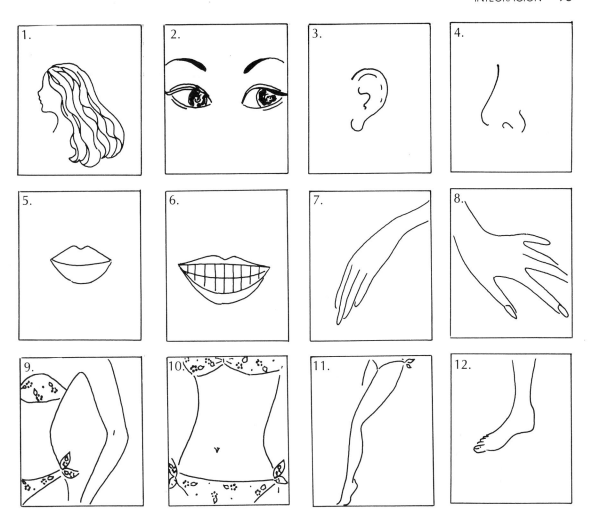

C. ORAL EXERCISE: THE PERSONAL **a**
Answer the questions on the tape according to the drawings.

Juanita   Mario

Example   (tape)   ¿A quién conoce Mario?
           (your response)   **Mario conoce a María.**

1. Juanita   Mario

2. Juanita   Mario

3. ¿Está Juanita?   Mario

4. Juanita   Mario

5. Pepe   Mónica

6. Pepe

7.

¿Dónde está mónica?

Pepe

8.

¿Cuál es el número?

Pepe

D.   ORAL EXERCISE: PRESENT-TENSE VERBS WITH IRREGULAR yo FORMS
Create two sentences with each cue, changing the verb to the **yo** form and to the **nosotros** form.

> Example   (tape)   hacer la tarea
> (your response)   **hago la tarea**
> **hacemos la tarea**

E.   WRITTEN EXERCISE: VERBS WITH IRREGULAR yo FORM
Write the answers to the nine questions on the tape. Each question will be given twice.

F.   ORAL EXERCISE: STEM-CHANGING VERBS
Repeat each sentence substituting the correct form of the verb.

> Example   (tape)   Yo entiendo la pregunta. Tú . . .
> (your response)   **Tú entiendes la pregunta.**

G.   ORAL EXERCISE: STEM-CHANGING VERBS + INFINITIVES
Answer the questions on the tape according to the drawings.

Example   (tape)   ¿Qué quiere hacer
usted?
(your response)   **Quiero nadar.**

1.

2.

3.

4.

5.

6.

7.

8.

9.

H.   WRITTEN EXERCISE: STEM-CHANGING VERBS
Write the answers to the eight questions on the tape. Each question will be given twice.

I.   ORAL EXERCISE: STEM-CHANGING VERBS WITH IRREGULAR **yo** FORM
Repeat each sentence, substituting the correct form of the verb.

Example   (tape)   Yo vengo temprano. Tú . . .
(your response)   **Tú vienes temprano.**

J.   ORAL EXERCISE: EXPRESSIONS WITH **tener**
Answer the questions on the tape according to the drawings.

Carlota

Example   (tape)   ¿Qué tiene Carlota?
(your response)   **Carlota tiene miedo.**

yo

Juan

3. Juan

4. nosotros

5. Carlota   Lupe

6. Carlos

7. la abuela

8. el padre

K.   ORAL EXERCISE: **tener que** + INFINITIVE, **tener ganas de** + INFINITIVE
Answer the questions on the tape according to the drawings.

Carmen

| Example | (tape) | ¿Qué tiene que hacer Carmen? |
| | (your response) | **Carmen tiene que tocar el piano.** |

1. Juan
2. Juan
3. yo
4. Carlos Teresa
5. Juan
6. Lupe
7. nosotros
8. yo

L.   WRITTEN EXERCISE: EXPRESSIONS WITH **tener**
      Write the answers to the eight questions on the tape. Each question will be
      given twice.

M.   DICTATION: **Los pasatiempos**
      Write the four sentences you hear. Each sentence will be read three times: the
      first time at normal speed, the second time with pauses for writing, and the
      third time at normal speed for correction.

■ REPASO DE VOCABULARIO ACTIVO

Sustantivos

la **boca**	el **estómago**	la **oreja**
el **brazo**	la **garganta**	el **pecho**
la **cabeza**	el **hombro**	el **pelo**
la **cara**	el **labio**	el **pie**
el **cuerpo**	la **lengua**	la **pierna**
el **dedo**	la **mano**	el **resfriado**
el **diente**	la **mentira**	la **verdad**
el **dolor**	la **nariz**	
la **espalda**	el **ojo**	

Verbos

abrazar	**entender (ie)**	**poner**
amar	**escuchar**	**preferir (ie)**
bailar	**fumar**	**querer (ie)**
besar	**hacer**	**repetir (i)**
buscar	**jugar (ue)**	**saber**
cantar	**leer**	**salir**
cerrar (ie)	**llamar**	**tener (ie)**
cocinar	**limpiar**	**tocar**
conocer	**manejar**	**traducir**
correr	**mirar**	**traer**
dar	**nadar**	**usar**
deber	**oír**	**venir (ie)**
decir (i)	**pedir (i)**	**ver**
descansar	**pintar**	**volver (ue)**
dormir (ue)	**poder (ue)**	

Expressions with **tener**

tener (mucho) calor	tener (mucha) sed
tener (mucho) frío	tener (mucho) sueño
tener (mucha) hambre	tener . . . años
tener (mucho) miedo	tener ganas de
tener razón	tener que
no tener razón	

■ EJERCICIOS DE REPASO

I. La a personal
¿Con o sin **a**?

1. Veo . . (mi amigo, la casa, los muchachos)
2. Conozco . . . (la señorita, el señor Lorca, la ciudad de Nueva York)

II. Verbos con yo irregular en el presente.
Complete las oraciones según el modelo.

Modelo   *oír* la televisión/yo, ellos
   Oigo la televisión.
   Oyen la televisión.

1. *traducir* las preguntas/yo, tú
2. *traer* el cuaderno/yo, ella
3. *salir* esta noche/yo, nosotros
4. *hacer* errores/yo, vosotros
5. *poner* el azúcar en el té/yo, ustedes
6. *ver* al médico/yo, usted
7. *dar* cincuenta pesos/yo, ellas
8. *conocer* a Carmen/yo, nosotros
9. *saber* cocinar/yo, tú

III. Los verbos con cambios en la raíz
Hágale preguntas a Carlos según el modelo.

Modelo   *entender* la lección
   Carlos, ¿entiendes la lección?

1. *dormir* en la clase
2. *pedir* una cerveza

3. *repetir* la conversación
4. *jugar* al béisbol
5. *preferir* descansar
6. *poder* salir ahora
7. *querer* cerrar la ventana
8. *volver* temprano

IV. Verbos con cambios en la raíz y con <u>yo</u> irregular

Conteste según el modelo.

Modelo   ¿Quién *dice* que el profesor es magnífico? (los estudiantes)
Los estudiantes dicen que el profesor es magnífico.

1. ¿Quién *viene* a la fiesta? (yo)
2. ¿Quiénes *vienen* de la ciudad? (nosotros)
3. ¿Quién *dice* la verdad? (yo)
4. ¿Quiénes no *dicen* mentiras? (nosotros)
5. ¿Quién *tiene* dolor de cabeza? (yo)
6. ¿Quiénes *tienen* dolor de estómago? (nosotros)

V. Expresiones con <u>tener</u>

Indique la expresión con **tener** que corresponde a cada (*each*) situación.

1. Voy a comer.
2. Voy a beber.
3. Van a dormir.
4. Carlota ve un ratoncito (*little mouse*).
5. ¡Vamos a abrir la ventana!
6. ¡Queremos sopa caliente y café caliente!
7. El profesor dice que yo tengo la respuesta correcta.
8. El profesor dice que tú no tienes la respuesta correcta.

VI. Repaso general

A. Conteste en oraciones completas.

1. ¿Cuáles son las partes de la cara?
2. ¿Qué partes del cuerpo usa usted para nadar?
3. ¿A qué hora sale usted esta noche?
4. ¿Qué comida trae usted a la fiesta?
5. ¿Duerme usted bien todas las noches?
6. ¿Prefieren ustedes los profesores fáciles o los profesores difíciles?
7. ¿Viene usted a clase a tiempo todos los días?
8. ¿Cuántos años tiene usted?
9. ¿Qué tiene usted que hacer hoy?
10. ¿Qué tiene usted ganas de hacer mañana?

B. Traduzca al español.

1. I know Robert.
2. I know how to swim well.
3. I am putting the pens and the pencils on (*en*) the desk.
4. What do you (familiar, singular) want to do now?
5. I can play the piano.
6. Do you (familiar, singular) play football?
7. He is looking for the child (m.); he sees the child; he is looking at the child.
8. We feel like going to the mountains.
9. I have to clean the house today.
10. I am very hungry.

[Handwritten answers:]

1. Yo ~~tengo~~ conozco Roberto
2. Yo ~~puedo~~ a nadar bien.
3. Yo pongo el lápiz y la pezera en la mesa
4. ¿Qué ~~tienes~~ tienes?
5. Yo juego el
6. ¿Juegas al futból?
7. el se busca del nino, el be el nino el es

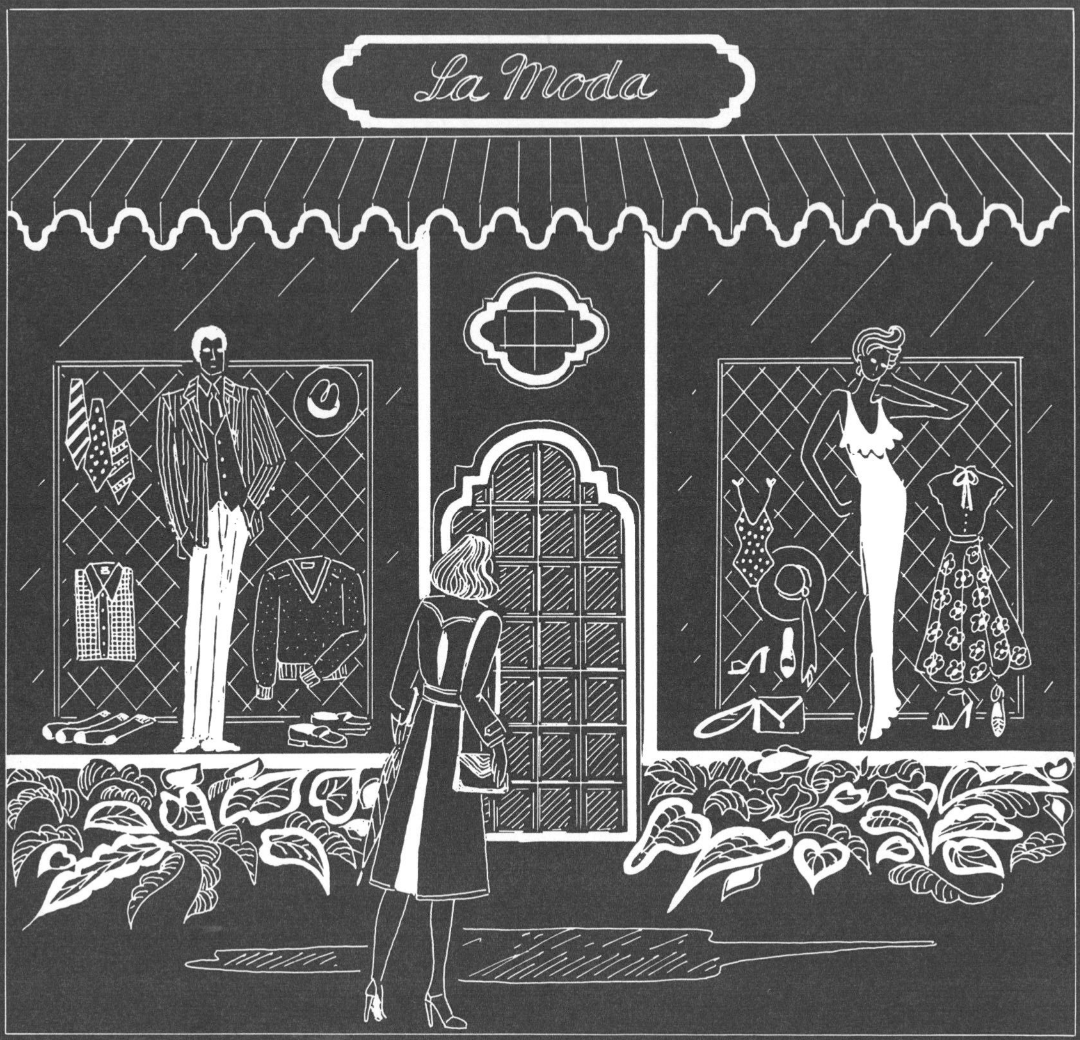
La Moda

■ VOCABULARIO *La ropa*

el **abrigo**	coat	el **suéter**	sweater
los **blujeans**	jeans	el **traje**	suit
la **blusa**	blouse	el **traje de baño**	bathing suit
la **bolsa**	purse, bag	el **vestido**	dress
las **botas**	boots	los **zapatos**	shoes
los **calcetines**	socks		
la **camisa**	shirt	**costar** (ue)	to cost
la **cartera**	wallet	**llevar**	to wear, take, carry
la **chaqueta**	jacket		
la **corbata**	tie	**ir de compras**	to go shopping
la **cosa**	thing		
la **falda**	skirt	**barato**	cheap
las **gafas**	glasses	**caro**	expensive
las **gafas de sol**	sunglasses	**corto**	short
el **impermeable**	raincoat	**largo**	long
las **joyas**	jewelry	**limpio**	clean
las **medias**	stockings	**sucio**	dirty
los **pantalones**	pants	**otro**	other, another
el **paraguas**	umbrella		
el **regalo**	gift	**amarillo**	yellow
el **reloj**	watch, clock	**azul**	blue
la **ropa**	clothing	**blanco**	white
la **ropa interior**	underwear	**gris**	grey
el **sombrero**	hat	**morado**	purple

negro	black		anoche	last night
pardo	brown		ayer	yesterday
rojo	red		el año pasado	last year
rosado	pink		la semana	
verde	green		pasada	last week

NOTE: Optional vocabulary of interest:

el **anillo**, *ring*; el **arete**, *earring*; el **collar**, *necklace*; la **pulsera**, *bracelet*; la **bata**, *robe*; los **calzoncillos**, *underpants*; la **camiseta**, *undershirt*; el **pijama**, *pajamas*; los **guantes**, *gloves*.

EJERCICIO 1   La ropa

Conteste en español en oraciones completas.
Según el dibujo:

1. ¿Qué ropa lleva el hombre-maniquí (*mannequin*)?
2. ¿Qué otros artículos ve usted allí?
3. ¿Cuántas corbatas ve usted?
4. ¿Qué lleva la mujer-maniquí?
5. ¿Es el vestido de la mujer-maniquí largo o corto?
6. ¿Qué otros artículos ve usted allí?
7. ¿Qué lleva la mujer que entra en la tienda?
8. ¿Cómo se llama la tienda? ¿Venden ropa cara o barata allí?

Preguntas generales:

9. ¿Qué ropa lleva usted hoy?
10. ¿Qué ropa lleva usted cuando va a un restaurante elegante?
11. ¿Qué ropa necesita usted llevar a Alaska? ¿y a Puerto Rico?
12. ¿De qué color es su camisa? ¿blusa? ¿vestido? ¿suéter?
13. ¿Prefiere usted faldas largas o faldas cortas?
14. ¿Lleva usted calcetines limpios o sucios hoy?
15. ¿Qué joyas llevan las mujeres? ¿y los hombres?
16. ¿Adónde va usted de compras?

EJERCICIO 2   Una cuestión de gusto (*A matter of taste*)

¿Qué va bien con (*goes well with*) estos (*these*) artículos de ropa?

1. una chaqueta azul
2. un suéter rojo
3. una corbata verde
4. calcetines negros
5. pantalones grises
6. una blusa blanca

La mujer guapa (*left*) lleva ropa tradicional y típica durante (*during*)
un festival sevillano. Sevilla, España. La mujer india (*right*) pasa horas largas
tejiendo (*weaving*) mantas (*blankets*) y artículos de ropa para vender
en el mercado. Oaxaca, México

EJERCICIO 3   ¿Cuánto cuesta? y ¿es caro o barato?

Diga usted cuánto cuestan los artículos; indique
si (*if*) en su opinión son caros o son baratos.

Modelo   la camisa (45 dólares)
La camisa cuesta cuarenta y cinco dólares.
¡Es cara!

1. el impermeable (60 dólares)
2. la bolsa (98 dólares)
3. el traje (75 dólares)
4. la cartera (59 dólares)
5. los zapatos (15 dólares)

Este año, hay mil posibili-
dades de combinar la moda:
Faldas, blusas, bermudas, chaquetas... Todo puede coordi-
narse en estilo y color. Con pocas prendas se puede cambiar
mucho, porque en Primavera
hay momentos alegres, sofisti-
cados, serenos o deportivos...
y una sóla moda:
La de El Corte Inglés.

El Corte Inglés es un almacén en España.

■ CONVERSACIÓN

Felipe va de compras a una tienda muy elegante. Busca un regalo para el cumpleaños de su madre.

DEPENDIENTA	**¿En qué puedo servirle, señor?**
FELIPE	**Estoy buscando un regalo especial para mi madre.**
DEPENDIENTA	**Muy bien. Tenemos toda clase de artículos para damas: vestidos, faldas, blusas, joyas. . . .**
FELIPE	**Quiero ver unas blusas, por favor, en la talla treinta y seis.**
DEPENDIENTA	**Esta blusa azul es muy elegante.**
FELIPE	**¿Cuánto cuesta?**
DEPENDIENTA	**Dos mil pesetas,[1] señor.**
FELIPE	**Muy bien, señora. Llevo la blusa, y aquí tiene mi tarjeta de crédito.**

NOTE 1: $1.00 U.S.A. = approximately 130 Spanish pesetas (1984).

Philip goes shopping at a very elegant store. He is looking for a birthday gift for his mother.

CLERK	*How can I help you, sir?*
PHILIP	*I'm looking for a special gift for my mother.*
CLERK	*Fine. We have all kinds of articles for women: dresses, skirts, blouses, jewelry. . . .*
PHILIP	*I would like to see some blouses, please, in size thirty-six.*
CLERK	*This blue blouse is very elegant.*
PHILIP	*How much does it cost?*
CLERK	*Two thousand pesetas, sir.*
PHILIP	*That'll be fine, ma'am. I'll take the blouse, and here is my credit card.*

■ ESTRUCTURA

I. El gerundio   *The present participle*

What in English we call the present participle, or *-ing* form of the verb, is referred to as the **gerundio** (gerund) in Spanish.

A. La formación del gerundio

To form the present participle, for infinitives ending in **-ar**, drop the **-ar** and add **-ando**. For infinitives ending in **-er** or **-ir**, drop the **-er** or **-ir** and add **-iendo**.

infinitive	stem	ending	
hablar	habl-	+ -ando	**hablando** (*speaking*)
comer	com-	+ -iendo	**comiendo** (*eating*)
vivir	viv-	+ -iendo	**viviendo** (*living*)

B. Algunos gerundios irregulares

decir (i)	**diciendo**	leer	**leyendo**
pedir (i)	**pidiendo**	oír	**oyendo**
repetir (i)	**repitiendo**	traer	**trayendo**
	dormir (u) **durmiendo**		

EJERCICIO 4   ¡Vamos a practicar!

Cambie los infinitivos al gerundio.

1.	besar	6.	fumar	11.	aprender	16.	pedir
2.	llamar	7.	escuchar	12.	entender	17.	decir
3.	llevar	8.	entrar	13.	ver	18.	oír
4.	escribir	9.	comer	14.	hacer	19.	leer
5.	nadar	10.	vivir	15.	dormir	20.	traer

II. El presente del progresivo *The present progressive*

<u>Function</u>: The present progressive stresses an action as being in progress at a given moment. In contrast, the present tense has a more general time reference.

Trabajo todos los días.   *I work (am working) every day.*
Estoy trabajando ahora.   *I am working now.*

<u>Formation</u>:

a conjugated form of <u>estar</u> + present participle →present progressive

Modelo   **hablar**   *to speak*

estoy hablando	*I am speaking (in the act of)*
estás hablando	*You are speaking*
está hablando	*You, he, she is (are) speaking*

estamos hablando	*We are speaking*
estáis hablando	*You are speaking*
están hablando	*They, you are speaking*

NOTE: The verbs **ir** and **venir** are not used in the progressive.

EJERCICIO 5   ¿Qué están haciendo?

Complete las oraciones según el modelo.

>   Modelo   . . . buscando mi reloj (yo)
>   **Estoy buscando mi reloj.**

1.   . . . escuchando la radio (tú, nosotros, usted)
2.   . . . aprendiendo el vocabulario (yo, Carlos y Carmen, vosotros)
3.   . . . durmiendo (los niños, la abuela, nosotros)

EJERCICIO 6   ¡Ahora!

Cambie las oraciones al presente del progresivo según el modelo.

>   Modelo   *Estudio* todos los días.
>   **Estoy estudiando ahora.**

1.   *Corro* todos los días.
2.   Los niños *duermen* la siesta todos los días.
3.   *Nadamos* todos los días.
4.   Él *toca* la guitarra todos los días.
5.   *Limpio* la casa todos los días.
6.   *Comemos* en el hotel todos los días.
7.   Ellos *miran* la televisión todos los días.
8.   Ella *repite* los ejercicios todos los días.

EJERCICIO 7   ¿Qué estás haciendo?

Hágale preguntas a un(a) estudiante según el modelo; escuche la respuesta.

>   Modelo   jugar (pregunta)   **¿Estás jugando?**
>   (respuesta)   **(Sí,) (No, no) estoy jugando.**

1.   fumar
2.   leer
3.   dormir
4.   escribir
5.   escuchar

III. El pretérito de verbos regulares *The preterit (past) tense of regular verbs*

A. Los verbos -ar

To form the preterit tense of regular **-ar** verbs, drop the **-ar** from the infinitive and to the remaining stem add the endings indicated.

-ar *endings*   Modelo   **cantar** *to sing*

Ending	Verb	Meaning
-é	cant**é**	I sang, did sing
-aste	cant**aste**	You sang, did sing
-ó	cant**ó**	You, she, he, it sang, did sing
-amos	cant**amos**	We sang, did sing
-asteis	cant**asteis**	You sang, did sing
-aron	cant**aron**	You, they sang, did sing

Ejemplos   Ellos **cantaron** en el programa anoche.
¿**Cantó** usted en el concierto la semana pasada?

B. Los verbos -er, -ir

To form the preterit tense of regular **-er** and **-ir** verbs, drop the **-er** or **-ir** from the infinitive and to the remaining stem add the endings indicated.

-er, **-ir** *endings*   Modelos   **comer** *to eat,*
vivir *to live*

Ending	Verb	Meaning	Verb	Meaning
-í	com**í**	I ate, did eat	viv**í**	I lived, did live
-iste	com**iste**	You ate, did eat	viv**iste**	You lived, did live
-ió	com**ió**	You, she, he, it ate, did eat	viv**ió**	You, she, he, it lived, did live
-imos	com**imos**	We ate, did eat	viv**imos**	We lived, did live
-isteis	com**isteis**	You ate, did eat	viv**isteis**	You lived, did live
-ieron	com**ieron**	You, they ate, did eat	viv**ieron**	You, they lived, did live

Ejemplos   **Comimos** langosta anoche.
¿**Comieron** ustedes en un restaurante caro?

NOTE 1: Spelling changes occur in the **yo** form of the preterit of verbs ending in **-gar**, **-car**, and **-zar** in order to maintain the same sound as the infinitive.

jugar: yo ju**gué**   llegar: yo lle**gué**
tocar: yo to**qué**   buscar: yo bus**qué**
abrazar: yo abra**cé**

NOTE 2: In the third person singular and plural endings in verbs like **leer** and **oír**, the **i** is changed to **y** when the **i** is preceded by a vowel.

leer: él le**y**ó, ellos le**y**eron   oír: él o**y**ó, ellos o**y**eron

EJERCICIO 8   ¡Vamos a practicar!

Conjugue los verbos en el pretérito.

1. comprar 2. aprender 3. escribir 4. llegar 5. leer

EJERCICIO 9   En el pasado

Cambie las oraciones según el modelo.

> Modelo   Anoche yo *miré* la televisión. (hablar con Carmen)
> **Anoche yo hablé con Carmen.**

1. Anoche yo *aprendí* el vocabulario. (comer un bistec) (beber una cerveza) (bailar en la discoteca)
2. Ayer mi madre *cocinó*. (limpiar la casa) (escribir a mi tío) (salir)
3. La semana pasada nosotros *compramos* una radio. (nadar en el lago) (descansar) (volver a la ciudad)
4. El año pasado ellos *jugaron* al fútbol. (trabajar en el restaurante) (estudiar el francés) (leer muchos libros)

EJERCICIO 10   ¿Cuándo? ¡Ayer!

Conteste según el modelo.

> Modelo   ¿Cuándo nadó usted? **Nadé ayer**.

1. ¿Cuándo salió usted?
2. ¿Cuándo trabajó usted?
3. ¿Cuándo comió usted?
4. ¿Cuándo llegó usted?
5. ¿Cuándo manejó usted?

> Modelo   ¿Cuándo nadaron ustedes?   **Nadamos ayer**.

6. ¿Cuándo limpiaron ustedes?
7. ¿Cuándo cocinaron ustedes?
8. ¿Cuándo salieron ustedes?
9. ¿Cuándo llamaron ustedes?
10. ¿Cuándo comieron ustedes?

EJERCICIO 11   Preguntas generales

Conteste en español en oraciones completas.

1. ¿Estudió usted aquí el año pasado?
2. ¿Dónde comió usted anoche?
3. ¿Jugó usted al tenis la semana pasada?
4. ¿Salió usted de la clase temprano ayer?
5. ¿Llegó usted a la clase a tiempo hoy?
6. ¿Qué compró usted para el cumpleaños (*birthday*) de su madre?
7. ¿Escribieron ustedes los ejercicios en el cuaderno?
8. ¿Bebieron ustedes toda la cerveza?

Estos (*these*) hombres de negocios
llevan la ropa tradicional de la región.
Otavalo, Ecuador

IV. Los posesivos *The possessives*

There are three ways to show possession in Spanish.

A. Posesión con <u>de</u>

Spanish uses **de** (*of*) to indicate possession; there is no *'s* in Spanish. Similarly, the
equivalent of *whose* is **¿de quién?**

Es el sombrero de Juan.	*It is John's hat.*
Son las gafas del profesor.	*They are the professor's glasses.*
¿De quién es el impermeable?	*Whose raincoat is it?*

EJERCICIO 12   ¿De quién es?

Conteste según el modelo.

> Modelo   ¿De quién es el sombrero? (Juan) *Whose hat is it?*
> **Es el sombrero de Juan**. *It's John's hat.*

MARÍA TERESA

Ropa linda para ellas. . . .

¡Prepare sus vacaciones!

BIKINIS   Gran surtido en estilos y colores
SOMBREROS DE PLAYA   Bellísimos y muy de moda
10% descuento con sólo mencionar el anuncio
Es muy fácil comprar a crédito

Diariamente abierto de 10:00 a.m. a 1:00 p.m. y de 4:00 p.m. a 8:00 p.m.

1. ¿De quién es la bolsa? (María)
2. ¿De quién es el abrigo? (la muchacha)
3. ¿De quién es el sombrero? (el hombre)
4. ¿De quién son las joyas? (la señora)
5. ¿De quién son las gafas? (Alfredo)
6. ¿De quién es el paraguas? (Roberto)

B. Los adjetivos de posesión antes del sustantivo   *Possessive adjectives used before the noun*

Possession can also be shown by use of possessive adjectives. The possessive adjectives used before the noun agree in number with the thing possessed. Only **nuestro** and **vuestro** have feminine forms and agree in gender.

mi, mis	*my*
tu, tus	*your*
su, sus	*your, his, her, its*
nuestro (-a, -os, -as)	*our*
vuestro (-a, -os, -as)	*your*
su, sus	*your, their*

Mi traje costó mucho.	*My suit cost a lot.*
Mis trajes son viejos.	*My suits are old.*
Nuestro coche está en el garaje.	*Our car is in the garage.*
Nuestra casa está en el campo.	*Our house is in the country.*
Es **su** libro.	*It is his (her, your, their) book.*
Son **sus** libros.	*They are his (her, your, their) books.*

NOTE: If the owner referred to by **su** or **sus** is not clear by context, clarify in the following manner:

su libro: el libro **de él, de ella, de usted, de ellos, de ellas, de ustedes**.
sus libros: los libros **de él, de ella**, etc.

EJERCICIO 13   Yo tengo mis cosas.

Cambie la oración para indicar que cada persona tiene sus cosas.

Modelos   Yo tengo el impermeable.
          Yo tengo mi impermeable.
          Él tiene las gafas.
          Él tiene sus gafas.

1. Yo tengo las botas.
2. Yo tengo el abrigo.
3. Rosita tiene los regalos.
4. Diego y Pepe tienen la radio
5. Nosotros tenemos los suéteres.
6. Nosotros tenemos la guitarra.
7. Vosotros tenéis las chaquetas.
8. Tú tienes el sombrero.

EJERCICIO 14   ¿Dónde está?

Conteste en español con la forma apropiada del posesivo.

1. Señor, ¿dónde está su cuaderno?
2. Señorita, ¿dónde está su bolsa?
3. Señor, ¿dónde están sus zapatos?
4. Señorita, ¿dónde están sus gafas?
5. Estudiantes, ¿dónde están sus libros?
6. Estudiantes, ¿dónde están sus plumas?

7. Estudiantes, ¿dónde está su profesor(a) de español?
8. Estudiantes, ¿dónde está su clase de español?

C. Los adjetivos de posesión después del sustantivo *Possessive adjectives used after the noun*

Possessive adjectives used after the noun agree in number and gender with the thing possessed.

mío (-a, -os, -as)	*mine, of mine*
tuyo (-a, -os, -as)	*yours, of yours*
suyo (-a, -os, -as)	*yours, of yours*
	his, of his
	hers, of hers
nuestro (-a, -os, -as)	*ours, of ours*
vuestro (-a, -os, -as)	*yours, of yours*
suyo (-a, -os, -as)	*yours, of yours*
	theirs, of theirs

Una amiga **mía** vive aquí.	*A friend of mine lives here.*
Muchos amigos **tuyos** están aquí.	*Many friends of yours are here.*
Los libros son **nuestros**.	*The books are ours.*
La medicina es **nuestra**.	*The medicine is ours.*
Conocí a una amiga **suya.**	*I met a friend of yours (his, hers, theirs).*
Conocí a unas amigas **suyas.**	*I met some friends of yours (his, hers, theirs).*

La lengua y cultura hispánicas son evidentes en muchos aspectos de la vida norteamericana. Queens, Neuva York

NOTE 1: If the owner meant by **suyo** (**-a**, **-os**, **-as**) is not clear by context, clarify in the following manner:

una amiga **suya**:   una amiga **de él, de ella, de usted, de ellos, de ellas, de ustedes**.
unas amigas **suyas**:   unas amigas **de él, de ella**, etc.

NOTE 2: The addition of the definite article to the after-the-noun form of the possessive adjective creates the possessive pronoun. After **ser** the article is omitted except for emphasis.

Tiene **mi** coche.→Tiene **el mío**.   *He has mine.*
Mis amigas vienen.→**Las mías** vienen.   *Mine are coming.*
Vendieron **nuestros** libros.→Vendieron **los nuestros.**   *They sold ours.*
Es **su** bolsa.→Es **suya**.   *It is hers.*

EJERCICIO 15   ¿De quién es?

Modelo   ¿De quién es la chaqueta? (yo)
         La chaqueta es mía.

1. ¿De quién es el suéter?
    (yo)
    (tú)
    (ellas)
2. ¿De quién son los regalos?
    (usted)
    (nosotros)
    (vosotros)

3. ¿De quién es la cartera?
    (yo)
    (tú)
    (él)
4. ¿De quién son las gafas de sol?
    (yo)
    (nosotros)
    (ellos)

EJERCICIO 16   Posesión

Cambie según el modelo.

Modelo   Vendieron *su coche.*
         Vendieron el suyo.

1. Comí *mis galletas.*
2. Busqué *mi reloj.*
3. Él buscó *su cartera.*
4. Ella llevó *su paraguas.*

5. Manejamos *nuestro coche.*
6. Vendimos *nuestros libros.*
7. ¿Llevaste *tus gafas*?
8. ¿Limpiaste *tu traje*?

PERSPECTIVA ORIGINAL

1. **La ropa**
    Bring to class a pictorial ad from a magazine or newspaper in which clothes are being modeled. Name and describe the article involved, including colors, price, etc.
2. Mini-drama: **en el almacén**
    Create a dialog which could be performed as a skit. You, or you and a friend,

go on a shopping excursion to buy a gift for your boyfriend or girlfriend. Suggested format:

a. Tell the sales clerk why you are at the department store.
b. Discuss what kind of gift you might buy.
c. Briefly describe your boyfriend or girlfriend to the sales clerk and try to determine the size needed and color preference (if you are buying apparel).
d. Eliminate items that are too big, too small, too ugly, too expensive.
e. Make your decision.
f. Pay for the merchandise.

SUPPLEMENTARY VOCABULARY

la **dependienta**	saleswoman	**demasiado**	too, too much
el **dependiente**	salesman	**grande**	large
el **precio**	price	**mediano**	medium
la **talla**	size	**pequeño**	small

■ PANORAMA CULTURAL

Los hispánicos en los Estados Unidos de América

Los españoles exploraron gran parte de los Estados Unidos en el *siglo* diez y seis. Exploradores famosos *como* Ponce de León, Cabeza de Vaca y Hernando de Soto[1] *descubrieron* las regiones que hoy llamamos la Florida, Texas, Nuevo México, Arizona, Nevada, Colorado y California.   *century* / *like* / *discovered*

La influencia española continúa hoy *por parte de* los catorce millones[2] de hispanoamericanos que viven en los Estados Unidos. Los ocho millones de chicanos (mexicano-americanos), un millón y medio de puertorriqueños, y los ochocientos mil cubanos forman los tres grupos más grandes.   *by means of*

El mural enorme representa la influencia política de los chicanos en los Estados Unidos. Los Ángeles, California

La concentración de los chicanos está en Texas, Nuevo México, Arizona, Colorado y California. La ciudad de los Ángeles tiene *más de* un millón y medio de chicanos. La *mayoría* de los puertorriqueños están en Nueva York, Nueva Jersey e Illinois, con más de un millón en la ciudad de Nueva York. Los cubanos que llegaron a este país recientemente, viven principalmente en Nueva York, Nueva Jersey, California, Illinois y la Florida. En el área metropolitana de Miami viven más de quinientos mil cubanos.

more than
majority

Para servir a esta población enorme *hay* doscientas ochenta estaciones de radio, sesenta estaciones de televisión y diecisiete *periódicos* de lengua española. La población hispánica *sigue creciendo* rápidamente y los hispánicos en todas partes y en muchas *maneras* están buscando su *propia* identidad en una cultura diferente, la norteamericana, pero una cultura que también es la suya.

there are
newspapers
continues/growing
ways/own

NOTE 1:   Ponce de León—(c. 1460-1521): Spanish explorer who in 1512 discovered Florida while in search of the legendary fountain of youth.

Cabeza de Vaca—(c.1490–1557): Spanish explorer who, after being shipwrecked, wandered and explored on foot the southeastern section of the U.S.A.

Hernando de Soto—(c. 1500–1542): Spanish explorer who discovered the Mississippi River in 1541.

NOTE 2:   Some estimates place the number as high as 20 million, a figure which is growing by 1 million a year.

¿CUÁNTO RECUERDAS?

Complete the statements given in Column A with the conclusions given in Column B.

A.   1. Uno de los famosos exploradores españoles es . . .
2. Los tres grupos más grandes de lengua española en los Estados Unidos son . . .
3. Ocho millones . . .
4. Uno de los estados de nombre español es . . .
5. Ochocientos mil . . .
6. Los españoles exploraron gran parte de los Estados Unidos . . .
7. Un millón y medio . . .
8. Más de un millón y medio de chicanos viven en . . .
9. En Nueva York viven . . .
10. La cultura española e hispanoamericana es . . .
11. Hay (*there are*) doscientas ochenta . . .
12. En Miami viven . . .

B.   a. . . . en el siglo diez y seis.
b. . . . Colorado.
c. . . . parte íntegra de este país
d. . . . más de un millón de puertorriqueños.
e. . . . estaciones de radio de lengua española en los Estados Unidos.
f. . . . de puertorriqueños viven en los Estados Unidos.
g. . . . cubanos viven en los Estados Unidos.
h. . . . Los Angeles.
i. . . . más de quinientos mil cubanos.
j. . . . los chicanos, los puertorriqueños y los cubanos.
k. . . . Hernando de Soto.
l. . . . de chicanos viven en los Estados Unidos.

EJERCICIO DE MAPA

Referring to the reading, shade those states in the United States which have a large Spanish-speaking population.

■ INTEGRACIÓN

A.   ORAL EXERCISE: **Conversación**
1. The dialog will be read twice. Listen the first time; the second time pauses will be provided for you to repeat each phrase.
2. Listen to the statements related to the dialog; indicate if the statements are true or false.

B.   ORAL EXERCISE: VOCABULARY, **la ropa**
Answer the questions on the tape according to the drawings; listen for the tape confirmation.

1.

Felipe

2.

Lupe

3.

Mónica

4.

Jaime

5.

Carlos

6.

Teresa

7.

8.
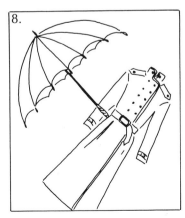

9.

C.   ORAL EXERCISE: PRESENT PROGRESSIVE
Change the present tense verbs in the sentences on the tape to present progressive.

> Example   (tape)   Él escucha la radio.
>   (your response) **Él está escuchando la radio.**

D.   ORAL EXERCISE: PRESENT PROGRESSIVE
Answer the questions on the tape according to the drawings.

Miguel

> Example
> (tape)   ¿Qué está haciendo Miguel?
> (your response) **Miguel está tocando la guitarra.**

1. Juan

2. Juanita   Mario

3. Teresa

4. nosotros

5. Miguel   Lupe

6. Teresa

Carlota Lupe   yo

E.   ORAL EXERCISE: PRETERIT TENSE
      Repeat each sentence substituting the correct form of the verb in the preterit
      tense.
          Example   (tape)   Yo entré en la clase. Tú . . .
                     (your response)   **Tú entraste en la clase.**

F.   ORAL EXERCISE: PRETERIT TENSE
      Change the present-tense verbs on the tape to the preterit.
          Example   (tape)   Yo nado.
                     (your response)   **Yo nadé.**

G.   ORAL EXERCISE: PRETERIT TENSE
      Answer the questions on the tape according to the drawings.
                          Example   (tape)   ¿Quién entró?
                                     (your response)   **Yo entré.**

yo

yo   yo

3.

tú

4.

tú

5.

él

6.

Teresa

7.

nosotros

8.

nosotros

9.

Juanita   Mario

10.

Juanita   Mario

H.   WRITTEN EXERCISE: PRETERIT TENSE
Write the answers to the ten questions on the tape. Each question will be given twice.

I.   ORAL EXERCISE: POSSESSIVE ADJECTIVES USED BEFORE THE NOUN
Answer the questions on the tape with the possessive adjective used before the noun that corresponds to the subjects and drawings provided.

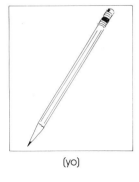

(yo)

Example   (tape)   ¿De quién es el lápiz?
          (your response)   **Es mi lápiz.**

1.

(yo)

2.

(yo)

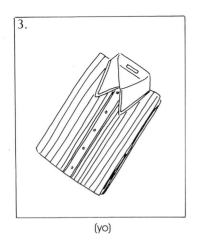

3.

(yo)

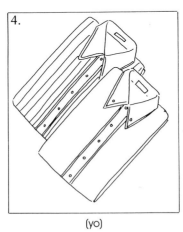

4.

(yo)

5.

(tú)

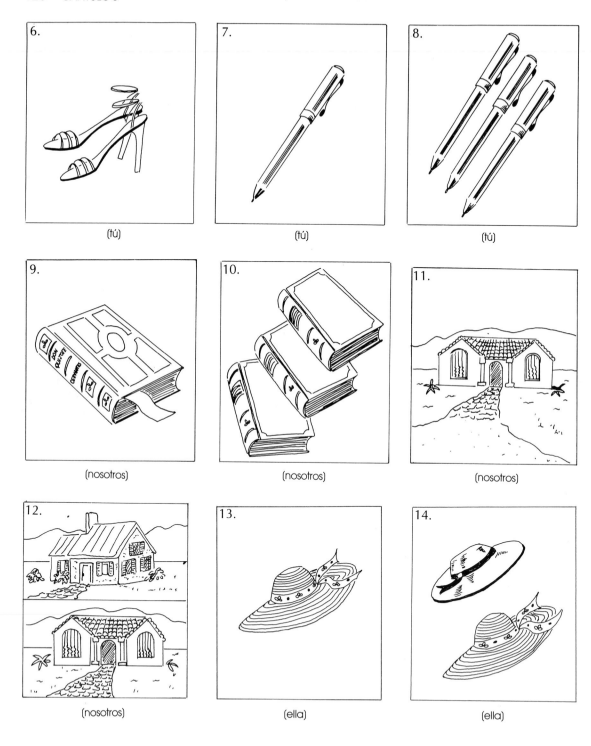

6. (tú)

7. (tú)

8. (tú)

9. (nosotros)

10. (nosotros)

11. (nosotros)

12. (nosotros)

13. (ella)

14. (ella)

(ellos)

(ellos)

J.   ORAL EXERCISE: POSSESSIVE ADJECTIVES USED AFTER THE NOUN
     Answer the questions on the tape with the possessive adjective used after the
     noun that corresponds to the subjects and drawings for Exercise H.
         Example   (tape)   ¿De quién es el lápiz?
                   (your response)   **El lápiz es mío.**

K.   WRITTEN EXERCISE: COMPREHENSION: **Los hispánicos en los Estados
     Unidos de América**
     You will hear a short paragraph which will be read twice. Write the answers
     to the three questions that follow.

L.   DICTATION: **Los hispánicos en los Estados Unidos de América**
     Write the four sentences you hear. Each sentence will be read three times.

■ REPASO DE VOCABULARIO ACTIVO

Adjetivos

barato	**sucio**	**negro**
caro	**amarillo**	**pardo**
corto	**azul**	**rojo**
largo	**blanco**	**rosado**
limpio	**gris**	**verde**
otro	**morado**	

Adjetivos de posesión (antes del sustantivo)

mi(-s)	**su(-s)**	**vuestro(-a, -os, -as)**
tu(-s)	**nuestro(-a, -os, -as)**	**su(-s)**

Adjetivos de posesión (después del sustantivo)

mío(-a, -os, -as)	**suyo(-a, -os, -as)**	**vuestro(-a, -os, -as)**
tuyo(-a, -os, -as)	**nuestro(-a, -os, -as)**	**suyo(-a, -os, -as)**

Sustantivos

el **abrigo**	la **camisa**	las **gafas**	el **paraguas**	el **suéter**
los **blujeans**	la **cartera**	las **gafas de sol**	el **regalo**	el **traje**
la **blusa**	la **chaqueta**	el **impermeable**	el **reloj**	el **traje de baño**
la **bolsa**	la **corbata**	las **joyas**	la **ropa**	el **vestido**
las **botas**	la **cosa**	las **medias**	la **ropa interior**	los **zapatos**
los **calcetines**	la **falda**	los **pantalones**	el **sombrero**	

Verbos

costar(ue)   **llevar**

Expresión idiomática

ir de compras

Expresiones de tiempo

anoche   **ayer**   **el año pasado**   **la semana pasada**

■ EJERCICIOS DE REPASO

I. El presente del progresivo
Cambie las oraciones al presente del progresivo.

Modelo   Él no *fuma*.
         Él no está fumando

1. El niño *duerme* la siesta.
2. *Leo* la novela.
3. Ellos *escriben* los ejercicios.
4. *Comemos* en el restaurante.
5. ¿*Miras* la televisión?
6. ¿*Escuchan* ustedes la radio?

II. El pretérito de verbos regulares.
Diga usted lo que las personas hicieron ayer.

Modelo   *llegar* tarde/Eduardo
         Eduardo llegó tarde.

1. *trabajar*/yo
2. *salir* temprano/yo
3. *comprar* un abrigo/tú
4. *comer* en el restaurante/tú
5. *llevar* un vestido nuevo/ella
6. *leer* el menú/ella
7. *bailar*/nosotros
8. *beber* vino/nosotros
9. *escuchar* la música/vosotros
10. *abrir* los regalos/vosotros
11. *manejar*/ellos
12. *volver* a casa/ellos

III. La posesión con <u>de</u>

Complete según el modelo.

> Modelo   el hijo (la señora López)
> **Es el hijo de la señora López.**

1. la niña (el señor Martínez)
2. el esposo (Elena)
3. la cartera (Felipe)
4. la bolsa (Carlota)

IV. Los posesivos

Complete según el modelo, usando las dos formas de los adjetivos de posesión.

> Modelo   ¿De quién es el sombrero? (yo)
> **Es mi sombrero.**
> **El sombrero es mío.**

1. ¿De quién es la pluma? (yo)
2. ¿De quién son las joyas? (ella)
3. ¿De quién son los regalos? (tú)
4. ¿De quién es el coche? (nosotros)
5. ¿De quién es la casa? (vosotros)
6. ¿De quién es la radio? (ellos)

V. Repaso general

A. Conteste en español en oraciones completas.

1. ¿Qué está usted haciendo en este momento?
2. ¿Qué ropa llevan las mujeres a un restaurante elegante?
3. ¿Qué ropa llevan los hombres a un restaurante elegante?
4. ¿Qué ropa va a llevar usted a Alaska?
5. ¿Qué ropa va a llevar usted a la Florida?
6. ¿De qué color es la manzana? ¿la lechuga? ¿el maíz?
7. ¿Estudió usted mucho anoche?
8. ¿Comió usted toda la torta?
9. ¿Bebieron ustedes toda la leche?
10. ¿Dónde están sus libros de español?
11. ¿Cuáles son los tres grupos más grandes de hispanoamericanos en los Estados Unidos?

B. Traduzca al español

1. I am not smoking! (in the act of)
2. We are repeating the sentences. (in the act of)
3. She wore the red blouse yesterday.
4. I called at six.
5. They did not understand the lesson.
6. My parents are going shopping tomorrow.
7. He is looking for his coat and mine.
8. Her new shoes are very expensive.
9. They bought our house last week.
10. Their friends are here now.

CAPÍTULO 6

■ VOCABULARIO *La ciudad*

el **centro**	*downtown, center*	el **rascacielos**	*skyscraper*
la **ciudad**	*city*	el **restaurante**	*restaurant*
el **pueblo**	*town, village*	el **teatro**	*theater*
la **gente**	*people*	la **tienda**	*store*
la **persona**	*person*		
		el **autobús**	*bus*
el **almacén**	*department store*	la **bicicleta**	*bicycle*
la **avenida**	*avenue*	el **metro**	*metro, subway*
el **banco**	*bank, bench*	la **motocicleta**	*motorcycle*
la **biblioteca**	*library*	el **taxi**	*taxi*
la **calle**	*street*		
la **catedral**	*cathedral*	**andar**	*to go, walk; to work,*
el **cine**	*movies*		*run (machinery)*
el **dinero**	*money*	**entrar** (en)	*to enter, go into*
el **edificio**	*building*	**esperar**	*to wait for, to hope*
la **iglesia**	*church*	**pensar** (ie)	*to think, to intend*
la **joyería**	*jewelry shop*		*+ infinitive*
la **librería**	*bookstore*	**recordar** (ue)	*to remember*
el **museo**	*museum*	**visitar**	*to visit*
el **parque**	*park*		
la **película**	*film*	**hay**[1]	*there is, there are*
la **peluquería**	*hairdresser's,*		
	beauty shop		

NOTE 1: **Hay** derives from the irregular auxiliary verb **haber**, *to have*, and denotes existence, not location.

133

EJERCICIO 1   En la ciudad

Conteste en español en oraciones completas.

Según el dibujo:

1. ¿Cómo se llama el banco?
2. ¿Cómo se llama el teatro?
3. ¿Cómo se llama la película?
4. ¿Cómo se llama el almacén?
5. ¿Cuántas personas entran en el almacén?
6. ¿Cómo se llama el restaurante?
7. ¿Qué beben las señoritas que están en el restaurante?
8. ¿Qué espera la señora que está sentada (*seated*) en el banco?
9. ¿Cuál es el número del autobús?
10. ¿Qué busca uno de los hombres?
11. ¿Qué edificio está en la distancia?

Preguntas generales:

12. ¿Piensa usted ir al cine esta noche?
13. ¿Qué ciudades piensan ustedes visitar?
14. ¿Recuerda usted en qué ciudad de los Estados Unidos viven muchos cubanos? ¿puertorriqueños? ¿chicanos?
15. ¿Recuerdan ustedes el número del autobús en el dibujo?
16. ¿Prefiere usted andar en el metro, en el autobús o en un taxi?
17. ¿Tiene usted una bicicleta? ¿una motocicleta? ¿anda bien?
18. ¿Hay muchos rascacielos en Nueva York? ¿Qué más (*what else*) hay en Nueva York?

EJERCICIO 2   ¿Adónde vamos?

¿Adónde va usted para (*in order to*) . . . ?

1. comprar joyas
2. comprar libros
3. comer una langosta
4. leer, estudiar y pensar
5. ver las obras (*works*) de artistas famosos
6. adorar a Dios (*God*)
7. buscar dinero
8. cortarse (*to cut*) el pelo
9. ver la película *E.T.*
10. ver "*Man of la Mancha*"
11. comprar ropas
12. descansar en el centro de la ciudad

■ CONVERSACIÓN

Roberto, un estudiante universitario, vuelve de vacaciones y hace una llamada por teléfono a su amiga, Rosita.

ROBERTO   **Rosita, ¿qué tal?**

ROSITA   **Bien, Roberto. Ana dice que pasaste las vacaciones en Barcelona.**

ROBERTO   **Sí, estuve allí toda la semana pasada.**

ROSITA   **¡Qué fantástico! Pues, ¿qué hiciste y adónde fuiste?**

ROBERTO   **Fui allí para visitar a unos parientes míos y para ver el famoso Paseo de Colón,[1] el puerto, la catedral y . . .**

ROSITA   **¿Fuiste al Museo de Arte Moderno para ver las obras de Picasso?**

ROBERTO   **¡Claro! y pasé una tarde en el Parque Güell[2] también. Bueno, ¿por qué no cenamos a las nueve en la Plaza Mayor y podemos hablar más?**

ROSITA   **¡Maravilloso! Te veo allí a las nueve. Adiós.**

NOTE 1:   Paseo de Colón—a major avenue fronting the port, a focal point of which is a statue of Columbus.

NOTE 2:   Parque Güell—a unique park designed by the famous architect Gaudí.

En la ciudad cosmopolita de Barcelona se puede visitar el puerto
y la estatua de Colón. Barcelona, España

Robert, a university student, returns from vacation and calls his friend Rosita on the telephone.

ROBERT   *Rosita, how are you?*
ROSITA   *Fine, Robert. Ana says that you spent your vacation in Barcelona.*
ROBERT   *Yes, I was there all last week.*
ROSITA   *How fantastic! Well, what did you do and where did you go?*
ROBERT   *I went there to visit some relatives of mine and to see the famous Paseo de Colón, the port, the cathedral and . . .*
ROSITA   *Did you go to the Museum of Modern Art to see the works of Picasso?*
ROBERT   *Of course! and I spent an afternoon at the Güell Park too. Say, why don't we have dinner at nine at the Plaza Mayor and we can talk some more?*
ROSITA   *Marvelous! I'll see you there at nine. Goodbye.*

■ ESTRUCTURA

I. El pretérito: verbos con cambios en la raíz *Preterit tense: stem-changing verbs*

Verbs ending in **-ir** that are stem-changing in the present tense (**o→ue, e→ie, e→i**) also change in the preterit. The change occurs in the third persons singular and plural (**o→u** and **e→i**).

Modelos

dormir (ue, u) *to sleep*   **preferir** (ie, i) *to prefer*   **pedir** (i, i) *to ask for*

dormí	dormimos	preferí	preferimos	pedí	pedimos
dormiste	dormisteis	preferiste	preferisteis	pediste	pedisteis
durmió	durmieron	prefirió	prefirieron	pidió	pidieron

Additional stem-changing verbs: **morir** (ue, u) *to die*, **repetir** (i, i) *to repeat*

Ejemplos   ¿**Durmieron** ustedes bien anoche? ¡Sí! **Dormimos** muy bien.
¿**Pidió** usted el pastel de chocolate? No, **pedí** el pastel de limón.

NOTE: Verbs that change **o→u, e→i** in the preterit make the same change in the **-ing** form.

Estoy **repitiendo** los ejercicios.
Muchos animales están **muriendo**.

EJERCICIO 3   ¡Vamos a practicar!

Conteste según el modelo.

Modelo   ¿Quién *prefirió* el bistec? (Nosotros)
Nosotros preferimos el bistec.

1. ¿Quién *durmió* bien anoche? (Yo, nosotros, ellos)
2. ¿Quién *pidió* las chuletas de cerdo? (Juan, vosotros, tú)
3. ¿Quién no *repitió* el vocabulario? (Yo, Ana y Lupe, nosotros)

EJERCICIO 4   Preguntas al profesor

Hágale preguntas al profesor (a la profesora) según el modelo; escuche la respuesta.

Modelo   *pedir* langosta en el restaurante
             (pregunta) **¿Pidió usted langosta en el restaurante?**

1. *dormir* bien anoche
2. *preferir* el examen largo o el examen corto
3. *pedir* vino en el restaurante
4. *repetir* la respuesta
5. *morir* su abuelo

EJERCICIO 5   Preguntas generales

Conteste en español en oraciones completas.

1. ¿Qué pidió usted en el banco?
2. ¿Qué pidieron ustedes en la joyería.
3. ¿Repitió usted el vocabulario?
4. ¿Repitieron ustedes el diálogo?
5. ¿Durmió usted en el dormitorio o en casa anoche?
6. ¿Durmieron ustedes en la clase de español ayer?
7. ¿Murió Kennedy el año pasado?
8. ¿Murieron muchas personas en accidentes el año pasado?
9. ¿Prefirió usted el helado de chocolate o la torta?
10. ¿Prefirieron ustedes el examen fácil o el examen difícil?

semáforo   escuela   topes

II. El pretérito: verbos irregulares *Preterit tense: irregular verbs*

A. The following verbs have irregular stems in the preterit tense and use the sets of irregular endings listed.

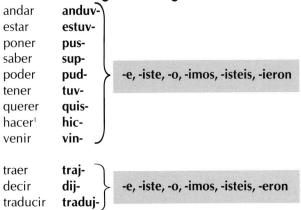

andar	anduv-
estar	estuv-
poner	pus-
saber	sup-
poder	pud-	-e, -iste, -o, -imos, -isteis, -ieron
tener	tuv-
querer	quis-
hacer¹	hic-
venir	vin-

traer	traj-
decir	dij-	-e, -iste, -o, -imos, -isteis, -eron
traducir	traduj-

NOTE 1:   The third person singular form of **hacer** is **hizo.**

Ejemplos   *Miguel no* **vino** *a clase ayer.*
              Tuvo *que visitar al médico.*
              *¿**Trajeron** ustedes los cuadernos?*
              *¿**Hizo** usted la tarea?*

EJERCICIO 6   ¿Qué hicieron?

Indique lo que hicieron las personas según el modelo.

   Modelo   Yo . . . (*traer* el postre)   **Yo traje el postre.**

1.   Yo . . . (*venir* temprano) (no *querer* salir)
2.   ¿Tú . . .? (no *poder* venir) (*tener* que trabajar)
3.   Camila . . . (*traducir* la oración) (*saber* las respuestas)
4.   Nosotros . . . (*poner* el dinero en el banco) (*andar* en el metro)
5.   ¿Vosotros . . .? (*estar* allí) (*decir* la verdad)
6.   Ellos . . . (*traer* la comida) (*hacer* la ensalada)

B. The following verbs are irregular in the preterit.
Note that **ser** and **ir** have the same forms.

ser *to be*		**ir** *to go*		**dar** *to give*	
fui	fuimos	fui	fuimos	di	dimos
fuiste	fuisteis	fuiste	fuisteis	diste	disteis
fue	fueron	fue	fueron	dio	dieron

Ejemplos   ¿Quién **fue**? **Fue** Alberto.

¿**Fuiste** al cine ayer? Sí. **Fui** con Roberto.

¿Quién **dio** el dinero? Mis tías **dieron** el dinero.

EJERCICIO 7   ¿Adónde fueron?

Complete según el modelo usando el verbo **ir** en el pretérito.

Modelo   ellos/al almacén   **Fueron al almacén.**

1. yo/al teatro
2. mis abuelos/al museo
3. mi novio(a)/a la biblioteca
4. ¿vosotros/a la librería?
5. ¿tú/al mercado?

EJERCICIO 8   ¿Qué dieron?

Complete según el modelo usando el verbo **dar** en el pretérito.

Modelo   mi primo/los regalos   **Dio los regalos.**

1. yo/el dinero
2. ¿ustedes/el reloj?
3. nosotros/el abrigo
4. ¿tú/la camisa?
5. ella/el suéter

EJERCICIO 9   Tú y yo

Hágale preguntas a un(a) estudiante según el modelo; escuche la respuesta.

Modelo   venir/a clase ayer
(pregunta)   **¿Viniste a clase ayer?**
(respuesta)   **(Sí,) (no, no) vine a clase ayer.**

1. hacer/la tarea
2. decir/la verdad al profesor
3. ir/al cine anoche
4. ir/a la biblioteca ayer
5. traer/el libro a la clase
6. poder/hacer la tarea
7. saber/traducir la lectura (*reading*)

EJERCICIO 10   Preguntas generales

Conteste en español en oraciones completas.

1. ¿Qué puso usted en la mesa?
2. ¿Qué hizo usted ayer?
3. ¿Adónde fue usted anoche?

Es costumbre tomar un refresco en un restaurante
al aire libre (*outdoor*). México, D. F.

4.   ¿Qué trajo usted a la clase hoy?
5.   ¿Qué tuvo usted que hacer ayer?
6.   ¿Quién dijo que no hay clase hoy?
7.   ¿Cuándo estuvo usted en el dormitorio?
8.   ¿Quién no quiso venir a clase hoy?
9.   ¿De dónde fueron sus bisabuelos (*great-grandparents*)?

III. Los meses, las estaciones, el tiempo   *Months, seasons, weather*

A. Meses

enero	*January*	**julio**	*July*
febrero	*February*	**agosto**	*August*
marzo	*March*	**septiembre**	*September*
abril	*April*	**octubre**	*October*
mayo	*May*	**noviembre**	*November*
junio	*June*	**diciembre**	*December*

NOTE: The names of the months are not capitalized in Spanish.

refran: **Al mal tiempo . . . buena cara.**

B. Estaciones

el **invierno**	winter	el **verano**	summer
la **primavera**	spring	el **otoño**	autumn

C. Tiempo

¿Qué tiempo hace?	What's the weather like?	**Hace sol.**	It's sunny.
Hace buen tiempo.	It's good weather.	**Hace viento.**	It's windy.
Hace mal tiempo.	It's bad weather.	**Llueve.**	It's raining.
Hace (mucho) frío.	It's (very) cold.	la **lluvia**	rain
Hace (mucho) calor.	It's (very) hot.	**Nieva.**	It's snowing.
Hace fresco.	It's cool.	la **nieve**	snow

EJERCICIO 11   Los meses, las estaciones y el tiempo

Conteste en español en oraciones completas.

1. ¿Cuáles son los meses del invierno?
2. ¿Cuáles son los meses de la primavera?
3. ¿Cuáles son los meses del verano?
4. ¿Cuáles son los meses del otoño?
5. ¿Cuál es su estación favorita?
6. ¿Cuál es su mes favorito?
7. ¿Qué tiempo hace hoy?
8. ¿Qué tiempo hace en el verano?
9. ¿Qué tiempo hace en el invierno?
10. ¿Llueve mucho en agosto?
11. ¿Nieva mucho en Alaska?
12. ¿Llueve mucho en Oregón?
13. ¿Nieva mucho en la Florida?
14. ¿En qué mes hace fresco aquí?
15. ¿Hace mucho viento en la playa?

refran: **Después de la lluvia sale el sol.**

EJERCICIO 12   El tiempo

Use una expresión de tiempo apropiada.

   Modelo   Voy a caminar en el parque.   **Hace buen tiempo. (o) Hace sol.**

1. Voy a la playa.
2. Llevo impermeable y paraguas.
3. Voy a esquiar (*ski*).

4. Llevo sombrero y gafas de sol.
5. Llevo suéter y abrigo.
6. Llevo chaqueta.

IV. Los números (100 y más)   *Numbers (100 and up)*

cien	*100*	**ochocientos(as)**	*800*
ciento un(o), una	*101*	**novecientos(as)**	*900*
doscientos(as)	*200*	**mil**	*1000*
trescientos(as)	*300*	**dos mil**	*2000*
cuatrocientos(as)	*400*	**cien mil**	*100.000*
quinientos(as)	*500*	**doscientos mil**	*200.000*
seiscientos(as)	*600*	**un millón (de)**	*1.000.000*
setecientos(as)	*700*	**dos millones (de)**	*2.000.000*

NOTE 1:   In large numbers in Spanish, the decimal point frequently replaces the comma used in the United States. In amounts of money, the comma is frequently used in place of the decimal point.

NOTE 2:   In Spanish, numbers above 1000 are never read by hundreds.

1971 = **mil novecientos setenta y uno**

NOTE 3:   When the number is a multiple of *100* and/or ends in *one*, it agrees in gender with the noun it modifies.

cuatrocientas una mujeres	*401 women*
ciento un hombres	*101 men*
ciento una mujeres	*101 women*

NOTE 4:   In Spanish there is no **y** between hundreds and a smaller number, even though we often say *and* in English.

205 = **doscientos cinco**
520 = **quinientos veinte**

EJERCICIO 13   Los números de cien

1. Vamos a contar de cien a mil—100, 150, 200, 250 . . .
2. Diga en español—
    201 hombres
    561 mujeres
    700 muchachas
    1.000.000 de dólares
    2.000.000 de personas
3. Diga en español
    1492   1898   1995   1984   1776

V. ¿Cuál es la fecha? *What is the date?*

The word order for dates in Spanish is:

article + number + de + month (+ de + year)

Es el cuatro de julio.
Es el diez y ocho de septiembre.
Es el primero de abril, de mil novecientos noventa.

NOTE: The ordinal number **primero**, not the cardinal **uno**, is used for first.

El centro de Madrid es moderno y atractivo. España

VOCABULARIO

la **fecha**	*date*
el **año**	*year*
el **cumpleaños**	*birthday*
la **Navidad**	*Christmas*
(**Feliz Navidad**)	(*Merry Christmas*)
el **Año Nuevo**	*New Year*
(**Próspero Año Nuevo**)	(*a prosperous new year*)
las **Pascuas**	*Christmas, Easter*
(**Felices Pascuas**)	(*Merry, happy, Christmas, Easter*)

EJERCICIO 14 ¿Cuándo vuelven?

Diga (*tell*) cuando las personas vuelven de España.

Modelo   María (junio/10)
María vuelve el diez de junio.

1. Juan (febrero/5)
2. Alberto (marzo/12)
3. Alicia (abril/13)
4. Lupe (mayo/14)

5. Teresa (agosto/15)
6. Carlota (septiembre/17)
7. Pepe (octubre/28)
8. Mario (noviembre/30)

EJERCICIO 15   ¿Cuál es la fecha?

Conteste en español en oraciones completas.

1. ¿Cuál es la fecha de hoy? (día, mes, año)
2. ¿Cuál es la fecha de su cumpleaños?
3. ¿Cuál es la fecha del Día de la Independencia de los Estados Unidos? (día, mes, año)
4. ¿Cuál es la fecha de la Navidad?
5. ¿Cuál es la fecha del Año Nuevo?

PERSPECTIVA ORIGINAL

1. Mini-drama: **En el restaurante**
   Using the following format as a guideline, create a dialog which could be performed as a skit.
   a. Call the waiter to your table; ask for the menu.
   b. The waiter can suggest certain dishes.
   c. Order from the menu: a soup, salad, main course, and beverage of your choice.
   d. Later the waiter asks if you want dessert; place your order.
   e. After the meal ask for the bill.
   f. Pay for your order; leave a tip.

SUPPLEMENTARY VOCABULARY

la **cuenta**	bill		la **propina**	tip
el **menú, la carta**	menu		**pagar**	to pay (for)
el **camarero**	waiter			

2. Presentación oral: **Mi visita a la ciudad de** . . . Prepare a brief oral presentation on your visit to any city of your choice. If possible, bring photos or pictures to illustrate your presentation. Using the preterit tense, tell your classmates such things as:
   a. When you visited the city (dates, season, how many days, etc., that you were there).
   b. What places you visited, what you did.
   c. Where you slept.
   d. Where and what you ate.

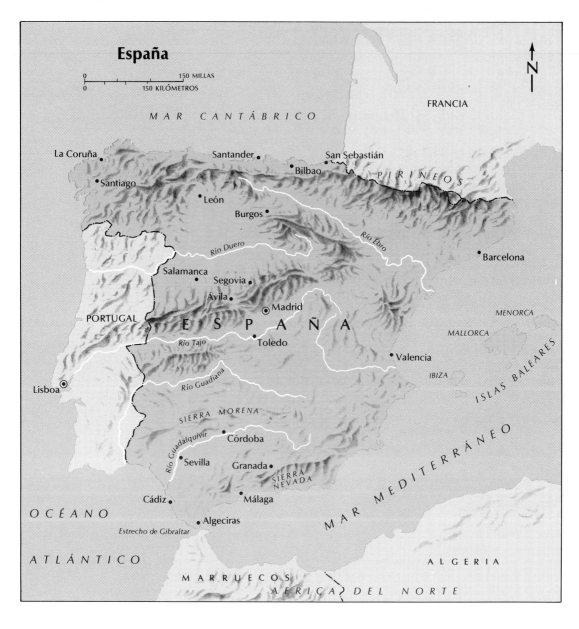

España

0   150 MILLAS
0   150 KILÓMETROS

N

FRANCIA

MAR CANTÁBRICO

La Coruña
Santiago
Santander
Bilbao
San Sebastián
PIRINEOS
León
Burgos
Río Ebro
Barcelona
Río Duero
Salamanca
Segovia
Ávila
Madrid
PORTUGAL
E S P A Ñ A
MENORCA
MALLORCA
Río Tajo
Toledo
Valencia
IBIZA
ISLAS BALEARES
Lisboa
Río Guadiana
SIERRA MORENA
Río Guadalquivir
Córdoba
Sevilla
Granada
SIERRA NEVADA
MAR MEDITERRÁNEO
Cádiz
Málaga
Algeciras
OCÉANO
Estrecho de Gibraltar
ATLÁNTICO
ALGERIA
MARRUECOS
ÁFRICA DEL NORTE

■ PANORAMA CULTURAL

España

España tiene una población de treinta y cinco millones de personas y está *limitada*   *bordered*
geográficamente por el Mar Cantábrico y Francia al norte, el Mar Mediterráneo al
este, el Océano Atlántico y Portugal al oeste, y el Estrecho de Gibraltar al sur.
España es un país montañoso que tiene cinco *ríos* de importancia. *Mientras*   *rivers/while*
la parte central es muy *seca*, en el norte hay mucha lluvia y la *tierra* es muy verde.   *dry/land*
En el sur y en el este la tierra es más fértil y allí se producen *aceitunas*, arroz, *trigo*,   *olives/wheat*
naranjas y muchos productos más.

La historia de España es variada por la serie de invasiones de la península
ibérica, pero de todos los invasores los romanos y los moros contribuyeron más a   *Iberian*
la formación de la España moderna. Los romanos, que *desde* 218 A.C. *hasta* 409   *from/B.C./until*
D.C. dominaron la península, *dejaron* su sistema de gobierno, el *derecho* romano,   *A.D./left/law*
una lengua común, *vías* de comunicación y monumentos artísticos. *Aún* hoy los   *routes, ways/even*
puentes y acueductos romanos dan evidencia de su larga presencia.   *bridges*

Los moros conquistaron la península en 711 y entre ese año y 1492 establecieron la civilización más brillante de todo el occidente. Construyeron ciudades
como Córdoba que se convirtió en el principal centro intelectual de Europa;
también contribuyeron mucho a los *conocimientos* científicos y técnicos del día,   *knowledge*
por ejemplo, matemáticas, medicina e ingeniería. Hoy día podemos ver ejemplos
de la magnífica arquitectura de los moros en la *Mezquita* de Córdoba y la Alham-   *Mosque*
bra de Granada.

La historia y las ricas tradiciones de España también son evidentes en los casti-
llos y catedrales de la Edad Media y el *Renacimiento*, y en los muchos monumen-   *Renaissance*
tos dedicados a personajes famosos como El Cid, Fernando e Isabel, *Colón*, Cer-   *Columbus*
vantes y Unamuno[1].

La España romántica, la España que *tal vez* el mundo conoce mejor, se mani-   *perhaps*
fiesta en el ritmo del baile flamenco, la música de la guitarra española, el drama de
la corrida de toros, el *sabor* del buen vino, y la *belleza* de las mujeres.   *taste/beauty*

NOTE 1: El Cid—historical figure of importance during the reconquest of the Spanish peninsula from the Moors and main character in the epic *Cantar de
Mío Cid* (1140).

Cervantes—author of the famous seventeenth-century novel of chivalry
El ingenioso hidalgo don Quijote de la Mancha, written in two parts,
1605 and 1615, respectively.

Fernando e Isabel—known as the Catholic Monarchs, ruled Castile and
Aragon from 1479 to 1517.

Unamuno—late nineteenth-and early twentieth-century Spanish philos-
opher, essayist, dramatist, poet, novelist, professor, rector (president) of
the University of Salamanca.

La influencia romana se nota en este impresionante
acueducto. Segovia, España

La Alhambra, el maravilloso palacio construído por los moros,
tiene en su patio central la hermosa fuente (*fountain*)
de los leones. Granada, España

¿CUÁNTO RECUERDAS?

Complete the statements given in Column A with the conclusions given in Column B.

A.
1. Al sur de España . . .
2. La historia de España es . . .
3. El norte de España . . .
4. Fernando e Isabel son dos . . .
5. La España romántica se ve . . .
6. Admiramos la magnífica arquitectura . . .
7. En el sur y en el este . . .
8. La parte central de España . . .
9. Los romanos dejaron . . .
10. Los moros conquistaron . . .
11. Córdoba se convirtió . . .
12. Los puentes y acueductos dan . . .

B.
a. . . . evidencia de la larga presencia de los romanos.
b. . . . está el Estrecho de Gibraltar.
c. . . . en el principal centro intelectual de Europa.
d. . . . variada por la serie de invasiones de la península ibérica.
e. . . . la península en 711.
f. . . . es muy verde.
g. . . . su sistema de gobierno y una lengua común.
h. . . . personajes famosos de la historia de España.
i. . . . es muy seca.
j. . . . en el ritmo flamenco, la corrida de toros, la belleza de las mujeres.
k. . . . producen naranjas, arroz, trigo y aceitunas.
l. . . . de los moros.

PREGUNTAS

Conteste en español según el mapa.

1. ¿Cuál es la capital de España?
2. ¿En qué parte de España está la capital?
3. ¿Cómo se llaman las montañas que están al norte de Barcelona?
4. ¿Cómo se llaman las islas que están en el Mar Mediterráneo?
5. ¿Cuál es el río que pasa por Lisboa, Portugal, y por Toledo, España?
6. ¿Qué continente está al sur de España?
7. ¿Qué país está al norte de España?
8. ¿Qué país está al oeste de España?

NOTE: Color photos of areas of Spain are found after page 224.

■ INTEGRACIÓN

A.   SONG: **Eres tú** (España)

Listen to the song the first time. The second time sing along with the tape.*

Como una promesa, eres tú, eres tú
Como una mañana de verano
Como una sonrisa, eres tú, eres tú
Así, así, eres tú.

Toda mi esperanza, eres tú, eres tú
Como lluvia fresca en mis manos
Como fuerte brisa, eres tú, eres tú
Así, así, eres tú.

Eres tú como el agua de mi fuente
Eres tú el fuego de mi hogar.

B.   ORAL EXERCISE: **Conversación**
   1.   The dialog will be read twice. Listen the first time; the second time pauses will be provided for you to repeat each phrase.
   2.   Listen to the statements related to the dialog; indicate if the statements are true or false.

C.   ORAL EXERCISE: VOCABULARY, **la ciudad**
   Answer the questions on the tape according to the drawings. Each drawing has two questions.

   *English translation:

Like a promise, you are, you are
Like a summer morning
Like a smile, you are, you are
Like that, like that, you are

All my hope you are, you are
Like fresh rain in my hands
Like a strong breeze, you are, you are
Like that, like that, you are.

You are like the water of my fountain
You are the fire of my home.

1.

2.
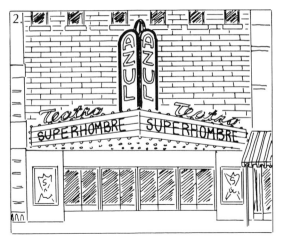

3.

4.

5.

6.

7.

8.

9.

10.

11.

12.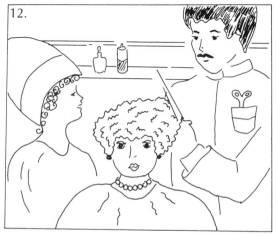

D. ORAL EXERCISE: THE PRETERIT OF STEM-CHANGING VERBS
    Repeat each sentence substituting the correct form of the verb in the preterit
    tense.

> Example   (tape)   Yo dormí en el hotel. Tú . . .
>   (your response) **Tú dormiste en el hotel.**

E. ORAL EXERCISE: THE PRETERIT OF STEM-CHANGING VERBS
    Answer the questions on the tape according to the drawings.

la planta

> Example   (tape)   ¿Qué murió?
>   (your response) **La planta murió.**

yo

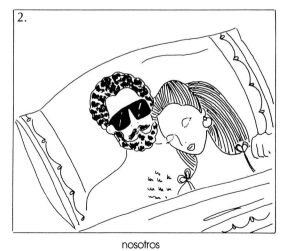

nosotros

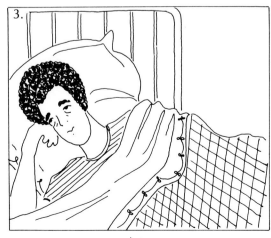

Juan

F.   ORAL EXERCISE: THE PRETERIT OF IRREGULAR VERBS
      Answer in Spanish with the correct form of the verb in the preterit tense.
          Example   ¿Quién supo el número del metro? Roberto . . .
              Roberto supo el número del metro.

G.   ORAL EXERCISE: THE PRETERIT OF IRREGULAR VERBS
      Answer the questions on the tape according to the drawings.

mi tío

          Example   (tape)   ¿Quién fue famoso?
                     (your response)   **Mi tío fue famoso.**

yo

Juanita   Mario

Carmen

yo

Pepe   Juan

nosotros

H.   WRITTEN EXERCISE: THE PRETERIT OF STEM-CHANGING AND IRREGU-
      LAR VERBS
      Write answers to the seven questions on the tape. Each question will be given
      twice.

I.   ORAL EXERCISE: MONTHS AND SEASONS
      Repeat the statements on the tape and add the two missing months.
         Example   (tape)   Los meses del invierno son diciembre,
                                           _____ y _____.

                    (your response)   **Los meses del invierno son diciembre, enero
                                      y febrero.**

J.   ORAL EXERCISE: THE WEATHER
      Answer the questions on the tape according to the drawings.

         Example   (tape)   ¿Qué tiempo hace hoy?
                    (your response)   **Hace sol.**

K.   ORAL EXERCISE: NUMBERS
      Give the answers to the following math problems.

L.   WRITTEN EXERCISE: COMPREHENSION, **España**
      You will hear a short paragraph which will be read twice. Write the answers
      to the three questions that follow.

M.   DICTATION: **España**
      Write the four sentences you hear. Each sentence will be read three times.

■ REPASO DE VOCABULARIO ACTIVO

Sustantivos

el **almacén**	el **cine**	la **lluvia**	la **persona**
el **año**	la **ciudad**	el **metro**	el **pueblo**
el **autobús**	el **cumpleaños**	la **motocicleta**	el **rascacielos**
la **avenida**	el **dinero**	el **museo**	el **restaurante**
el **banco**	el **edificio**	la **Navidad**	el **taxi**
la **biblioteca**	la **fecha**	la **nieve**	el **teatro**
la **bicicleta**	la **gente**	el **parque**	la **tienda**
la **calle**	la **iglesia**	las **Pascuas**	
la **catedral**	la **joyería**	la **película**	
el **centro**	la **librería**	la **peluquería**	

Verbos

andar	**esperar**	**pensar (ie)**	**visitar**
entrar (en)	**morir (ue)**	**recordar (ue)**	**hay**

Meses

enero	**abril**	**julio**	**octubre**
febrero	**mayo**	**agosto**	**noviembre**
marzo	**junio**	**septiembre**	**diciembre**

Estaciones

el **invierno**   la **primavera**   el **verano**   el **otoño**

Tiempo

¿Qué tiempo hace?	**Hace (mucho) frío.**	**Hace sol.**	**Nieva.**
Hace buen tiempo.	**Hace (mucho) calor.**	**Hace viento.**	
Hace mal tiempo.	**Hace fresco.**	**Llueve.**	

Números (de cien)

cien	**quinientos**	**novecientos**
doscientos	**seiscientos**	**mil**
trescientos	**setecientos**	**un millón (de)**
cuatrocientos	**ochocientos**	

■ EJERCICIO DE REPASO

I. El pretérito de verbos con cambios en la raíz
Hágales preguntas a Ana y a Carlos y Felipe según el modelo.

> Modelo   *repetir* el verbo
> **Ana, ¿repitió usted el número?**
> **Carlos y Felipe, ¿repitieron ustedes el número?**

1. *dormir* bien
2. *preferir* el helado de fresa
3. *pedir* el arroz con pollo
4. *repetir* el poema

II. El pretérito de verbos irregulares
Conteste según el modelo.

> Modelo   ¿Quién *tradujo* la lectura? (Yo)
> **Yo traduje la lectura.**

1. ¿Quién *vino* a clase temprano? (yo, usted)
2. ¿Quién no *supo* la respuesta? (yo, ellos)
3. ¿Quién no *pudo* hacer el ejercicio? (ella, nosotros)
4. ¿Quién *tuvo* que salir? (vosotros, tú)
5. ¿Quién *anduvo* en motocicleta? (yo, mi hermana)
6. ¿Quién *fue* al museo? (nosotros, mis primos)
7. ¿Quién *dio* el dinero? (yo, mis padres)
8. ¿Quién no *estuvo* allí? (Carmen, mis amigos)
9. ¿Quién *quiso* volver a casa? (nosotros, tú)

III. Los meses, las estaciones, el tiempo
Indique los meses y el tiempo que corresponden a la estación.

> Modelo   la primavera
> meses: **marzo, abril, mayo**
> tiempo: **hace fresco, hace sol, llueve**

1. el verano
2. el otoño
3. el invierno

IV. Los números (de cien)

Diga en español:

1. 222   2. 333   3. 444   4. 555
5. 666   6. 777   7. 888   8. 999
9. 1986   10. 1898

V. Repaso general

A. Conteste en español.

1. ¿Qué pidió usted en el restaurante?
2. ¿Adónde fue usted la semana pasada?
3. ¿Qué hizo usted anoche?
4. ¿Dónde puso usted los libros?
5. ¿Quién dijo que no hay examen hoy?
6. ¿Cuál es la fecha de la Navidad? ¿y del Año Nuevo?
7. ¿Qué ve usted en las calles o avenidas en el centro de la ciudad?
8. En una ciudad, ¿en qué edificios puede usted ir de compras?
9. En una ciudad, ¿qué edificios puede usted visitar?
10. ¿Recuerda usted qué invasores contribuyeron más a la formación de la España moderna?
11. ¿Cuál es la capital de España?
12. ¿Qué país está al norte de España? ¿al oeste? ¿Qué continente está al sur?

B. Traduzca al español

1. The children slept here all night.
2. He went to Madrid and visited the museum.
3. My mother put the cookies on (en) the table.
4. They came early and brought the drinks.
5. He is waiting for a taxi.
6. Do they intend to visit Spain?
7. What's the weather like in Venezuela?
8. What is the date?
9. Is there a beauty shop downtown?
10. My watch doesn't work well.

VII. Repaso de verbos

Cambie los verbos según los tiempos (*tenses*) indicados.

Modelo   nosotros/esperar el autobús
          presente—**Esperamos el autobús.**
          presente del progresivo—**Estamos esperando el autobús.**
          pretérito—**Esperamos el autobús**

1. él/dormir en el sofá
2. él/pedir un favor
3. yo/hacer los ejercicios
4. yo/decir la verdad

■ VOCABULARIO *El campo*

el **campo**	country, field		la **selva**	jungle
la **hacienda**	ranch, farm		la **tierra**	land, earth
			el **valle**	valley
el **animal**	animal			
la **araña**	spider		la **arena**	sand
el **burro**	donkey		el **barco**	boat
el **caballo**	horse		el **lago**	lake
el **cerdo**	pig		el **mar**	sea
la **culebra**	snake		el **océano**	ocean
la **gallina**	chicken, hen		el **río**	river
el **gato**	cat			
el **insecto**	insect		el **cielo**	sky
la **mosca**	fly		la **estrella**	star
el **mosquito**	mosquito		la **luna**	moon
la **oveja**	sheep		la **nube**	cloud
el **pájaro**	bird		el **sol**	sun
el **perro**	dog			
la **vaca**	cow		**pasar**	to spend (time), pass, happen
el **árbol**	tree		**viajar**	to travel
el **bosque**	woods, forest			
el **desierto**	desert		**hacer un viaje**	to take a trip
la **flor**	flower			
la **hierba**	grass		**muchas veces**	often
la **isla**	island		**una vez**	once

EJERCICIO 1   En el campo

Conteste en español en oraciones completas.

Según el dibujo:

1. ¿Cuántos caballos ve usted? ¿y cuántas vacas?
2. ¿Qué animal está mirando los cerdos?
3. ¿Qué animales están comiendo el maíz?
4. ¿Cuántas gallinas ve usted?
5. ¿Qué ve usted en el cielo?
6. ¿Qué ve usted en la distancia?
7. ¿Hay un lago o un río en la distancia?
8. ¿Qué tiempo hace?
9. ¿Dónde están todos los animales?

Preguntas generales:

10. ¿Prefiere usted pasar las vacaciones en el campo o en la ciudad?
11. ¿Prefiere usted nadar en el océano, en un lago, o en un río?
12. ¿Qué ve usted en el cielo por la noche?
13. ¿De qué color es la hierba? ¿el cielo?
14. ¿De qué color son las nubes? ¿las flores?
15. ¿Tiene usted un perro? ¿un gato?
16. ¿Viajó usted el verano pasado? ¿adónde? ¿Cuánto tiempo (*time*) pasó usted allí?
17. ¿Va usted a hacer un viaje este (*this*) verano? ¿adónde?
18. ¿Qué es el Amazonas? ¿el Sahara? ¿Puerto Rico?
19. ¿Quiere usted visitar la selva Amazonas? ¿una vez o muchas veces?

EJERCICIO 2   Identificación

Dé (*give*) la palabra que corresponde a la definición.

Modelo   Toma leche.   **el gato**

1. Produce leche.
2. Muchos árboles.
3. Es amigo del hombre.
4. Canta muy bonito.
5. Produce huevos.
6. Su carne se llama jamón.
7. Tierra entre (*between*) montañas.
8. Producen lluvia.
9. Lo que usamos en lagos, ríos, etc.
10. Los suéteres vienen de este (*this*) animal.
11. Muchas personas tienen miedo de este reptil.
12. Está en el cielo por la noche; es grande.
13. Son de muchos colores bonitos.
14. Hay muchas en el cielo de noche.
15. Lo contrario (*opposite*) de agua.

■ CONVERSACIÓN

Ricardo y Jaime, amigos de hace años, se encuentran en un bar y hablan de su juventud.

RICARDO	Jaime, ¿recuerdas que como muchacho yo te visitaba cada verano en el campo?
JAIME	Sí. ¡Cómo no! Tú pasabas un mes con nosotros y todos los días trabajábamos y jugábamos mucho.
RICARDO	Sí, pero nos levantábamos tan temprano por la mañana para dar de comer a los animales. ¡Caramba! ¡Cuántos animales había!
JAIME	¿Recuerdas que un día tú y yo fuimos al lago para pescar y vimos esa culebra grande? ¡Cuánto miedo tuvimos!
ROBERTO	Sí, y una noche fuimos al bosque donde vimos un animal grande entre los árboles. Creímos que era un monstruo.
JAIME	¡Qué gracioso! El próximo día supimos que era una vaca de mi papá.
ROBERTO	Bien, mi amigo. Tengo que volver al trabajo. ¿Por qué no venimos aquí otro día para hablar más de nuestras experiencias?
JAIME	¡Buena idea! Nos vemos entonces; hasta luego.

Richard and James, friends from years ago, meet in a bar and talk about their youth.

RICHARD	*James, do you remember how as a boy I visited you each summer in the country?*
JAMES	*Yes. Of course! You used to spend a month with us, and every day we would work and play a lot.*
RICHARD	*Yes, but we got up so early in the morning to feed the animals. My gosh! There were so many animals!*
JAMES	*Do you remember that one day you and I went to the lake to fish and we saw that large snake? We were really scared!*
ROBERT	*Yes, and one night we went to the woods where we saw a large animal among the trees. We thought that it was a monster.*
JAMES	*How funny! The next day we found out that it was one of my father's cows.*
ROBERT	*Well, my friend. I have to return to work. Why don't we come here another day to talk more about our experiences?*
JAMES	*Good idea! We'll see each other then; goodbye.*

■ ESTRUCTURA

I. El imperfecto *The imperfect tense*

Spanish has two simple past tenses: the preterit and the imperfect. The imperfect tense, indicating an uncompleted or continuous action, will be explained and contrasted with the preterit after its forms are introduced.

A. Formación de los verbos regulares en el imperfecto

Los verbos **-ar**

To form the imperfect tense, regular **-ar** verbs drop the **-ar** from the infinitive and add the endings indicated.

-ar *endings*   Modelo   **cantar**   *to sing*

-aba	**cantaba**	*I was singing, used to sing, sang*
-abas	**cantabas**	*You were singing, used to sing, sang*
-aba	**cantaba**	*He, she, it was, you were singing, used to sing, sang*
-ábamos	**cantábamos**	*We were singing, used to sing, sang*
-abais	**cantabais**	*You were singing, used to sing, sang*
-aban	**cantaban**	*They, you were singing, used to sing, sang*

Los verbos **-er**, **-ir**

To form the imperfect tense, regular **-er** and **-ir** verbs drop the **-er** or **-ir** from the infinitive and add the endings indicated.

-er, -ir *endings*   Modelo   **comer**   *to eat*

-ía	**comía**	*I was eating, used to eat, ate*
-ías	**comías**	*You were eating, used to eat, ate*
-ía	**comía**	*He, she, it was, you were eating, used to eat, ate*
-íamos	**comíamos**	*We were eating, used to eat, ate*
-íais	**comíais**	*You were eating, used to eat, ate*
-ían	**comían**	*They, you were eating, used to eat, ate*

Modelo   **vivir**   *to live*

vivía	*I was living, used to live, lived*
vivías	*You were living, used to live, lived*
vivía	*He, she, it was, you were living, used to live, lived*
vivíamos	*We were living, used to live, lived*
vivíais	*You were living, used to live, lived*
vivían	*They, you were living, used to live, lived*

Ejemplos   Carlos **miraba** la televisión y Pepe **dormía.**
¿Dónde **vivían** ustedes? **Vivíamos** en Miami.
¿Qué **hacían** los niños? **Comían** galletas.
Todos los días **trabajábamos** y **jugábamos** mucho.

EJERCICIO 3   En la playa

Diga usted lo que las personas hacían en la playa. Sustituya según el modelo.

Modelo   *Llevábamos* gafas de sol. (yo)
Yo llevaba gafas de sol.

1. *Vivían* en el hotel. (yo, él, nosotros)
2. *Jugaba* en el océano. (vosotros, ustedes, tú)
3. *Escuchabas* la radio. (yo, ella, nosotros)
4. *Comía* helado. (tú, ellos, usted)
5. *Dormían* en el sol. (nosotros, Alfonso, ellas)
6. *Leíamos* novelas. (las chicas, yo, Lisa)

B. Los verbos irregulares en el imperfecto

There are only three irregular verbs in the imperfect tense.

ser *to be*		**ir** *to go*		**ver** *to see*	
era	éramos	iba	íbamos	veía	veíamos
eras	erais	ibas	ibais	veías	veíais
era	eran	iba	iban	veía	veían

Ejemplos   Cuando **éramos** niños, **íbamos** a la hacienda de mi tío.
Ellos **veían** a la señora vieja todos los días.

EJERCICIO 4   Ir, ser y ver.

Haga una oración en el imperfecto con los verbos indicados.

Modelo   ir . . . yo/al museo
Iba al museo.

1. ir . . . tú/a la hacienda
2. ir . . . nosotros/al valle
3. ir . . . ellos/a la selva
4. ser . . . mi abuelo/carpintero
5. ser . . . mis tíos/artistas
6. ser . . . yo/un alumno malo
7. ver . . . ¿tú/a Lupe los domingos?
8. ver . . . ¿ustedes/a los muchachos en la clase?
9. ver . . . Elena/a Ricardo en el parque

EJERCICIO 5   ¿Qué hacía(n)?

Conteste en español según el modelo.

Modelo   Cuando usted era joven, ¿qué hacía?
(*tocar* el piano)
Cuando yo era joven, tocaba el piano.

1. Cuando usted era niño(a), ¿qué hacía?
(*hablar* mucho)
(*jugar* en la calle)
(*dormir* la siesta)
(*mirar* la televisión)

2. Cuando ustedes eran niños(as), ¿qué hacían?
   (*nadar* en el río)
   (*ir* a la playa)
   (*beber* leche)
   (*escuchar* la radio)
3. Cuando el presidente viajaba, ¿qué hacía?
   (*besar* a los niños)
   (*decir* mentiras)
   (*comer* mucho)
   (*manejar* un Cadillac)

EJERCICIO 6   Cuando estabas en la escuela secundaria (*high school*) . . .

Hágale preguntas a un(a) estudiante usando el imperfecto; escuche la respuesta.

Modelo   estudiar el español
       (pregunta)   **¿Estudiabas el español?**
       (respuesta)   **(Sí,) (No, no) estudiaba el español.**

1. *tener* muchos amigos
2. *ser* muy tímido(a)
3. *bailar* en las discotecas
4. *ir* a las fiestas
5. *beber* vino
6. *fumar* cigarrillos
7. *jugar* al fútbol
8. *estar* enamorado(a) (*in love*)

El hombre y su caballo reúnen (*gather*) las ovejas en la Tierra del Fuego. Argentina

II. Pretérito versus imperfecto

Although both the preterit and the imperfect tenses show past time, they convey different meanings.

A. Preterit denotes:

1.   A single completed past action.

Cerré la puerta.	*I closed the door.*
Murió.	*He died.*
Llamamos a María a las diez.	*We called Mary at 10:00.*

2.   An action with a specific limitation of time, that is, a designated beginning and/or ending.

Ayer comí demasiado.	*Yesterday I ate too much.*
La semana pasada tuvimos que trabajar por la noche.	*Last week we had to work at night.*
El año pasado los americanos compraron muchos automóviles.	*Last year Americans bought many automobiles.*

B. Imperfect denotes:

1.   A continuous or repeated past action that was occurring or used to occur over a period of time, without a stated beginning or end.

Veía a Roberto todas las noches.	*She used to see Robert every night.*
Íbamos al cine muchas veces.	*We went to the movies often.*

2.   Background description (often accompanied by interrupting action in the preterit).

Llovía y hacía sol.	*It was raining and the sun was shining.*
Caminábamos en el parque cuando vimos el cuerpo.	*We were walking in the park when we saw the body.*

3. Description of mental or emotional attitudes or physical characteristics.

No sabíamos la respuesta.   *We did not know the answer.*
Roberto amaba a su novia.   *Robert loved his girlfriend.*
Era muy bonita.   *She was very pretty.*

4. Telling time in the past.

Era la una de la tarde.   *It was one o'clock in the afternoon.*
Eran las dos y media.   *It was 2:30.*

EJERCICIO 7   En el pasado

Haga oraciones usando el imperfecto y el pretérito según el modelo.

Modelo   todos los días yo . . .   anoche yo . . .
          jugar al tenis
          Todos los días jugaba al tenis.   Anoche jugué al tenis.

1. *comer* mucho
2. *ir* a la biblioteca
3. *hacer* mi tarea
4. *tocar* el piano
5. *esperar* a mi novio(a)
6. *llamar* a mis padres
7. *llegar* a tiempo
8. *mirar* la televisión
9. *limpiar* el apartamento
10. *ver* a mi amigo

EJERCICIO 8   Un testigo (*a witness*)

Una noche usted no duerme bien. Oye un ruido (*noise*) en la casa de su vecino (*neighbor*). ¡Usted es testigo de un robo (*robbery*)! Más tarde usted narra la historia (*tell the story*) a su amigo. (Use el pretérito o el imperfecto según las indicaciones.)

1. *Son* las dos de la mañana.
2. *Hace* viento.
3. La luna *está* en el cielo.
4. La casa *es* grande y vieja.
5. Un hombre *entra* por (*through*) la ventana.
6. El hombre *es* alto y flaco.
7. El hombre *lleva* un sombrero negro.
8. Yo *llamo* a un policía.
9. El hombre *pasa* diez minutos en la casa.
10. El hombre *sale* con una bolsa grande.
11. El hombre *ve* el auto del policía.
12. El policía *dice*, "¡Alto!" (*stop*)
13. Pero (*but*) el hombre *corre* en la otra dirección.

EJERCICIO 9   ¿Qué hacía usted cuando . . . ?

Conteste en español en oraciones completas.

1.   ¿Esperaba usted en la calle cuando llegó el autobús?
2.   ¿Dormía usted cuando llamó su amigo?
3.   ¿Besaba usted a su novio(a) cuando entró la madre?
4.   ¿Estaba usted enfermo(a) cuando llegó el doctor?
5.   ¿Hablaban ustedes cuando entró el profesor?

> refranes: **El árbol se conoce por sus frutos.**
> **Los pájaros de la misma pluma vuelan juntos.**
> **En boca cerrada no entran moscas.**

III. Hacer en expresiones de tiempo   *Hacer in expressions of time*

A. To indicate an action that has been going on for a period of time and still is, Spanish uses:

> **Hace + time + que + present tense**

Hace mucho tiempo¹ que vivo aquí.   *I have been living here for a long time (much time).*

Hace dos años que toco el piano.   *I have been playing the piano for two years.*

NOTE 1:   In this context **tiempo** means *time* and does not refer to weather.

NOTE 2:   To indicate an action that had been going on for some time and still was up to the moment referred to or implied, Spanish uses: **Hacía** + time + **que** + imperfect tense.

Hacía mucho tiempo que vivía allí.
I had been living there for a long time.

EJERCICIO 10   ¿Cuánto tiempo hace?

Conteste en español según el modelo.

Modelo   ¿Cuánto tiempo hace que juega usted al fútbol?   *(How long have you been playing football?)*
   Hace tres años que juego al fútbol.   *(I have been playing footall for three years.)*

1.   ¿Cuánto tiempo hace que estudias español?
2.   ¿Cuánto tiempo hace que vives en el dormitorio?

3. ¿Cuánto tiempo hace que conoces al profesor de español?
4. ¿Cuánto tiempo hace que sales con tu novio(a)?
5. ¿Cuánto tiempo hace que la puerta está cerrada (abierta)?
6. ¿Cuánto tiempo hace que el profesor (la profesora) habla?

B. To indicate an action that took place sometime ago, Spanish uses:

> **preterit tense + hace + time**

Llegó hace dos horas.   *He arrived two hours ago.*
Salieron hace cinco minutos.   *They left five minutes ago.*

NOTE: An alternate word order is: **Hace dos horas que llegó.**

Las calles estrechas (*narrow*), las flores y plantas abundantes y los balcones de hierro (*wrought iron*) dan una imagen romántica de España. Sevilla, España

EJERCICIO 11   ¿Hace mucho tiempo?

Conteste en español en oraciones completas usando la construcción *preterit* + **hace** + *time*.

Modelo   ¿Cuánto tiempo hace que usted   *(How long ago did you buy a*
compró un abrigo?   *coat?)*
Compré un abrigo hace dos   *(I bought a coat two years ago.)*
años.

1. ¿Cuánto tiempo hace que usted compró zapatos nuevos?
2. ¿Cuánto tiempo hace que usted escribió a sus padres?
3. ¿Cuánto tiempo hace que usted comió?
4. ¿Cuánto tiempo hace que usted limpió su cuarto (*room*)?
5. ¿Cuánto tiempo hace que usted fue a un restaurante?

IV. Los demostrativos *Demonstratives*

A. Los adjetivos demostrativos

Demonstrative adjectives are used to point out or clarify a specific object or objects. In Spanish there are two words for *that*—one for objects near the person spoken to and one for objects "over there" or far away. Like all adjectives, demonstratives agree with the word they describe in gender and number.

	near speaker		near person spoken to		over there
este	*this* (m.)	**ese**	*that* (m.)	**aquel**	*that* (m.)
esta	*this* (f.)	**esa**	*that* (f.)	**aquella**	*that* (f.)
estos	*these* (m.)	**esos**	*those* (m.)	**aquellos**	*those* (m.)
estas	*these* (f.)	**esas**	*those* (f.)	**aquellas**	*those* (f.)

Este libro es mío.	*This book is mine.*
Estos libros son míos.	*These books are mine.*
Esa blusa es suya.	*That blouse is hers.*
Esas gafas son suyas.	*Those glasses are hers.*
Aquel parque es bonito.	*That park is pretty.*
Aquellas montañas son magníficas.	*Those mountains are magnificient.*

EJERCICIO 12   ¡Vamos a practicar!

Sustituya según el modelo.

Modelo   Necesito este *libro.* (pluma)
Necesito esta pluma.

1. Van a comprar este *gato.* (vaca, perros, caballo, gallinas)
2. Voy a visitar ese *teatro.* (parque, catedral, tiendas, museos)
3. Mañana vamos a aquel *lago.* (montañas, desierto, valles, isla)

Esta niña es muy bonita.
Tarragona, España.

EJERCICIO 13   Aquí, allí y en la distancia

Cambie según el modelo.

Modelo   La pluma es mía.
Esta pluma es mía.
Esa pluma es mía.
Aquella pluma es mía.

1. La bicicleta es suya.
2. El lago es pequeño.
3. Las flores son bonitas.
4. Los árboles son grandes.

B. Los pronombres demostrativos

The demonstrative adjective becomes a pronoun with the addition of a written accent over the first **e**. There is no difference in pronunciation.

este libro	→ **éste**	*this one*
esa mujer	→ **ésa**	*that one*
esos hombres	→ **ésos**	*those* (near you)
aquellas personas	→ **aquéllas**	*those* (over there)

EJERCICIO 14   Vamos de compras.

Usted y su amigo(a) van de compras en un almacén muy grande. Indiquen (indicate) los artículos que ustedes prefieren según el modelo.

Modelo   el impermeable
       (estudiante 1)   **Yo prefiero este impermeable.**
       (estudiante 2)   **Yo prefiero ése.**

1. el libro
2. las gafas
3. la camisa
4. los zapatos
5. la cartera
6. las botas
7. el suéter
8. los calcetines

C. Los demostrativos neutros   *Neuter demonstratives*

Neuter demonstratives are used only when the identity is unknown or extremely general.

esto   *this (unspecified or unidentifiable)*
eso   *that (unspecified or unidentifiable)*

¿Qué es **esto?**   *What is this?*
¿Qué es **eso?**   *What is that?*
¡Eso es horrible!   *That is horrible!*

EJERCICIO 15   ¿Qué dicen?

¿Qué expresión corresponde a cada (*each*) situación?

Expresiones: **¿Qué es esto? ¿Qué es eso?**
             ¡Eso es ridículo! ¡Eso es horrible!
             ¡Eso es maravilloso!

Situaciones:

1. El profesor dice que mañana hay tres exámenes y que los alumnos tienen que escribir quince ejercicios. ¿Qué dicen los alumnos?
2. Usted está en la cafetería y mira su plato (*plate*) de comida que tiene muchas cosas difíciles de identificar. ¿Qué dice usted?
3. Usted y su amigo caminan en el bosque y ven un animal muy extraño (*strange*). ¿Qué dicen ustedes?
4. Usted vio una película anoche. Al fin (*at the end*) de la película, todas las personas y todos los animales murieron. ¿Qué dijo usted?
5. El profesor dice que mañana no hay clase, que este semestre no hay examen y que los estudiantes tienen vacaciones de un mes. ¿Qué dicen los estudiantes?

PERSPECTIVA ORIGINAL

A.   **¿Eres artista?** En la pizarra o en papel . . .

Draw a good-sized rectangle in the shape of a picture frame. Draw a line across the middle from left to right. Follow the instructions to complete your drawing.

1. La línea representa el horizonte. Son las seis de la tarde. Dibuja el sol en el horizonte.
2. Hay muchos pájaros en el cielo. Dibuja tres o cuatro pájaros.

3. Podemos ver muchas nubes. Dibuja dos o tres nubes en el cielo.

4. En el centro está la casa de tus abuelos. Dibuja una casa con puerta y ventanas.

5. Enfrente de (*in front of*) la casa hay flores y hierba. Dibuja la hierba y muchas flores bonitas.

6. También vemos algunos árboles. Dibuja tres o cuatro árboles.

7. Tus abuelos tienen muchos animales. Dibuja un caballo, una vaca y dos gallinas.

8. En la distancia vemos un lago. Dibuja un lago pequeño, con un barco en el lago.

9. Ahora escribe el nombre del dibujo, el nombre del artista (tu nombre) y el precio (*price*) del dibujo.

B. Composición: **En la playa o en el campo**

Write a composition in Spanish describing a scene at the beach or in the country (the weather, sky, clouds, activities, and so on). Use the imperfect and the preterit tense as necessary.

■ PANORAMA CULTURAL

El carácter español

Las diversas influencias—su posición estratégica entre Europa y África, su variada historia, la fusión de varios grupos étnicos, la serie de invasiones de la península ibérica, la grandeza de su *pasado*, y la decadencia de su importancia militar—*se han combinado* durante los siglos para producir el carácter español, un carácter singular. El español es a *la vez* austero y frívolo, *irrespetuoso* y religioso, práctico e idealista, independiente y patriótico. Este carácter se manifiesta en tres personajes literarios de fama universal: El Cid, don Quijote y don Juan Tenorio.

past
have combined
at the same time/
*   disrespectful*

El Cid es el héroe de uno de los grandes poemas épicos de la literatura europea, "El Cantar de Mío Cid", escrito en el siglo XII[1]. Pero El Cid, como hombre de su época, era más que un campeón en batallas *contra* los moros; era religioso, inteligente y prudente; era vasallo *fiel* a su *rey* pero independiente *por* sus altos *valores* morales; era un buen padre y esposo. En resumen, era un símbolo de las aspiraciones de una nación nueva porque era el héroe nacional con quien la gente española podía y puede identificarse.

against
faithful/king/
*   because of/*
*   values*

Don Quijote es el protagonista central de la primera novela moderna, "El ingenioso hidalgo don Quijote de la Mancha". Esta novela es una sátira de los libros de *caballería*, pero representa también una visión total y *compleja* de la vida española. Don Quijote y su compañero Sancho Panza son antitéticos: donde uno es valiente, el otro es *cobarde*; donde uno es idealista, el otro es práctico. Los dos se complementan para formar una imagen de España y del español del siglo XVII *tanto como* del español de hoy.

chivalry/complex

coward

as much as

Don Juan Tenorio, personaje de ficción en dos dramas, uno del siglo XVII y el otro del siglo XIX, es un hombre irrespetuoso, cínico, satírico, irresponsable, egoísta, gran amante de las mujeres, héroe rebelde y finalmente símbolo del machismo latino. Pero es una personalidad que, por su espíritu de independencia, *li-*

El Cid Campeador era el más famoso de los héroes épicos españoles. Burgos, España

En el centro de Madrid vemos la estatua de Cervantes, autor de la famosa novela *Don Quijote de la Mancha*, y los dos personajes literarios Don Quijote y Sancho Panza. Madrid, España

bertad, y *deseo* de *romper* con los convencionalismos sociales *cautiva* la imaginación de todo el mundo.

*liberty/desire/
break/captivates*

Los tres personajes reflejan la singularidad del carácter español y *siguen* contribuyendo hoy como en el pasado a la gran tradición literaria española.

continue

NOTE 1:   In Spanish, centuries are written in Roman numerals.

¿CUÁNTO RECUERDAS?

Write the initials of the character (E.C. = El Cid, D.Q. = Don Quijote, D.J. = Don Juan) next to the characteristic or phrase that best applies.

1. _____ rebelde
2. _____ idealista
3. _____ campeón contra los moros
4. _____ Sancho Panza
5. _____ drama del siglo XVII
6. _____ buen padre y esposo
7. _____ cínico
8. _____ religioso
9. _____ visión total de la vida española
10. _____ poema épico del siglo XII
11. _____ egoísta

12. _____ drama del siglo XIX
13. _____ libros de caballería
14. _____ romper con los convencionalismos sociales
15. _____ fiel a su rey
16. _____ símbolo del machismo latino
17. _____ héroe nacional
18. _____ símbolo de las aspiraciones de una nación nueva
19. _____ la primera novela moderna
20. _____ gran amante de las mujeres

■ INTEGRACIÓN

A. ORAL EXERCISE: **conversación**
    1. The dialog will be read twice. Listen the first time; the second time pauses
        will be provided for you to repeat each phrase.
    2. Listen to the statements related to the dialog; indicate if the statements are
        true or fales.

B. ORAL EXERCISE: VOCABULARY, **el campo**
    Answer the questions according to the drawings, naming the items in each
    picture. Listen for the tape confirmation.

1.

2.

3.

4.

5.

6.

7.

8.

9.

10.

C.   ORAL EXERCISE: IMPERFECT TENSE
      Complete the sentences with the correct form of the verb in the imperfect
      tense.
           Example   (tape)   trabajar allí/yo
                      (your response)   **Yo trabajaba allí.**

D.   ORAL EXERCISE: IMPERFECT TENSE IRREGULAR VERBS **ser**, **ir**, AND **ver**
      Repeat each sentence substituting the correct form of the verb in the imper-
      fect tense.
           Example   (tape)   Yo era rico. Tú . . .
                      (your response)   **Tú eras rico.**

E.   ORAL EXERCISE: IMPERFECT TENSE
      Answer the questions on the tape according to the drawing, using the imper-
      fect tense. Listen for the tape confirmation.

F.   WRITTEN EXERCISE: IMPERFECT TENSE

Change the sentences on the tape from the present to the imperfect tense.

Example   (tape)   Él habla mucho.
          (your written response)   **Él hablaba mucho.**

G.   ORAL EXERCISE: PRETERIT AND IMPERFECT

Answer the questions on the tape according to the drawings.

Juanita   Teresa

Example   (tape)   ¿Qué hacía Teresa
                              cuando Juanita entró?
          (your response)   **Teresa escribía cuando
                              Juanita entró.**

Juanita   Teresa

Juanita   Teresa

Juanita   Mario   Juanita   Mario

los estudiantes

los estudiantes

H. ORAL EXERCISE: **hacer** + **que** + PRESENT TENSE (DURATION OF TIME)
    Answer the questions on the tape according to the drawings.

(media hora)

Example   (tape)   ¿Cuánto tiempo hace
                             que Lupe canta?

           (your response) **Hace media hora que
                             Lupe canta.**

(dos días)

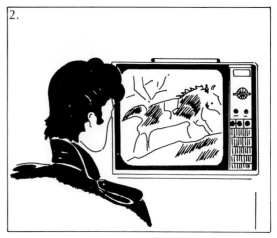

(dos horas)

(media hora)

(veinte minutos)

(quince minutos)

(ocho horas)

I.   ORAL EXERCISE: PRETERIT + **hace** + TIME (AGO)
     Answer the questions on the tape using the times indicated.
     Example   (tape)   ¿Cuándo vendió usted el coche?—una se-
                                        mana
                    (your response)   **Vendí el coche hace una semana.**

J.   ORAL EXERCISE: DEMONSTRATIVES
     Give the demonstrative adjectives corresponding to each object in each pic-
     ture.

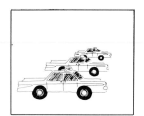

Example   (tape)   taxi
          (your response)   **este taxi**
                              ese taxi
                              aquel taxi

1.

2.
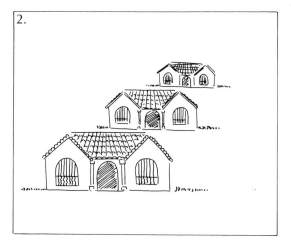

3.

4.

K.   WRITTEN EXERCISE: COMPREHENSION, **El carácter español**
     You will hear a short paragraph which will be read twice. Write the answers
     to the three questions that follow.

L.   DICTATION: **El carácter español**
     Write the four sentences you hear. Each sentence will be read three times.

■ REPASO DE VOCABULARIO ACTIVO

Sustantivos

el **animal**	la **estrella**	la **nube**
la **araña**	la **flor**	el **océano**
el **árbol**	la **gallina**	la **oveja**
la **arena**	el **gato**	el **pájaro**
el **barco**	la **hacienda**	el **perro**
el **bosque**	la **hierba**	el **río**
el **burro**	el **insecto**	la **selva**
el **caballo**	la **isla**	el **sol**
el **campo**	el **lago**	el **tiempo**
el **cerdo**	la **luna**	la **vaca**
el **cielo**	el **mar**	el **valle**
la **culebra**	la **mosca**	
el **desierto**	el **mosquito**	

Verbos   *Expresiones idiomáticas*

pasar   **hacer un viaje**
viajar   **muchas veces**
              una vez

Adjetivos demostrativos   *Demostrativos neutros*

este	**ese**	**aquel**	**esto**	**eso**
esta	**esa**	**aquella**		
estos	**esos**	**aquellos**		
estas	**esas**	**aquellas**		

■ EJERCICIOS DE REPASO

I. El imperfecto

Diga usted lo que las personas hacían cuando eran niños.

Modelo   *tomar* jugo de naranja . . . yo
         Tomaba jugo de naranja.

1. *abrazar* a mi abuela . . . yo
2. *correr* en el parque . . . yo
3. *amar* a tu perro . . . tú
4. *leer* muchos libros . . . tú
5. *pedir* galletas . . . él
6. *andar* en bicicleta . . . él
7. *querer* jugar . . . nosotros
8. *visitar* a nuestros tíos . . . nosotros

9. *salir* por la tarde . . . vosotros
10. *caminar* en la avenida . . . vosotros
11. *comer* mucho helado . . . ustedes
12. *hablar* todo el día . . . ustedes

II. ¿Pretérito o imperfecto?

Complete con la forma **yo** del verbo en el pretérito o en el imperfecto según las indicaciones.

> Modelo   (*ir* de compras) ayer . . .
> **Ayer fui de compras**

1. (*ir* a la playa) El verano pasado . . .
2. (*ir* a la playa) Todos los sábados . . .
3. (*nadar* en el lago) Una vez . . .
4. (*nadar* en el lago) Muchas veces . . .
5. (*ver* el programa) Todos los días . . .
6. (*ver* el programa) Anoche . . .
7. (*hacer* el viaje) Hace dos años . . .
8. (*hacer* el viaje) Todos los veranos . . .
9. (*llamar* por teléfono) La semana pasada . . .
10. (*llamar* por teléfono) Todos los domingos . . .

III. Hacer en expresiones de tiempo

Conteste según el modelo.

> A. Modelo   ¿Cuánto tiempo hace que vives aquí?—un año
> **Hace un año que vivo aquí.**

1. ¿Cuánto tiempo hace que trabajas aquí?—dos años
2. ¿Cuánto tiempo hace que juegas al tenis?—tres meses
3. ¿Cuánto tiempo hace que conoces a María?—una semana

> B. Modelo   ¿Cuánto tiempo hace que usted vendió el coche?—dos días
> **Vendí el coche hace dos días.**

1. ¿Cuánto tiempo hace que usted salió?—dos horas
2. ¿Cuánto tiempo hace que usted limpió la casa?—tres días
3. ¿Cuánto tiempo hace que usted fue al cine?—un mes

IV. Los demostrativos

Cambie según el modelo.

> Modelo   Compré los zapatos.   **Compré estos zapatos, ésos y aquéllos.**

1. Compré el vestido.
2. Prefiero las galletas.
3. Conozco a la mujer.
4. Abrí los regalos.

V. Repaso general

A. Conteste en español

1. ¿Qué animales ve usted en una hacienda grande?
2. ¿Cuáles son los animales domésticos?
3. ¿Qué ve usted en el parque?
4. ¿Qué contrastes ve usted en la geografía del mundo (*world*)?
5. ¿Qué hacía usted cuando era niño?
6. ¿Qué hacían los estudiantes cuando el profesor entró?
7. ¿Es tuyo este libro?
8. ¿Quién es el héroe de un famoso poema épico español?
9. ¿Cómo se llama el compañero de Don Quijote de la Mancha?
10. ¿Quién es el gran amante de las mujeres, personaje famoso de dos dramas españoles?

B. Traduzca al español.

1. She was very pretty.
2. It was midnight.
3. The stars were in the sky.
4. I was sleeping when my father returned.
5. They arrived at 10:00.
6. I have been studying Spanish for five months.
7. I ate an hour ago.
8. This is easy!
9. These flowers are pretty!
10. These horses are ours; that one is my brother's.

VI. Repaso de verbos

Escriba oraciones cambiando el verbo a los tiempos indicados. Use la forma **yo** del verbo.

1. ser estudiante   2. estar en el desierto   3. ir al lago

a) presente **Yo . . .**
b) pretérito
c) imperfecto

CAPÍTULO 8

■ VOCABULARIO *La casa*

la **alcoba**	*bedroom*	la **bañera**	*bathtub*	
el **baño**	*bathroom, bath*	la **ducha**	*shower*	
la **cocina**	*kitchen*	el **inodoro**	*toilet*	
el **comedor**	*dining room*	el **jabón**	*soap*	
el **cuarto**	*room*	el **lavabo**	*sink* (bath)	
la **escalera**	*stairs*	la **toalla**	*towel*	
el **garaje**	*garage*			
el **hogar**	*home*	la **estufa**	*stove*	
el **jardín**	*garden*	el **fregadero**	*sink* (kitchen)	
el **piso**	*floor, story*	el **refrigerador**	*refrigerator*	
la **sala**	*living room*			
el **sótano**	*basement*	la **cuchara**	*spoon*	
		el **cuchillo**	*knife*	
la **alfombra**	*carpet, rug*	el **plato**	*plate, dish*	
el **armario**	*bureau, closet*	la **servilleta**	*napkin*	
la **cama**	*bed*	la **taza**	*cup*	
las **cortinas**	*curtains*	el **tenedor**	*fork*	
el **disco**	*phonograph record*	el **vaso**	*glass*	
el **espejo**	*mirror*			
la **lámpara**	*lamp*	**alquilar**	*to rent*	
la **luz**	*light*	**apagar**	*to turn off*	
los **muebles**	*furniture*	**bajar**	*to go down,*	
el **sillón**	*easy chair*		*to get off*	
el **sofá**	*sofa*	**encender** (ie)	*to turn on* (lights)	
el **tocadiscos**	*record player*	**lavar**	*to wash*	

preparar	*to prepare*	el **fin de semana**	*weekend*
subir	*to go up, climb,*	la **semana que viene**	*next week*
	to get on	el **año que viene**	*next year*

EJERCICIO 1   La casa

Conteste en español en oraciones completas.

Según el dibujo:

1. ¿Qué muebles hay en la sala?
2. ¿Qué hay en el comedor?
3. ¿Qué hay en la cocina?
4. ¿Qué muebles tiene la alcoba?
5. ¿Qué hay en el baño?
6. ¿Cuántas toallas ve usted?
7. ¿Tiene una ducha este baño?
8. ¿Qué ve usted en el cuarto que tiene el escritorio?
9. ¿Cuántas ventanas hay en la casa?
10. ¿Dónde está la escalera?
11. ¿En qué cuarto hay un espejo?

Preguntas generales:

12. ¿Cuántos cuartos hay en su casa? ¿cuántas alcobas? ¿cuántos baños?
13. ¿Cuántos pisos tiene su casa?
14. ¿Tiene su casa muebles nuevos o muebles viejos?
15. ¿Tiene su casa un jardín? ¿un garaje? ¿y un sótano?

EJERCICIO 2   Identificación

Dé la palabra que corresponde a la definición.

1. El cuarto donde preparamos la comida.
2. El cuarto donde comemos.
3. El cuarto donde dormimos.
4. El cuarto donde tomamos una ducha.
5. El cuarto donde visitamos con nuestros amigos.
6. Lo que usamos para lavar el cuerpo.
7. Lo que miramos para ver nuestra reflexión.
8. Lo que usamos para subir y bajar.
9. Lo que apagamos de día y encendemos de noche.
10. Lo que hacemos cuando no queremos comprar la casa.
11. Lo que usamos para limpiar la boca.
12. Lo que usamos para tomar la sopa.
13. Lo que usamos para tomar el café.
14. Lo que usamos para tomar el agua.
15. Lo que usamos para comer la carne. (dos cosas)
16. Donde lavamos los platos.
17. Donde lavamos la cara y las manos.

Los patios interiores y los arcos (*arches*) dan evidencia de la arquitectura colonial. Cuzco, Perú

■ CONVERSACIÓN

El Sr. Gómez está buscando información sobre una casa para alquilar. Llama por teléfono al propietario.

SR. GÓMEZ	¿Aló? Buenos días. Vi su anuncio en el periódico y quiero saber más de la casa.
PROPIETARIO	¡Por supuesto, señor! Es una casa nueva y con muebles.
SR. GÓMEZ	¡Qué bueno! ¿Cuántos cuartos tiene la casa?
PROPIETARIO	Tiene una sala grande, un comedor, dos alcobas, baño, cocina y un patio con un jardín bonito.
SR. GÓMEZ	¿Será posible ver la casa esta tarde a las tres?
PROPIETARIO	¡Claro! La dirección es calle Santiago, número 870.
SR. GÓMEZ	Muchas gracias. Llegaré a las tres en punto.

Mr. Gómez is seeking information about a house for rent. He calls the owner on the telephone.

MR. GÓMEZ   Hello? Good morning. I saw your advertisement in the paper and I'd like to know more about the house.
OWNER   Certainly, sir. It's a new house with furniture.
MR. GÓMEZ   Great! How many rooms does the house have?
OWNER   It has a large living room, a dining room, two bedrooms, a bath, a kitchen, and a patio with a pretty garden.
MR. GÓMEZ   Will it be possible to see the house this afternoon at three?
OWNER   Of course! The address is Santiago Street, number 870.
MR. GÓMEZ   Thank you very much. I'll arrive at three o'clock sharp.

■ ESTRUCTURA

I. El futuro   *The future tense*

The future tense tells what will happen.

A. Formación del futuro
The future tense of regular -**ar**, -**er**, or -**ir** verbs is formed by adding to the *complete infinitive* the endings indicated.

endings   Modelos   **hablar, comer, vivir**

-é	hablaré	I will speak	comeré	I will eat, etc.	viviré	I will live, etc.
-ás	hablarás	You will speak	comerás		vivirás	
-á	hablará	He, she, you will speak	comerá		vivirá	
-emos	hablaremos	We will speak	comeremos		viviremos	
-éis	hablaréis	You will speak	comeréis		viviréis	
-án	hablarán	They, you will speak	comerán		vivirán	

Ejemplos   **Llegaré** a las tres en punto.
Será una reunión muy importante.
Compraremos la casa.

EJERCICIO 3   ¡Vamos a practicar!

Diga (*tell*) usted lo que las personas van a hacer; use el tiempo futuro.

Modelo   Jaime . . . (*ir* a su cuarto)
Jaime irá a su cuarto.

1. Yo . . . (*vender* mi VW) (*comprar* un Honda)
2. Tú . . . (*viajar* a Europa) (*visitar* Londres)
3. Ellos . . . (*ir* a la sala) (*hablar*)
4. Nosotros . . . (*apagar* la luz) (*dormir*)

5. Vosotros . . . (*entrar*) (*esperar*)
6. Ella . . . (*pasar* dos días allí) (*volver* pronto)

EJERCICIO 4   Este verano

Pregúntele a un(a) estudiante lo que va a hacer este verano.

Modelo *estudiar* (pregunta)   **¿Estudiarás el español?**
                 (respuesta)   **(Sí,) (No, no) estudiaré el español.**

1. *trabajar*
2. *comprar* un coche
3. *ir* a la playa
4. *viajar* a México
5. *descansar*
6. *beber* mucha cerveza
7. *vivir* con la familia

B. Verbos irregulares en el futuro

The following verbs have irregular stems, which are used with the future tense
endings.

decir:	**dir-**	
hacer:	**har-**	**-é**
poder:	**podr-**	**-ás**
poner:	**pondr-**	**-á**
querer:	**querr-**	**-emos**
saber:	**sabr-**	**-éis**
salir:	**saldr-**	**-án**
tener:	**tendr-**	
venir:	**vendr-**	

Ejemplos

¿A qué hora **saldrán** ustedes?
Saldremos a las ocho.
¿Tendrás que volver el domingo?
No. **Tendré** que volver el miércoles.

¡Qué vista panorámica tienen estas casas antiguas
situadas en los precipicios (*cliffs*) de Cuenca! España

EJERCICIO 5   ¿Qué harán?

Indique lo que harán las personas según el modelo.

>   Modelo   yo . . (*salir* temprano)
>   **Yo saldré temprano.**

1.   Yo . . . (*hacer* la tarea) (*saber* la respuesta)
2.   Ellos . . . (*tener* sueño) (no *venir* a la clase)
3.   Nosotros . . . (*poner* el tocadiscos en la sala) (*querer* bailar)
4.   Tú . . . (*decir* la verdad) (*poder* salir)

EJERCICIO 6   ¿Qué van a hacer? ¿Qué harán?

Cambie las oraciones al futuro según el modelo.

>   Modelo   Yo *voy a comer.*   **Comeré.**

1.   Yo *voy a venir.*
2.   Yo *voy a preparar* la comida.
3.   Tú *vas a leer.*
4.   Tú *vas a encender* la luz.
5.   Lolita *va a fumar.*
6.   Lolita *va a bailar* el tango.
7.   Nosotros *vamos a salir* la semana que viene.
8.   Nosotros *vamos a alquilar* un apartamento.

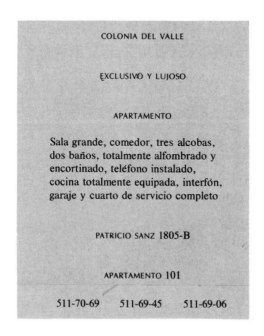

COLONIA DEL VALLE

EXCLUSIVO Y LUJOSO

APARTAMENTO

Sala grande, comedor, tres alcobas,
dos baños, totalmente alfombrado y
encortinado, teléfono instalado,
cocina totalmente equipada, interfón,
garaje y cuarto de servicio completo

PATRICIO SANZ 1805-B

APARTAMENTO 101

511-70-69   511-69-45   511-69-06

EJERCICIO 7   Preguntas generales

Conteste en español en oraciones completas.

1.   ¿Qué tendrá usted que hacer mañana?
2.   ¿Qué hará usted este fin de semana?
3.   ¿Qué traerá usted a la fiesta?
4.   ¿Qué pondrá usted en el armario? ¿y en la mesa?
5.   ¿Qué países (*countries*) visitará usted en el futuro?
6.   ¿Podrá usted aprender el español en un año?
7.   ¿Usará usted un poco de español en el futuro?
8.   ¿Qué tipo (*type*) de casa comprará usted?
9.   ¿Volverá usted a la universidad el año que viene?

II. El condicional *The conditional*

The conditional tells what would happen.

A. Formación del condicional

The conditional of regular **-ar**, **-er**, or **ir** verbs is formed by adding to the complete infinitive the endings indicated. Note that the conditional endings are identical to the imperfect tense endings for **-er** and **-ir** verbs.

endings   Modelos   **hablar, comer, vivir**

endings		
-ía	hablaría	I would speak
-ías	hablarías	You would speak
-ía	hablaría	He, she, you would speak
-íamos	hablaríamos	We would speak
-íais	hablaríais	You would speak
-ían	hablarían	They, you would speak

comería	I would eat, etc.	viviría	I would live, etc.
comerías		vivirías	
comería		viviría	
comeríamos		viviríamos	
comeríais		viviríais	
comerían		vivirían	

Ejemplos Con cien mil dólares, yo **compraría** una casa nueva.
¿**Viajarían** ustedes a Europa?
¿**Darías** dinero a los pobres?

En la selva tropical una choza (*hut*) de bambú y paja (*straw*) protege de los elementos.

EJERCICIO 8   Hoy no hay clase

Imagine usted que hoy no hay clase de español. Diga usted lo que las personas harían (*would do*).

1. Yo . . . (*lavar* la ropa) (*preparar* la comida)
2. Tú . . . (*ir* a un restaurante) (*andar* en bicicleta)
3. Vosotros . . . (*jugar* al fútbol) (*descansar*)
4. Marta . . . (*besar* a su novio) (*mirar* la televisión)
5. Paco y Pepe . . . (*escuchar* la radio) (*beber* Coca-Cola)
6. Nosotros . . . (*nadar*) (*dormir*)

B. Verbos irregulares en el condicional

The following verbs have irregular stems which are used with the conditional endings. These irregular stems are the same as those of the future.

decir:	**dir-**	
hacer:	**har-**	
poder:	**podr-**	**-ía**
poner:	**pondr-**	**-ías**
querer:	**querr-**	**-ía**
saber:	**sabr-**	**-íamos**
salir:	**saldr-**	**-íais**
tener:	**tendr-**	**-ían**
venir:	**vendr-**	

Ejemplos   ¿Qué **harías** en esa situación?
Yo **saldría.**
Nosotros **diríamos** la verdad.
Él **tendría** miedo.

EJERCICIO 9   Un(a) estudiante ideal

¿Qué harías para ser un(a) estudiante ideal?

Complete según el modelo.

Modelo   *poner* una manzana en la mesa del profesor
Pondría una manzana en la mesa del profesor.

1. *hacer* la tarea
2. *venir* a clase todos los días
3. *saber* las respuestas
4. no *decir* mentiras
5. no *salir* de la clase temprano
6. no *tener* miedo de los exámenes
7. *poder* hacer todos los ejercicios
8. *querer* estudiar

La elegancia y la originalidad de la arquitectura de la mansión indican los gustos de una familia rica. México, D. F.

EJERCICIO 10 Preguntas generales

Conteste en español en oraciones completas.

1. ¿Qué haría usted con un millón de dólares?
2. ¿Qué haría usted en Miami?
3. ¿Qué diría usted a un cubano que no habla inglés?
4. ¿Dónde pondría usted las flores? ¿los platos sucios? ¿la ropa limpia?
5. ¿Podría usted lavar los platos, hacer la cama y tomar una ducha en media hora?
6. ¿Vendrían ustedes a la clase sin la tarea?
7. ¿Viviría usted en Alaska? ¿por qué? ¿y en Puerto Rico?

III. Palabras afirmativas y negativas *Affirmative and negative words*

alguien	*someone, somebody*
alguno (-a, -os, -as)	*some one, some*
algo	*something*
siempre	*always*
a veces	*sometimes, at times*
también	*also*
o . . . o	*either . . . or*
nadie	*no one, nobody*
ninguno (-a)	*not one, none, not any*
nada	*nothing, not anything*
nunca	*never, not ever*
tampoco	*neither, not either*
ni . . . ni	*neither . . . nor*

NOTE 1: In a negative sentence in Spanish, the verb is either preceded by **no** and followed by the longer negative or preceded by the longer negative alone.

no + verb + negative

Carlos **no** cocina **nunca**.
No estaba abierta **ninguna** ventana.

negative + verb

Carlos **nunca** cocina.
Ninguna ventana estaba abierta.

NOTE 2: **Alguien** and **nadie**, as objects of the verb, are preceded by a personal **a**.

Veo **a** alguien en la casa.
No veo **a** nadie allí.

NOTE 3:   **Alguno** and **ninguno** become **algún** and **ningún** before a masculine singular noun. **Ninguno** has no plural form.

Vamos a México **algún** día.
No veo **ningún** disco.

EJERCICIO 11   Una persona negativa

Usted es una persona negativa que contradice todo lo que su amigo(a) dice. Use la construcción **no** + verbo + palabra negativa.

Modelo   Su amigo(a) dice: *Siempre* tengo hambre.
         Usted dice: **¡No tengo hambre nunca!**

1.   Hay *alguien* en la cocina.
2.   Hay *algo* interesante en la televisión.
3.   Tengo *algunos* discos nuevos.
4.   *Siempre* limpio mi alcoba.
5.   Lavo la ropa *también*.
6.   Voy de compras *o* el viernes *o* el sábado.

EJERCICIO 12   Otra persona negativa

Exprese en la forma negativa usando la construcción: palabra negativa + verbo.

Modelo   *No* cocino *nunca*.
         Nunca cocino.

1.   *No* está pasando *nada*.
2.   *No* viene a la fiesta *nadie* interesante.
3.   *No* como helado *nunca*.
4.   *No* como torta *tampoco*.
5.   *No* puede usar mi tocadiscos *ninguna* persona.

EJERCICIO 13   Una persona positiva

Usted es una persona positiva; responda usted a su amigo(a) en oraciones afirmativas.

Modelo   Su amigo(a) dice: *Nunca* salgo con mis amigos.
         Usted dice: **Siempre salgo con mis amigos.**

1.   *No* conozco a *nadie* interesante.
2.   *Nunca* llamo a mis amigos.
3.   *No* hice *nada* anoche.
4.   *No* fui a la fiesta *tampoco*.
5.   *No* compré *ningún* regalo.

EJERCICIO 14   Preguntas generales

Conteste en español en oraciones completas.

1. ¿Tiene usted algo en la mano?
2. ¿Dice usted la verdad siempre, nunca, o a veces?
3. ¿Hay alguien en su alcoba?
4. ¿Hay algunos programas buenos en la televisión? ¿Cuáles?
5. ¿Algún día quiere usted hacer un viaje a la luna?
6. ¿Hay algo en este escritorio?
7. ¿Ve usted a alguien importante en frente de (*in front of*) la clase?

> refrán: **¡Más vale tarde que nunca!**

IV. Formación de los adverbios *Formation of adverbs*

You already know some Spanish adverbs such as **ahora**, **hoy**, **mañana**, **tarde**, **bien**, **mal**, **aquí**, **allí**, **muy**. However, many other adverbs end in **-mente**, the Spanish equivalent of the English **-ly**. The ending **-mente** is added to the feminine singular form of the adjective, or directly to adjectives which end in **e** or a consonant.

rápido	→**rápida**	→**rápidamente**	*rapidly*
perfecto	→**perfecta**	→**perfectamente**	*perfectly*
posible		**posiblemente**	*possibly*
personal		**personalmente**	*personally*

VOCABULARIO

fácil	*easy*	**posible**	*possible*
frecuente	*frequent*	**probable**	*probable*
general	*general*	**profesional**	*professional*
lento	*slow*	**rápido**	*rapid, fast*
perfecto	*perfect*	**reciente**	*recent*
personal	*personal*		

EJERCICIO 15   ¡Vamos a practicar!

Sustituya según el modelo.

> Modelo   *Probablemente* alquilaremos la casa. (posible)
> **Posiblemente alquilaremos la casa.**

1. Ella baila *perfectamente*. (lento)
2. Él escribió los ejercicios *fácilmente*. (rápido)
3. *Posiblemente* vamos al teatro el sábado. (probable)
4. *Generalmente* no quiere estudiar. (reciente)
5. Mónica conoce a Carlos *profesionalmente*. (personal)
6. Hablan español *lentamente*. (perfecto)

7. *Generalmente* él no sabe nada. (profesional)
8. Toca la guitarra *fácilmente*. (frecuente)

PERSPECTIVA ORIGINAL

1. Presentación oral: **Mi casa (real o imaginada)**
   Bring photos or draw a picture of a house which you will describe. Tell your classmates such things as size, number of rooms, floors, style, interesting features, etc.

SUPPLEMENTARY VOCABULARY

el **ladrillo**	*brick*	la **cancha de tenis**	*tennis court*
la **madera**	*wood*	la **chimenea**	*chimney, fireplace*
el **vidrio**	*glass*	el **desván**	*attic*
		la **pared**	*wall*
el **balcón**	*balcony*	la **piscina**	*pool*

2. Composición: **Mi vida en veinte años**
   Write a brief composition describing your life twenty years from now (where you will live, what work you will be doing, your marital and family status, trips you will take, things you will want to do).

La majestuosa Pirámide del Sol domina Teotihuacán, antigua ciudad indígena, anterior en su construcción a la cultura azteca. Teotihuacán, México

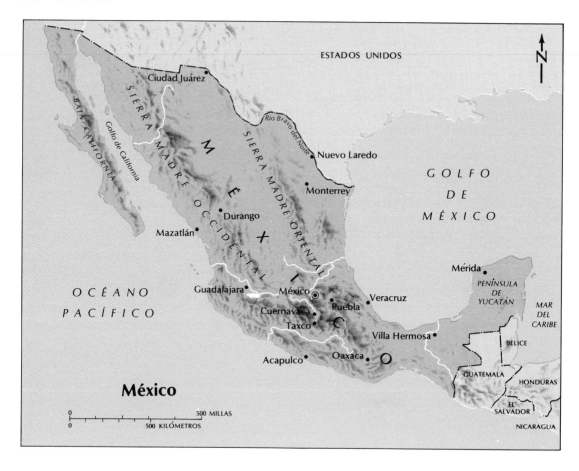

México

■ PANORAMA CULTURAL

México

México, tres veces más grande que España, es un país *bastante* moderno y progre-sista. Con una población de más de setenta millones de personas es muy impor-tante en la política y la economía del Nuevo *Mundo*.

    Hay mucha variedad en el clima, en la geografía y en la gente. Hay costas y selvas tropicales, montañas y volcanes magníficos y desiertos áridos. La mayor parte de la población es mestiza, una *mezcla* de indio y español.

    Antes de la llegada de los españoles, las civilizaciones más importantes eran *la de* los aztecas, situada en la *meseta* central, y la de los mayas, situada en la Penín-sula de Yucatán, Guatemala y Honduras. Las ilustres civilizaciones indias dan al país una originalidad que no tiene otro país del mundo. El famoso calendario az-teca, las pirámides de San Juan Teotihuacán, las *antiguas* ciudades de Palenque y Chichén-Itzá en el sur, y los muchos monumentos y *artesanías*, dan buena eviden-

quite

world

mixture
before/that of
plateau

ancient
artifacts

cia de los avances científicos, arquitectónicos y culturales de los imperios preco-
lombinos.

Hernán Cortés conquistó a los aztecas en 1521 después de una *lucha* de dos   *struggle*
años. El imperio de los mayas ya estaba en decadencia y no *ofreció* a los españoles   *offered*
una resistencia bien organizada. En 1810 México declaró su independencia de España pero la influencia española se ve todavía en las catedrales impresionantes,
las casas, haciendas y pueblos coloniales.

La fusión de lo indígena y lo español *ha creado* una cultura *única*, evidente en   *has created/*
los murales de Diego Rivera y José Clemente Orozco[1], en el espectáculo del Ballet   *unique*
Folklórico, en las *canciones* del pueblo y la música de los mariachis[2], en las arte-   *songs*
sanías de cerámica y *plata*, y en los colores vivos del sarape. Conociendo esta   *silver*
cultura e historia, el viajero puede empezar a entender el *orgullo* del mexicano   *pride*
cuando dice, "Soy mexicano".

NOTE 1: José Clemente Orozco and Diego Rivera are two of Mexico's outstanding
twentieth-century painters focusing on social and revolutionary themes.
NOTE 2: Mariachis are musicians who play a popular style of music generally on
the guitar, violin, and trumpet.

Las impresionantes ruinas de Palenque, ciudad
construída por los mayas, están situadas en la selva
tropical de Yucatán. México

PREGUNTAS

Conteste en español según el mapa.

1. ¿Con qué países tiene fronteras México?
2. ¿Cuál es la capital de México?
3. ¿Cuál es una famosa ciudad turística que está en el Océano Pacífico?
4. ¿Cómo se llama la península que está al norte de Guatemala?
5. ¿Cómo se llama el río que divide México y los Estados Unidos de América?

Conteste en español según la lectura.

1. ¿Cuántas personas viven en México?
2. ¿Cómo es la geografía de México?
3. ¿Qué significa la palabra "mestizo"?
4. Antes de la llegada de los españoles, ¿cuáles eran las dos civilizaciones de más importancia?
5. ¿Dónde estaba situada la civilización azteca? ¿la maya?
6. ¿En qué año conquistó Cortés a los aztecas?
7. ¿Ofrecieron los mayas una resistencia bien organizada?
8. ¿En qué año declaró México su independencia?
9. ¿La cultura mexicana es una fusión de qué elementos?

■ INTEGRACIÓN

A. SONG: **Cielito lindo** (México)
   Listen to the song the first time. The second time sing along with the tape.*

   De la sierra morena,
   cielito lindo, vienen bajando
   un par de ojitos negros
   cielito lindo, de contrabando. [repita]

   (CORO)
   ¡Ay! ¡Ay, ay, ay!
   Canta y no llores
   porque cantando se alegran,
   cielito lindo, los corazones.

   *English translation:

From the shadowy range,	¡Ay! ¡Ay, ay, ay!
pretty littly sky, come down	Sing and don't cry
a pair of furtive eyes,	because by singing
pretty little sky.	hearts rejoice, pretty little sky.

   "Cielito Lindo." Performance by Arcadio Elias Mariachi Nacional, from "Viva Mariachi" (Audiofidelity Stereodisc album AFSD 6159). Used by permission of Audiofidelity Enterprises, Inc.

B. ORAL EXERCISE: **conversación**
    1. The dialog will be read twice. Listen the first time; the second time pauses will be provided for you to repeat each phrase.
    2. Listen to the statements related to the dialog; indicate if the statements are true or false.

C. ORAL EXERCISE: VOCABULARY, **la casa**
    Answer the questions on the tape according to the drawings.

la sala

la cocina

la mesa

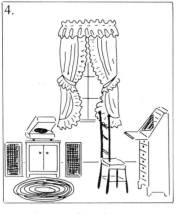
el cuarto

la alcoba

el baño

D. ORAL EXERCISE: FUTURE TENSE
    Repeat each sentence substituting the correct form of the verb in the future tense.

    Example   (tape)   Yo dormiré en el sofá. Tú . . .
               (your response)   **Tú dormirás en el sofá.**

E. ORAL EXERCISE: FUTURE TENSE
    Using the future tense, indicate that the following actions will take place.
        Example (tape)   Voy a subir la escalera.
                 (your response) **Subiré la escalera.**

F. ORAL EXERCISE: FUTURE TENSE
    Answer the questions on the tape according to the drawings.

Example (tape)   ¿Quién no comerá?
         (your response) **Lupe no comerá.**

Carlota   Lupe

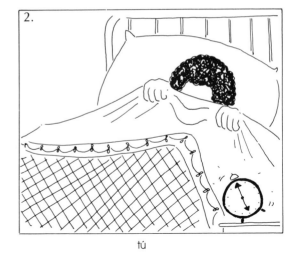

1. yo   Pepe

2. tú

3. Pepe   Carlos

4. las chicas   Teresa

5. Carlota   Lupe

6. el padre   nosotros

G. WRITTEN EXERCISE: FUTURE TENSE
Answer the five questions on the tape. Each question will be given twice.

H. ORAL EXERCISE: CONDITIONAL
Tell what each of the persons would do if they won the lottery.

Example   (tape)   ir a Europa/Carlos
          (your response)   **Carlos iría a Europa.**

I. ORAL EXERCISE: CONDITIONAL
    Answer the questions on the tape according to the drawings.

Example   (tape)   ¿Qué haría usted con el
                            periódico?
          (your response) **Yo leería el periódico.**

yo

1.

yo

2.

Carmen

3.

Pepe

4.

Juan

5.

nosotros

6.

yo

J.   WRITTEN EXERCISE: CONDITIONAL
     Answer the five questions on the tape. Each question will be given twice.

K.   ORAL EXERCISE: AFFIRMATIVE AND NEGATIVE WORDS
     Answer the questions on the tape according to the drawings. Listen for the
     tape confirmation.

1.
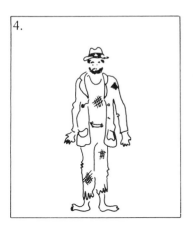

2.

3.

4.

5.
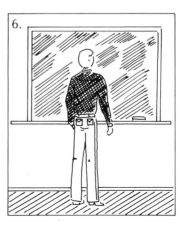

6.
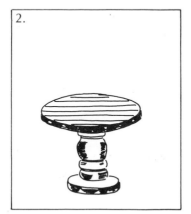

L.   WRITTEN EXERCISE: COMPREHENSION, **México**
     You will hear a short paragraph read twice. Listen to it carefully. Write the an-
     swers to the three questions that follow.

M.   DICTATION: **México**
     Write the four sentences you hear on the tape. Each sentence will be read
     three times.

■ REPASO DE VOCABULARIO ACTIVO

Adjetivos

fácil	**lento**	**posible**	**rápido**
frecuente	**perfecto**	**probable**	**reciente**
general	**personal**	**profesional**	

Sustantivos

la **alcoba**	la **cuchara**	el **inodoro**	la **sala**
la **alfombra**	el **cuchillo**	el **jabón**	la **servilleta**
el **armario**	el **disco**	el **jardín**	el **sillón**
la **bañera**	la **ducha**	la **lámpara**	el **sofá**
el **baño**	la **escalera**	el **lavabo**	el **sótano**
la **cama**	el **espejo**	la **luz**	la **taza**
la **cocina**	la **estufa**	los **muebles**	el **tenedor**
el **comedor**	el **fregadero**	el **piso**	la **toalla**
las **cortinas**	el **garaje**	el **plato**	el **tocadiscos**
el **cuarto**	el **hogar**	el **refrigerador**	el **vaso**

Verbos

alquilar	**bajar**	**lavar**	**subir**
apagar	**encender(ie)**	**preparar**	

Palabras afirmativas y negativas

algo	**nada**	**ni . . . ni**	**tampoco**
alguien	**nadie**	**o . . . o**	
alguno (-a, -os, -as)	**ninguno (-a)**	**siempre**	
a veces	**nunca**	**también**	

Expresiones

el año que viene   **la semana que viene**
el fin de semana

■ EJERCICIOS DE REPASO

I. El futuro

Diga usted lo que las personas van a hacer en el año 2000.

>   Modelo   Carlos/*vivir* en Buenos Aires
>   **Carlos vivirá en Buenos Aires.**

1. Juanita y Mario/*tener* muchos hijos
2. Yo/*alquilar* una casa en Acapulco
3. Mi esposo(a) y yo/*pasar* un año en Europa

4. Tú/*hacer* un viaje a Madrid
5. Vosotros/*volver* a la universidad
6. Carlota/*ir* a Italia

7. Alberto/*ser* millonario
8. Nosotros/*poder* ir a la luna
9. Ustedes/*trabajar* en Nueva York

II. El condicional
Diga usted lo que las personas harían con un millón de dólares.

Modelo   Carlos/*comprar* una casa
          Carlos compraría una casa.

1. Yo/*comprar* un Mercedes
2. Alicia/*dar* el dinero a los pobres
3. Pepe/*poner* el dinero en el banco
4. Nosotros/*viajar* a la América del Sur

5. Mónica y Lupe/*salir* de la universidad
6. Tú/*tener* muchas vacaciones
7. Ustedes/*comer* en restaurantes muy caros

III. Palabras afirmativas y negativas
Conteste en oraciones negativas.

1. ¿Hay alguien en la bañera?
2. ¿Hay algo en la estufa?
3. ¿Tiene usted algunas toallas limpias?

4. ¿Usted siempre prepara la comida?
5. ¿Lava usted los platos también?

IV. Repaso General
A. Conteste en español en oraciones completas.

1. ¿Qué cuartos hay en su casa?
2. ¿Qué muebles hay en la alcoba?
3. ¿Qué hay en el baño?
4. ¿Qué hay en la mesa?
5. ¿Qué hará usted este sábado?
6. ¿Qué haría usted en Acapulco?

7. ¿Maneja usted rápidamente o lentamente?
8. ¿Cuál es la capital de México?
9. Antes de la llegada de los españoles, ¿cuáles eran las dos civilizaciones de más importancia en México?
10. ¿Qué hizo Hernán Cortés?

B. Traduzca al español.

1. I would sell the car for (*por*) $900.
2. Would you (familiar, singular) rent that house?
3. He said that they would leave on the first of April.
4. We will put the rug in the bedroom.
5. I will turn on the light.

6. They will look for the glasses.
7. Who will bring the cake?
8. I know someone that has a record player.
9. There is something in my soup!
10. He probably will arrive next week.

V. Repaso de verbos
Escriba oraciones cambiando el verbo a los tiempos indicados. Use la forma **yo** del verbo.

1. tener que esperar

a) presente **Yo** . . .
b) pretérito
c) imperfecto

2. salir a las cinco

d) futuro
e) condicional

CAPÍTULO 9

■ VOCABULARIO *El correo, el banco*

el **buzón**	mailbox	**depositar**	to deposit
la **carta**	letter	**empezar(ie)**[1]	to begin
la **casa de correos**	post office	**encontrar(ue)**	to find
el **correo**	mail	**firmar**	to sign
el **correo aéreo**	airmail	**ganar**	to earn, win
la **dirección**	address	**gastar**	to spend
el **paquete**	package		(money)
el **sello**	stamp	**invitar**[1]	to invite
el **sobre**	envelope	**mandar**	to send, com-
la **tarjeta postal**	postcard		mand
		mostrar(ue)	to show
el (la) **cajero(a)**	teller, cashier	**pagar**	to pay (for)
el **cambio**	change, exchange	**perder(ie)**	to lose
el **cheque**	check	**preguntar**	to ask (ques-
el **cheque de viajeros**	traveler's check		tion)
la **firma**	signature	**prestar**	to lend
la **ventanilla**	cashier's window	**recibir**	to receive
		sacar	to take out
la **calculadora**	calculator	**terminar**	to finish
la **computadora**	computer		
la **máquina de escribir**	typewriter	**acabar de** + *infini-*	
el **teléfono**	telephone	*tive*	to have just . . .
		tratar de + *infini-*	
cambiar	to change, ex-	*tive*	to try to . . .
	change	**echar al correo**	to mail
cobrar	to cash	**escribir a máquina**	to type
contestar	to answer		

211

NOTE 1:   **Empezar** and **invitar** require the preposition **a** before a following infinitive.

Él **empezó a** trabajar.   *He began to work.*
Me **invitaron a** comer.   *They invited me to eat.*

EJERCICIO 1   En el correo y en el banco

Conteste en español en oraciones completas.

A. Según el primer (*first*) dibujo:

1. ¿Dónde están las personas?
2. El hombre que lleva pantalones largos, ¿está comprando sellos o está escribiendo una carta?
3. ¿Qué tiene en las manos la mujer joven?
4. ¿Cuál es la fecha?
5. ¿Qué hace el niño?
6. El hombre que lleva gafas, ¿qué puede comprar en la casa de correos?
7. ¿Qué va a mandar la señora vieja?

B. Según el segundo (*second*) dibujo:

1. ¿Dónde están las personas?
2. ¿Qué hace la mujer que está al escritorio? ¿y qué puede hacer?
3. ¿Qué instrumentos están en el escritorio?
4. ¿Cómo se llama la persona que está en la ventanilla?
5. ¿Qué puede hacer la cajera?
6. ¿Qué pueden hacer los clientes?
7. ¿Qué hora es?

EJERCICIO 2   Preguntas generales

Conteste en español en oraciones completas.

1. ¿Qué escribe usted en el sobre?
2. ¿Cuánto paga usted por una tarjeta postal?
   (**centavos** = *cents*)
3. ¿Qué tipo de sellos compra usted cuando quiere mandar una carta a Europa rápidamente?
4. ¿Recibe usted muchos cheques de sus padres?
5. ¿Acaba usted de escribir a sus padres?
6. ¿Trata usted de contestar todas las cartas que usted recibe?
7. ¿Qué tiene usted que hacer con los cheques de viajeros?
8. ¿Sabe usted escribir a maquina? ¿a cuántas palabras por minuto?
9. ¿Cuánto cuesta una calculadora? ¿y una computadora?
10. Generalmente, ¿qué horas están abiertos los bancos?
11. ¿Trabajó usted el verano pasado? ¿Cuánto ganó usted?
12. ¿Quiénes gastan más dinero, los hombres o las mujeres?
13. ¿Qué es lo contrario (*opposite*) de empezar? ¿perder? ¿preguntar? ¿mandar? ¿sacar?

■ CONVERSACIONES

En la casa de correos.

DEPENDIENTE	**Buenos días, señorita. ¿En qué puedo servirle?**
LINDA	**Quiero mandar esta carta a mis amigos en los Estados Unidos.**
DEPENDIENTE	**¿Cómo quiere mandarla? ¿Por correo aéreo o certificada?**
LINDA	**Correo aéreo, por favor.**
DEPENDIENTE	**Le cuesta veinte pesos en sellos.**
LINDA	**Gracias, señor. ¿Dónde debo echarla?**
DEPENDIENTE	**Allí, a la derecha, en el buzón.**

At the post office.

CLERK	*Good morning, miss. How can I help you?*
LINDA	*I want to send this letter to my friends in the United States.*
CLERK	*How do you want to send it? Air mail or certified?*
LINDA	*Air mail, please.*
CLERK	*That will cost you twenty pesos in stamps.*
LINDA	*Thank you, sir. Where should I deposit (mail) it?*
CLERK	*There, to the right, in the mailbox.*

En el banco.

CAJERA	**Buenos días, señor. ¿En qué puedo servirle?**
CLIENTE	**Quiero cobrar este cheque de viajeros, por favor.**
CAJERA	**Muy bien, ¿Puede mostrarme su identificación?**
CLIENTE	**Aquí la tiene. ¿A cuánto está el cambio hoy?**

CAJERA	**Se lo digo en un momento. A ver . . . ciento cuarenta al dólar americano.**
CLIENTE	**¿Puede darme el dinero en billetes de cincuenta y cien?**
CAJERA	**Sí, señor. ¿Me hace el favor de firmar el cheque?**
CLIENTE	**Ah, sí . . . Aquí está . . . Muchas gracias por su ayuda.**

In the bank.

TELLER	*Good morning, sir. How can I help you?*
CLIENT	*I want to cash this traveler's check, please.*
TELLER	*Very well. Can you show me your identification?*
CLIENT	*Here it is. What is the exchange rate today?*
TELLER	*I will tell you in a moment. Let's see . . . one hundred forty to the American dollar.*
CLIENT	*Can you give me the money in bills of fifty and one hundred?*
TELLER	*Yes, sir. Will you do me the favor of signing the check?*
CLIENT	*Oh, yes . . . Here it is . . . Many thanks for your help.*

■ ESTRUCTURA

I. Pronombres de complemento directo *Direct object pronouns*

The direct object receives the action directly through the verb. The following forms are used when the direct object is a pronoun.

me	*me*	**nos**	*us*
te	*you*	**os**	*you*
lo	*you* (m.), *him, it* (m.)	**los**	*you* (m.), *them* (m.)
la	*you* (f.), *her, it* (f.)	**las**	*you* (f.), *them* (f.)

In Spanish, the direct object pronoun is placed directly before a conjugated verb, and generally after and attached to an infinitive or present participle.

María **me** ve.	*Mary sees me.*
No **lo** compraron.	*They did not buy it.*
Carlos **nos** llamó anoche.	*Carlos called us last night.*
Alex quiere conocer**te**.	*Alex wants to meet you.*
Estamos buscándo**los**.	*We are looking for them.*

NOTE: An accent mark is added to the present participle to preserve the original stress pattern.

EJERCICIO 3   Las invitaciones

Manolo va a tener una fiesta. Él invita a todas las personas que quieren ir a la fiesta. Indique usted a quién invita él según el modelo.

Modelo   *Paco* quiere ir.
          Manolo **lo** invita.

1. *Yo* quiero ir. **Manolo** . . .
2. *Nosotros* queremos ir.
3. *Tú* quieres ir.
4. *Cecilia* quiere ir.
5. *Vosotros* queréis ir.
6. *Carlota y Lupe* quieren ir.
7. *Juanita y Mario* quieren ir.
8. *Eduardo* quiere ir.

EJERCICIO 4   ¿Conoce usted a las personas?

Indique usted, según el modelo, si usted conoce a las personas personalmente.

Modelo   Henry Kissinger
          (Sí,) (No, no) lo conozco personalmente.

1. las mujeres de esta clase
2. el presidente de la universidad
3. Michael Jackson
4. los hombres de esta clase
5. Margaret Thatcher
6. sus primas
7. el (la) profesor(a) de español.

EJERCICIO 5   Juanita y Mario

Indique usted que Mario hace las mismas (*same*) cosas que hace Juanita. Siga (*follow*) los modelos.

Modelo   Juanita terminó *el examen*.
          Mario **lo** terminó también.

1. Juanita recibió *la invitación*.
2. Juanita contestó *las cartas*.
3. Juanita compró *los sellos*.
4. Juanita mandó *el paquete*.

Modelo   Juanita va a terminar *el examen*.
          Mario va a terminar**lo** también.

5. Juanita tiene que encontrar *la calculadora*.
6. Juanita trató de usar *la computadora*.
7. Juanita acaba de firmar *los documentos*.
8. Juanita va a buscar *las direcciones*.

Modelo   Juanita está terminando *el examen*.
          Mario está terminándo**lo** también.

9. Juanita está limpiando *el comedor*.

10. Juanita está preparando *las tortas*.
11. Juanita está lavando *los platos*.
12. Juanita está escuchando *la radio*.

EJERCICIO 6   Tú y yo

Hágale preguntas a un(a) estudiante según los modelos; escuche la respuesta.

> Modelo   *visitarme* hoy
> (pregunta)   **¿Me visitas hoy?**
> (respuesta)   **(Sí,) (No, no) te visito hoy.**

1. *quererme* mucho
2. *conocerme*
3. *amarme*
4. *llevarme* al cine

> Modelo   *querer* visitarme
> (pregunta)   **¿Quieres visitarme?**
> (respuesta)   **(Sí,) (No, no) quiero visitarte.**

5. *querer* llamarme esta noche
6. *poder* entenderme
7. *querer* invitarme a la fiesta
8. *poder* contestarme

¿Adónde mandamos las cartas?
Casa de Correos, San José, Costa Rica

II. Pronombres de complemento indirecto *Indirect object pronouns*

The indirect object receives the action indirectly through the verb. It tells to whom or for whom the action is performed. The following forms are used when the indirect object is a pronoun. (It may be necessary to clarify a third-person indirect object pronoun with the forms shown in parentheses.)

me	*to me*	**nos**	*to us*
te	*to you*	**os**	*to you*
le	*to you* (**a usted**)	**les**	*to you* (**a ustedes**)
	to him (**a él**)		*to them* (**a ellos**)
	to her (**a ella**)		*to them* (**a ellas**)

The indirect object pronoun is placed directly before a conjugated verb, and generally after and attached to an infinitive or present participle.

Jorge **me** da la carta.	*Jorge gives the letter to me.*
Le traigo el cheque **a ella**.	*I am bringing the check to her.*
Quiero paga**rte** el dinero.	*I want to pay you the money.*
Está escribiéndo**nos** una carta.	*He is writing a letter to us.* (note accent on participle)

EJERCICIO 7   Un tío muy generoso

Un tío muy generoso les dió a todas las personas en la familia lo que necesitaban. Indique usted lo que el tío dio a cada (*each*) persona según el modelo.

Modelo   *Mi hermana* necesitaba un reloj.
          Él **le** dio un reloj.

1. *Yo* necesitaba una calculadora.
2. *Mi madre* necesitaba un vestido.

Es fácil cambiar los cheques de viajeros. México, D. F.

3. *Mi padre* necesitaba un traje.
4. *Mis hermanas* necesitaban un tocadiscos.
5. *Mis hermanos* necesitaban una radio.
6. *Tú* necesitabas una computadora.
7. *Nosotros* necesitábamos un coche.
8. *Vosotros* necesitabais una televisión.

EJERCICIO 8   ¿A quién escribió usted?

Conteste en español según el modelo.

> Modelo   ¿Escribió usted *al abogado?*
> Sí, **le** escribí.

1. ¿Escribió usted *a su madre?*
2. ¿Escribió usted *a sus hermanos?*
3. ¿Escribió usted *a sus amigas?*
4. ¿Escribió usted *al presidente?*

> Modelo   ¿Quiere usted mandar la carta *al abogado?*
> Sí, quiero mandar**le** la carta.

5. ¿Quiere usted mandar la carta *a su madre?*
6. ¿Quiere usted mandar la carta *a sus amigas?*
7. ¿Quiere usted mandar la carta *a sus hermanos?*
8. ¿Quiere usted mandar la carta *al presidente?*

III. Dos complementos del verbo   *Indirect and direct object pronouns with the verb*

When a verb takes both an indirect and a direct object pronoun, the indirect always precedes.

Te lo mando.   *I am sending it to you.*
Quiere dár**noslos**.   *He wants to give them to us.*

NOTE: An accent mark is added to an infinitive that has two objects to preserve the original stress pattern.

When both the indirect and direct object pronouns are in the third person, the indirect object pronouns **le** and **les** change to **se**.

$$
\begin{matrix} \text{le} \\ \text{les} \end{matrix} \; + \; \begin{matrix} \text{lo} \\ \text{la} \\ \text{los} \\ \text{las} \end{matrix} \; \rightarrow \; \text{se} \begin{matrix} \text{lo} \\ \text{la} \\ \text{los} \\ \text{las} \end{matrix}
$$

Se lo traigo a ellos.   *I am bringing it to them.*
Él tiene que mandár**selos** a ella.   *He has to send them to her.*

EJERCICIO 9   Vamos al correo y al banco.

Cambie las oraciones según los modelos.

Modelo   La señorita me trae *los sobres.*
          La señorita me **los** trae.

1. La señorita me da *el paquete.*
2. La señorita me trae *las cartas.*
3. La señorita me vende *los sellos.*
4. La señorita me muestra *el buzón.*

Modelo   La cajera va a traernos *el cambio.*
          La cajera va a traérnos**lo**.

5. La cajera va a prestarnos *la pluma.*
6. La cajera va a pedirnos *las identificaciones.*
7. La cajera va a cobrarnos *los cheques.*
8. La cajera va a cambiarnos *el dinero.*

EJERCICIO 10   Las posesiones de Juan

Juan va a salir de la escuela por un año. Diga usted lo que Juan hará con sus posesiones; sustituya según el modelo.

Modelo   Juan le dará *los discos* a Marta.
          Juan **se** los dará (a ella).

1. Juan le venderá *la bicicleta* a Pepe.
2. Juan les prestará *el tocadiscos* a Ana y a Teresa.
3. Juan le dará *los libros* a Susana.
4. Juan le llevará *las plantas* a Elena.
5. Juan les traerá *los discos* a Andrés y a Tomás.

EJERCICIO 11   Una nueva computadora.

Imagine que usted tiene una nueva computadora. ¿La comparte (*do you share it*)
con sus amigos? Conteste según el modelo.

Modelo   ¿La dio usted a *Eduardo*?
               (Sí,) (No, no) **se** la di (a él).

1. ¿La dio usted a *Ricardo*?
2. ¿La dio usted a *Amelia*?
3. ¿La mostró usted a *sus amigos*?
4. ¿La mostró usted a *sus amigas*?
5. ¿La prestó usted a *Felipe*?
6. ¿La prestó usted a *Felina*?

Los Andes altos e impresionantes forman
el espinazo (*backbone*) del continente. Chile

TARJETA VISA
Para comprar sin dinero, con sólo su firma, en todo el mundo.

BANCO EXTERIOR DE ESPAÑA
El banco sin fronteras

CAMBIO DE MONEDA
Nuestra experiencia, operando directamente en 29 países, le facilita la resolución de sus operaciones en moneda extranjera, a través de nuestras 412 oficinas en España.

CRÉDITO AGRÍCOLA
Facilidades financieras para las necesidades del campo, con líneas especiales de crédito establecidas en colaboración con el Banco de Crédito Agrícola.

EJERCICIO 12   ¿Por qué?

Diga usted por qué Pablo hace lo que hace.

> Modelo   Pablo me los vende. ¿Por qué?
> **¡Porque quiere vendérmelos!**

1. Pablo te lo dice. ¿Por qué?
2. Pablo me las da. ¿Por qué?
3. Pablo nos lo trae. ¿Por qué?
4. Pablo se los vende a ella. ¿Por qué?
5. Pablo se la manda a él. ¿Por qué?

EJERCICIO 13   Preguntas generales

1. Señorita, usted no lleva sus joyas hoy. ¿Las perdió usted?
2. Yo no sé quién pagó la cuenta (*the bill*) en el restaurante anoche. ¿La pagó usted?
3. Usted va a la playa este verano. ¿Me mandará usted una tarjeta postal?
4. Mañana es mi cumpleaños. ¿Va usted a darme un regalo?
5. Señor, usted tiene un abrigo muy elegante y yo tengo frío. ¿Me lo presta usted?
6. Señorita, usted tiene una bolsa muy cara. ¿Me la muestra usted?
7. Es la hora de cenar y yo tengo mucha hambre. Veo el arroz con pollo. ¿Puede usted pasármelo?

IV. Gustar *To be pleasing (to like)*

Gustar in Spanish means *to be pleasing* and is used to translate the English *to like.* Thus, *I like the house* becomes in Spanish *The house is pleasing to me*, requiring the use of the indirect object pronoun.

Gustar is used in the third person singular and plural. The singular form is used when one thing is liked. The plural form is used when several things are liked.

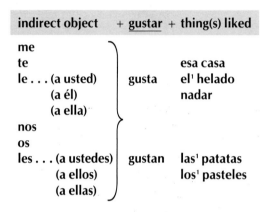

indirect object	+ **gustar** +	thing(s) liked
me		
te		esa casa
le . . . (a usted)	gusta	el¹ helado
(a él)		nadar
(a ella)		
nos		
os		
les . . . (a ustedes)	gustan	las¹ patatas
(a ellos)		los¹ pasteles
(a ellas)		

Me gusta esa casa.	*I like that house.*
¿Te gustan las patatas fritas?	*Do you like fried potatoes?*
¿Le gusta a él nadar?	*Does he like to swim?*
Nos gusta comer helado.	*We like to eat ice cream.*
Les gustan los pasteles.	*They like the pies.*

NOTE 1:   Remember that in Spanish the definite article is placed before nouns used in an abstract or general sense.

NOTE 2:   The verbs **parecer** (*to seem*) and **faltar** (*to lack, need*) function like the verb **gustar**.

Me parece inteligente.	*He seems intelligent to me.*
Nos falta dinero.	*We lack (need) money.*

EJERCICIO 14   Vamos de compras

A. Usted, su hermano(a) y una amiga están de compras en un almacén muy grande. Conteste usted las preguntas de su hermano(a) según el modelo.

Modelo   ¿Te gusta este reloj?
   Sí, me gusta, pero a ella no le gusta.

1.   ¿Te gusta esta corbata?
2.   ¿Te gusta este sombrero?
3.   ¿Te gusta esta blusa?
4.   ¿Te gustan estos zapatos?

A los españoles les gusta charlar por la tarde. España

5.   ¿Te gustan estos pantalones?
6.   ¿Te gustan estos camisas?

B.   Usted, su familia y algunos amigos de la familia van a comprar muebles. Conteste usted las preguntas del dependiente (*clerk*) según el modelo.

   Modelo   ¿Les gusta (a ustedes) el sofá?
         Sí, nos gusta, pero a ellos no les gusta.

1.   ¿Les gusta este sillón?
2.   ¿Les gusta esta mesa?
3.   ¿Les gusta esta cama?
4.   ¿Les gustan estas lámparas?
5.   ¿Les gustan estas sillas?
6.   ¿Les gustan estos armarios?

EJERCICIO 15   Preguntas personales

Conteste en español en oraciones completas.

1.   ¿Le gusta a usted más (*more*) dormir o comer?
2.   ¿Cuál le gusta a usted más, la comida italiana, la comida china, o la comida mexicana?

3.   ¿Le gusta a usted fumar?
4.   ¿Le gustan a usted las películas románticas?
5.   ¿Le gustó a usted más la película Guerra de las Galaxias (*Star Wars*) o E.T.?
6.   ¿Les gustan a ustedes las patatas fritas de McDonald's?
7.   ¿Les gusta a ustedes la clase de español?
8.   ¿Les gustan a ustedes los exámenes difíciles?
9.   ¿Le falta a usted más el dinero o el amor?
10. ¿Cuál le parece a usted peor, el sexo o la violencia en la televisión?

PERSPECTIVA ORIGINAL

Composición: **Una carta a un(a) amigo(a) español(a)**
Write a letter to your new Spanish-speaking friend telling him or her about such things as:

1.   yourself (name, age, physical description),
2.   your likes and dislikes;
3.   your family;
4.   your home;
5.   things you would like to show your friend;
6.   places you would like to take your friend when he/she comes to visit you.

SUPPLEMENTARY VOCABULARY

Querido(a)   *dear*
Con cariño   *affectionately*

Este hermoso castillo, el Alcázar de Segovia, fue construído en la Edad Media. Segovia, España

El baile flamenco es pura manifestación de la España romántica. Sevilla, España

ESPAÑA

Los molinos de viento y las ruinas de un castillo nos hacen pensar en Don Quijote. "La Mancha," España

Una vista panorámica de la
hermosa ciudad de Granada
revela el famoso palacio de La
Alhambra y la Sierra Nevada.

Esta estrecha calle, llamada Calle de las Flores, es típica de
Córdoba. Se ve la mezquita al fondo. Córdoba, España

En los mercados públicos hay oportunidad de comprar,
vender, y charlar (*chat*).

Los olivos y las amapolas (*poppies*) forman una escena
tranquila y bella del sur de España. Sevilla, España

Por todo el mundo se conoce el Ballet Folklórico por su representación de la tradición e historia de México.

Los mariachis, tocando la música típica y tradicional mexicana, se encuentran en muchos restaurantes. Cuernavaca, México

MÉXICO

En las murallas y los frescos de Diego Rivera, famoso artista mexicano del siglo 20, se ven temas de la vida india y de la revolución mexicana.

En el Museo de Antropología, magnífico ejemplo de la arquitectura contemporánea, podemos ver un panorama de las civilizaciones precolombinas de México. México, D. F.

Los jóvenes también revelan en varias formas sus talentos artísticos. Acapulco, México

Una visita a México debe incluir Taxco, famosa y pintoresca ciudad colonial, conocida por sus artesanías de plata.

La gente indígena de Oaxaca teje los colores vivos de los sarapes. Oaxaca, México

■ PANORAMA CULTURAL

México—mosaico artístico

Muchas facetas de la cultura mexicana reflejan la importancia del arte en todos los aspectos de la vida diaria. Estas facetas forman el mosaico artístico que es el México de ayer y de hoy. Parece que *cada* mexicano, pobre o rico, *campesino* de un pueblo remoto o habitante de una ciudad cosmopolita, tiene una *sensibilidad* intrínseca de lo que es el arte. Este arte, en *cualquier* forma en que *aparezca*—la música, la pintura, la arquitectura, la escultura, las *artesanías*, la ropa, etc.—es el producto de una combinación de tradición e innovación. De más importancia, este arte revela la individualidad, el espíritu y la identidad del mexicano contemporáneo.

each/farmer
sensitivity
any/appears
crafts

   Las imágenes del mosaico se encuentran por todas partes—en las catedrales, las plazas, las casas modestas o elegantes, los parques, los *centros comerciales*, los edificios profesionales, las *murallas* y las *aceras*. *Aún* los taxis, coches y autobuses presentan evidencia de los gustos artísticos y personales de sus conductores.

shopping centers
walls/sidewalks/
   Even

NOTE: Refer to color photos of Mexico on the preceding two color pages.

¿CUÁNTO RECUERDAS? (de la lectura y de las fotos)

Complete las frases de la Columna A con las conclusiones de la Columna B.

COLUMNA A	COLUMNA B
El arte de México es	un famoso pintor mexicano de temas indio-revolucionarios.
Diego Rivera es	ejemplo de la música típica y tradicional mexicana.
El Museo de Antropología es	una representación de la historia mexicana en danzas regionales, etc.
Los mariachis son	una famosa ciudad colonial, conocida por sus artesanías de plata.
Taxco es	un buen ejemplo de la arquitectura contemporánea.
El Ballet Folklórico es	producto de una combinación de tradición e innovación.

■ INTEGRACIÓN

A.   ORAL EXERCISE: **Conversaciones**
     The dialogs will be read twice. Listen the first time; the second time pauses
     will be provided for you to repeat each phrase.
B.   ORAL EXERCISE: VOCABULARY, **el correo, el banco**
     Answer in Spanish according to the drawings.

1.

2.

3.
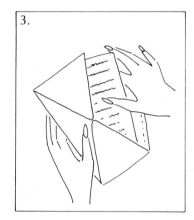

4.
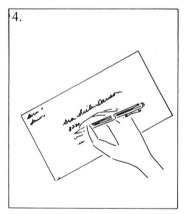

5.

6.

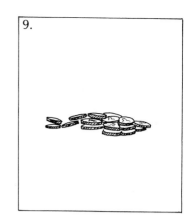  

  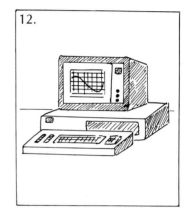

C.   ORAL EXERCISE: DIRECT OBJECT PRONOUNS

Complete the sentences on the tape with the direct object pronoun equivalent of the persons or objects in the pictures. Place the pronoun before the conjugated verb.

(yo)

Example   (tape)   Él ve.
          (your response)   **Él me ve.**

1. (tú)

2. (usted)

3. (Juan)

4. (María)

5. (nosotros)

6. (ustedes)

7. (Juan y Alfonso)

8. (Isabel y María)

9. (el lápiz)

10. (la carta)

11. (los libros)

12. (las tarjetas postales)

D. ORAL EXERCISE: DIRECT OBJECT PRONOUNS
    Complete the sentences on the tape with the direct object pronoun equiva-
    lent of the persons or objects in the pictures in Exercise C. Place the pronoun
    after the infinitive.

(yo)

Example   (tape)   Él quiere ver _____.
          (your response)   **Él quiere verme.**

E. ORAL EXERCISE: INDIRECT OBJECT PRONOUNS
    Complete the sentences on the tape with the indirect object pronoun equiva-
    lent of the persons in the pictures. Place the pronoun before the conjugated
    verb.

(yo)

Example   (tape)   Carlos da el dinero.
          (your response)   **Carlos me da el dinero.**

1.

(tú)

2.

(usted)

3.

(Juan)

4.

(María)

| (nosotros) | (ustedes) | (Juan y Alfonso) | (Isabel y María) |

F.   ORAL EXERCISE: INDIRECT OBJECT PRONOUNS
     Complete the sentences on the tape with the indirect object pronoun equiva-
     lent of the persons in the pictures in Exercise E. Place the pronoun after the
     infinitive.

(yo)

Example   (tape)   Carlos debe dar el di-
                              nero.

          (your response)   **Carlos debe darme el
                              dinero.**

G.   WRITTEN EXERCISE: DIRECT AND INDIRECT OBJECT PRONOUNS.
     Substitute the direct or indirect object noun with a pronoun. Each sentence
     will be repeated twice.
     Examples: (tape)   Compré la blusa.
                 (your written response)   **La compré.**
                 (tape)   Di el regalo a Ricardo.
                 (your written response)   **Le di el regalo (a él).**

H. ORAL EXERCISE: INDIRECT AND DIRECT OBJECT PRONOUNS

Complete the sentences on the tape with the indirect and direct object pronoun equivalents of the persons and objects in the pictures. Place the pronouns before the conjugated verb.

Indirect Object   Direct Object

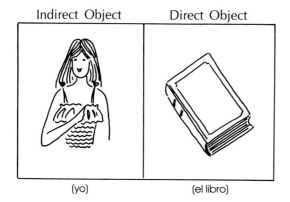

(yo)   (el libro)

Example   (tape)   Carlos da . . .
           (your response) **Carlos me lo da.**

Indirect Object   Direct Object

1.

(yo)   (la taza)

Indirect Object   Direct Object

2.

(tú)   (las cucharas)

3.

(nosotros)   (el cuaderno)

4.

(usted)   (los discos)

Indirect Object	Direct Object		Indirect Object	Direct Object

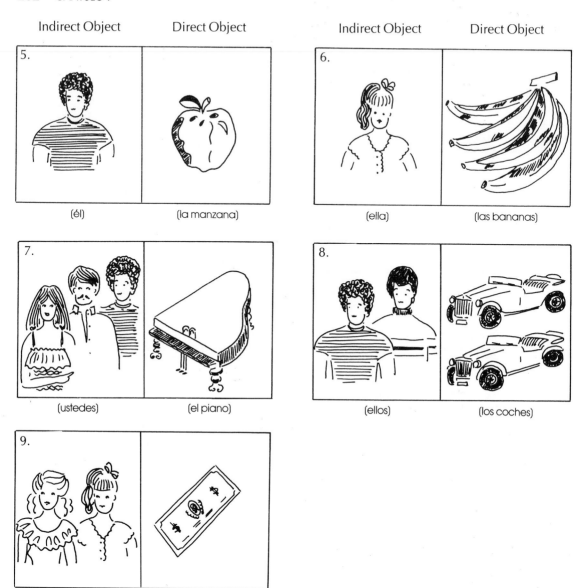

5. (él)   (la manzana)

6. (ella)   (las bananas)

7. (ustedes)   (el piano)

8. (ellos)   (los coches)

9. (ellas)   (el dinero)

I.   ORAL EXERCISE: INDIRECT AND DIRECT OBJECT PRONOUNS
      Complete the sentences on the tape with the indirect and direct object pro-
      noun equivalents of the persons and objects in the pictures in Exercise H.
      Place the pronouns after the infinitive.

Indirect Object   Direct Object

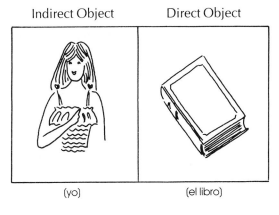

(yo)   (el libro)

Example
(tape)   Carlos no puede dar . . .
(your response)   **Carlos no puede dár-
                    melo.**

J.   ORAL EXERCISE: **gustar**
      Create a sentence by linking:
1.   indirect object pronouns represented in the pictures plus;
2.   the correct form of **gustar** plus;
3.   the thing(s) liked.

Indirect object + **gustar** + thing(s) liked

(yo)

Example
(your sentence)   **Me gusta el libro.**
(tape confirmation) Me gusta el libro.

1.

(yo)

K.   WRITTEN EXERCISE: **gustar**
Write the answers to the eight questions on the tape. Each question is given twice.

L.   DICTATION: **México—mosaico artístico**
Write the three sentences you hear on the tape. Each sentence is repeated three times.

■ REPASO DE VOCABULARIO ACTIVO

Pronombres de complemento directo

me	lo	nos	los
te	la	os	las

Pronombres de complemento indirecto

me	le	os
te	nos	les

Sustantivos

el **buzón**	el **correo aéreo**
el (la) **cajero(a)**	la **dirección**
la **calculadora**	la **firma**
el **cambio**	la **máquina de escribir**
la **carta**	el **paquete**
la **casa de correos**	el **sello**
el **cheque**	el **sobre**
el **cheque de viajeros**	la **tarjeta postal**
la **computadora**	el **teléfono**
el **correo**	la **ventanilla**

Verbos

cambiar	ganar	perder (ie)
cobrar	gastar	preguntar
contestar	invitar	prestar
depositar	gustar	recibir
empezar (ie)	mandar	sacar
encontrar (ue)	mostrar (ue)	terminar
faltar	pagar	
firmar	parecer	

Expresiones idiomáticas

acabar de + infinitive	echar al correo
tratar de + infinitive	escribir a máquina

■ EJERCICIOS DE REPASO

I. Pronombres de complemento directo

A. El tío Antonio va a Cancún para las vacaciones. Él va a llevar a todas las personas que quieren ir.

Indique usted a quién él va a llevar según el modelo:

Modelo   *Elena* quiere ir.
Antonio va a llevar**la**.

1. *Yo* quiero ir.
2. *Nosotros* queremos ir.
3. *Ustedes* quieren ir.
4. *Mis hermanas* quieren ir.
5. *Mis hermanos* quieren ir.
6. *Pepito* quiere ir.
7. *Tú* quieres ir.

B. Su familia está haciendo los preparativos para el viaje. Conteste las preguntas de su hermano según el modelo:

Modelo   ¿Encontraste *el traje de baño*?
Sí, **lo** encontré.

1. ¿Perdiste *las gafas de sol*?
2. ¿Depositaste *el dinero*?
3. ¿Sacaste *los cheques*?
4. ¿Pagaste *la cuenta* (*bill*)?
5. ¿Apagaste *las luces*?

II. Pronombres de complemento indirecto

Su tía vive en Quito, Ecuador. Indique usted a quiénes ella escribe muchas cartas. Siga los modelos.

Modelo   *Yo* recibo cartas.
Ella **me** escribe.

1. *Nosotros* recibimos cartas.
2. *Tú* recibes cartas.
3. *Vosotros* recibís cartas.
4. *María* recibe cartas.
5. *Usted* recibe cartas.

Modelo   *José* acaba de recibir una carta.
Ella acaba de escribir**le**.

6. *Yo* acabo de recibir una carta.
7. *Ustedes* acaban de recibir una carta.
8. *Mis abuelos* acaban de recibir una carta.
9. *Tú* acabas de recibir una carta.
10. *Nosotros* acabamos de recibir una carta.

III. Dos complementos del verbo

Cambie según los modelos.

Modelo   Andrés me mostró *los discos*.
Andrés me **los** mostró.

1. Andrés me mostró *la tarjeta postal*.
2. Andrés me mostró *los sellos*.
3. Andrés nos mostró *el escritorio nuevo*.
4. Andrés nos mostró *las plantas*.

Modelo   Voy a prestar *el libro al profesor.*
Voy a prestár**selo** (a él).

5. Voy a prestar *la calculadora a Teresa.*
6. Voy a prestar *el dinero a mis hermanos.*
7. Voy a prestar *los discos a mis primas.*
8. Voy a prestar *las botas a Manolo.*

IV. El verbo *gustar*

Cambie las oraciones según el modelo.

Modelo   *Me gusta* el helado. (nosotros)
Nos gusta el helado.

1. *Me gusta* la sandía. (ellos, tú, nosotros)
2. *Les gusta* comer. (yo, Alberto, nosotros)
3. No *nos gustan* las habichuelas. (ellas, yo, usted)
4. ¿*Le gustan* los camarones? (ustedes, vosotros, tú)

V. Repaso General

A. Conteste en español en oraciones completas.

1. ¿Qué escribe usted en el sobre?
2. ¿Qué puede hacer usted en el correo?
3. ¿Qué puede hacer usted en el banco?
4. ¿Qué instrumentos puede encontrar usted en una oficina?
5. Cuando usted empieza un proyecto, ¿trata usted de terminarlo?
6. ¿Me presta usted su libro de español?
7. ¿Alguien le escribió a usted la semana pasada?
8. ¿Qué le gusta a usted hacer?
9. ¿Hay comidas que no le gustan a usted? ¿cuáles?
10. ¿Quién es un famoso pintor mexicano de temas indio-revolucionarios?
11. ¿Recuerda usted un ejemplo de la música mexicana? ¿de la arquitectura? ¿del baile?

B. Traduzca al español

1. She does not know me.
2. I see them (m.).
3. I am doing it (m.) (in the act of).
4. He sent the package to us.
5. I want to give it (m.) to her.
6. He sold it (m.) to me.
7. I read it (m.) to them.
8. We do not like those vegetables!

IV. Repaso de verbos

Escriba oraciones cambiando el verbo a los tiempos indicados. Use la forma **yo** del verbo.

1. darle el regalo   2.   traérselo

a) presente
b) pretérito
c) imperfecto
d) futuro
e) condicional

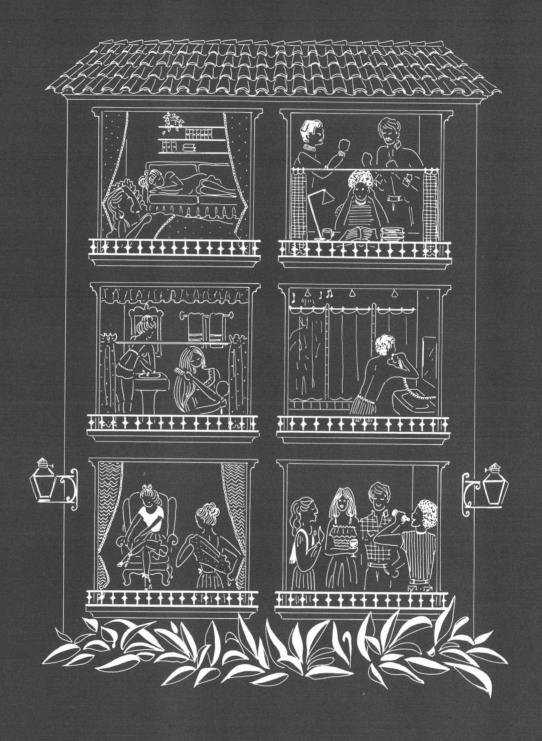

CAPÍTULO 10

■ VOCABULARIO *El dormitorio*

el **dormitorio**, la **residencia estudiantil**	*dormitory*	**cepillarse**	*to brush*
		comprometerse	*to get engaged*
el (la) **compañero(a) de cuarto**	*roommate*	**cortarse**	*to cut oneself*
		despertarse (ie)	*to wake up*
el **cepillo**	*brush*	**divertirse (ie, i)**	*to have a good time*
el **cepillo de dientes**	*toothbrush*	**dormirse (ue, u)**	*to go to sleep*
el **champú**	*shampoo*	**enamorarse**	*to fall in love*
la **crema de afeitar**	*shaving cream*	**enojarse**	*to get angry*
		irse	*to go away*
la **marca**	*brand, mark*	**lavarse**	*to wash (oneself)*
la **máquina de afeitar**	*electric shaver*	**levantarse**	*to get up*
la **navaja**	*razor*	**peinarse**	*to comb one's hair*
el **papel higiénico**	*toilet paper*	**ponerse**	*to put on*
la **pasta de dientes**	*toothpaste*	**preocuparse (por)**	*to worry (about)*
		quitarse	*to take off*
el **peine**	*comb*	**secarse**	*to dry*
el **secador de pelo**	*hair dryer*	**sentarse (ie)**	*to sit down*
		vestirse (i, i)	*to get dressed*
acostarse(ue)	*to go, put to bed*		
afeitarse	*to shave*	**estar enamorado(a) (de)**	*to be in love (with)*
bañarse	*to take a bath, bathe*	**estar comprometido(a)**	*to be engaged*
casarse	*to marry, get married*		

239

EJERCICIO 1 El dormitorio

Conteste en español en oraciones completas según el dibujo. Son las once de la noche en el dormitorio.

En el tercer (*third*) piso:

> Modelo La chica que está en la cama, ¿se levanta o se acuesta?
> **Se acuesta.**

1. La otra chica, ¿se duerme en el sofá o se duerme en la cama?
2. El chico que trata de estudiar, ¿se preocupa por los exámenes o se divierte?
3. Los otros chicos, ¿se enojan o se divierten?

En el segundo (*second*) piso:

4. La chica que está enfrente de (*in front of*) la ventana, ¿se lava o se peina?
5. La chica que está enfrente del lavabo, ¿se lava o se peina?
6. El chico que está enfrente del espejo, ¿se afeita la cara o se afeita las piernas?
7. El chico que está cantando, ¿se baña en la ducha o se baña en la bañera?

En el primer (*first*) piso:

8. la chica que está sentada en el sillón ¿se pone los calcetines o se pone los zapatos?
9. La chica que está enfrente de la ventana, ¿se quita la falda o se quita la blusa?
10. Los estudiantes que están en la fiesta, ¿se preocupan por los exámenes o se divierten?
11. ¿Qué están haciendo los estudiantes que están en la fiesta?

EJERCICIO 2 Las cosas que usamos

¿Qué cosas usa usted en las siguientes (*following*) actividades?

1. cepillarse los dientes:
2. afeitarse:
3. cepillarse el pelo:
4. lavarse el pelo:
5. lavarse el cuerpo:
6. secarse el cuerpo:
7. secarse el pelo:

EJERCICIO 3 Preguntas personales

Conteste en español en oraciones completas.

1. ¿Qué marca de pasta de dientes prefiere usted? ¿y de champú? ¿y de papel higiénico?
2. ¿Vive usted en una residencia estudiantil? ¿Le gusta a usted vivir allí?
3. ¿Tiene usted un(a) compañero(a) de cuarto? ¿Son ustedes buenos(as) amigos(as)?
4. ¿Está usted enamorado(a)? ¿de quién?
   ¿Estuvo usted enamorado(a) el año pasado?
5. ¿Está usted comprometido(a)? ¿Cuánto tiempo hace que usted está comprometido(a)?
6. En su opinión, ¿cuál es la edad (*age*) ideal para casarse?

■ CONVERSACIÓN

Ricardo llama a la puerta del baño y le dice a su hermana:

RICARDO	**Oye, Anita. ¿Cuánto tiempo vas a estar bañándote?**
ANITA	**Espera un momento, por favor. Yá estoy cepillándome los dientes.**
RICARDO	**Date prisa. Casi es la hora de salir.**
ANITA	**¿Quieres afeitarte?**
RICARDO	**¡No! Quiero peinarme.**
ANITA	**¡Caramba, Ricardo! ¡Tú tienes un espejo en tu cuarto donde puedes mirarte!**
RICARDO	**¡Dios mío, Anita! ¡Hace dos horas que estás allí!**

Richard knocks on the bathroom door and says to his sister:

RICHARD	*Listen, Anita. How long are you going to be in there bathing?*
ANITA	*Wait a minute, please. I'm already brushing my teeth*
RICHARD	*Hurry up! It's almost time to leave.*
ANITA	*Do you want to shave?*
RICHARD	*No! I want to comb my hair.*
ANITA	*Good grief, Ricardo! You've got a mirror in your room where you can look at yourself!*
RICHARD	*My God,* Anita! You've been in there for two hours!*

■ ESTRUCTURA

I. Pronombres y verbos reflexivos   *Reflexive pronouns and verbs*

A. Pronombres reflexivos

Some verbs add the reflexive pronouns to show that the doer of the action also receives the action.

me	*myself*	**nos**	*ourselves*
te	*yourself*	**os**	*yourselves*
se	*yourself*	**se**	*yourselves*
	himself		*themselves*
	herself		

Reflexive pronouns, like direct and indirect object pronouns, are placed before a conjugated verb and generally after and attached to an infinitive or present participle. Note the following distinctions.

Yo corté la carne.   *I cut the meat.*   **Yo me corté.**   *I cut myself.*
(not reflexive)   (reflexive)

---

*Spanish uses such expressions frequently, and they are considered perfectly acceptable.

Ellas están lavando la ropa. (not reflexive)	*They are washing the clothes.*
Ellas están lavándose. *(reflexive)*	*They are washing themselves.*

Debemos vestir a los niños. (not reflexive)	*We should dress the children.*
Debemos vestirnos. (reflexive)	*We should dress ourselves (get dressed).*

NOTE 1:   **Nos** and **se** in addition to *ourselves, yourselves,* and *themselves* also mean *each other.*

Nos queremos.	*We love each other.*
Se besan.	*They are kissing each other.*

NOTE 2:   With reflexive verbs, and in other cases where the reference is clear, the definite article, not the possessive adjective, is commonly used in referring to a part of one's body or article of clothing.

Quiero lavarme **el** pelo.	*I want to wash my hair.*
Va a ponerse **las** botas.	*He is going to put on his boots.*

B. Conjugación de los verbos reflexivos

Modelo   **lavarse**   *to wash*

(Yo) **me lavo**	*I wash myself*
(Tú) **te lavas**	*You wash yourself*
(Usted) **se lava**	*You wash yourself*
(Él) **se lava**	*He washes himself*
(Ella) **se lava**	*She washes herself*

(Nosotros) **nos lavamos**	*We wash ourselves*
(Vosotros) **os laváis**	*You wash yourselves*
(Ustedes) **se lavan**	*You wash yourselves*
(Ellos) **se lavan**	*They wash themselves*
(Ellas) **se lavan**	*They wash themselves*

EJERCICIO 4   ¡Vamos a practicar!

Conteste según el modelo.

Modelo   ¿Quién *se preocupa* por los exámenes? (yo)
          Yo me preocupo por los exámenes.

1. ¿Quién *se acuesta* a las once? (yo, tú, él)
2. ¿Quién *se levanta* temprano? (nosotros, vosotros, ellos)

3. ¿Quién *quiere sentarse* en el sofá? (yo, mi hermana, tú)
4. ¿Quién *está bañándose*? (yo, los niños, nosotros)

Ejercicio 5   ¿Y después (*afterwards*)?

Indique usted las actividades de las personas según el modelo.

   Modelo   Carlos/*lavar* el coche.
   Carlos lavará el coche y después se lavará.

1. Yo/*bañar* a mi niño.
2. Nosotros/*lavar* la ropa.
3. Mi madre/*peinar* a Elenita.
4. Mis padres/*vestir* a Pepito.
5. Tú/*acostar* a tu hijo.

EJERCICIO 6   Tú y yo.

Hágale preguntas a un(a) estudiante según los modelos; escuche la respuesta.

   Modelo   acostarse/temprano
   (pregunta) **¿Te acuestas temprano?**
   (respuesta) **(Sí,) (No, no) me acuesto temprano.**

1. levantarse/tarde
2. peinarse/frecuentemente
3. vestirse/rápidamente
4. enojarse/fácilmente
5. preocuparse/mucho

   Modelo   dormirse/¿a qué hora?
   (pregunta) **¿A qué hora te duermes?**
   (respuesta) **Me duermo a las once.**

6. acostarse/¿a qué hora?
7. despertarse/¿a qué hora?
8. bañarse/¿cuándo?
9. afeitarse/¿cuándo?
10. divertirse/¿con quién?
11. casarse/¿con quién?

EJERCICIO 7   Dos aventuras

A.   Usted y sus amigos se preparan para un día en las montañas. Indique las acciones que van a ocurrir según el modelo.

   Modelo   *Nos despertamos* a las cuatro de la mañana.
   Vamos a despertarnos a las cuatro de la mañana.

1. *Nos levantamos* muy temprano.
2. *Nos quitamos* los pijamas.
3. *Nos bañamos*.

4. *Nos vestimos.*
5. *Nos ponemos* suéteres, abrigos y botas.
6. *Nos divertimos.*

B.   La historia (*story*) de amor de Juanita y Mario. Indique que las acciones ya ocurrieron (*already occurred*).

> Modelo   Van a encontrarse.
> **¡Ya se encontraron!**

1. Van a conocerse.
2. Van a hablarse.
3. Van a entenderse.
4. Van a enamorarse.
5. Van a comprometerse.
6. Van a casarse.

EJERCICIO 8   Preguntas personales

Conteste en español en oraciones completas.

1. ¿Cuántas veces al día se cepilla usted los dientes?
2. ¿Se afeita usted con una navaja o con una máquina de afeitar?
3. ¿Necesita usted cortarse el pelo? ¿A qué peluquería o barbería va usted? ¿Cuánto cuesta para cortarse el pelo?
4. ¿Se seca usted el pelo con toalla o con un secador de pelo?
5. Usted y sus amigos, ¿se preocupan mucho por los exámenes?
6. Usted y sus amigos, ¿se divertirán este fin de semana? ¿Qué harán ustedes?
7. ¿Recibió usted dinero por su cumpleaños? ¿Qué se compró usted?
8. ¿Se peinó usted esta mañana? ¿Se lavó usted la cara? ¿Se puso usted calcetines limpios?
9. ¿Le gusta a usted levantarse temprano? ¿acostarse tarde?
10. ¿Quiere usted casarse? ¿cuándo?
11. Usted y su novio(a), ¿se quieren (*each other*) mucho? ¿Se besan mucho?
12. ¿Adónde se va usted para las vacaciones?

> refrán: **La ropa sucia se lava en casa.**

II. Se—otros usos *Se—other uses*

Se is used in Spanish with a third person singular verb when the subject does not refer to a particular person but rather to a general or anonymous reference (one, they, you, etc.).

No se debe fumar.	*One should not smoke.*
Se dice que es una profesora excelente.	*They say that she is an excellent teacher.*

Dos compañeros de cuarto estudian y se divierten
en la residencia estudiantil. Sevila, España

Se is frequently used in Spanish with a third person singular or plural verb to express a passive construction (the subject is acted upon rather than performing the action).

¿Se habla español aquí?	*Is Spanish spoken here?*
¿Se necesitan muchos libros en esa clase?	*Are many books needed in that class?*
¿Dónde se venden cepillos de dientes?	*Where are toothbrushes sold?*

EJERCICIO 9   Preguntas impersonales

Conteste en español en oraciones completas.

1. ¿Dónde se compran sellos?
2. ¿Dónde se vende ropa?
3. ¿Dónde se compra pan?
4. ¿Dónde se habla español?
5. ¿Dónde no se debe fumar?
6. ¿Qué se hace en una peluquería?
7. ¿Cómo se dice "What time is it?" en español?
8. Generalmente, ¿a qué hora se abren los almacenes?
9. Generalmente, ¿a qué hora se cierran los bancos?

refrán: **Donde una puerta se cierra, otra se abre.**

III. Preposiciones *Prepositions*

A. Preposiciones comunes

a	*to, at*[1]	**detrás de**	*behind*
en	*in, at*[2]	**delante de, enfrente de**	*in front of*
al	*upon*	**al lado de**	*beside*
de	*from, of, about*	**en vez de**	*instead of*
con	*with*	**debajo de**	*beneath, under*
sin	*without*	**encima de**	*on top of, above*
entre	*between, among*	**cerca de**	*near*
como	*like*	**lejos de**	*far from*
antes de	*before*	**dentro de**	*inside*
después de	*after*	**fuera de**	*outside*

NOTE 1:   *at* as in *Who is at the door?*   **¿Quién está a la puerta?**
NOTE 2:   *at* as in *He is at home (in the house).*   **Está en casa.**

EJERCICIO 10   Mi gato Rodolfo

Para indicar los gustos de su gato Rodolfo, cambie las oraciones usando la preposición de significado contrario.

Modelo   Rodolfo prefiere su comida *sin* leche.
　　　　　Rodolfo prefiere su comida **con** leche.

1. Rodolfo viene *a* la casa.
2. Rodolfo duerme *debajo de* la cama.
3. Rodolfo está *detrás del* sofá.
4. Rodolfo está *lejos de* la mesa.
5. Rodolfo sale *después del* desayuno.
6. Rodolfo corre *dentro de* la casa.

EJERCICIO 11   Preguntas generales

Conteste en español en oraciones completas.

1. ¿Tiene usted un libro como el mío?
2. ¿Quién en esta clase mira la televisión en vez de estudiar?
3. ¿Quiere usted sentarse al lado de su novio(a)? ¿al lado de su profesor(a)?
4. ¿Entre qué personas prefiere usted sentarse?
5. ¿Qué hace usted por la mañana al levantarse?
6. ¿Qué lleva usted debajo del abrigo?
7. ¿Toma usted la ensalada con o sin cebollas?
8. ¿Tiene usted un perro? ¿Duerme dentro o fuera de la casa?
9. ¿Viven sus padres lejos o cerca de la universidad? ¿Dónde viven?
10. Los sábados, ¿se levanta usted antes o después del mediodía?

La mayoría de los jóvenes latinoamericanos se casan en la iglesia católica. Juchitán, México

B. Las preposiciones por y para

Por and **para** both mean *for*, but they convey different ideas and can be translated in different ways.

CONTRASTING USES

por—*for (because of), (on account of), (for the sake of), (on behalf of)*

para—*for (in order to)*

Looking back to the cause	Purpose, pointing to the goal
←	→

Trabaja por su familia.
He works for (for the sake of) his family.
Es inocente por ser joven.
He is innocent because of being young.

Estudio para aprender.
I study in order to learn.
Se acostó para descansar.
He went to bed in order to rest.

por—*for (during)*

para—*for (by)*

Duration of time	Future limit in time
	→

Viajamos por tres días.
We traveled for three days.

Escriba el ejercicio para mañana.
Write the exercise for tomorrow.

por—*(along, down, by, through)*   **para**—*for (headed for or toward), (des-tined for)*

Movement in and around a given place	**Destination, recipient**

Caminamos por la avenida.
We walked along the avenue.
Viajamos por las montañas.
We traveled through the mountains.

Salió para Madrid.
He left for (headed for) Madrid.
El regalo es para su hermano.
The gift is for (destined for) her brother.

ADDITIONAL USES

por—*for*

in exchange for

Compró una camisa por cincuenta pesos.
He bought a shirt for fifty pesos.

por—*for*

To get with verb of motion

Voy al mercado por leche.
I am going to the market for milk.

para—*for*

In the employment of

Trabaja para IBM.
He works for IBM.

EJERCICIO 12   Para y **por**

Conteste las preguntas según el modelo.

Modelo   ¿Para qué trabajas? (comprar una casa)
          Trabajo para comprar una casa.

1. ¿Para qué estudias? (aprender) (ser abogado)
2. ¿Para cuándo debes terminar la tarea? (mañana) (el viernes)
3. ¿Para quién es el regalo? (mi madre) (el profesor)
4. ¿Para qué compañía trabaja tu padre? (Iberia) (Del Monte)
5. ¿Por quién lo hiciste? (mi abuela) (mi hermano enfermo)
6. ¿Por cuánto tiempo viajaste? (tres días) (cinco meses)
7. ¿Por dónde andabas? (el río) (la calle)
8. ¿Por cuánto vendiste el coche? (500 dólares) (3,800 dólares)
9. ¿Por qué volviste al cuarto? (mi libro) (mi abrigo)

EJERCICIO 13   ¡A Buenos Aires!

Haga usted oraciones con **por** o **para** según las indicaciones.

> Modelo   Pasé/el Brasil
> **Pasé por el Brasil.**

1. Salimos/Buenos Aires
2. Estuvimos allí/una semana
3. Hicimos reservaciones/el ocho de octubre
4. Caminamos/la Avenida de Mayo
5. Mi madre estaba cansada. Fuimos de compras/ella
6. Fuimos al almacén/comprar regalos
7. Compramos las bolsas/mis tías
8. Compramos los zapatos/mil pesos
9. Fuimos al centro/ver la Plaza de Mayo
10. Volví al hotel/mi cámara
11. Hicimos planes/visitar los Andes

C. Preposiciones con infinitivos

In Spanish, a verb following a preposition is in the infinitive form.

Antes de **salir**, voy a tomar una ducha.   *Before leaving, I am going to take a shower.*

Después de **estudiar**, vamos al cine.   *After studying, we are going to the movies.*

GRACIAS POR PONER
LA BASURA EN SU LUGAR

EJERCICIO 14   Expresión personal

Complete las oraciones con los infinitivos apropiados.

1. Me lavo las manos antes de . . .
2. Siempre pienso antes de . . .
3. Miramos la televisión en vez de . . .
4. Dormimos en vez de . . .
5. Iremos al teatro después de . . .
6. No debemos manejar después de . . .
7. No podré ganar dinero sin . . .
8. No podría vivir sin . . .

D. Pronombres complementos de preposiciones *Object of preposition pronouns*

The following pronouns are used with prepositions. Except for **mí** and **ti** they are the same as the object pronouns

OBJECT OF PREPOSITION PRONOUNS

mí	*me*	**nosotros (as)**	*us*
ti	*you* (familiar)	**vosotros (as)**	*you* (familiar)
usted	*you* (formal)	**ustedes**	*you* (formal)
él	*him*	**ellos**	*them*
ella	*her*	**ellas**	*them*

Ejemplos   ¿Este regalo es para **mí**?
¡Sí! Lo compré para **ti**.
Y compré uno para **ella** también.

NOTE: The preposition **con** + **mí** or **ti** becomes **conmigo** (with me) or **contigo** (with you), respectively.

¿Quieres venir **conmigo**?
¡Sí! Voy **contigo**.

EJERCICIO 15   ¿Para quién? y ¿Con quién?

A.   Indique usted para quién(es) las personas compraron regalos según el modelo.

Modelo   *Ellos* compraron un regalo para *ti*. Tú . . .
Tú compraste un regalo para ellos.

1. *Yo* compré un regalo para *él*. Él . . .
2. *Nosotros* compramos un regalo para *ellos*. Ellos . . .
3. *Tú* compraste un regalo para *mí*. Yo . . .
4. *Ustedes* compraron un regalo para *nosotros*. Nosotros . . .

B.   Indique usted con quién las personas bailaron según el modelo.

Modelo   *Ella* bailó *conmigo*. Yo . . .
Yo bailé con ella.

1. *Yo* bailé con *él*. Él . . .
2. *Tú* bailaste *conmigo*. Yo . . .

El Canal de Panamá, construído en parte por los Estados Unidos, permite tránsito marítimo entre los océanos Atlántico y Pacífico. Panamá

3. *Él* bailó con *ella*. Ella . . .
4. *Ellas* bailaron con *nosotros*. Nosotros . . .

EJERCICIO 16   Preguntas generales

1. ¿Quieres hablar conmigo? ¿con él? ¿con ella?
2. ¿Puedes ir al cine con nosotros?
3. ¿Quieres sentarte cerca de ella?
4. ¿Estudias con él?
5. ¿Es esta bolsa para mí?
6. ¿Hablarías de mí fuera de la clase?

PERSPECTIVA ORIGINAL

1. Presentación oral: **en la residencia estudiantil**
    Prepare an oral presentation in which you describe the activities and/or conversations occurring in a room or rooms of the introductory dormitory picture. Use your imagination!
2. Composición: **Vamos a salir**
    Write a description in paragraph form of your activities in preparation for going out on a date.

■ PANORAMA CULTURAL

La América Central y las Antillas

La América Central, *puente* entre la América del Norte y la del Sur, es una tierra de contrastes y de una *belleza* geográfica que *cautivan* la imaginación. Estos países, unidos por la lengua y la cultura españolas, son siete en total: Guatemala, *Belice*,[1] Honduras, El Salvador, Nicaragua, Costa Rica y Panamá.

bridge
beauty/captivate

Los *paisajes* fantásticos, el clima *templado*, el carácter histórico indio-español— todos fascinan al viajero. Por todas partes se pueden contemplar panoramas que cambian constantemente: las montañas floridas y frescas de Guatemala, los grandes volcanes de El Salvador y Nicaragua, las abruptas montañas *cubiertas* de pinos de Honduras, los grandes lagos interiores de Nicaragua, las playas bonitas de Costa Rica y las densas selvas tropicales de Panamá. *Claro que* no debemos *olvidar* una *maravilla* de ingeniería moderna, el canal de Panamá, que permite tránsito marítimo entre los océanos Atlántico y Pacífico. Tampoco podemos perder la oportunidad de visitar las ruinas impresionantes de la civilización maya. En Guatemala y Honduras la grandeza de esta civilización se ve en las ciudades antiguas de Tikal y Copán, ahora en ruinas. La población india y mestiza de estos países es evidente en los pueblos remotos de las montañas y en pueblos famosos como Chichicastenango.[2]

landscapes/temperate

covered

of course
forget/marvel

Viajando en automóvil, el viajero puede ver evidencia del énfasis en la agricultura, industria dominante de los países centroamericanos: las plantaciones grandes de bananas y otras frutas, de cacao, de café y de azúcar—todos productos que contribuyen a la vida económica de esta parte del Nuevo Mundo. Un *peligro* en viajar por estos países en automóvil es el gran número de animales (caballos, vacas, cerdos, gallinas, etc.) que se encuentran en los caminos. El peligro principal y el más *corriente*, *sin embargo*, es el conflicto político y revolucionario que domina gran parte de esta región, *sobretodo*, en El Salvador y Nicaragua. Frecuentemente se ven pueblos donde hay evidencia de una batalla reciente. La tragedia es que este conflicto entre los comunistas y los ultra-conservadores está destruyendo la productividad agrícola y la estabilidad de esta región, y es una vez más la gente pobre que sufre.

danger

current/nevertheless/above all

* * * * * *

Los países hispánicos de las Antillas son tres: Cuba, la República Dominicana y Puerto Rico. Cuba, la "perla de las Antillas," situada dentro de la zona tropical a la entrada del Golfo de México, es la isla *mayor* de las Antillas. Las profundas y bien formadas *bahías a lo largo de* su costa constituyen excelentes puertos y playas. *Además de* su belleza geográfica, la isla es rica en productos agrícolas y en depósitos minerales. Su población está compuesta por descendientes de españoles y por elementos de la raza negra. Esta población ha creado una literatura considerable

largest
bays/along
besides

---

[1]Belice is an exception, as its official language is English.

[2]Chichicastenango is a beautiful Indian village in the highlands of Guatemala.

Chichicastenango tiene uno
de los mercados más grandes
e importantes de Guatemala.

siendo uno de los escritores más representativos José Martí, campeón de la independencia cubana.

La República Dominicana, que ocupa la parte *oriental* de la isla llamada Española, fue descubierta por Cristóbal Colón en 1492 y es una de las naciones más modernas del Mar Caribe. También fue el *punto* de *partida* de exploradores, conquistadores y colonizadores que salieron para el continente. En Santo Domingo, la capital, se encuentra la Universidad de Santo Domingo, el primer centro de *enseñanza superior* en el Nuevo Mundo, y también el primer hospital. La República hoy es un país esencialmente agrícola que produce para exportación azúcar, cacao, café y frutas.

Puerto Rico, la *tercera* isla hispánica de las Antillas, está situado a unas mil millas de la Florida. La isla, que separa el Océano Atlántico del Mar Caribe, tiene un clima agradable, playas blancas y bonitas, y hoteles excelentes. Por estas *razones* muchos turistas de los Estados Unidos visitan la isla para sus vacaciones. Porque Puerto Rico es un "commonwealth," sus *ciudadanos* pueden *mudarse* a los Estados Unidos sin restricciones y visitantes norteamericanos pueden entrar y salir sin pasaportes u otros documentos. Hoy día algunos puertorriqueños quieren que Puerto Rico *sea* otro estado de los Estados Unidos y otros buscan la independencia y la nacionalidad puertorriqueña. Por su *herencia* e historia españolas la lengua principal es el español, pero muchos habitantes también hablan inglés. Hace algunos años la economía se basaba en productos agrícolas pero hoy la industria y el turismo contribuyen más a la base económica de la isla.

En el futuro tendremos que estudiar y conocer mejor todos los países de la América Central y de las Antillas porque su dirección y estabilidad de muchas maneras influyen las decisiones políticas y económicas de las Américas y de gran parte del mundo.

eastern

point/departure

learning/higher

third

reasons

citizens/move

be
heritage

¿CUÁNTO RECUERDAS?

Complete las frases de la Columna A con las conclusiones de la Columna B.

COLUMNA A

1. La América Central es . . .
2. La grandeza de la civilización maya se ve . . .
3. Los países hispánicos de las Antillas son . . .
4. La población de Guatemala y Honduras es . . .
5. El punto de partida de exploradores, etc., para el continente era . . .
6. Una maravilla de ingeniería moderna es . . .
7. El peligro principal en la América Central es . . .
8. El campeón de la independencia cubana era . . .
9. A unas mil millas de la Florida está . . .
10. Los países de la América Central . . .

COLUMNA B

a. . . . india y mestiza.
b. . . . son unidos por la lengua y la cultura españolas.
c. . . . el conflicto político y revolucionario.
d. . . . José Martí.
e. . . . en las ciudades antiguas de Tikal y Copán.
f. . . . la isla de Puerto Rico.
g. . . . Cuba, la República Dominicana y Puerto Rico.
h. . . . puente entre la América del Norte y la del Sur.
i. . . . la República Dominicana.
j. . . . el canal de Panamá.

La belleza de las playas y las bahías de Puerto Rico atraen a muchos visitantes.

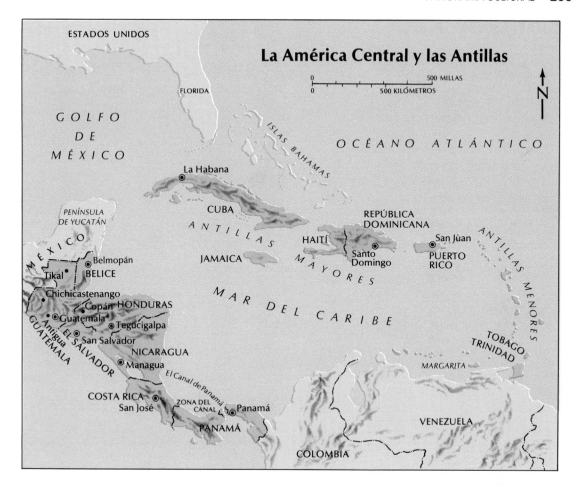

La América Central y las Antillas

PREGUNTAS

Conteste en español según el mapa.

1. ¿Cuál es la capital de Guatemala? ¿de Cuba? ¿de Puerto Rico?
2. ¿Con qué países tiene fronteras Guatemala?
3. ¿Con qué países tiene fronteras Panamá?
4. Pasando por el Canal de Panamá, ¿en qué dirección vamos? ¿del este al oeste, o del norte al sur?
5. ¿En qué mar están situadas las Antillas?
6. ¿Cuál es la isla mayor de las Antillas?
7. ¿Dónde está Cuba en relación geográfica con la Florida? ¿en relación con la Península de Yucatán?
8. ¿Dónde está Puerto Rico en relación con la República Dominicana?
9. ¿Con qué país tiene fronteras la República Dominicana?

■ INTEGRACIÓN

A.   SONG: Guantanamera (Cuba)
     Listen to the song the first time. The second time sing along with the tape.*

Guantanamera, guajira guantanamera**
Guantanamera, guajira guantanamera

Yo soy un hombre sincero
De donde crece la palma; (repita)
Y antes de morirme quiero
Echar mis versos del alma.

Guantanamera, guajira guantanamera
Guantanamera, guajira guantanamera

Mi verso es de un verde claro
Y de un carmín encendido; (repita)
Mi verso es un ciervo herido
Que busca en el monte amparo.

*English translation:
Guantanamera, guajira guantanamera
Guantanamera, guajira guantanamera

I am a sincere man
from where the palm tree grows;
And before dying I want
To cast my verses from the soul.

Guantanamera, guajira guantanamera
Guantanamera, guajira guantanamera

My verse is of a light green
And of a burning red;
My verse is a wounded deer
That seeks in the mount refuge.

**guajira guantanamera = girl from Guantánamo Bay, Cuba

B. ORAL EXERCISE: **Conversación**
    1. The dialog will be read twice. Listen the first time; the second time pauses
        will be provided for you to repeat each phrase.
    2. Listen to the statements related to the dialog; indicate if the statements are
        true or false.

C. ORAL EXERCISE: VOCABULARY, **el dormitorio**
    Answer the questions on the tape according to the drawings.

1.
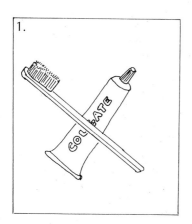

2.
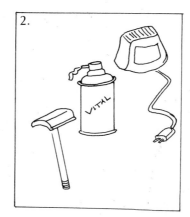

3.
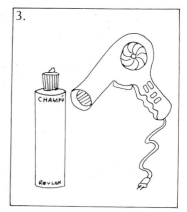

4.

Mónica

5.

Juanita   Mario

6.

Carmen

D. ORAL EXERCISE: REFLEXIVE VERBS
    Repeat each sentence substituting the correct reflexive pronoun and present
    tense verb form.

    Example   (tape)   Yo me levanto a las seis. Tú . . .
              (your response) **Tú te levantas a las seis.**

E.   ORAL EXERCISE: REFLEXIVE VERBS
     Answer the questions on the tape according to the drawings.

yo

Example   (tape)   ¿Quién se quita el som-
                                brero?
          (your response)   **Yo me quito el som-
                            brero.**

1. ella

2. yo

3. tú

4. yo

5. el padre   la madre

6. nosotros

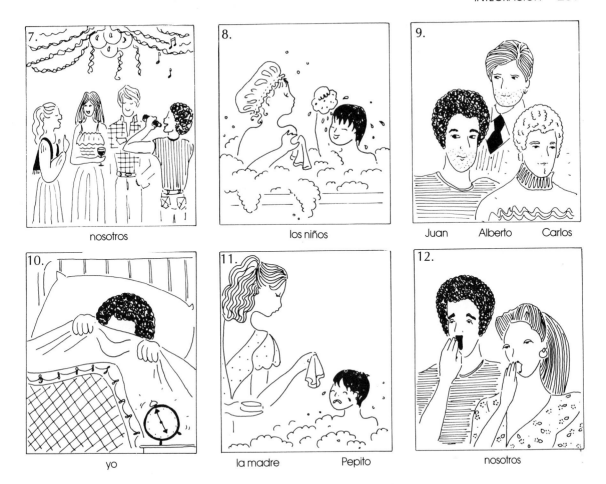

F.   WRITTEN EXERCISE: REFLEXIVES
     Write the answers to the eight questions on the tape. Each question will be
     given twice.

G.   ORAL EXERCISE: **Se**—OTHER USES
     Answer the questions on the tape according to the example.
         Example   (tape)   ¿Dónde se compran sellos?
                   (your response)   **Se compran sellos en la casa de correos.**

H. ORAL EXERCISE: PREPOSITIONS
Answer the questions on the tape according to the drawing.

I. ORAL EXERCISE: PREPOSITIONS
Answer the questions on the tape according to the drawings.

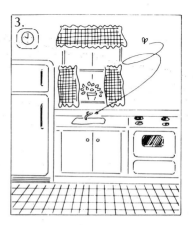

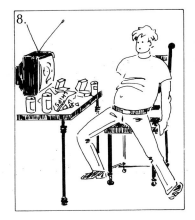

J.   ORAL EXERCISE: Por VS. Para

Answer the questions on the tape according to the drawings.

nosotros   yo   Juanita   Mario

Carlos

Carlos

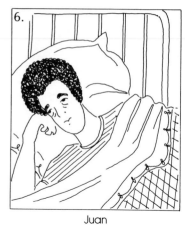

Juan

K.   WRITTEN EXERCISE: COMPREHENSION, **La América Central y las Antillas**
You will hear a short paragraph read twice. Listen to it carefully. Write the answers to the three questions that follow.

L.   DICTATION: **La América Central y las Antillas**
Write the three sentences you hear on the tape. Each sentence will be read three times.

■ REPASO DE VOCABULARIO ACTIVO

Preposiciones

a	**con**	**detrás de**	**fuera de**
al	**de**	**en**	**lejos de**
al lado de	**debajo de**	**encima de**	**sin**
antes de	**delante de**	**enfrente de**	
cerca de	**dentro de**	**entre**	
como	**después de**	**en vez de**	

Pronombres complementos de preposiciones

mí	**él**	**vosotros (as)**	**ellas**
ti	**ella**	**ustedes**	
usted	**nosotros (as)**	**ellos**	

Pronombres reflexivos

me	**se**	**os**
te	**nos**	**se**

Sustantivos

el **cepillo**
el **cepillo de dientes**
el **champú**
el **compañero(a) de cuarto**
la **crema de afeitar**
el **dormitorio,** la **residencia estudiantil**
la **marca**

la **máquina de afeitar**
la **navaja**
el **papel higiénico**
la **pasta de dientes**
el **peine**
el **secador de pelo**

Verbos

acostarse (ue)	**divertirse (ie, i)**	**ponerse**
afeitarse	**dormirse (ue, u)**	**preocuparse (por)**
bañarse	**enamorarse**	**quitarse**
casarse	**enojarse**	**secarse**
cepillarse	**irse**	**sentarse (ie)**
comprometerse	**lavarse**	**vestirse (i, i)**
cortarse	**levantarse**	
despertarse (ie)	**peinarse**	

Expresiones idiomáticas

estar enamorado(a) (de)
estar comprometido(a)

■ EJERCICIOS DE REPASO

I. Pronombres y verbos reflexivos

Son las ocho de la mañana en el dormitorio. Indique usted las actividades de las varias personas.

Modelo   Linda/*levantarse*
          Linda se levanta.

1. Mi compañera de cuarto/*despertarse*
2. Yo/*levantarse*
3. Tú/*quitarse* los pijamas
4. Vosotros/*vestirse*
5. Nosotros/*preocuparse* por el examen
6. Ana y Susana/*enojarse*
7. Yo/*irse*

Modelo   Diego/*levantarse*
          Diego acaba de levantarse.

8. Yo/*bañarse*
9. Felipe/*secarse*
10. Tú/*lavarse* la cara
11. Nosotros/*afeitarse*
12. Ellos/*cepillarse* los dientes
13. Yo/*peinarse*
14. Pedro/*ponerse* los calcetines

II. Las preposiciones

A. Cambie las oraciones usando la preposición de significado contrario.

1. Quiero el bistec *con* cebollas.
2. Carlos está *detrás de* María.
3. Vamos a hablar *antes de* comer.
4. El gato está *debajo del* sofá.
5. Vivimos *cerca de* las montañas.
6. El perro duerme *dentro de* la casa.

B. Conteste según las indicaciones.

1. ¿Para quién trabajaste? (el Banco Nacional)
2. ¿Para qué trabajaste? (ir a México)
3. ¿A qué hora saliste para México? (a las cinco)
4. ¿Por cuántos días estuviste allí? (diez días)
5. ¿Para quién compraste la blusa? (Lupe)
6. ¿Cuánto pagaste por la blusa? (700 pesos)

III. Repaso general

A. Conteste en español en oraciones completas.

1. ¿Qué hace usted después de levantarse?
2. ¿Qué usa usted para lavarse el pelo? ¿secarse el pelo? ¿peinarse? ¿cepillarse los dientes?
3. ¿Quiere usted casarse algún día?
4. En la clase de español, ¿quién se sienta al lado de usted? ¿y detrás? ¿y delante?
5. ¿Qué va usted a hacer esta noche después de comer? ¿y después de estudiar?
6. ¿Limpiaría usted la casa por su madre?
7. ¿Le gustaría a usted ir a España conmigo? ¿con sus padres? ¿con su amigo(a)?
8. ¿Dónde se puede estudiar?
9. ¿Cuáles son los países de la América Central?
10. ¿Cómo son unidos los países de la América Central?
11. ¿Cuáles son los países de las Antillas de lengua española?
12. ¿Cuál de los países de las Antillas es un "commonwealth"?

B. Traduzca al español.

1. They fell in love and they got engaged.
2. We have to go to bed at ten thirty.

3. At 6:00 I get up, take a bath, shave, and get dressed.
4. Where is toothpaste sold?
5. We ought to finish the book by tomorrow.
6. We walked through the forest and along the river.
7. I need to go to the bank for (to get) traveler's checks.
8. I am going to listen to a record instead of looking at television.
9. He lives near me.
10. I don't want to go with you (familiar, singular).
11. Is this present for us? No! It is for him.

IV. Repaso de verbos

Escriba oraciones cambiando el verbo a los tiempos indicados.

1. despertarse (ie) . . . yo   2. vestirse (i,i) . . . él

a) presente
b) presente del progresivo
c) pretérito
d) imperfecto
e) futuro
f) condicional

■ VOCABULARIO *La estación de ferrocarril*

la **estación de ferrocarril**	*railroad station*
el **tren (expreso)**	*train (express)*
el **horario**	*schedule*
la **salida**	*exit, departure*
la **llegada**	*arrival*
la **taquilla**	*ticket window*
el **boleto**	*ticket*
de **ida y vuelta**	*round-trip*
de **primera clase**	*first class*
de **segunda clase**	*second-class*
la **maleta**	*suitcase*
el **equipaje**	*luggage*
el **quiosco**	*newsstand*
la **revista**	*magazine*
el **periódico**	*newspaper*
la **noticia**	*news*
la **caricatura**	*cartoon*
el **servicio**	*restroom*
la **guía telefónica**	*phone book*
la **línea**	*line*
la **llamada**	*call*

de **cobro revertido**	*collect*
de **larga distancia**	*long distance*
el (la) **operador(a)**	*operator*
el **país**	*country*
el **teléfono público**	*public telephone*
dejar	*to leave (behind), to let*
marcar	*to dial*
telefonear	*to telephone*
ocupado	*busy*
bastante	*enough*
demasiado	*too, too much*
ya	*already*
hacer una llamada	*to make a call*
hacer la maleta	*to pack*
ponerse impaciente	*to become impatient*

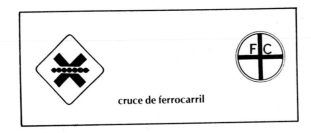

cruce de ferrocarril

EJERCICIO 1   En la estación de ferrocarril

Conteste en español en oraciones completas según el dibujo.

1. ¿Qué quiere comprar el hombre que está enfrente de la taquilla?
2. Probablemente, ¿qué clase de boletos hay?
3. ¿Tiene el hombre mucho equipaje?
4. ¿Cuántas maletas tiene?
5. ¿Con quiénes habla la señora?
6. ¿Qué está haciendo la señorita que lleva la falda corta?
7. ¿Qué quiere comprar el hombre que está enfrente del quiosco?
8. ¿Qué lee el señor que está sentado (*seated*) en el banco?
9. Los jóvenes que están al lado del hombre, ¿se conocen bien? ¿se aman mucho?
10. ¿Qué mira la señorita que tiene el pelo muy largo?
11. ¿A qué hora sale el tren para Toledo?
12. ¿A qué hora llega el tren a Granada?
13. ¿Qué hora es según el reloj de la estación de ferrocarril?
14. ¿Qué ve usted detrás de los niños? ¿Dónde puede usted buscar el número de teléfono?

EJERCICIO 2   Preguntas generales

1. ¿Cuál es su número de teléfono?
2. ¿Hace usted muchas llamadas de larga distancia? ¿a quién?
3. ¿Hace usted llamadas de cobro revertido frecuentemente? ¿a quién?
4. Cuando la línea está ocupada, ¿se pone usted impaciente?
5. ¿En qué otras ocasiones se pone usted impaciente?
6. Al comprar un periódico, ¿qué lee usted primero, las noticias o las caricaturas? ¿Cuál es su caricatura favorita?
7. ¿Está usted ocupado ahora? ¿Qué está haciendo usted?
8. ¿Tiene usted bastante tiempo para estudiar? ¿dormir? ¿divertirse?
9. ¿Come usted demasiado? ¿Bebe usted demasiado?

EJERCICIO 3   Definiciones

Indique la palabra que corresponde a la definición.

1. El cuarto de baño en un lugar (*place*) público.
2. La llamada de un país a otro país.
3. La otra persona paga esta llamada.
4. La persona que puede asistir en hacer llamadas.
5. El acto de usar el teléfono.
6. El acto de indicar el número en el teléfono.
7. Donde se venden boletos.
8. El acto de salir.
9. El acto de llegar.
10. El boleto que usted compra cuando quiere ir y volver.
11. Lo contrario de traer.
12. El acto de poner las cosas en la maleta.
13. Un tren muy rápido.

■ CONVERSACIÓN

Un pasajero llega de prisa a la taquilla de la estación de ferrocarril.

PASAJERO   **Buenas tardes. Lo siento pero he llegado un poco tarde. ¿Ha salido el tren para Sevilla?**

BOLETERO   **No, señor. El tren saldrá en cinco minutos.**

PASAJERO   **¡Qué suerte! Necesito un boleto de ida y vuelta, por favor.**

BOLETERO   **¿De primera o de segunda clase, señor?**

PASAJERO   **De segunda. No he tenido tiempo para cambiar mi dinero. ¿Aceptan ustedes cheques de viajeros?**

BOLETERO   **Sí, ¡cómo no! . . . Aquí tiene el boleto y su cambio. Y, señor, a la derecha usted puede encontrar un horario.**

PASAJERO   **Muchísimas gracias.**

BOLETERO   **¡Buen viaje!**

A passenger arrives hurriedly at the ticket window of the railroad station.

PASSENGER   *Good afternoon. I'm sorry but I have arrived a bit late. Has the train left for Seville?*

TICKET AGENT   *No, sir. The train will leave in five minutes.*

PASSENGER   *What luck! I need a round trip ticket, please.*

TICKET AGENT   *First or second class, sir?*

PASSENGER   *Second. I haven't had time to change my money. Do you accept traveler's checks?*

TICKET AGENT   *Yes, of course! . . . Here is the ticket and your change. And, sir, to the right you can find a schedule.*

PASSENGER   *Thank you very much.*

TICKET AGENT   *Have a good trip!*

■ ESTRUCTURA

I. El participio pasado   *The past participle*

A. La formación de los participios pasados

The Spanish past participle (equivalent to *closed, eaten, written, heard,* and so on) is formed as follows:

Participios pasados regulares

> **verb stem + <u>ado</u> (for -ar verbs) = past participle**

cerr + **ado** = **cerrado** (*closed*)

> **verb stem + <u>-ido</u> (for -er and -ir verbs) = past participle**

viv + **ido** = **vivido** (*lived*)
com + **ido** = **comido** (*eaten*)

Algunos participios pasados irregulares

decir	**dicho** (*said, told*)		volver	**vuelto** (*returned*)
hacer	**hecho** (*done, made*)		romper	**roto** (*broken*)
escribir	**escrito** (*written*)		abrir	**abierto** (*opened*)
ver	**visto** (*seen*)		morir	**muerto** (*died, dead*)
poner	**puesto** (*put, placed*)			

EJERCICIO 4   ¡Vamos a practicar!

Cambie el infinitivo al participio pasado.

Modelo   cambiar   **cambiado**

1. venir
2. caminar
3. traer
4. recordar
5. ir
6. preparar
7. recibir
8. escuchar
9. entender
10. dar
11. leer
12. pagar
13. perder
14. dejar
15. pedir
16. gastar
17. ser
18. apagar
19. abrir
20. decir
21. volver
22. hacer
23. poner
24. escribir

B. Participios pasados usados como adjetivos

The past participle can be used as an adjective to describe a noun, in which case it agrees in gender and number with the noun modified.

Se venden coches **usados** allí.
Tiene una cámara **hecha** en el Japón.

With **ser** the past participle is used as an adjective to indicate that the subject is acted upon by (**por**) an agent, expressed or implied.

La taza **fue rota** por mi hermano menor.
Las puertas **fueron cerradas** a las diez en punto.

With **estar** the past participle is used as an adjective to indicate the resultant condition of a completed action. (See Chapter 2, uses of **estar**.)

Las puertas **estaban cerradas** cuando llegué.
El animal **estaba muerto.**

EJERCICIO 5   Preguntas generales

Conteste en español en oraciones completas.

1. ¿Cuál es un producto (automóvil, cámara, etc.) hecho en Alemania? ¿en Hongkong? ¿en México? ¿en España?
2. ¿Cuál es el nombre de una novela escrita por un español? ¿por un alemán? ¿un francés? ¿un ruso?

¿A qué hora sale el tren? Estación Atocha, Madrid, España

Donde una puerta se cierra, otra se abre.

3.   En la residencia estudiantil, ¿hay muchas cosas rotas? ¿qué cosas?
4.   ¿Está usted cansado(a)? ¿por qué?
5.   ¿Están cerradas o abiertas las ventanas de este cuarto?
6.   ¿Tienen sus padres un coche nuevo o usado? ¿y usted?
7.   ¿Por quién fue conquistada la civilización azteca?
8.   ¿Por quién fue asesinado el Presidente Lincoln?

II. El presente perfecto *The present perfect tense*

The present perfect tense in Spanish, as in English, shows action in the past that continues or influences the present.
Formation:

the present tense of <u>haber</u> (*to have*) + **the past participle** = **present perfect**

Modelo   **cerrar**   *to close*

	haber (present tense)	past participle
he	*I have*	
has	*You have*	
ha	*He, she, it has, you have*	+ **cerrado** *closed*
hemos	*We have*	
habéis	*You have*	
han	*They, you have*	

Ejemplos   **He llegado** un poco tarde.
　　　　　¿Ha salido el tren?
　　　　　No **hemos tenido** tiempo para cambiar el dinero.

NOTE 1:   **Haber** means *to have* only as a helping verb before a past participle. **Tener** means *to have* in the sense of possession.

NOTE 2:   All object pronouns directly precede the helping verb **haber** and follow **no** if the sentence is negative.

Lo he terminado.
I have finished it.

No **los** hemos vendido.
We haven't sold them.

EJERCICIO 6   Los preparativos para el viaje

Indique quién se ha preparado para el viaje según el modelo.

Modelo   ¿Quién *ha telefoneado* a la estación? (yo)
         Yo he telefoneado a la estación.

1.   ¿Quién *ha hecho* la maleta? (yo, tú, Jaime)
2.   ¿Quiénes *se han vestido*? (nosotros, vosotros, ellos)
3.   ¿Quién *ha llamado* el taxi? (yo, los profesores, Pablo)
4.   ¿Quién *ha visto* el horario? (nosotros, tú, Sonia)
5.   ¿Quién *ha comprado* los boletos? (yo, nosotros, Lupe y Linda)

EJERCICIO 7   Tú y yo

Hágale las preguntas siguientes a un(a) estudiante; escuche la respuesta.

Modelo   ¿Has escrito a tus padres recientemente?
         (Sí,) (No, no) he escrito a mis padres recientemente.

1.   ¿Has vuelto a casa recientemente?
2.   ¿Has roto algo recientemente?
3.   ¿Has ido al cine recientemente?
4.   ¿Has abierto el libro de español recientemente?
5.   ¿Has dicho algo interesante recientemente?
6.   ¿Has hecho algo interesante recientemente?
7.   ¿Has dejado algo en la clase recientemente?
8.   ¿Te has puesto impaciente recientemente?
9.   ¿Te has peinado recientemente?
10. ¿Te has enamorado recientemente?

EJERCICIO 8   Las noticias

Usted es un periodista (*newspaper reporter*). Indique las noticias importantes del día según el modelo.

Modelo   Los soldados (*soldiers*) están *saliendo* de la isla.
         ¡Los soldados ya han salido de la isla!

1. Los soldados *están volviendo* al país.
2. Los astronautas *están llegando* a la luna.
3. El presidente *está visitando* China.
4. El presidente *está firmando* los documentos.
5. Muchas personas *están muriendo* de hambre.
6. *Estamos mandando* comida a los pobres.
7. *Estamos perdiendo* en los Juegos Olímpicos.
8. La Universidad de México *está ganando*.

EJERCICIO 9   ¿Que han hecho?

Conteste según el modelo.

>   Modelo   ¿Qué has hecho? (levantarse)
>   **Me he levantado.**

1. ¿Qué has hecho? (bañarse) (peinarse) (afeitarse)
2. ¿Qué han hecho ustedes? (divertirse) (enamorarse) (comprometerse)
3. ¿Qué han hecho ellos? (cambiarlo) (firmarlos) (terminarla)
4. ¿Qué ha hecho ella? (decírmelo) (traérnoslo) dármelo)

III. El pasado perfecto   *The past perfect tense*

The past perfect tense refers to action in the distant past that continued or influenced the time under discussion.
Formation:

> **the imperfect tense of <u>haber</u> + the past participle = past perfect**

Modelo   **comer**   *to eat*

haber (imperfect tense)		past participle
había	*I had*	
habías	*You had*	
había	*You, he, she, it had*	
habíamos	*We had*	+ **comido** *eaten*
habíais	*You had*	
habían	*You, they had*	

Ejemplos   ¿Qué **habían hecho?**
¡**Habían roto** la ventana!
Jaime **había salido.**
Nosotros **habíamos llamado** por teléfono.

NOTE: 1   The past perfect tense is also referred to as the *pluperfect* or in Spanish the **pluscuamperfecto.**

NOTE 2:   The future perfect tense is formed by using **haber** in the future plus the past participle.

Habré ido.   *I will have gone.*
Habrás ido.   *You will have gone,* etc.

NOTE 3:   The conditional perfect is formed by using **haber** in the conditional plus the past participle.

Habría ido.   *I would have gone.*
Habrías ido.   *You would have gone,* etc.

EJERCICIO 10   Una visita de mi tío

Indique los preparativos que había hecho la familia antes de la llegada del tío. Use el pasado perfecto según el modelo.

Modelo   Nosotros/*lavar* el coche.
          Habíamos lavado el coche.

1. Mi padre/*cortar* la hierba.
2. Mi madre/*preparar* la comida.
3. Nosotros/*limpiar* la casa.

¿Adónde va este tren? Estación Atocha, Madrid, España

4. Tú/*hacer* las camas.
5. Vosotros/*lavar* el perro.
6. Nosotros/*bañarse*.
7. Yo/*vestirse* en mi mejor ropa.
8. Mis hermanas/*poner* flores en la mesa.

IV. Las comparaciones *Comparisons*

A. Las comparaciones de igualdad   *Equal comparisons*

To compare equally two things or persons with regard to a general quality, use:

> **tan** + adjective (or adverb) + **como** = *as . . . as*

Las españolas son **tan bonitas como** las francesas.
Spanish women are as pretty as French women.
No cantamos **tan bien como** ustedes.
We do not sing as well as you.

To compare equal quantities, use:

> **tanto (-a, -os, -as)** + noun + **como** = *as much (many) . . . as*

Nosotros tenemos **tanto dinero como** ellos.
We have as much money as they do.
Ellos compraron **tantas revistas como** usted.
They bought as many magazines as you did.

NOTE: When the noun reference is omitted, and two actions are compared equally, **tanto como** is used.

Él comió **tanto como** tú.
He ate as much as you.

Also, **tanto** has the additional meaning of *so much, so many*.

¡El tiene **tantos** coches!
He has so many cars!

EJERCICIO 11   ¡Vamos a comparar!

Haga una comparación de igualdad según los modelos.

Modelo   Juana es *hermosa*. Camila es *hermosa*.
          Juana es tan hermosa como Camila.

1. Paco es *alto*. Pepe es *alto*.
2. Doña González es *flaca*. Su hija es *flaca*.
3. Nosotros somos *simpáticos*. Ustedes son *simpáticos*.

4. Yo estoy *ocupado(a)*. Mi amigo está *ocupado*.
5. Las mujeres están *contentas*. Los hombres están *contentos*.

    Modelos   Rosita comió *galletas*. Sancho comió *galletas*.
           Rosita comió tantas galletas como Sancho.

6. Los padres comieron *helado*. Los niños comieron *helado*.
7. Él trajo *comida*. Nosotros trajimos *comida*.
8. Juan compró *discos*. Paco compró *discos*.
9. Susana durmió cuatro *horas*. Yo dormí cuatro *horas*.
10. Yo tenía *frío*. Él tenía *frío*.

EJERCICIO 12 Preguntas de comparación

Conteste en español en oraciones completas.

1. ¿Es usted tan inteligente como su profesor(a)?
2. ¿Es usted tan fuerte como su padre?
3. ¿Tiene usted tanta ropa como su hermano(a)?
4. ¿Tiene usted tanto dinero como sus amigos?
5. ¿Estudia usted tanto como su compañero(a) de cuarto?
6. ¿Come usted tanto como Fat Albert?

B. Las comparaciones de desigualdad *Unequal comparisons*

1. Formación de los comparativos y los superlativos

The comparative is formed by placing **más** (*more*) or **menos** (*less*) before the adjective.

The superlative is formed by placing *the article* + **más** or **menos** before the adjective. After the superlative, **de** is the Spanish equivalent to the English *in*.

María es **bonita.**	*Mary is pretty.*
Lupe es **más bonita**.	*Lupe is prettier.*
Estela es **la más bonita de** la universidad.	*Estela is the prettiest in the university.*
Esta lección es **difícil**.	*This lesson is difficult.*
Esa lección es **menos difícil**.	*That lesson is less difficult.*
Aquella lección es **la menos difícil del** libro.	*That lesson is the least difficult in the book.*

NOTE: *Than* is translated by **que** except before a number, in which case **de** is used.

Ella es más bonita **que** su hermana.
She is prettier than her sister.
Él tiene más **de** cincuenta dólares.
He has more than fifty dollars.

2. Los comparativos y los superlativos irregulares

A few adjectives have irregular comparative and superlative forms and do not use **más** and **menos**.

mejor	*better*	**mayor**	*older (referring to age)*
el mejor	*the best*	**el mayor**	*the oldest*
peor	*worse*	**menor**	*younger (referring to age)*
el peor	*the worst*	**el menor**	*the youngest*

Es **bueno**.	*He is good.*
Es **mejor**.	*He is better.*
Es **el mejor de** la ciudad.	*He is the best in the city.*

Es **malo**.	*He is bad.*
Es **peor**.	*He is worse.*
Es **el peor del** mundo.	*He is the worst in the world.*

Es mi hermano **mayor**.	*He is my older brother.*
Es **el mayor de** los hermanos.	*He is the oldest of the brothers.*

Es mi **hermana menor**.	*She is my younger sister.*
Es **la menor de** la familia.	*She is the youngest in the family.*

EJERCICIO 13   Al superlativo

Complete según el modelo.

> Modelo   Juana es *débil*. (Lupe) (Linda)
> **Lupe es más débil.**
> **Linda es la más débil de las tres.**

1. Susana es *bonita*. (Lola) (Isabel)
2. Este libro es *fácil*. (ese libro) (aquel libro)
3. Mis tíos son *simpáticos*. (mis abuelos) (mis padres)
4. Yo soy *malo*. (mi hermano menor) (mi hermano mayor)
5. La ensalada es *buena*. (el pollo) (el postre)

EJERCICIO 14   Preguntas generales

Conteste en español en oraciones completas.

1. ¿Quién tiene más de diez dólares? ¿Me los presta usted?
2. ¿Es usted mayor o menor que su profesor(a)?
3. ¿Es usted más guapo(a) que su profesor(a)? ¿más fuerte? ¿más rico(a)?
4. ¿Es el Mercedes mejor o peor que el Toyota?
5. ¿Es su profesor(a) de español más fácil o más difícil que su profesor(a) de inglés?
6. ¿Es su madre más generosa o menos generosa que su padre?

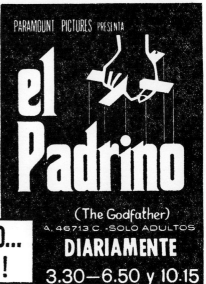

EJERCICIO 15 En su opinión

Indique la persona o la cosa que, en su opinión, corresponde a cada (*each*) categoría.

Modelo La mejor película
La mejor película es "Star Wars."

1. El mejor restaurante de esta ciudad.
2. La actriz más hermosa.
3. El actor más guapo.
4. El mejor programa de televisión.
5. La clase más interesante.
6. El disco más popular.
7. La persona más importante de mi vida (*life*).
8. El peor problema de mi vida.

PERSPECTIVA ORIGINAL

1. Mini-drama: **En la estación de ferrocarril**
   Using the following format as a guideline, create a dialog which could be performed as a skit.
   a. Ask for the schedule of arrivals and departures.

Las llamas son parte del paisaje (*landscape*) andino. Lago Millumi, Bolivia

b. Request a ticket (specifying kind) to your destination.
c. Pay for your ticket, either in cash or with a traveler's check; do not forget your change.
d. Ask where you can buy a newspaper or magazine.

2. Composición: **¿Quién es mejor?**
   Compare yourself or compare your boyfriend or girlfriend to a famous actor or actress. Use the equal and the unequal comparative constructions as appropriate.

3. Inventando preguntas.
   Using the present perfect tense, formulate five questions appropriate to each of the following situations:
   a. A teacher asking the students immediately after their arrival to class (Have you done your homework, etc.?);
   b. A mother asking a young child (Have you brushed your teeth, etc.?).

■ PANORAMA CULTURAL

La América del Sur

La América del Sur es un continente muy grande con todas las posibles variaciones geográficas. Hay montañas altas, desiertos, lagos hermosos, valles fértiles y
selvas tropicales. En la Argentina existe la *pampa* más grande del mundo, tierra
natal del *gaucho*. En el Brasil hay una inmensa selva que *cubre* gran parte de la región del río Amazonas. Pasando por *avión* entre Santiago y Buenos Aires, el viajero tiene que cruzar los Andes, magnífica *cordillera* que se extiende *desde* Colombia en el norte *hasta* la Argentina y Chile en el sur.

    También hay en el continente una variedad de tipos raciales. En el Brasil
(donde se habla portugués) y en las costas tropicales hay un gran número de negros. En Chile, la Argentina, el Uruguay y el Brasil hay muchos inmigrantes europeos, principalmente de Italia, España, Portugal y Alemania. El indio es el elemento predominante en países como el Perú, el Ecuador y Bolivia, donde existía
el imperio inca. En las montañas de los Andes, cerca de Cuzco, Perú, se encuentran las ruinas de Machu Picchu, vieja y *última* capital de los incas, situada a más
de doce mil pies *de altura*. Esta ciudad, como otros sitios históricos, es monu-
mento al *desarrollo* militar, social y cultural de este imperio conquistado por Pizarro en 1532.

plain
native/cowboy/
covers/airplane
mountain
range/from/to

last
high
development

Machu Picchu, la antigua ciudad perdida de los incas,
está situada a más de 12.000 pies de altura en los Andes. Perú

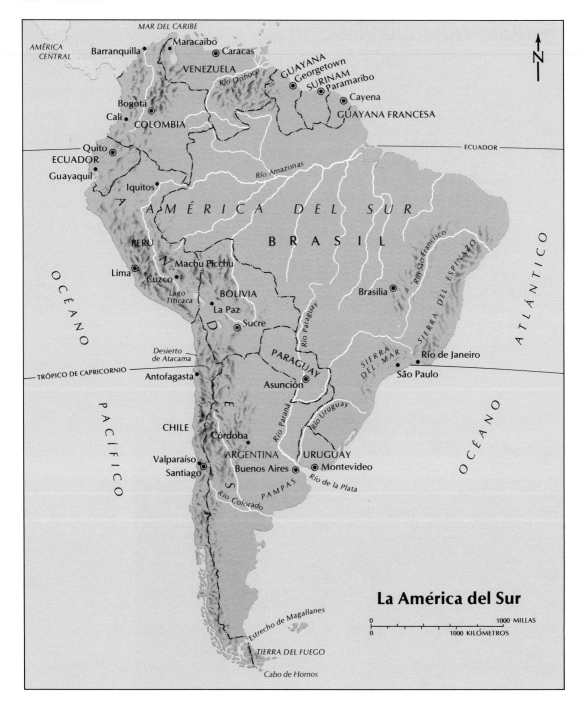

La América del Sur

El gaucho y la pampa son como uno. Argentina

Después de la desintegración del imperio incaico, los españoles solidificaron su posición en la América del Sur con exploraciones por las dos costas del continente, *creando* pueblos y *fortalezas* en sitios que ahora son ciudades famosas y grandes como Buenos Aires, Caracas y Santiago. El continente pasó por tres siglos de colonización, período en el cual la iglesia católica, las universidades, el sistema económico y político y la estructura social se establecieron *bajo* un estricto régimen español. Para mantener control *sobre* un territorio tan vasto y tan lejos de la patria, los españoles no querían dar privilegios, derechos o posiciones de gran importancia a los indios, a los mestizos o a los criollos (personas *nacidas* en América de padres españoles). A los *fines* del siglo diez y ocho las ideas liberales de Europa llegaban a Sudamérica a la *misma* vez que se *debilitaba* el poder militar de España. Los líderes como Bolívar, O'Higgins y San Martín y otros reconocieron el momento en que iniciar la *lucha* por su independencia y libertad. Para 1830 la mayoría de los países hispanoamericanos habían ganado su independencia y buscaban la oportunidad de formular su propio sistema de gobierno.

Los años después de la independencia han sido marcados por la inestabilidad política. Llegaron a *poder* jefes políticos llamados *caudillos*, que en muchos casos se hicieron dictadores crueles.

Muchos problemas sociales todavía existen en la América del Sur y se manifiestan en varias formas—la pobreza, las *sublevaciones*, los *golpes de estado*, la inflación increíble, las dictaduras, la revolución, la falta de una buena educación para todos, y más. Pero estos problemas son los que, en muchos casos, han dado origen a una literatura que iguala la de los otros países del mundo. Autores como Gabriela Mistral y Pablo Neruda de Chile, Jorge Luis Borges y Julio Cortázar de la Argentina, Gabriel García Márquez de Colombia y otros han ganado fama internacional por sus obras literarias.

Mirando al futuro podemos ver que este continente enorme, con su población de más de doscientos millones, con sus *riquezas* minerales, su petróleo, su gran

creating/fortresses

under
over

born
end
same/weakened

struggle

power/political
bosses

uprisings/coups
d'etat

resources

capacidad agrícola e industrial y su enorme extensión tendrá una influencia cada vez más profunda en la economía, la política, el pensamiento intelectual y el balance de poder del mundo.

¿CUÁNTO RECUERDAS?

¿Cuál es la referencia en la Columna B que corresponde a la descripción en la Columna A?

COLUMNA A

a. Hay muchos que viven en el Brasil y en las costas tropicales.
b. Elemento racial predominante en países donde existía el imperio inca.
c. El río grande que se extiende por la selva del Brasil.
d. Período en que se establece la estructura social, económica y política de los españoles.
e. El vaquero (*cowboy*) que vive en la pampa argentina.
f. Personas nacidas en América de padres españoles.
g. El país de Sudamérica que tiene la pampa más grande del mundo.
h. Jefes políticos que en muchos casos se hicieron dictadores.
i. Europeos que viven principalmente en Chile, el Brasil, la Argentina y el Uruguay.
j. El país que tiene una inmensa selva.
k. Autores de fama internacional.
l. La última capital de los incas.
m. La tierra natal del gaucho.
n. La cordillera que se extiende desde Colombia hasta el sur de Chile.
o. Su imperio existía principalmente en el Perú, el Ecuador y Bolivia.
p. La lengua que se habla en el Brasil.
q. Conquistador del imperio inca.
r. Líderes de la lucha por la independencia sudamericana.

COLUMNA B

1. la Argentina
2. la pampa
3. el Brasil
4. colonización
5. portugués
6. criollos
7. los Andes
8. Bolívar, O'Higgins, San Martín
9. los incas
10. caudillos
11. Machu Picchu
12. Mistral, Neruda, Borges, Cortázar, García Márquez
13. Pizarro
14. el indio
15. el Amazonas
16. los inmigrantes
17. los negros
18. el gaucho

PREGUNTAS

Conteste en español según el mapa.

1. ¿Cuál es el país más grande de la América del Sur?
2. ¿Con qué países tiene fronteras la Argentina?
3. ¿Cuál es la capital de la Argentina? ¿de Chile? ¿del Brasil? ¿de Venezuela? ¿de Colombia? ¿del Perú?
4. ¿Dónde está el río Amazonas?
5. ¿En qué países se ve la cordillera de los Andes?
6. ¿Cómo se llaman los países pequeños que están al norte del Brasil?
7. ¿En qué río están situadas las ciudades de Buenos Aires y Montevideo?
8. ¿Dónde está el desierto de Atacama?
9. ¿Cómo se llama el lago situado en la frontera entre el Perú y Bolivia?

■ INTEGRACIÓN

A. SONG: **María Isabel** (La América del Sur)
   Listen to the song the first time. The second time sing along with the tape.*

La playa estaba desierta,
El sol bañaba tu piel,
Cantando con mi guitarra
Para ti, María Isabel. (repita)

(Coro)
Coge tu sombrero y póntelo,
Vamos a la playa, ¡qué lindo el sol! (repita)

Chiribiribí, po po po po
Chiribiribí, po po po po (repita)

En la arena escribí tu nombre,
Y luego yo lo borré,
Para que nadie pisara
Tu nombre, María Isabel (repita)   (Coro)

B. ORAL EXERCISE: **Conversación**
   1. The dialog will be read twice. Listen the first time; the second time pauses will be provided for you to repeat each phrase.
   2. Listen to the statements related to the dialog; indicate if the statements are true or false.
C. ORAL EXERCISE: VOCABULARY, **la estación de ferrocarril**
   Answer the questions on the tape according to the drawings.

*English translation:

The beach was deserted,
The sun bathed your skin,
Singing with my guitar
For you, María Isabel.

Take your hat and put it on,
Let's go to the beach,
The sun is warm.

Chi ri bi ri bí
Popopopo

In the sand I wrote your name,
And then I erased it,
So that nobody would step
On your name, María Isabel.

1.

MENDOZA

2.

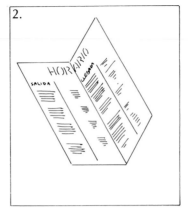

HORARIO
SALIDA
LLEGADA

3.

BOLETO
VUELTA
IDA

4.

5.

La Prensa

6.

TIEMPO

7.

SAN
ANTONIO

8.

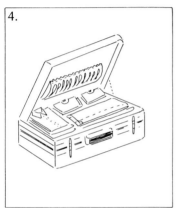

9.

D. ORAL EXERCISE: PRESENT PERFECT TENSE

Complete the sentences with the correct form of the verb in the present perfect tense.

Example　(tape)　　　　　　comer allí—yo
　　　　　　(your response)　**Yo he comido allí.**

E. ORAL EXERCISE: PRESENT PERFECT TENSE

Answer the questions according to the drawings.

yo

Example　(tape)　　　　　　¿Quién ha recibido
　　　　　　　　　　　　　　una A?
　　　　　　(your response)　**Yo he recibido una A.**

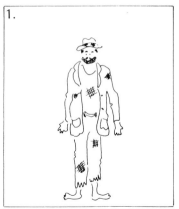

1.

Jorge

2.

tú

3.

yo

4.

tú

5.

nosotros

6.

nosotros

7. Carlota

8. Juan   Alberto   Carlos

9. yo

10. la profesora

11. Carmen

12. Pepe   Mónica

F.   WRITTEN EXERCISE: PRESENT PERFECT TENSE
     Write the answers to the nine questions on the tape. Each question is given
     twice.

G.   ORAL EXERCISE: PAST PERFECT TENSE
     Change the verbs in the sentences from the present perfect to the past perfect
     tense.

     Example   (tape)   Hemos vuelto temprano.
               (your response)   **Habíamos vuelto temprano.**

H.   ORAL EXERCISE: EQUAL COMPARISONS (QUALITIES)
     Using the cues provided, make a sentence of equal comparison. Use the pat-
     tern **tan** + adjective + **como**.

Alberto   Miguel

     Example   (tape)   rico
               (your response)   **Alberto es tan rico
                                 como Miguel.**

1. Andrés Paco	2. Elena Marta
3. Juan Teresa	4. Jorge Pancho

I.   ORAL EXERCISE: EQUAL COMPARISONS (QUANTITIES)

Using the cues provided, make a sentence of equal comparison. Use the pattern **tanto** (**-a, -os, -as**) + noun + **como**.

Alberto   Miguel

Example   (tape)   coches
          (your response)   **Alberto tiene tantos
                              coches como Miguel.**

1. Alberto   Miguel

2. Carlos   Juan

3. Carlos   Juan

4. Carlos   Juan

J.   ORAL EXERCISE: UNEQUAL COMPARATIVES AND SUPERLATIVES
Complete the comparisons following the example.

Tomás Luis Paco

Example   (tape)   Tomás es alto.
           (your sentences)   **Luis es más alto. Paco
                               es el más alto.**

1.

Carlos   Miguel   Alberto

2.

Carlos   Miguel   Alberto

3.

su   tu   mi
examen   examen   examen

4.

mi   tu   su
examen   examen   examen

K.   ORAL EXERCISE: UNEQUAL COMPARISONS WITH **QUE**
Answer the questions on the tape according to the drawings.
Follow the example.

Carlos   Teresa

Example   (tape)   ¿Tiene Carlos más o
                            menos libros que
                            Teresa?
           (your response) **Carlos tiene más libros
                            que Teresa.**

1. Juan   Carlota

2. el abuelo   Pepito

3. el elefante   el mosquito

4. Daniel   Enrique

5. Juan   José

6. Mónica   Alicia

L.   WRITTEN EXERCISE: COMPREHENSION, **La América del Sur**
You will hear a short paragraph which will be read twice. Write the answers
to the three questions that follow.

M.   DICTATION: **La América del Sur**
Write the three sentences you hear. Each sentence will be read three times.

■ REPASO DE VOCABULARIO ACTIVO

Adjetivo

ocupado

Adverbios

bastante   **menos**
demasiado   **ya**
más

Sustantivos

el **boleto**	la **llamada**	el **periódico**
de **ida y vuelta**	de **cobro revertido**	el **quiosco**
de **primera clase**	de **larga distancia**	la **revista**
de **segunda clase**	la **llegada**	la **salida**
la **caricatura**	la **línea**	el **servicio**
el **equipaje**	la **maleta**	la **taquilla**
la **estación de ferrocarril**	la **noticia**	el **teléfono público**
la **guía telefónica**	el (la) **operador(a)**	el **tren (expreso)**
el **horario**	el **país**	

Verbos

dejar   **marcar**
haber   **telefonear**

Expresiones idiomáticas

hacer una llamada   **ponerse impaciente**
hacer la maleta

Expresiones de comparación

tan . . . como
tanto(-a, -os, -as) . . . como

■ EJERCICIOS DE REPASO

I. El presente perfecto

Indique lo que las personas han hecho en el Ecuador.

Modelo   Nosotros/*llegar* al Ecuador.
          Hemos llegado al Ecuador.

1. Yo/*caminar* por la ciudad de Quito.
2. Nosotros/*visitar* la catedral.
3. Tú/*tomar* fotos de la plaza.
4. Inés/*ir* al mercado público.
5. Vosotros/*comprar* muchas flores.
6. Mis amigos/*escribir* muchas tarjetas postales.
7. Usted/*viajar* por los Andes.
8. Yo/*subir* las montañas.
9. Tú/*ver* la selva.
10. Ustedes/*conocer* el puerto de Guayaquil.
11. Yo/*hacer* muchas cosas interesantes.
12. Nosotros/*volver* a los Estados Unidos.

II. El pasado perfecto
Cambie las oraciones al pasado perfecto.

Modelo   *Hemos escuchado* al profesor.
          Habíamos escuchado al profesor.

1. El profesor lo *ha dicho*.
2. *Hemos hecho* la tarea.
3. Lupe y Cecilia *han escrito* los ejercicios.
4. *He estudiado* el vocabulario.
5. ¿Los *has terminado*?
6. ¿Ustedes *han leído* la lectura (*reading*)?

III. Las comparaciones de igualdad
Haga comparaciones de igualdad según los modelos.

Modelo   la clase de inglés/la clase de español (difícil)
          **La clase de inglés es tan difícil como la clase
          de español.**

1. hombres/mujeres (inteligentes)
2. Roberto/Miguel (alto)
3. Lisa/Rosario (simpática)

Modelo   los Gutiérrez/los Gómez (hijas)
          **Los Gutiérrez tienen tantas hijas como los
          Gómez.**

4. los Gutiérrez/los Gómez (dinero)
5. los Gutiérrez/los Gómez (coches)
6. los Gutiérrez/los Gómez (ropa)

IV. Las comparaciones de desigualdad
Haga comparaciones de desigualdad según el modelo.

Modelo   Rodolfo es *honesto*. (Felipe) (Alberto)
Felipe es más honesto.
Alberto es el más honesto de los tres.

1. La clase de historia es *difícil*. (la clase de inglés) (la clase de matemáticas)
2. Yo soy *fuerte*. (mi hermano) (mi primo)
3. El pastel es *bueno*. (el helado) (la torta de chocolate)

V. Repaso general

A. Conteste en español en oraciones completas.

1. ¿Qué tipos de boletos de tren hay?
2. ¿Dónde se compran boletos? ¿y periódicos?
3. ¿Dónde busca usted las llegadas y salidas de los trenes?
4. Si (*if*) usted no sabe el número de teléfono, ¿qué puede usted hacer? (dos cosas)
5. ¿Qué ha hecho usted hoy?
6. ¿Han estudiado ustedes bastante? ¿demasiado?
7. ¿Es usted tan simpático(a) como su profesor(a)?
8. ¿Es usted mayor o menor que su profesor(a)?
9. ¿Cuál era la civilización india que existía en El Perú, El Ecuador y Bolivia?
10. ¿Cómo se llama el río principal del continente? ¿y la cordillera principal?
11. ¿Cuál es la capital de la Argentina? ¿de Colombia? ¿de Venezuela?

B. Traduzca al español.

1. The novel (*novela*) ''Don Quijote'' was written by Cervantes.
2. The records are broken!
3. Have you (fam. sing.) left your books in the room?
4. I have packed.
5. He has already dialed the number.
6. We haven't finished it.
7. I am as sad as he is.
8. He read as many magazines as I did.
9. We worked as much as they did.
10. He is poorer than I am.

VI. Repaso de verbos

Escriba oraciones cambiando el verbo a los tiempos indicados. Use la forma **yo** del verbo, y traduzca las oraciones al inglés.

hacerlo

1. presente	**Lo hago**	I do (am doing) it.
2. presente del progresivo		
3. pretérito		
4. imperfecto		
5. futuro		
6. condicional		
7. presente perfecto		
8. pasado perfecto		

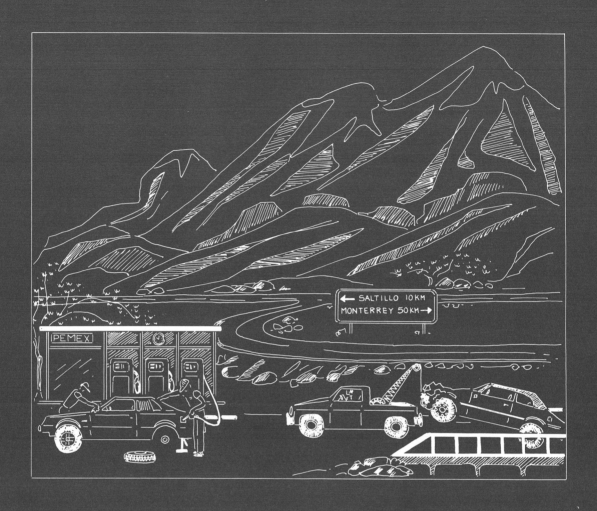

CAPÍTULO 12

■ VOCABULARIO *La carretera*

el **accidente**	*accident*	**llenar**	*to fill*
el **aceite**	*oil*	**pararse**	*to stop*
el **camino**	*road*	**revisar**	*to check*
el **camión**	*truck*	**seguir (i, i)**	*to continue, follow*
la **carretera**	*highway*		
la **cuadra, man-**			
zana	*block*	**a la derecha**	*to the right*
la **esquina**	*corner*	**a la izquierda**	*to the left*
la **estación de ser-**		**recto, derecho**	*straight, straight ahead*
vicio	*gas station*		
la **gasolina**	*gasoline*		
la **glorieta**	*traffic circle*	**darse prisa**	*to hurry up*
la **frontera**	*border*	**tener cuidado**	*to be careful*
la **llanta**	*tire*	**ahora mismo**	*right now*
el **parabrisas**	*windshield*	**otra vez**	*again*
el **policía**	*policeman*		
el **puente**	*bridge*	**despacio**	*slowly*
el **semáforo**	*traffic light*	**pronto**	*soon, right away*
el **tanque**	*tank*		
el **tráfico**	*traffic*	**¡Caramba!**	*My goodness!*
		¡Claro!	*Of course!*
arreglar	*to fix*	**¡Socorro!**	*Help!*
callarse	*to be quiet*	**¡Lo siento mucho!**	*I'm so sorry!*
cruzar	*to cross*	**¡Qué barbaridad!**	*How awful!*
doblar	*to turn*	**¡Qué lástima!**	*What a shame!*
estacionarse	*to park*	**¡Qué lío!**	*What a mess!*
funcionar	*to work* (machine)		

297

EJERCICIO 1   La carretera

Conteste en español en oraciones completas.

Según el dibujo:

1. ¿Dónde está el coche?
2. ¿Cómo se llama la estación de servicio?
3. ¿Qué ponen en el tanque?
4. ¿Qué limpia el hombre que está delante del coche?
5. ¿Qué tienen que cambiar?
6. ¿Ha cruzado el puente el camión?
7. ¿Qué ha tenido el coche que está detrás del camión?
8. ¿Se dobla a la derecha o a la izquierda para ir a Saltillo? ¿y a Monterrey?
9. ¿A cuántos kilómetros está Monterrey? ¿y Saltillo?
10. ¿Qué ve usted en la distancia?

Preguntas generales:

11. ¿Ha tenido usted un accidente? ¿dónde?
12. ¿Tiene usted cuidado cuando maneja?
13. ¿Manejan los hombres más rápidamente que las mujeres?
14. ¿Qué puede usted hacer en la estación de servicio?
15. ¿Tiene usted que pagar para estacionarse en el centro?
16. ¿Ha cruzado usted la frontera entre México y los Estados Unidos?
17. ¿Qué color de luz en el semáforo indica pararse? ¿seguir? ¿ir despacio?
18. ¿Sabe usted arreglar el motor de su coche cuando no funciona?

EJERCICIO 2   Situaciones

¿Qué diría usted en las siguientes situaciones?

Modelo   Usted ha tenido un accidente en el coche de su padre.
          ¡Qué barbaridad!

1. El coche nuevo de su amigo fue destruído (*destroyed*) en una catástrofe natural.
2. Usted está manejando en el desierto de Arizona y . . . ¡no hay más gasolina en su tanque!
3. Usted está en el centro de la ciudad de Nueva York y su llanta necesita aire.
4. Su padre le pregunta a usted si quiere un coche nuevo.
5. Usted se estaciona en un lugar (*place*) donde no debe estacionarse y recibe una multa (*fine*) del policía.
6. Llueve mucho y su limpiaparabrisas (*windshield wiper*) no funciona.
7. Hace mucho tiempo que usted no limpia su coche. Está muy, muy sucio.
8. Usted dobla a la derecha donde no debe hacerlo, y un policía lo (la) ve.
9. Yo le digo a usted que mi coche es muy viejo y ya no funciona.
10. Un amigo suyo ha tenido un accidente horrible y está en el hospital.

■ CONVERSACIÓN

El viajero acaba de pararse en la estación de servicio después de muchas horas en el camino.

VIAJERO	¡Qué bien! En esta estación de servicio puedo pararme un poco.
EMPLEADO	Buenos días, señor. ¿Qué clase de gasolina quiere?
VIAJERO	Regular. Llene el tanque, por favor.
EMPLEADO	¿Qué tal el aceite? ¿Quiere que lo revise?
VIAJERO	Sí, y hágame el favor de limpiar el parabrisas.
EMPLEADO	Muy bien. Y voy a revisar las llantas también. . . . Bueno, todo está listo.
VIAJERO	¿Cuánto le debo?
EMPLEADO	Mil doscientos pesos, señor. . . . Gracias. ¡Que tenga un buen viaje!

The traveler has just stopped at the service station after many hours on the road.

TRAVELER	*Oh good! I can stop awhile at this service station.*
EMPLOYEE	*Good day, sir. What kind of gasoline do you want!*
TRAVELER	*Regular. Fill the tank, please.*
EMPLOYEE	*How's the oil? Do you want me to take a look at it?*
TRAVELER	*Yes, and please clean the windshield.*
EMPLOYEE	*Fine. And I'll check the tires also. . . . Okay, everything is ready.*
TRAVELER	*How much do I owe you?*
EMPLOYEE	*A thousand two hundred pesos, sir. . . . Thank you. Have a good trip!*

curva
peligrosa

hombres
trabajando

■ ESTRUCTURA

I. El subjuntivo *The subjunctive mood*

The indicative is an objective mood for stating facts or communicating specific knowledge. All the tenses that you have studied to this point (present, preterit, imperfect, present perfect, past perfect, future, future perfect, conditional, conditional perfect) are indicative tenses.

The subjunctive, in contrast, is a subjective mood for conveying a speaker's attitudes, including commanding, requesting, emotion, disbelief, denial, uncertainty, or unreality.

In this chapter and subsequent chapters you will learn the forms for the four tenses of the subjunctive (present, present perfect, imperfect, past perfect), plus the uses of the subjunctive forms as they are found (1) in direct commands, (2) in indirect or implied commands, (3) with expressions of emotion, (4) with expressions of doubt, denial, disbelief, (5) after indefinite and negative antecedents, (6) after conjunctions of purpose and proviso, and (7) after conjunctions of time.

II. El presente de subjuntivo *The present subjunctive*

A. Formación del presente de subjuntivo

The present subjunctive of regular -ar, -er, or -ir verbs is formed by using the **yo** form of the present indicative minus **-o** and adding the endings indicated.

stem	+ -ar verb endings	-er, -ir verb endings
yo form of the present indicative minus **-o**	-e -es -e	-a -as -a
	-emos -éis -en	-amos -áis -an

Modelos

hablar	habló	habl	hable hables hable	hablemos habléis hablen
comer	comó	com	coma comas coma	comamos comáis coman
vivir	vivó	viv	viva vivas viva	vivamos viváis vivan

conocer	**conozcó**	**conozc**	**conozca**	**conozcamos**
			conozcas	**conozcáis**
			conozca	**conozcan**
tener	**tengó**	**teng**	**tenga**	**tengamos**
			tengas	**tengáis**
			tenga	**tengan**

NOTE 1: The present subjunctive is usually translated like the present indicative, although it can also have the meaning of *may* or *will* (although a future subjunctive exists, it is very rarely used).

NOTE 2: Stem-changing verbs ending in **-ar** and **-er** have stem changes in the present subjunctive in the same persons as the present indicative.

pensar (ie)		**volver (ue)**	
piense	**pensemos**	**vuelva**	**volvamos**
pienses	**penséis**	**vuelvas**	**volváis**
piense	**piensen**	**vuelva**	**vuelvan**

NOTE 3: Stem-changing verbs ending in **-ir** have an additional change (**o→u** and **e→i**) in the **nosotros** and **vosotros** forms.

dormir (ue, u)		**preferir (ie, i)**		**pedir (i, i)**	
duerma	**durmamos**	**prefiera**	**prefiramos**	**pida**	**pidamos**
duermas	**durmáis**	**prefieras**	**prefiráis**	**pidas**	**pidáis**
duerma	**duerman**	**prefiera**	**prefieran**	**pida**	**pidan**

B. Los verbos irregulares en el presente de subjuntivo

dar		**ir**		**estar**	
dé	**demos**	**vaya**	**vayamos**	**esté**	**estemos**
des	**deis**	**vayas**	**vayáis**	**estés**	**estéis**
dé	**den**	**vaya**	**vayan**	**esté**	**estén**

saber		**ser**		**haber**	
sepa	**sepamos**	**sea**	**seamos**	**haya**	**hayamos**
sepas	**sepáis**	**seas**	**seáis**	**hayas**	**hayáis**
sepa	**sepan**	**sea**	**sean**	**haya**	**hayan**

NOTE: The present subjunctive forms of **haber** are used to form the present perfect subjunctive (which you will meet later); **haya** is also the subjunctive form of **hay** (*there is, there are*).

La glorieta forma un enfoque (*focus*) artístico y práctico
para la intersección del Paseo de la Reforma y otras
avenidas en el centro de la capital. México, D. F.

EJERCICIO 3   ¡Vamos a practicar!

Conjugue los verbos en el presente de subjuntivo.

1. cantar
2. aprender
3. abrir
4. salir
5. venir
6. cerrar (ie)
7. dormir (ue, u)
8. repetir (i, i)
9. ir
10. saber

III. Los mandatos usted y ustedes   *The usted and ustedes formal command forms*

You have been using command forms of verbs from Chapter 1—**escriba el ejercicio**, for example. These forms are really subjunctive, since commanding is an attitude that is expressed by the subjunctive. The **usted** and **ustedes** affirmative and negative commands are the same as the third person singular and plural present subjunctive forms.

¡Hable usted!	*Speak!*
¡Hablen ustedes!	*Speak!* (plural)
¡No hable usted!	*Do not speak!*
¡No hablen ustedes!	*Do not speak!* (plural)

NOTE 1:   In all affirmative commands the object pronouns are attached at the end;
an accent mark is placed on the syllable normally stressed in the command form.

¡Hágalo usted!   *Do it!*
¡Levántense ustedes!   *Get up!* (plural)

NOTE 2:   In all negative commands the object pronouns are placed before the verb.

¡No lo haga usted!   *Do not do it!*
¡No se levanten ustedes!   *Do not get up!* (plural)

EJERCICIO 4   Estudiantes y profesores

A. Usted es un(a) estudiante en la clase de español. Dé usted mandatos al profesor
(a la profesora).

Modelo   abrir la ventana
Abra la ventana, por favor.

1. hablar más despacio
2. escribir la respuesta en la pizarra
3. traducir la oración
4. repetir (i, i) la pregunta
5. cerrar (ie) la puerta
6. escuchar a los estudiantes
7. leer la oración otra vez

B. Usted es el (la) profesor(a) de la clase de español. Dé usted mandatos a los estudiantes.

Modelo   estudiar el vocabulario
Estudien el vocabulario.

1. hacer la tarea
2. venir a clase a tiempo
3. aprender los verbos
4. contestar las preguntas
5. ir a la pizarra
6. sentarse, por favor
7. callarse, por favor
8. darse prisa, por favor
9. volver pronto

EJERCICIO 5   En la estación de servicio

Haga usted mandatos afirmativos y negativos al empleado de la estación de servicio según el modelo.

Modelo   llenar (el tanque)
Llénelo.
No lo llene.

1. arreglar (el motor)
2. revisar (el aceite)
3. cambiar (la llanta)
4. limpiar (las ventanas)
5. traerme (el mapa)

EJERCICIO 6   Las direcciones

Dé usted direcciones a unas personas que buscan la universidad.

> Modelo   ir a la calle Juárez.
> > **Vayan a la calle Juárez.**

1. seguir recto cuatro cuadras
2. pararse en la esquina de Juárez y Morelos
3. doblar a la izquierda
4. cruzar el puente
5. pasar cinco semáforos
6. doblar a la derecha en la glorieta
7. seguir tres cuadras más
8. estacionarse enfrente de la biblioteca

EJERCICIO 7   Consejos (*advice*) para Doña Mercedes

Dígale usted a Doña Mercedes lo que debe hacer en cada situación.

> Modelo   Doña Mercedes tiene sed.
> > **¡Beba una Coca-Cola!**

1. Doña Mercedes tiene mucha hambre.
2. Doña Mercedes tiene mucho frío.
3. Doña Mercedes ha recibido un paquete muy grande en el correo.
4. Doña Mercedes tiene un libro muy interesante que usted quiere leer.
5. Doña Mercedes ha trabajado demasiado y está muy cansada.
6. Doña Mercedes está muy enferma.
7. Doña Mercedes tiene tres coches y le falta dinero.
8. Doña Mercedes está caminando por el parque y hay nieve y hielo en el camino.
9. Doña Mercedes ha preparado unas galletas deliciosas y usted tiene hambre.
10. Doña Mercedes tiene ganas de visitar a sus nietos.

IV. Los mandatos nosotros   *The let's commands*

There are two ways in Spanish of expressing the command or suggestion *let's*.

A. El mandato nosotros: subjuntivo

The first person plural—**nosotros** form—of the present subjunctive can be used to form the *let's* command.

Las carreteras modernas y anchas (*wide*) nos llevan
por las ciudades de Latinoamérica. Caracas, Venezuela

¡Comamos!	*Let's eat!*
¡No comamos!	*Let's not eat!*
¡Paguémoslo!	*Let's pay it!*
¡No lo paguemos!	*Let's not pay it!*

NOTE 1: To form the affirmative *let's* command of reflexive verbs, the final **-s** is
dropped before adding the reflexive pronoun **nos**.

levantemos→levantemo + nos→¡Levantémonos!
but the negative is:
¡No nos levantemos!

NOTE 2: The verb **ir** or **irse** has an irregular affirmative *let's* command:

¡Vamos! or **¡Vámonos!** *Let's go!*
But the negative is the same as the subjunctive:
¡No vayamos! or **¡No nos vayamos!** *Let's not go!*

B. El mandato <u>nosotros</u>: <u>vamos a</u>

The affirmative *let's* command can also be formed by using **vamos a** + infinitive.
However, the negative *let's* command returns to the subjunctive form.

¡Vamos a nadar!	*Let's swim!*
But **¡No nademos!**	*Let's not swim!*

EJERCICIO 8   Ideas

Es la primavera y usted y sus amigos han terminado todos sus exámenes finales.
Presente usted ideas de lo que pueden hacer; escuche las respuestas negativas de
su amigo(a).

> Modelo   salir ahora mismo
> **¡Salgamos ahora mismo!**
> **¡No salgamos ahora mismo!**

1. tener una fiesta
2. invitar a todos los alumnos
3. bailar toda la noche
4. beber mucho
5. hacer un viaje

6. ir a la playa
7. jugar al volibol
8. descansar
9. nadar en el océano
10. divertirnos (ie, i)

EJERCICIO 9   ¡Vamos!

Cambie según el modelo.

> Modelo   ¡Durmamos!
> **¡Vamos a dormir!**

1. ¡Comamos!
2. ¡Sentémonos!
3. ¡Levantémonos!
4. ¡Empecemos!
5. ¡Terminemos!

El Río Paraná y las cataratas (*waterfalls*)
de Iguazú forman parte de la
frontera entre el Brasil y la Argentina.

V. Los mandatos tú   *The tú (familiar) commands.*

A. El mandato tú negativo

The negative **tú** command form is the same as the **tú** form of the present subjunctive.

¡No hables!	*Do not speak!*
¡No comas!	*Do not eat!*
¡No lo repitas!	*Do not repeat it!*
¡No fumes!	*Do not smoke!*
¡No te acuestes!	*Do not go to bed!*

EJERCICIO 10   ¡No lo hagas!

Dígale a su hermano(a) menor que no haga las siguientes cosas.

Modelo   comerlo
         ¡No lo comas!

1.	beberlo	7.	salir ahora
2.	hacerlo	8.	usar el tocadiscos
3.	tocarlo	9.	irte
4.	repetirlo	10.	sentarte allí
5.	decirme mentiras	11.	levantarte
6.	hablar tanto	12.	enojarte

refranes: **No digas en secreto lo que no quieres oír en público.**
No hagas a otro lo que no quieres que te hagan.

B. El mandato tú afirmativo

The **tú** affirmative commands do not use the subjunctive form. The regular **tú** command forms are identical to the third person singular (**él**, **ella**, **usted**) form of the present tense indicative.

¡Habla!	*Speak!*
¡Come!	*Eat!*
¡Repítelo!	*Repeat it!*
¡Piensa!	*Think!*
¡Acuéstate!	*Go to bed!*

The irregular **tú** affirmative commands are:

tener	**ten**	decir	**di**
salir	**sal**	ir	**ve**
poner	**pon**	ser	**sé**
venir	**ven**	hacer	**haz**

EJERCICIO 11   ¡Hazlo!

Dígale a su hermano(a) menor que haga las siguientes cosas.

Modelo   comerlo
   ¡Cómelo!

1. tomarlo	12. lavarte
2. dejarlo	13. peinarte
3. encontrarlo (ue)	14. vestirte (i, i)
4. mostrármelo (ue)	15. irte
5. traérmelo	16. decírmelo
6. abrir la puerta	17. ser bueno
7. subir la escalera	18. hacerlo
8. encender (ie) la luz	19. venir aquí pronto
9. darte prisa	20. ponerlo en la mesa
10. callarte	21. salir ahora mismo
11. cepillarte los dientes	22. tener cuidado

EJERCICIO 12   Una persona indecisa

Esta persona no puede decidir lo que quiere. Indique su indecisión según el modelo.

Modelo   Mostrármelo
   ¡Muéstramelo!
   ¡No, no me lo muestres!

1. dármelo	6. volver (ue) mañana
2. prestármelo	7. venderlo
3. comprarlo	8. repetirlo (i, i)
4. llevarlo	9. hacerlo
5. llamarme	10. salir

EJERCICIO 13   Consejos para Juan

Dígale a Juan lo que debe hacer o lo que no debe hacer en cada situación.

Modelos   Juan tiene hambre y está mirando las galletas.
   ¡Cómelas!
   Juan está fumando y empieza a toser (*cough*).
   ¡No fumes!

1. Juan tiene una clase a las diez. Son las diez menos cinco y todavía (*still*) está en la cama durmiendo.
2. Juan tiene un examen muy importante el miércoles y está nervioso.
3. Son las cuatro de la mañana y Juan está tratando de estudiar pero está demasiado cansado.
4. Hace mucho frío y Juan va a salir del dormitorio sin el abrigo.
5. Juan tiene hambre y está mirando un sandwich que ha estado en el escritorio por cinco días.

6. Juan ha bebido muchas cervezas y quiere manejar al centro.
7. Juan está bañándose en la bañera y quiere usar su máquina de afeitar.
8. Juan ha comido muchas cebollas y quiere besar a su novia.

refrán: **Dime con quien andas y te diré quien eres.**

EJERCICIO 14   Repaso

Dé usted los mandatos en las formas indicadas.

		Usted	Ustedes	Nosotros	Tú no	Tú
Modelo	**hablar**	**hable**	**hablen**	**hablemos**	**no hables**	**habla**

1. estudiar
2. terminar
3. escribir
4. sentarse (ie)
5. salir

NOTE: The plural familiar **vosotros** commands, used commonly in Spain, are replaced in Spanish America with the **ustedes** form. The affirmative **vosotros** command is formed by dropping the **-r** from the infinitive and adding **-d** (**hablar→hablad, comer→comed, vivir→vivid**). When the reflexive pronoun **os** is attached to the affirmative form the **d** is dropped (**acostaos**). The negative **vosotros** command is identical to the **vosotros** subjunctive form (**no habléis, no comáis, no viváis, no os acostéis**).

PERSPECTIVA ORIGINAL

1. Una actividad: ¡**Socorro!**

   Have one student leave the classroom. While he or she is absent, rearrange the chairs in the classroom to form a labyrinth. Someone blindfolds the absent student, who is then directed through the labyrinth by commands (go straight ahead, turn to the right, stop, etc.). Have a surprise waiting for the student at the end of the trip!

2. Composición: **Un viaje en automóvil**

   Describe a car trip that you have taken, telling such things as:
   a. when you took the trip;
   b. the route that you took;
   c. things that you saw;
   d. places you visited;
   e. events along the way (flat tire, etc.).

■ PANORAMA CULTURAL *¡Vamos a viajar!*

(In this and the following travel-oriented readings, we have left out marginal vocabulary. Now you will see how well your accumulated knowledge benefits you in comprehending these passages, just as they might appear in advertisements, brochures, and pamphlets. Don't worry if you do not understand every word. You're on your own! ¡Buen viaje!)

Nuevos Horizontes: La Carretera Panamericana

Cada día más personas, en sus campers, vans o automóviles, cruzan la frontera entre los Estados Unidos y México para seguir la extensa Carretera Panamericana y entrar en un mundo de aventuras y nuevas experiencias.

Siguiendo esta carretera, nosotros, los viajeros, pasamos por una vasta cadena de montañas que se extienden por las Américas. Pasamos por México y los países pequeños pero interesantes de la América Central—Guatemala, El Salvador, Honduras, Nicaragua y Costa Rica—llegando por fin a Panamá, término de la primera parte de nuestra aventura. Aquí una densa selva ha impedido la construcción de esta parte de la carretera. Para llegar a Sudamérica vamos en barco con nuestros vehículos desde Panamá hasta un puerto en Colombia o Venezuela, donde, al desembarcar, podemos continuar nuestro camino.

Vamos al oeste para llegar a los Andes y a los panoramas espectaculares del Ecuador y del Perú donde visitamos las capitales de Quito y Lima. En las alturas andinas pasamos de Cuzco con su ambiente colonial e indio a la ciudad antigua de Machu Picchu. Continuamos a la frontera entre el Perú y Bolivia para explorar el misterioso lago Titicaca, origen legendario de los Incas. Seguimos a La Paz, Bolivia, la capital más alta del mundo,* situada a unos 12.000 pies de altura. De allí

_____

*The legal capital of Bolivia is Sucre, but La Paz, a more accessible city, is the actual seat of government.

tomamos una ruta que nos lleva a Chile, donde tenemos que cruzar cientos de millas del desierto Atacama antes de llegar a los valles fértiles de Chile y a la bella capital, Santiago, con el mar Pacífico a un lado y la sierra de los Andes al otro. Cruzamos los Andes por el Paso Bermejo, donde vemos la estatua del Cristo de los Andes, y en dos días, pasada la pampa argentina, estamos en Buenos Aires, una de las ciudades más grandes del mundo. Queremos pasar un rato en esta ciudad cosmopolita antes de continuar el viaje por el Uruguay y la costa del Brasil en camino a Río de Janeiro. Saliendo de la selva tropical vemos esta ciudad maravillosa con sus famosas y bonitas playas de Copacabana e Ipanema, las montañas que bajan al mar, y los rascacielos ultramodernos. Una nueva carretera brasileña nos lleva al interior, a la nueva capital de Brasilia, última parte del extenso viaje.

¿Por qué hacer un viaje en automóvil de más de once mil millas cuando se puede volar? Porque en automóvil conocemos la tierra, conocemos a la gente, y así nos sentimos una parte más íntima del continente. Podemos hacer campamento en las ciudades, en un lugar bonito a la orilla de un lago o río, en una playa solitaria, o en las montañas con vista magnífica de los picos y los valles.

En el campo o en la ciudad, nuestro viaje terrestre más que nada nos da la oportunidad de hacernos amigos del latinoamericano, y de recibir su saludo amable, ''Ya sabes donde tienes tu casa.''

Seguimos la Carretera Panamericana por una tierra llena
(*filled*) de misterios y de aventuras. El desierto de Atacama, Chile

PREGUNTAS

1. ¿Por qué cruzan más personas la frontera entre los Estados Unidos y México?
2. ¿Qué se extiende por todas las Américas?
3. ¿Por qué no han terminado la carretera de Panamá a Colombia?
4. ¿Dónde están Cuzco y Machu Picchu?
5. ¿Dónde está el misterioso lago Titicaca?
6. ¿Cuál es la capital más alta del mundo?
7. ¿Cómo se llama la capital de Chile? ¿Dónde está situada?
8. ¿Cómo es Buenos Aires?
9. ¿Cuáles son las playas famosas de Río de Janeiro?
10. ¿Cómo se llama la nueva capital del Brasil: ¿Dónde está situada?
11. ¿Qué conocemos viajando en automóvil?
12. ¿Dónde podemos hacer campamento?
13. ¿Qué dice el latinoamericano a su amigo, el viajero?

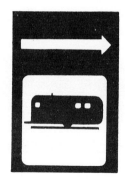

■ INTEGRACIÓN

A. ORAL EXERCISE: **Conversación**
   1. The dialog will be read twice. Listen the first time; the second time pauses will be provided for you to repeat each phrase.
   2. Listen to the statements related to the dialog; indicate if the statements are true or false.

B.   ORAL EXERCISE: VOCABULARY, **la carretera**
Answer the questions on the tape according to the drawings.

1.
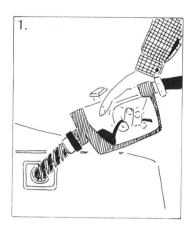

2.

3.

4.

5.

6.

7.
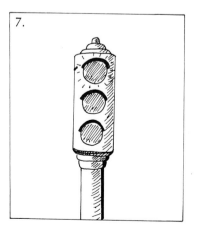

8.

9.
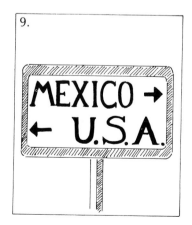

C.   ORAL EXERCISE: usted AND ustedes COMMANDS
Using the cues provided, give an **usted** command to the first person in the picture and an **ustedes** command to both persons.

Example   (tape) estudiar
(your responses)   **¡Estudie usted!**
¡Estudien ustedes!

1.

2.

3.

4.

5.

6.

7.

8.

D. ORAL EXERCISE: **usted** AND **ustedes** COMMANDS + OBJECT
Give the negative form of the affirmative **usted** or **ustedes** commands.

    Example   (tape)   ¡Báñese usted!

             (your response)   **¡No se bañe usted!**

E. ORAL EXERCISE: **usted** AND **ustedes** COMMANDS + OBJECT
Give the affirmative of the negative **usted** or **ustedes** commands.

    Example   (tape)   ¡No se bañe usted!

             (your response)   **¡Báñese usted!**

F. ORAL EXERCISE: GIVING DIRECTIONS

This exercise has two variations.

First, following the dotted lines from 1 to 8, repeat each direction as given.

Second, you give the directions and listen for the tape confirmation.

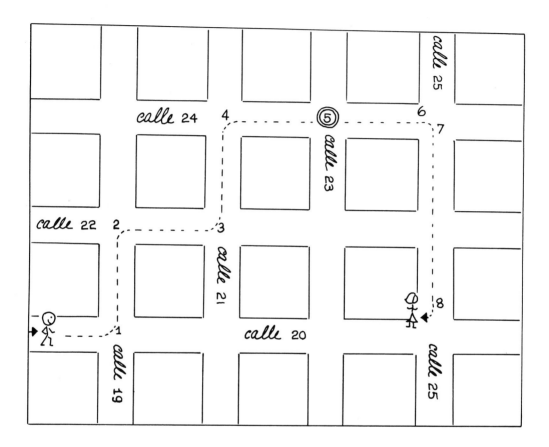

G. ORAL EXERCISE: *Let's* COMMANDS

Using the cues provided, give an affirmative and negative *let's* command appropriate to each drawing.

Example	(tape)	Vamos a jugar al tenis.
	(your response)	**Juguemos al tenis.**

H.   ORAL EXERCISE: **tú** COMMANDS, NEGATIVE
     Give the negative **tú** command form of the infinitives.

     Example   (tape)   comer
                (your response)   **¡No comas!**

I.   ORAL EXERCISE: **tú** COMMANDS, AFFIRMATIVE
     Using the cues provided, give an affirmative **tú** command appropriate to each
     drawing.

Example   (tape)   tener cuidado
          (your response)   **¡Ten cuidado!**

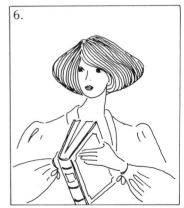

J.   ORAL EXERCISE: **tú** COMMANDS, AFFIRMATIVE TO NEGATIVE
      Give the negative form of the following affirmative **tú** commands.
      Example   (tape)   ¡Cómelo!
                 (your response)   **¡No lo comas!**

K.   WRITTEN EXERCISE: COMPREHENSION, **La carretera panamericana**
      You will hear a short paragraph which will be read twice. Write the answers
      to the three questions that follow.

L.   DICTATION: **La carretera panamericana**
      Write the four sentences you hear. Each sentence will be read three times.

■ REPASO DE VOCABULARIO ACTIVO

Adverbios

despacio
pronto

Sustantivos

el **accidente**	la **gasolina**
el **aceite**	la **glorieta**
el **camino**	la **llanta**
el **camión**	el **parabrisas**
la **carretera**	el **policía**
la **cuadra, manzana**	el **puente**
la **esquina**	el **semáforo**
la **estación de servicio**	el **tanque**
la **frontera**	el **tráfico**

Verbos

arreglar	**funcionar**
callarse	**llenar**
cruzar	**pararse**
doblar	**revisar**
estacionarse	**seguir (i, i)**

Expresiones idiomáticas

ahora mismo	**otra vez**
darse prisa	**tener cuidado**

Expresiones

¡Caramba!	**¡Qué barbaridad!**
¡Claro!	**¡Qué lástima!**
¡Socorro!	**¡Qué lío!**
¡Lo siento mucho!	

Direcciones

a la derecha
a la izquierda
recto, derecho

■ EJERCICIOS DE REPASO

I. Los mandatos usted y ustedes
Cambie según el modelo.

Modelo   hacerlo (usted)
          ¡Hágalo! ¡No lo haga!

1. esperar (usted)
2. usarlo (usted)
3. comerlo (usted)
4. volver (usted)
5. ir (usted)
6. escribirme (ustedes)
7. traérmelo (ustedes)
8. decírmelo (ustedes)
9. levantarse (ustedes)
10. sentarse (ustedes)

II. Los mandatos nosotros
Cambie según el modelo.

Modelo   cantar
          Vamos a cantar; cantemos; no cantemos.

1. bailar
2. hacerlo
3. venderlo
4. acostarnos

III. Los mandatos tú, afirmativos y negativos
Cambie según el modelo.

Modelo   comer
          come; no comas

1. cantar
2. dejarlo
3. dormirte
4. casarte

5. hacerlo   8. venir
6. decirlo   9. irte
7. salir   10. ponerlo aquí

IV. Repaso general

A. Conteste en español en oraciones completas.

1. ¿Qué revisa el empleado en la estación de servicio? ¿Qué llena? ¿Qué limpia? ¿Qué cambia?
2. ¿Qué es lo contrario (*opposite*) de hablar mucho? ¿de romper? ¿de seguir?
3. ¿Qué es lo contrario de rápidamente? ¿y de más tarde?
4. ¿Qué dice usted cuando el motor de su coche no funciona? ¿y cuando hay una tragedia?
5. ¿Cómo se llama la línea que divide dos países?
6. ¿Qué usamos para cruzar un río?
7. ¿Qué miramos para saber cuándo cruzar la calle?
8. ¿Cómo se llama la intersección de dos calles?
9. ¿A quién llama usted cuando hay un accidente?
10. ¿Cómo se llama la carretera que se extiende desde Alaska hasta los países de la América del Sur?

B. Traduzca al español.

1. (usted) Go to the right.
2. (usted) Turn to the left at the corner.
3. (usted) Continue straight ahead four blocks.
4. (ustedes) Wait at the traffic circle.
5. (ustedes) Repeat the address again, please.
6. (ustedes) Don't park there!
7. (tú) Hurry up!
8. (tú) Be careful!
9. (tú) Don't worry!
10. Let's leave right now.

V. Repaso de verbos

A. Escriba oraciones cambiando el verbo a los tiempos indicados.
Use la forma **yo** del verbo, y traduzca las oraciones al inglés.

volver a tiempo

1. presente
2. pretérito
3. imperfecto
4. futuro
5. condicional
6. presente perfecto
7. pasado perfecto

B. Escriba los mandatos y traduzca los mandatos al inglés.

volver

1. usted
2. ustedes
3. nosotros
4. tú (negativo)
5. tú (afirmativo)

CAPÍTULO 13

■ VOCABULARIO *El aeropuerto*

la **aduana**	*customs*	el **pasaporte**	*passport*
el **aeropuerto**	*airport*	el **piloto**	*pilot*
la **agencia de viajes**	*travel agency*	la **reservación**	*reservation*
		la **sala de espera**	*waiting room*
el **asiento**	*seat*	la **sala de reclamación**	*baggage claim*
el **auxiliar de vuelo**	*steward*	**de equipajes**	*room*
el **avión**	*airplane*	el **vuelo**	*flight*
la **azafata**	*stewardess*		
el **cinturón**	*seatbelt*	**abrocharse**	*to fasten*
el **documento**	*document*	**ayudar**	*to help*
la **línea aérea**	*airline*	**despedirse (de) (i, i)**	*to say goodbye (to)*
el **lugar**	*place*	**facturar**	*to check (baggage)*
el **mundo**	*world*	**recoger**	*to pick up*
el **oficial**	*official*	**volar (ue)**	*to fly*
el **pasajero**	*passenger*		

EJERCICIO 1   En el aeropuerto

Conteste en español en oraciones completas.

Según el dibujo:

1. ¿Dónde está el avión?
2. ¿Los pasajeros van a subir al avión o bajar del avión?
3. ¿Cuántos pasajeros hay?
4. ¿Quién está en el avión para ayudar a los pasajeros?
5. ¿Llevan maletas los pasajeros?
6. ¿Cuál es el número del vuelo?

7. ¿Cómo se llama la línea aérea?
8. ¿Es una línea local o internacional?

Preguntas generales:

9. ¿Qué lugares interesantes ha visitado usted?
10. ¿Ha viajado usted en avión? ¿adónde?
11. ¿A qué parte del mundo quiere usted viajar? ¿a Asia? ¿a Europa? ¿al Oriente?
    ¿a África? ¿al Polo Sur?
12. ¿Con qué línea aérea prefiere usted volar?
13. ¿Dónde se pueden hacer reservaciones?
14. Al hacer un viaje largo y por mucho tiempo, ¿es difícil despedirse de sus pa-
    dres? ¿de su novio(a)?
15. ¿Factura usted el equipaje antes o después de subir al avión?
16. ¿Le gustaría a usted ser piloto? ¿auxiliar de vuelo? ¿azafata?
17. Cuando se sientan los pasajeros, ¿qué deben hacer?
18. ¿Prefiere usted sentarse en la sección de fumar o de no fumar?
19. ¿Dónde recoge usted el equipaje?
20. ¿Dónde se revisan los pasaportes o los documentos?

■ CONVERSACIÓN

Un pasajero se acerca a una señorita que está sentada en la sala de espera del aeropuerto.

INSPECCION

aduana

PASAJERO	**Perdóneme, señorita. ¿Está ocupada esta silla?**
PASAJERA	**No, señor. Siéntese.**
PASAJERO	**Acabo de llegar al aeropuerto y me dicen que hay un problema. ¿Sabe usted cuál es?**
PASAJERA	**No estoy segura, pero los oficiales temen que haya una bomba en uno de los aviones.**
PASAJERO	**¡Qué barbaridad! ¡No creo que sea posible!**
PASAJERA	**Tampoco yo. Espero que la encuentren pronto porque si no, ¿quién sabe qué va a pasar?**
PASAJERO	**¡Esto es ridículo! Hay tantos locos en el mundo hoy. Pues, voy a hablar con los oficiales; tal vez tengan más información.**

A passenger approaches a young lady who is seated in the waiting room of the airport.

PASSENGER	*Excuse me, ma'am. Is this chair occupied?*
PASSENGER	*No, sir. Sit down.*
PASSENGER	*I have just arrived at the airport and they tell me that there is a problem. Do you know what it is?*
PASSENGER	*I'm not sure, but the officials are afraid that there is a bomb in one of the air-planes.*
PASSENGER	*How awful! I don't believe that it's possible!*

PASSENGER   *Me either. I hope that they find it soon because if not, who knows what will happen?*

PASSENGER   *This is ridiculous! There are so many crazy people in the world today. Well, I'm going to speak with the officials; perhaps they have more information.*

■ ESTRUCTURA

I. El subjuntivo: en mandatos indirectos *The subjunctive: in indirect (implied) commands*

You have already used the subjunctive form in the last chapter to express a direct command (**¡Hable!**, **¡No vayas!**). An indirect or implied command, however, expresses the speaker's will or bias (desire, preference, recommendation, request, and so on) that someone else do something.

Quiero   **que usted hable.**
Independent clause   Dependent clause
 I want you to speak (that you speak).

Recomiendo   **que no vayas.**
Independent clause   Dependent clause
 I recommend that you not go.

Notice that the independent clause, expressing the speaker's will or bias (I want . . . ; I recommend . . .) is in the indicative, and the dependent clause (. . . you to speak; . . . that you not go) is in the subjunctive. In Spanish the two clauses are linked by **que**.

expression of will/bias + que + subjunctive		
(subject #1—influences)		(subject #2—influenced)

Some expressions indicating indirect or implied command (will/bias) include:

querer (ie)   *to wish, want*

  Él quiere que lo hagas.   *He wants you to do it.*[1]

preferir (ie, i)   *to prefer*

  Prefiero que vengas.   *I prefer that you come.*

recomendar (ie)   *to recommend*

  Ella recomienda que volvamos ahora. *She recommends that we return now.*

insistir (en)   *to insist*

  Insisto (en) que ellos vayan.   *I insist that they go.*

pedir (i, i)²	*to ask for*
Les pedimos que salgan.	*We are asking them to leave.¹*
decir²	*to say, tell*
Ella me dice que lo compre.	*She is telling me to buy it.¹*
es necesario	*it is necessary*
importante	*important*
urgente	*urgent*
mejor	*better*
¡Es necesario (importante, urgente, etc.) **que lo termines ahora!**	*It is necessary (important, urgent, etc.) that you finish it now!*

NOTE 1: Note that in some instances English uses an object plus infinitive after the expression of will/bias whereas Spanish uses **que** + subjunctive.

NOTE 2: **Pedir** and **decir** are most commonly used with indirect object pronouns.

NOTE 3: If there is no change of subject after the expression of will/bias, use the infinitive, not **que** + subjunctive.

Quiero venderlo.   *I want to sell it.*

EJERCICIO 2   ¿Qué quiere usted que hagan?

Dígales a las personas lo que usted quiere que hagan; siga el modelo.

Modelo   Yo quiero que *vayas.* (hacerlo)
Yo quiero que lo hagas.

1. Yo prefiero que Isabel *vaya al aeropuerto.* (venir conmigo) (ayudarme)
2. Yo recomiendo que Rita *busque el horario.* (despedirse de su novio) (facturar el equipaje)
3. Es importante que *lleves los documentos.* (abrocharte el cinturón) (no fumar)
4. Es urgente que Lola y Lupe *compren los boletos.* (llamarme) (subir al avión)
5. Les pido a ustedes que *lleguen temprano.* (hacer reservaciones) (traer los pasaportes)

EJERCICIO 3   Profesores y padres

A. Indique usted lo que el profesor quiere que hagan los estudiantes.

Modelo   recomendar/hacer la tarea
El profesor recomienda que los estudiantes hagan la tarea.

1. recomendar/estudiar mucho
2. decirles/repetir el vocabulario
3. pedirles/llegar a clase a tiempo
4. insistir (en)/no dormir en la clase

5. querer/ir a la pizarra
6. preferir/escribir con pluma

B. Indique usted lo que sus padres quieren que usted haga (o no haga).

> Modelo   querer/vender la motocicleta
> **Mis padres quieren que yo venda la motocicleta.**

1. querer/no gastar tanto dinero
2. preferir/no acostarme tarde
3. insistir (en)/levantarme temprano
4. decirme/no volver después de la medianoche
5. recomendar/limpiar mi cuarto
6. pedirme/no beber mucho vino

EJERCICIO 4   ¡Otra persona!

Cambie las oraciones según el modelo.

> Modelo   Quiero *venderlo.* (Paco)
> **Quiero que Paco lo venda.**

1. Quiero *hacerlo.* (Mónica)
2. Quiero *leerlo.* (mi hermano)

NO ESCONDA
LO QUE NECESITE
VENDER.

ANUNCIELO
EN LOS
CLASIFICADOS
DE
DIARIO
LAS
AMERICAS.

Al llegar al aeropuerto tendremos
que facturar el equipaje. Santiago de Chile

3. Recomiendo *firmarlo*. (el abogado)
4. Recomiendo *arreglarlo*. (mi padre)
5. Prefiero *comprarlo*. (ellos)
6. Prefiero *traerlo*. (ellas)
7. Es necesario *entenderlo*. (tú)
8. Es mejor *verlo*. (tú)

II. El subjuntivo: con expresiones de emoción *The subjunctive: with expressions of emotion*

When the subject expresses emotion/feelings (glad, hopeful, sorry, and so on) about the actions of someone else, Spanish uses the subjunctive in the dependent clause.

> **expression of emotion + que + subjunctive**
> **(subject #1)   (subject #2)**

Some expressions of emotion include:

esperar *to hope*

   Carlos espera que usted juegue bien.   *Carlos hopes that you play well.*

sentir (ie, i) *to feel, regret, be sorry*

   Siento que estés enfermo.   *I am sorry that you are sick.*

temer, tener miedo *to fear, be afraid*

   Temo que haya un problema aquí.   *I am afraid that there is a problem here.*

alegrarse (de) *to be happy, glad*

   Nos alegramos de que estés aquí.   *We are glad that you are here.*

es una lástima *it is a pity, it is a shame*

   Es una lástima que ella no esté aquí.   *It is a shame that she is not here.*

NOTE: If there is no change of subject after the expression of emotion, use the infinitive, not **que** + subjunctive.

Espero ir.   *I hope to go.*

EJERCICIO 5   ¡Vamos a practicar!

Cambie las oraciones según el modelo.

   Modelo   Espero que *venga.* (traer dinero)
          Espero que traiga dinero.

1. Espero que *vuelvas.* (tener cuidado) (decir la verdad)
2. Tememos que ella *llegue tarde.* (no recordar el número) (perder la dirección)
3. Se alegran (de) que *estemos aquí.* (trabajar para Iberia) (ganar mucho dinero)
4. Es una lástima que no *puedan hacerlo.* (querer hacerlo) (saber hacerlo)

EJERCICIO 6   Su reacción

Indique su reacción a cada situación usando **me alegro de que . . .** o **siento que . . .** según los modelos.

   Modelos   No *tenemos* un examen hoy.
          Me alegro de que no tengamos un examen hoy.
          Carlos está enfermo.
          Siento que Carlos esté enfermo.

1. *Hace* sol hoy.
2. *Hace* mucho frío hoy.
3. El examen *es* muy difícil.
4. Mi hermano *tiene* una temperatura de 102°F.

5. El profesor no *está* aquí hoy.
6. Mi hermano mayor *dice* mentiras.
7. El semestre *termina* pronto.
8. *Vamos* a la playa.

III. El subjuntivo: con expresiones de duda, negación e incredulidad *The subjunctive: with expressions of doubt, denial, and disbelief*

When the subject expresses doubt, uncertainty, or disbelief about the actions of someone else, or denies those actions, Spanish uses the subjunctive in the dependent clause.

expression of doubt/denial/disbelief + que + subjunctive
(subject #1)   (subject #2)

Some expressions of doubt, uncertainty, denial, and disbelief include:

dudar	*to doubt*
Dudo que él lo traiga.	*I doubt that he will bring it.*
no estar seguro de	*to be not sure of*
No estoy seguro de que él llegue.	*I am not sure that he will arrive.*
negar (ie)	*to deny*
Ella niega que yo pueda hacerlo.	*She denies that I can do it.*
no creer	*not to believe (think)*
No creo que él venga.	*I do not think that he is coming.*
es posible	*it is possible*
imposible	*impossible*
probable	*probable*
improbable	*improbable*
Es posible que él recuerde el número.	*It is possible that he remembers the number.*
no es verdad, no es cierto	*it is not true*
No es cierto que tenga mucho dinero.	*It's not true that he has a lot of money.*

NOTE 1:   **No dudar**, **no negar**, **creer**, **estar seguro**, **es verdad**, and **es cierto** as expressions of certainty would use the indicative, not the subjunctive.

Creo que él sabe la respuesta.	*I believe (am sure) that he knows the answer.*

NOTE 2:   Expressions of certainty may become expressions of doubt when used in
the interrogative form.

¿Crees que él sepa la respuesta?   *Do you think (not sure) that he knows*
the answer?

EJERCICIO 7   Dudas (*doubts*) y negaciones

Conteste en español según las indicaciones.

Modelo   ¿Qué duda usted? . . . El avión *puede* volar.
          Dudo que el avión pueda volar.

1.   ¿Qué duda usted? . . . El avión *llega* a tiempo.
                         El equipaje *está* en el avión.
2.   ¿Qué niega usted? . . . *Hay* un piloto aquí.
                         Él *tiene* las instrucciones.
3.   ¿Qué no cree usted? . . . *Hace* buen tiempo.
                         Vamos a California.
4.   ¿Qué es posible? . . . *Cambian* el vuelo.
                         Esperan una hora más.
5.   ¿Qué es improbable? . . . *Ganamos* la lotería.
                         Viajamos a Venus.

EJERCICIO 8   Opiniones

Indique si usted cree o duda las declaraciones siguientes.

Modelo   Los coches americanos *son* inferiores.
          Yo creo que los coches americanos son inferiores. (o)
          Yo dudo que los coches americanos sean inferiores.

1.   Los franceses *son* simpáticos.
2.   Los hombres hispánicos *son* machos.
3.   Las mujeres *son* más inteligentes que los hombres.
4.   Los profesores *son* más inteligentes que los alumnos.
5.   Los hombres *prefieren* a las mujeres rubias.
6.   El gobierno (*government*) americano *es* bueno.
7.   La guerra (*war*) *es* inevitable.
8.   La inflación *es* incontrolable.

EJERCICIO 9   ¿Qué crees tú?

Cambie las oraciones usando el subjuntivo o el indicativo según las indicaciones.

Modelo   Carmen *viene* mañana.
          (Dudo que . . .) **Dudo que Carmen venga mañana.**
          (Es cierto que . . .) **Es cierto que Carmen viene mañana.**

1.   Ella *tiene* problemas. (No estoy seguro(a) de que . . .) (Es posible . . .) (Es verdad que . . .)

2. Sus padres lo *saben*. (Niego que . . .) (Es imposible que . . .) (Estoy seguro(a) que . . .)
3. El doctor *está* aquí. (Dudo que . . .) (No dudo que . . .) (No niego que . . .)
4. Ella *puede* salir esta noche. (Es improbable . . .) (No creo que . . .) (Creo que . . .)

EJERCICIO 10   Preguntas generales

Conteste en español en oraciones completas.

1. ¿Siente usted que el profesor esté aquí?
2. ¿Quiere usted que el profesor salga?
3. ¿Qué quiere usted que hagan sus padres?
4. ¿Duda usted que el Presidente diga la verdad?
5. ¿Cree usted que el dinero sea indispensable? ¿y el amor?
6. ¿Teme usted que los exámenes sean difíciles?
7. ¿Es una lástima que esta clase termine pronto?
8. ¿Es urgente que los americanos estudien el ruso? ¿el chino? ¿el español?

EJERCICIO 11   Expresión personal

Complete con frases originales.

> Modelo   Quiero que él . . .
> **Quiero que él salga.**

1. Temo que él . . .
2. Mi novio(a) prefiere que yo . . .
3. Yo siento que usted . . .
4. No creo que ellos . . .
5. Es posible que tú . . .
6. Es una lástima que ella . . .

Muchos europeos visitan las
playas de San Sebastián
en el norte de España.

IV. El subjuntivo: después de los antecedentes indefinidos y negativos *The subjunctive: after indefinite and negative antecedents*

An adjective clause is a clause that functions like an adjective in that it describes a noun or pronoun.

Do you know a man   who wants to buy my car?
independent clause   dependent adjective clause describing the man

In Spanish the subjunctive is used in the dependent adjective clause when the noun or pronoun described (the antecedent) is indefinite or negative.

A. Indefinite antecedent (unidentified, hypothetical, or unknown)

¿Conoce usted un hombre que quiera comprar mi coche?[1]
             unknown   subjunctive
Do you know a man who wants to buy my car?

Sí, conozco a un hombre que quiere comprar su coche.
             known   indicative
Yes, I know a man   who wants to buy your car.

En Chile podemos escapar a las playas
del Pacífico como ésta en Viña del Mar.

B. Negative antecedent (nonexistent)

No conozco a nadie que   quiera comprar su choche.
          negative   subjunctive
I do not know anyone who wants to buy your car.

NOTE 1:   When the direct object noun refers to a hypothetical person, the personal
a is not used.

EJERCICIO 12   Una investigación

Cambie las oraciones según el modelo.

Modelo   Busco a *la persona* que entiende la situación.
           (una persona)
           Busco una persona que entienda la situación.

1.   Necesito a *la secretaria* que habla ruso. (una secretaria)
2.   Busco *al oficial* que revisa los documentos. (un oficial)
3.   Quiero *la computadora* que tiene la información. (una computadora)
4.   Hay *alguien* aquí que sabe usarla. (nadie)
5.   Hay *algo* aquí que es muy extraño (*strange*). (nada)
6.   Tengo *algunos pasaportes* que están falsificados (*forged*). (ningún pasaporte)

EJERCICIO 13   Preguntas generales

Conteste según el modelo.

Modelo   ¿Conoce usted a alguien que tenga mucho dinero?
Sí, conozco a alguien que tiene mucho dinero.
No, no conozco a nadie que tenga mucho dinero.

1. ¿Conoce usted a alguien que cante muy bien?
2. ¿Conoce usted a alguien que pueda escribir a máquina?
3. ¿Tiene usted un amigo que hable español?
4. ¿Tiene usted un pariente que sea muy rico?
5. ¿Tiene usted un(a) compañero(a) de cuarto que entienda sus problemas?
6. ¿Hay un buen restaurante que esté cerca de aquí?

V. El presente perfecto de subjuntivo *The present perfect subjunctive*

Formation:

the present subjunctive of <u>haber</u> (*to have*) + **the past participle**

Modelo   **estudiar**   *to study*

haya estudiado	*I have studied*
hayas estudiado	*You have studied*
haya estudiado	*You have, he, she has studied*
hayamos estudiado	*We have studied*
hayáis estudiado	*You have studied*
hayan estudiado	*You, they have studied*

Ejemplos   Es una lástima que no lo **haya terminado.**
It is a shame that he hasn't finished it.
Espero que **hayas estudiado.**
I hope (that) you have studied.

NOTE: The present perfect subjunctive is translated like the present perfect indicative although it also can have the meaning of *may have.*

EJERCICIO 14   ¡Vamos a practicar!

Cambie los verbos al presente perfecto de subjuntivo según el modelo.

Modelo   Espero que usted *vaya.*
Espero que usted haya ido.

1. Espero que usted *coma* bien.
2. Ella siente que nosotros *estemos* enfermos.

3. No creo que ellos *fumen*.
4. Busco a un alumno que *estudie* mucho.
5. No conozco a nadie que *toque* la guitarra.

EJERCICIO 15   Las contradicciones

Cambie las oraciones según las indicaciones.

    Modelo   Es cierto que Carmen ha salido. (No es cierto . . .)
              No es cierto que Carmen haya salido.

1. Es verdad que se han enojado. (No es verdad . . .)
2. No niegan que yo lo he hecho bien. (Niegan . . .)
3. No dudamos que han tratado de ayudar. (Dudamos . . .)
4. Yo estoy seguro(a) de que ha perdido la cartera. (No estoy seguro(a) de que . . .)
5. Yo sé que han pagado. (Es probable . . .)

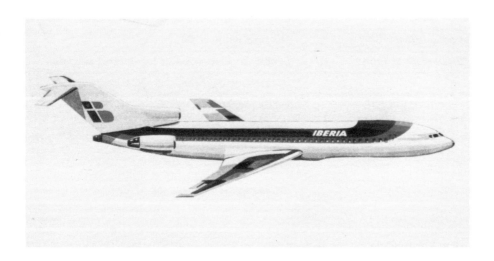

PERSPECTIVA ORIGINAL

1. Mini-drama: **En el aeropuerto**
   You are traveling abroad on a business trip and arrive at the airport. Create a dialog which could be performed as a skit, in which you and the airline official discuss such things as:
   a. The arrival of the flight (on time, late, etc.);
   b. Checking your ticket, luggage, seat preference;
   c. What documents you have to show, location of customs;
   d. Where you can buy reading material, get something to eat, make a phone call.

2. Composición: ¿**El matrimonio?**

Pretend that you are seriously considering becoming engaged. Express the pros and cons of possible marriage to that individual. For example:

a. Your feelings toward the individual, or certain qualities or characteristics of the individual;

b. Your expectations, demands, and/or wants of that individual;

c. Your preferences and hopes about where the two of you will live; what you will do together; where you will work;

d. Recommendations/suggestions that friends and parents may give about your possible engagement.

■ PANORAMA CULTURAL *Vamos a viajar*

Excursiones a Puerto Rico

En nuestro tercer año de operación, ofrecemos lo mejor de Puerto Rico en fantásticas excursiones de 4 y 7 días. La isla, con su belleza natural, sus paisajes pintorescos, sus playas de arena blanca, y sus brisas frescas, tiene excelentes hoteles de lujo y de primera clase. En la histórica ciudad de San Juan, capital de este paraíso, se refleja el pasado español: las calles antiguas y coloniales, el Fuerte del Morro, la Capilla del Cristo, y otros lugares históricos que hacen de San Juan una ciudad encantadora.

Pero San Juan no es todo lo que Puerto Rico tiene que ofrecer. Sus majestuosas y verdes montañas le impresionarán. ¿Qué tal una visita al Yunque que es una de las regiones más lluviosas y bellas del mundo? ¿Cómo le gustaría retirarse a playas tranquilas con el agua tan clara que se ven los colores de los peces? Y si le gustan los mariscos, gozará de un buen filete de pescado en restaurantes donde el ambiente es elegante pero informal. Éstos y muchos tesoros secretos, para que usted los descubra, le esperan en Puerto Rico, la isla del encanto.

El día que guste puede volar a San Juan, y en muy pocas horas está en esta hermosa ciudad del Caribe pasando unas vacaciones fantásticas. Con nosotros usted vuela más rápido, más cómodo, con los mejores horarios, atendido con las tradicionales cortesías. Estudie el itinerario condensado que sigue y llámenos inmediatamente para hacer su reservación en nuestro Vuelo Champagne (de primera clase, champaña gratis a todos los pasajeros adultos, películas y estéreo) o en nuestro Vuelo Capitán (en clase turista donde se siente la atmósfera cordial, tan típica de Puerto Rico).

Reservaciones: Éstas se pueden hacer por teléfono o en persona en nuestras oficinas de boletos o por conducto de su agente de viajes. Se suplica a los pasajeros obtener sus boletos con anticipación al día de vuelo.

Reconfirmación: Los pasajeros deberán reconfirmar sus reservaciones 24 horas antes de la salida de su vuelo, de lo contrario sus reservaciones serán automáticamente canceladas.

Llegada al aeropuerto: Se recomienda que los pasajeros deban presentarse en el aeropuerto una hora antes de la salida.

Una de las atracciones más históricas y populares de Puerto
Rico es la fortaleza El Morro, construída por los españoles.

Transportación: La transportación entre el aeropuerto y la ciudad y viceversa, es por cuenta del pasajero.

Documentación: Ninguna es necesaria para vuelos a Puerto Rico.

Equipaje: Se aceptan 30 kilos de equipaje en vuelos internacionales de Primera Clase. En Clase Turista y Económica 25 kilos.

Itinerario condensado

A San Juan de	Vuelo	Clase	Sale	Llega	Frecuencia
Nueva York	638	P/T	08:00	13:00	Diario
Washington	520	P/T	10:30	14:30	Diario
Miami	120	P/T/E	13:00	15:00	Diario

Equipo Jet Boeing 707
Jet Boeing 720-B
Jet Boeing 737
Jet DC-10

Itinerarios y tarifas sujetos
a cambios sin previo aviso.
Todas las horas especificadas
son locales en las ciudades
correspondientes.

Clases:
P—Primera
T—Turista
E—Económica

Solicite informes
de nuestras tarifas reducidas.
Consulte a su agente de viajes.
Tel: 533-20-00

Tarifa regular de pasaje en dólares (viaje de ida y vuelta)

San Juan	Primera	Turista	Económica
Nueva York	$650	$611	_____
Washington D.C.	$525	$490	_____
Miami	$275	$258	$235

PREGUNTAS

1. ¿Qué clase de hoteles hay en Puerto Rico?
2. ¿De cuántos días son las excursiones?
3. ¿Dónde se refleja el pasado español?
4. ¿Cómo se llama una de las regiones más lluviosas del mundo?
5. ¿Cuál prefiere usted, el Vuelo Champagne o el Vuelo Capitán? ¿por qué?
6. ¿Por qué deben los pasajeros reconfirmar sus reservaciones?
7. ¿Cuánto tiempo antes de la salida deben llegar los pasajeros?
8. ¿Quién tiene la responsabilidad de arreglar la transportación entre el aeropuerto y la ciudad?
9. ¿Qué documentación es necesaria?
10. ¿Cuántos kilos de equipaje pueden llevar los pasajeros de Clase Turista?
11. ¿Cómo se pueden hacer las reservaciones?
12. ¿Cuánto cuesta el viaje de ida y vuelta, Clase Primera entre Washington, D.C., y San Juan?

■ INTEGRACIÓN

A. ORAL EXERCISE: **Conversación**
   1. The dialog will be read twice. Listen the first time; the second time pauses will be provided for you to repeat each phrase.
   2. Listen to the statements related to the dialog; indicate if the statements are true or false.
B. ORAL EXERCISE: VOCABULARY, **el aeropuerto**
   Answer the questions on the tape according to the drawings.

1.

2.

3.

C.   ORAL EXERCISE: THE SUBJUNCTIVE: INDIRECT OR IMPLIED COMMAND.
     Repeat each sentence substituting the verb in the second clause. Use the
     que + subjunctive construction.

>   Example   (tape)   El profesor quiere que yo aprenda. (estudiar)
>   (your response)   **El profesor quiere que yo estudie.**

D.   ORAL EXERCISE: THE SUBJUNCTIVE, INDIRECT OR IMPLIED COMMAND
     Answer the questions on the tape according to the drawings using the
     que + subjunctive construction.

Margarita   Graciela

>   Example   (tape)   ¿Qué quiere Margarita?
>   (your response)   **Margarita quiere que**
>   **Graciela juegue al**
>   **tenis.**

el padre   Juanita   ellos   la profesora

Miguel   Lupe   la madre   Pepito

E.   ORAL EXERCISE: THE SUBJUNCTIVE, EMOTION
     Answer the questions on the tape according to the drawings using the
     que + subjunctive construction.

Carmen

Example   (tape)   ¿Qué siente Carmen?
          (your response)   **Carmen siente que Ma-
                              nuel no esté aquí.**

F.   ORAL EXERCISE: THE SUBJUNCTIVE, DOUBT, DENIAL, AND DISBELIEF
     Answer the questions on the tape according to the drawings using the
     que + subjunctive construction.

	Example	(tape)	¿Qué duda Juan?
		(your response)	**Juan duda que ellos vengan.**

1. ¿Lo hacen?

Alicia

2. ¿Llegan hoy?

Juan

3. ¡No están aquí!

Juan

4. ¡No lo saben!

Alicia

G.   WRITTEN EXERCISE: THE SUBJUNCTIVE
Answer the six questions using a two-clause structure with the subjunctive in
the dependent clause. Each question will be given twice.

  Example   (tape)   ¿Qué prefiere usted?
            (possible answer)   **Prefiero que Juan vaya.**

H.   ORAL EXERCISE: THE SUBJUNCTIVE, INDEFINITE ANTECEDENTS.
Repeat each sentence, then make a new sentence with the cue provided +
que + subjunctive.

  Example   (tape)   ¿Conoce usted a la mujer que habla francés?
                                (una mujer)
            (your response)   **¿Conoce usted una mujer que hable francés?**

I.   ORAL EXERCISE: THE SUBJUNCTIVE, NEGATIVE ANTECEDENTS.
     Repeat each sentence; then make a new sentence with the cue provided +
     que + subjunctive.

          Example   (tape)   Conozco a alguien que tiene un coche. (na-
                                      die)
                     (your response) **No conozco a nadie que tenga un coche.**

J.   ORAL EXERCISE: PRESENT PERFECT SUBJUNCTIVE
     Change the present subjunctive verbs to the present perfect subjunctive.

          Example   (tape)   Dudo que ella venga.
                     (your response) **Dudo que ella haya venido.**

K.   WRITTEN EXERCISE: COMPREHENSION, **Excursiones a Puerto Rico**
     You will hear a short paragraph which will be read twice. Write the answers
     to the three questions that follow.

L.   DICTATION: **Excursiones a Puerto Rico**
     Write the three sentences you hear. Each sentence is repeated three times.

■ REPASO DE VOCABULARIO ACTIVO

Sustantivos

la **aduana**	el **lugar**
el **aeropuerto**	el **mundo**
la **agencia de viajes**	el **oficial**
el **asiento**	el **pasajero**
el **auxiliar de vuelo**	el **pasaporte**
el **avión**	el **piloto**
la **azafata**	la **reservación**
el **cinturón**	la **sala de espera**
el **documento**	la **sala de reclamación de equipajes**
la **línea aérea**	el **vuelo**

Verbos

abrocharse	**insistir (en)**
alegrarse de	**negar (ie)**
ayudar	**recoger**
creer	**recomendar (ie)**
despedirse (de) (i, i)	**sentir (ie)**
dudar	**temer**
esperar	**volar (ue)**
facturar	

Expresiones

es importante	**es probable**
es imposible	**es una lástima**
es improbable	**es urgente**
es mejor	**no es cierto**
es necesario	**no es verdad**
es posible	**no estar seguro de**

■ EJERCICIOS DE REPASO

I. El subjuntivo—mandatos indirectos, expresiones de emoción, duda y negación.

A. Conteste según el modelo.

Modelo   ¿Quieres ayudarlo? (Rita)
          No, quiero que Rita lo ayude.

1.   ¿Quieres llamarla? (Juan)
2.   ¿Prefieres llevarlo? (Lisa)
3.   ¿Recomiendas dejarlo? (ellos)
4.   ¿Insistes en dormirte? (tú)
5.   ¿Esperas irte? (tú)
6.   ¿Sientes estar aquí? (ellos)
7.   ¿Temes perderlo? (ustedes)
8.   ¿Dudas saberlo? (ella)
9.   ¿Niegas tenerlo? (él)

B. Conteste según el modelo.

Modelo   ¿Trabajan mucho? (Es necesario . . .)
          Es necesario que trabajen mucho.

1.   ¿Recuerdan el número? (Es urgente . . .)
2.   ¿Espera el avión? (Es importante . . .)
3.   ¿Prepara la comida? (Es mejor . . .)
4.   ¿Llegamos tarde? (Es una lástima . . .)
5.   ¿Hacemos el viaje? (Es posible . . .)
6.   ¿Terminamos a tiempo? (Es imposible . . .)
7.   ¿Tienen el dinero? (No es verdad . . .)

II. El subjuntivo después de los antecedentes indefinidos y negativos

Cambie la oración según las indicaciones.

Modelo   Conozco a una persona que baila bien.
          (Busco . . .)
          Busco una persona que baile bien.

1. Tengo un amigo que vende computadoras. (Necesito . . .)
2. Vivo en una casa que está cerca del centro. (Quiero comprar . . .)
3. Conozco a un profesor que no da exámenes. (Busco . . .)
4. Tengo algo que te gusta. (. . . nada . . .)
5. Hemos encontrado a alguien que puede hacerlo. (. . . a nadie . . .)

III. El presente perfecto de subjuntivo

Cambie las oraciones según el modelo.

> Modelo   Me alegro que usted *venga*.
> **Me alegro que usted haya venido.**

1. Temo que mi amigo no *llegue*.
2. No creo que tú *vayas*.
3. Es una lástima que nosotros no lo *hagamos*.
4. Es posible que ellos *estén* en el hotel.

IV. Repaso general

A. Conteste en español en oraciones completas.

1. ¿Dónde puedes hacer una reservación para un vuelo a Madrid?
2. Antes de subir al avión, ¿qué debes hacer con el equipaje?
3. ¿Dónde debes mostrar el pasaporte? ¿y a quién?
4. ¿Quiénes están en el avión para ayudar a los pasajeros?
5. ¿Qué deben hacer los pasajeros al sentarse?
6. ¿Qué hacen los pasajeros en la sala de reclamación de equipajes?
7. ¿Qué quieren los profesores que hagan los estudiantes?
8. ¿Se alegra usted de que el semestre termine pronto?
9. ¿Conoce usted a alguien que haya viajado por todo el mundo?
10. ¿Duda usted que esta universidad sea la mejor de todas?

B. Traduzca al español.

1. I want you to come with me.
2. We are asking them to drive more slowly.
3. I hope that you (fam. sing.) haven't spent the money.
4. I am afraid that they will worry.
5. It is important that they see it.
6. It is a shame that we cannot go to the movies tonight.
7. I do not think that he studies enough.
8. I doubt that he has received the gift.
9. Do you (formal sing.) know anyone who has the address?
10. No, I don't know anyone who has it (f.).

V. Repaso de verbos

Escriba oraciones cambiando el verbo a los tiempos indicados. Use la forma **yo** del verbo y traduzca las oraciones al inglés.

venir en avión

1. presente
2. pretérito
3. imperfecto
4. futuro
5. condicional
6. presente perfecto
7. pasado perfecto
8. presente de subjuntivo. **Esperan que** . . .
9. presente perfecto de subjuntivo. **Esperan que** . . .

CAPÍTULO 14

■ VOCABULARIO *El hotel*

el **aire acondicionado**	*air conditioning*	el **recepcionista**	*desk clerk*
la **almohada**	*pillow*		
el **ascensor**	*elevator*	el **baño privado**	*private bath*
la **calefacción**	*heating*	el **cuarto para uno**	*single room*
la **cobija, manta**	*blanket*	el **cuarto doble** (o)	
la **cuenta**	*bill*	de **matrimonio**	*double room*
la **habitación**, el		el **servicio de**	
cuarto	*room*	**cuartos**	*room service*
el **hotel**	*hotel*		
la **información**	*information*	**desayunar**	*to have break-*
la **llave**	*key*		*fast*
la **piscina**	*swimming pool*	**almorzar** (ue)	*to have lunch*
la **planta baja**	*main floor*	**cenar**	*to dine, have*
el **precio**	*price*		*dinner*
la **propina**	*tip*	**quedarse**	*to stay, remain*
el **recado**	*message*		
la **recepción**	*front desk*	**bienvenido**	*welcome*
el **recibo**	*receipt*		
la **sábana**	*sheet*	**primero(a)**	*first*
la **tarjeta de crédito**	*credit card*	**segundo(a)**	*second*
el **vestíbulo**	*lobby*	**tercero(a)**	*third*
		cuarto(a)	*fourth*
el **botones**	*bellboy*	**quinto(a)**	*fifth*
la **camarera**	*waitress*	**sexto(a)**	*sixth*
el **camarero**	*waiter*	**séptimo(a)**	*seventh*
la **criada**	*maid*	**octavo(a)**	*eighth*
el **huésped**	*guest*	**noveno(a)**	*ninth*
el **portero**	*door-man*	**décimo(a)**	*tenth*

349

NOTE 1: **Primero** and **tercero** become **primer** and **tercer** before a masculine singular noun.

NOTE 2: For ordinal numbers higher than **décimo**, the cardinal numbers (**once** and so on) are used.

EJERCICIO 1   En el hotel

Conteste en español en oraciones completas.

Según el dibujo:

1. ¿En qué parte del hotel estamos?
2. ¿Está la recepción en la planta baja o en el primer piso?
3. ¿Qué necesita la mujer?
4. ¿Quién le da la llave a la mujer?
5. ¿Es la mujer de la clase alta o de la clase baja? ¿Cómo lo sabe usted?
6. ¿Quién lleva las maletas?
7. ¿Está el restaurante a la derecha o a la izquierda de la recepción?
8. ¿Cómo se llama el restaurante? ¿Quién es el señor que está allí?
9. ¿Cuántas personas están sentadas en el vestíbulo?
10. ¿Cuántos ascensores ve usted?
11. ¿Qué hora es?
12. ¿Es el hotel elegante o económico?

Preguntas generales:

13. ¿Qué cosas puede usted pedir en la recepción?
14. ¿Le gusta a usted desayunar en los hoteles? ¿almorzar? ¿cenar?
15. ¿Es importante que el hotel tenga una piscina? ¿Por qué?
16. ¿Qué debe tener la habitación cuando hace mucho calor? ¿y cuando hace mucho frío?
17. En un hotel elegante, ¿cuál es el precio de un cuarto doble?
18. En un hotel, ¿paga usted la cuenta al salir o al entrar? ¿Paga usted con tarjeta de crédito? ¿Pide usted un recibo?
19. ¿Prefiere usted quedarse en un hotel o en un motel?
20. Después del primer piso, ¿a qué piso sube usted? ¿después del tercero? ¿del quinto? ¿del séptimo? ¿del noveno?

EJERCICIO 2   Definiciones

Indique la palabra que corresponde a la definición.

1. Un saludo muy cordial, usado cuando una persona simpática llega a su casa, a su país, etc.
2. Lo que usted puede usar para pagar la cuenta si usted no tiene dinero en su cartera.
3. Lo que usamos para subir del primer piso al décimo piso.
4. Lo que usted paga al botones cuando él lleva las maletas al cuarto.
5. Lo que usamos para abrir la puerta de la habitación.

6. Donde ponemos la cabeza al acostarnos.
7. Las cosas que ponemos en la cama cuando la hacemos.
8. La persona que sirve la comida en un restaurante.
9. La señorita que limpia las habitaciones en un hotel.
10. La ayuda que usted recibe cuando llama de su habitación.
11. La persona que visita el hotel.
12. El hombre que abre la puerta principal en un hotel grande y elegante.
13. Lo que cuesta la habitación.
14. Una comunicación que una persona deja para otra persona.

■ CONVERSACIÓN

Alicia y Orlando están de luna de miel y pasan por un pueblo pequeño donde deciden buscar una habitación en un hotel pintoresco.

ORLANDO	**Buenas tardes, señor. Quisiéramos saber si ustedes tienen una habitación para dos personas.**
RECEPCIONISTA	**No creo que tengamos, señor, pero voy a ver si hay una cancelación. Un momento. . . . ¡Ustedes tienen suerte!**
ALICIA	**¿Verdad? ¡Qué bueno! ¿Es posible que la habitación tenga vista al mar? Estamos de luna de miel y preferimos un cuarto que sea muy especial.**
RECEPCIONISTA	**¡Qué casualidad! ¡Tenemos la habitación perfecta para ustedes! Tiene un baño privado, aire acondicionado y . . . ¡la vista al mar!**
ORLANDO	**¡Perfecto! Si tuviéramos más tiempo, nos quedaríamos aquí varios días, pero solamente tenemos el fin de semana.**
RECEPCIONISTA	**Está bien. La habitación está en el segundo piso. El botones tiene la llave y puede subir las maletas.**
ALICIA	**Muchísimas gracias, señor.**
RECEPCIONISTA	**De nada y, en caso de que ustedes necesiten algo, llámenme en seguida. ¡Felicitaciones!**

Alicia and Orlando are on their honeymoon, and they are passing through a small town where they decide to look for a room in a quaint (picturesque) hotel.

ORLANDO	*Good afternoon, sir. We would like to know if you have a room for two persons.*
RECEPTIONIST	*I don't believe that we have, sir, but I'll see if there is a cancellation. One moment. . . . You're in luck!*
ALICIA	*Really? Wonderful! Is it possible to have a room with a view of the sea? We're on our honeymoon and prefer a room that is very special.*
RECEPTIONIST	*What a coincidence! We have the perfect room for you! It has a private bath, air conditioning and. . . . the view of the sea!*
ORLANDO	*Perfect! If we had more time we would stay here several days, but we only have the weekend.*

RECEPTIONIST   *That's fine. The room is on the second floor. The bellboy has the key and he can bring up your suitcases.*

ALICIA   *Thank you so much, sir.*

RECEPTIONIST   *You're welcome and, in the event that you need something, call me right away. Congratulations!*

■ ESTRUCTURA

I. El subjuntivo: después de conjunciones de finalidad y de condición *The subjunctive: after conjunctions of purpose and condition or proviso*

In Spanish the subjunctive is always used in dependent clauses introduced by conjunctions denoting purpose (so that . . .) and condition or proviso (unless . . . , provided that . . . , in case . . .).

Conjunctions denoting purpose and condition or proviso include:

para que

so that, in order that

Voy a hacerlo para que usted lo entienda.

I am going to do it so that you will understand it.

a menos que

unless

A menos que usted lo encuentre, no diga nada.

Unless you find it, do not say anything.

con tal que

provided that

Vamos con tal que él llegue a tiempo.

We are going provided that he arrives on time.

en caso de que

in case

Llámanos en caso de que quieras ir.

Call us in case you want to go.

NOTE: When there is no change of subject, the conjunction **para que** most commonly becomes the preposition **para** + infinitive.

Vuelvo a casa para descansar.

EJERCICIO 3   ¿Para qué van?

Usted va a llevar a sus padres a España. Indique para qué usted los lleva según el modelo.

   Modelo   Voy a llevarlos . . . (*conocer* la ciudad de Madrid)
      Voy a llevarlos para que conozcan la ciudad de Madrid.

1.   Voy a llevarlos . . . (*conocer* a la gente) (*ver* la corrida de toros)
2.   Quiero llevarlos . . . (*poder* ver los museos) (*tomar* muchas fotos)
3.   Espero llevarlos . . . (*comer* una paella) (*beber* el vino magnífico)
4.   Pienso llevarlos . . . (*aprender* el español) (*divertirse*)

EJERCICIO 4   Siempre hay condiciones

Indique usted las condiciones que puedan influir su viaje a España. Use la conjunción entre paréntesis + el subjuntivo para formar una oración.

   Modelo   (a menos que) Vamos a España este verano.
                  Mi tía nos *visita*.
      Vamos a España este verano a menos que mi tía nos visite.

1.   (con tal que) Vamos a España este verano.
            Tenemos el dinero.
2.   (con tal que) Saldremos en julio.
            Encontramos a alguien para alquilar la casa.
3.   (a menos que) Nos quedaremos un mes.
            El cambio *es* malo.
4.   (a menos que) Volveremos en agosto.
            Vamos a Francia también.
5.   (en caso de que) Llevaremos los impermeables.
            Llueve.
6.   (en caso de que) Llevaremos los suéteres.
            Hace fresco por la noche.

II. El subjuntivo: después de conjunciones temporales *The subjunctive: after conjunctions of time*

In Spanish the subjunctive is used when the conjunction of time (when, until, after, and so on) introduces an action or state of being that is future, yet to happen. If future time is not implied (the actions are habitual or in the past), the indicative is used. Note the contrasts in the examples.

En la recepción, los jóvenes buscan información
y hacen planes para el día. México, D. F.

Conjunctions of time include:

cuando   *when*

(future action—subjunctive)
**Cuando vuelvas a casa, tráeme un   *When you return home, bring me a
   regalo.**   gift.*
(habitual action—indicative)
**Cuando mi tío vuelve a casa, siem-   *When my uncle returns home, he al-
   pre me trae un regalo.**   ways brings me a gift.*

hasta que   *until*

(future action—subjunctive)
Me quedaré aquí hasta que llegue.   *I will stay here until he arrives.*
(past action—indicative)
Me quedé aquí hasta que llegó.   *I stayed here until he arrived.*

después de que   *after*

(future action—subjunctive)
**Después de que terminen, vamos a   *After they finish, we are going to a
   un restaurante.**   restaurant.*
(past action—indicative)
**Después de que terminaron, fuimos   *After they finished, we went to a res-
   a un restaurante.**   taurant.*

tan pronto como	*as soon as*

(future action—subjunctive)

Limpiaré el cuarto tan pronto como pueda.	*I will clean the room as soon as I can.*

(past action—indicative)

Limpié el cuarto tan pronto como pude.	*I cleaned the room as soon as I could.*

antes de que[1]	*before*
Debes llamarlo antes de que él salga.	*You should call him before he leaves.*

NOTE 1:   The conjunction **antes de que**, because of its meaning, is always followed by the subjunctive.

NOTE 2:   When there is no change of subject, the conjunctions **hasta que**, **después de que**, and **antes de que** most commonly become the prepositions **hasta**, **después de**, **antes de** + infinitive.

Voy a bañarme antes de salir.
but
Voy a bañarme antes de que él salga.

EJERCICIO 5   Las actividades en el hotel

Indique usted cuando las personas hicieron las siguientes actividades según las indicaciones.

   Modelo   *Fui* a la piscina tan pronto como *pude*. (Iré . . .)
                  Iré a la piscina tan pronto como pueda.

1. *Desayuné* en el hotel tan pronto como *abrieron* el restaurante. (Desayunaré . . .)
2. *Hablé* con el recepcionista tan pronto como *recibimos* el recado. (Hablaré . . .)
3. *Me quedé* en el hotel hasta que Carlos me *llamó*. (Voy a quedarme . . .)
4. *Esperé* en el vestíbulo hasta que Carlos *llegó*. (Voy a esperar . . .)
5. *Di* la propina al botones después de que me *trajo* las maletas. (Voy a dar . . .)
6. *Llamé* al portero después de que *encontramos* la llave. (Voy a llamar . . .)
7. *Puse* el aire acondicionado cuando *volvimos* a la habitación. (Voy a poner . . .)
8. *Pagamos* la cuenta cuando *salimos*. (Vamos a pagar . . .)

EJERCICIO 6   Las actividades del día

Conteste las preguntas según el modelo.

   Modelo   ¿Cuándo vamos a desayunar?
                  cuando/tu padre/despertarse
                  Vamos a desayunar cuando tu padre se despierte.

1. ¿Cuándo vamos al banco?
   antes de que/las tiendas/abrirse
2. ¿Cuándo vamos al centro?
   tan pronto como/tu hermano/volver
3. ¿Cuándo vamos a almorzar?
   después de que/tu tía/salir del museo
4. ¿Cuándo podemos comprar los boletos?
   antes de que/llegar/el autobús
5. ¿Cuándo podemos ir al teatro?
   cuando/nosotros/terminar la cena
6. ¿Para qué volvemos a la habitación?
   para que/tu padre/buscar la tarjeta de crédito
7. ¿Para qué volvemos al hotel?
   para que/tu tía/descansar

III. El imperfecto de subjuntivo *The imperfect (past) subjunctive*

A. Formación

The imperfect subjunctive of **-ar**, **-er**, or **-ir** verbs is formed by using the **ellos** form of the preterit tense indicative minus **-ron** and adding the endings indicated.

stem	+	endings
ellos form of the preterit tense indicative minus **-ron**	+	-ra -ramos -ras -rais -ra -ran

Modelos

hablar	**hablaron**	**habla**	**hablara**
			hablaras
			hablara
			habláramos
			hablarais
			hablaran
comer	**comieron**	**comie**	**comiera**
			comieras
			comiera
			comiéramos
			comierais
			comieran
vivir	**vivieron**	**vivie**	**viviera**
			vivieras
			viviera
			viviéramos
			vivierais
			vivieran

ser	fueron	fue	fuera
			fueras
			fuera
			fuéramos
			fuerais
			fueran
pedir	pidieron	pidie	pidiera
			pidieras
			pidiera
			pidiéramos
			pidierais
			pidieran

NOTE: The imperfect subjunctive is translated like the imperfect indicative although it also can have the meaning of *might* or *would* (since there is no conditional subjunctive).

EJERCICIO 7   ¡Vamos a practicar!

Cambie al imperfecto de subjuntivo según el modelo.

   Modelo   caminar *caminaron* (yo, tú, nosotros)
            caminara, caminaras, camináramos

1. bajar *bajaron* (yo, tú, él)
2. pagar *pagaron* (yo, nosotros, ellos)
3. subir *subieron* (yo, tú, él)
4. escribir *escribieron* (yo, nosotros, vosotros)
5. volver *volvieron* (yo, tú, usted)
6. ir *fueron* (yo, nosotros, ustedes)
7. dar *dieron* (yo, tú, ella)
8. estar *estuvieron* (yo, nosotros, vosotros)
9. hacer *hicieron* (yo, nosotros, ellos)
10. poder *pudieron* (yo, tú, ella)
11. poner *pusieron* (yo, nosotros, ustedes)
12. querer *quisieron* (yo, tú, usted)
13. saber *supieron* (yo, nosotros, ellos)
14. tener *tuvieron* (yo, tú, él)
15. traer *trajeron* (yo, nosotros, ustedes)

En Caracas, Venezuela hay muchos hoteles elegantes que sirven al viajero.

B. La función del imperfecto de subjuntivo

The imperfect subjunctive is used for past events, usually under the same requirements as the present subjunctive:

1. in indirect (implied commands);
2. with expressions of emotion;
3. with expressions of doubt, denial and disbelief;
4. after indefinite and negative antecedents;
5. after conjunctions of purpose and condition or proviso;
6. after conjunctions of time (because of its meaning almost exclusively **antes de que**)

In such sentences if the verb in the independent clause is in a past tense, the imperfect subjunctive is used in the dependent clause.

Quiero que vayas.	*I want you to go.*
Quería que fueras.	*I wanted you to go.*
Dudo que él esté aquí.	*I doubt that he is here.*
Dudaba que él estuviera aquí.	*I doubted that he was here.*

EJERCICIO 8   En años pasados

Conteste las preguntas según las indicaciones usando el imperfecto de subjuntivo.

> Modelo   Cuando estabas en la escuela secundaria (*high school*), ¿qué querías?
> mi novio(a)/*invitarme* a la fiesta
> **Quería que mi novio(a) me invitara a la fiesta.**

1. Cuando estabas en la escuela secundaria, . . .
   ¿qué querías? mis padres/*prestarme* el coche
   mi novio(a)/*llevarme* al cine
   los profesores/no *darme* mucha tarea
   ¿qué esperabas? mi novio(a)/*llamarme*
   nosotros/*hacer* un viaje
   las vacaciones/*ser* muy largas
2. Cuando eras niño(a), . . .
   ¿qué dudabas? mi tío/*volver* del Brasil
   mis padres/*saber* las respuestas
   mi abuela/*poder* entenderme
   ¿qué temías? mis hermanos/*dejarme* en el tren
   Santa Claus/nunca *venir*
   mi gato Rodolfo/*morir*

EJERCICIO 9   Un hotel muy económico.

Hable de su experiencia desafortunada en un hotel muy económico. Cambie las oraciones al pasado según las indicaciones.

> Modelo   *Es urgente* que *llamemos* a la criada.
> (Era urgente . . .) **Era urgente que llamáramos a la criada.**

1. *Es una lástima* que la calefacción no *funcione*. (Era una lástima . . .)
2. *No estoy seguro(a)* de que el baño *tenga* papel higiénico.
   (No estaba seguro(a) . . .)
3. *Tememos* que las sábanas *estén* sucias. (Temíamos . . .)
4. *Es improbable* que el ascensor *suba*. (Era improbable . . .)
5. *Buscamos* a alguien que *arregle* el inodoro. (Buscábamos . . .)
6. *No hay nadie* en la recepción que *conteste* el teléfono. (No había nadie . . .)
7. *Cierro* la ventana para que no *entren* los insectos. (Cerré . . .)
8. *Tenemos* que quedarnos a menos que *encontremos* otro hotel. (Teníamos . . .)

EJERCICIO 10   Expresión personal

Complete con frases originales según el modelo.

Modelo   Prefería que ellos . . .
        Prefería que ellos no lo hicieran.

1. Mi madre insistía que yo . . .
2. Me alegraba de que él . . .
3. Sentía que ellos . . .
4. No era verdad que nosotros . . .
5. Era posible que ella . . .
6. No vi a nadie que . . .
7. Lo terminé antes de que mi hermano . . .

Solicite su tarjeta

y úsela

como si fuera dinero.

IV. Cláusulas con <u>si</u> *If clauses*

When an *if* clause expresses a condition that is contrary to fact or unlikely to occur,
it requires a verb in the past subjunctive.
   The verb in the clause expressing the result is in the conditional.

> **if (si) + imperfect subjunctive + conditional**
> **contrary-to-fact clause   result clause**

Si yo fuera usted, no haría eso.
Si él nos visitara, nos alegraríamos.

If I were you, I would not do that.
If he were to vist us (very unlikely), we
    would be happy.

NOTE: When an *if* clause does not express a condition that is contrary to fact or unlikely to occur, the indicative is used.

Si estoy cansado, no estudio.   *If I am tired, I do not study.*

EJERCICIO 11   Condiciones y resultados

Complete las oraciones combinando las condiciones de la Columna A con los re-
sultados de la Columna B.

Columna A	Columna B
Si yo tuviera el tiempo . . .	. . . tomaría una siesta.
Si yo pudiera . . .	. . . viviría en una isla.
Si él no estuviera en la clase . . .	. . . me alegraría.
Si yo ganara la lotería . . .	. . . volaría a la luna.
Si yo recibiera una ''A'' en español . . .	. . . iría al almacén.
Si yo fuera usted . . .	. . . no trabajaría.
Si el (la) profesor(a) no nos diera exá-	. . . bebería una cerveza.
menes . . .	. . . estaría muy preocupado.
	. . . compraría un condominio.
	. . . nadaría en el océano.
	. . . viajaría a Buenos Aires.

EJERCICIO 12   Si pudiéramos cambiar las circunstancias . . .

Indique usted lo que las personas harían si pudieran cambiar sus circunstancias.

Modelo   Felipe *está* cansado. (*limpiar* la casa)
Si Felipe NO estuviera cansado, limpiaría la casa.

1.   Carlota *es* gorda. (*comer* toda la torta)
2.   Juan *tiene* que estudiar. (*salir* con sus amigos)
3.   Alicia *trabaja*. (*ir* a España)
4.   Linda *está* enferma. (*venir* al cine conmigo)
5.   Ricardo *necesita* el dinero. (no *trabajar* allí)
6.   Elena *vive* en Las Vegas. (*vivir* en San Francisco)

EJERCICIO 13   Preguntas personales

Conteste en español en oraciones completas.

1.   Si no tuvieras que estudiar, ¿qué te gustaría hacer?
2.   Si tuvieras un millón de dólares, ¿qué harías?
3.   Si estuvieras en una tienda de ropa, ¿qué comprarías?
4.   Si estuvieras en un restaurante elegante, ¿qué pedirías?
5.   Si pudieras hacer un viaje, ¿adónde irías?
6.   Si pudieras, ¿a quién besarías?
7.   Si fueras profesor, ¿qué harías?

8. Si tienes diez dólares, ¿qué puedes comprar?
9. Si hace frío, ¿qué llevas?

> refrán: **Si el mozo supiera
> y el viejo pudiera
> no habría cosa
> que no se hiciera.**

V. El pasado perfecto de subjuntivo *The past perfect subjunctive*

Formation:

> **the imperfect subjunctive of <u>haber</u> (to have) + the past participle**

Modelo   **estudiar**   *to study*

hubiera estudiado	*I had studied*
hubieras estudiado	*You had studied*
hubiera estudiado	*You, he, she had studied*
hubiéramos estudiado	*We had studied*
hubierais estudiado	*You had studied*
hubieran estudiado	*You, they had studied*

Ejemplos   Él esperaba que yo lo **hubiera hecho**.
He hoped that I had done it.
Temían que no **hubiéramos llegado**.
They were afraid that we had not arrived.

NOTE: The past perfect subjunctive is translated like the past perfect indicative although it also can have the meaning of *might have* or *would have*.

EJERCICIO 14   ¡Vamos a practicar!

Cambie las oraciones según las indicaciones.

Modelo   *Siento* que lo *hayas* perdido. (Sentía . . .)
Sentía que lo hubieras perdido.

1. *Me alegro* de que lo *hayas* dicho. (Me alegraba . . .)
2. *No creo* que lo *hayan* hecho. (No creía . . .)
3. *Es posible* que ya *haya* salido. (Era posible . . .)
4. *Busco* a alguien que *haya* escrito los ejercicios. (Buscaba . . .)
5. *Niega* que lo *hayamos* pagado. (Negaba . . .)

VI. Correspondencia de los tiempos   *Sequence of tenses*

As you have observed, in Spanish the tense of the verb in the independent indicative clause dictates the tense of the verb in the dependent subjunctive clause. The most frequently used sequences of tenses are:

Independent clause	Dependent clause
present indicative	present subjunctive
future indicative	or
command form	present perfect subjunctive

Quiero que me haga una reservación.
Le pediré que me haga una reservación.
Dígale que me haga una reservación.
Espero que me haya hecho una reservación.

imperfect indicative	imperfect (past) subjunctive
preterit indicative	or
conditional	past perfect subjunctive

Quería que me hiciera una reservación.
Le pedí que me hiciera una reservación.
Esperaba que me hubiera hecho una reservación.
Me haría una reservación si tuviera las fechas.

EJERCICIO 15   En camino al examen final

Lea la conversación y conteste las preguntas en oraciones completas.
    Ana y Roberto están hablando en camino al examen final de español.

ROBERTO   **Ana, ¿sabes que después de que tomemos el examen final es probable que no nos veamos hasta septiembre?**

ANA   **Sí. ¿Por qué no hacemos planes para vernos durante el verano? Me gustaría que vinieras a visitarnos en nuestra casa que está en la playa.**

ROBERTO   **¡Buena idea! Es necesario que yo trabaje casi (*almost*) todo el verano, pero es posible que tome una o dos semanas de vacaciones.**

ANA   **¡Magnífico! Escríbeme cuando llegues a casa para que podamos hacer los planes. Debo confesar, Roberto, que me alegro de que hayas estado en esta clase y de que seamos "amigos españoles".**

ROBERTO   **Gracias, Ana, y ¡buena suerte en el examen!**

1.   ¿Qué era probable?
2.   ¿Qué le gustaría a Ana?
3.   ¿Qué decía Roberto que era necesario?

4.   ¿Qué era posible?
5.   ¿Por qué debía Roberto escribirle a Ana pronto?
6.   ¿De qué se alegraba Ana?

PERSPECTIVA ORIGINAL

1.   Presentación oral: **El agente de viajes**
     Develop a travelog including narration and audio-visual aids describing a place of your choice. Tell:
     a.   Where it is (country, region, climate);
     b.   What it offers (hotels, attractions, recreation, food);
     c.   Appropriate clothing to take;
     d.   How you get there (air, rail, bus, car);
     e.   Cost
2.   Composición: **Un vuelo de fantasía**
     Write a composition in which you imagine what your life would be like in one of the following circumstances:
     a.   If you were to win the lottery;
     b.   If you were to find yourself on a tropical island far from civilization;
     c.   if . . . (original)

■ PANORAMA CULTURAL: *Vamos a viajar*

En el hotel (con el "Jet Set")

Sus vacaciones empiezan al aproximarse a la bahía de Acapulco a bordo de su jet. Su guía estará esperando para recibirle y llevarle a su confortable hotel, situado entre las flores y las palmeras de una sección remota de la playa, donde usted encontrará su espacioso búngalow con vista al mar. La belleza de Acapulco se ve por todas partes: las flores, las nubes, las puestas de sol, los pájaros, las montañas, la playa, el mar y la gente.

Nosotros, preocupados por los problemas diarios no nos damos el tiempo para ver y para participar en la vida. Ahora, por lo menos, durante el tiempo de vacaciones cambiemos de ritmo y divirtámonos.

¿Qué ofrecemos?

El alojamiento: Usted vivirá en unos búngalows que evocan el estilo de las bellas haciendas mexicanas, pero con todo el confort moderno: aire condicionado, camas "Queen-size", baño-ducha, terraza privada, fondo musical F.M. y servicio telefónico directo.

Tarifas:	Plan	Sencillo	Doble (pesos)
	Americano	$9.000.00	$10.600.00*
	Europeo	$7.250.00	$ 7.000.00*

*Los menores de 12 años se benefician de una reducción del 20%.

Acapulco—un paraíso tropical de palmeras, playas
bonitas y brisas suaves (*soft*) del Pacífico. México.

La comida: ¡Para la persona que no nos conoce, la comida es cosa de ima-
ginarse! Primero, el desayuno: es fantástico encontrarse, vestido con traje de
baño, entre la calma y la frescura de las grandes mesas adornadas de flores y frutas,
dulces, pasteles sabrosos, jarras de yogurt, leche fresca, jugo, miel, mantequilla,
chocolate, platillos de huevos frescos y jamón, quesos y mermeladas y el aroma
del más delicioso té o café. El almuerzo: una mañana llena de actividades le abrirá
el apetito para el almuerzo—un bufet donde se encuentra una fantástica selección
de ensaladas, platillos preparados fríos o calientes, de pollo, carne, pescado, legumbres y deliciosos panes con mantequilla. También hay un grill donde podrá
elegir su carne o pescado favorito, acompañado de deliciosos platillos típicos del
país. ¡Hemos olvidado los postres—una avalancha de frutas, pasteles, tortas, al-
mendras! La cena: ¡La cena es otra cosa! Es servida en mesas para dos o cuatro personas con música y luces de velas. Tendrán ustedes el placer de descubrir su menú
con cinco platillos. Y el vino . . . cada día en la comida y la cena, grandes jarras de
vino adornan las mesas. Podrá elegir entre el fresco y ligero vino rosado o el buen
vino del país, rojo y delicioso.

Deportes: podrá practicar los siguientes deportes, ya que todo está comprendido en el precio especial de vacaciones:

(Volibol Ping Pong)	Buceo Libre	Tenis	Surf
Esquí Acuático	Buceo con Botellas	Yoga	Excursiones Paseos en el Mar
Vela	Piscina	Paseos a Caballo	Golf

Hay también actividades extraordinarias como las excursiones en barco, teatro, cursos de danza, noche de baile al son de una orquesta, grupos folklóricos, discoteca y conciertos de música clásica.

Clima: temperatura media de 27 a 34 grados en verano y 22 a 27 grados en invierno.

F (Fahrenheit)

32°	50°	68°	86°	98°	122°	212°
0°	10°	20°	30°	37°	50°	100°

C (Celsius)

Ropa: trajes de baño y sandalias son lo acostumbrado en el hotel. Pero para vestirse, como para todo lo demás, la libertad es absoluta.

Formalidades: pasaportes y la visa de turista mexicana son obligatorios. La lengua oficial es el español. La moneda local es el peso.

PREGUNTAS:

1. ¿Quién estará esperando en el aeropuerto?
2. ¿Dónde está el hotel?
3. ¿Qué debemos hacer durante el tiempo de las vacaciones?
4. ¿Dónde vivirá usted en el hotel?
5. Si usted y su esposo(a) quieren quedarse en el hotel una noche, ¿cuántos pesos les costará?
6. ¿Qué tomará usted en el desayuno? ¿Qué hay para beber?
7. ¿Por qué tendrá usted apetito bueno para el almuerzo?
8. ¿Cómo sirven la cena?
9. ¿Qué tipo de vino sirven?
10. ¿Cuáles son los deportes acuáticos?
11. ¿Qué ropa se ve más en el hotel?
12. ¿Hace frío en Acapulco?
13. ¿Cuál es la moneda local?

■ INTEGRACIÓN

A.   ORAL EXERCISE: **Conversación**
1.   The dialog will be read twice. Listen the first time; the second time pauses will be provided for you to repeat each phrase.
2.   Listen to the statements related to the dialog; indicate if the statements are true or false.

B.   ORAL EXERCISE: VOCABULARY, **el hotel**
Answer the questions on the tape according to the drawings.

5.

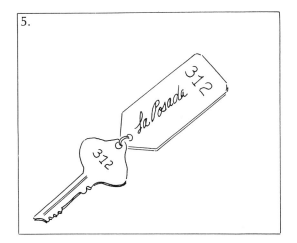

6.

7.

8.

C. ORAL EXERCISE: THE SUBJUNCTIVE, AFTER CONJUNCTIONS OF PURPOSE AND CONDITION OR PROVISO.
   Link the two sentences with the conjunction given on the tape; change the verb in the second clause to the subjunctive.

   Example   (tape)   para que . . .
                                  Voy a trabajar. Él va a la escuela.
            (your response)   **Voy a trabajar para que él vaya a la escuela.**

D. ORAL EXERCISE: THE SUBJUNCTIVE, AFTER CONJUNCTIONS OF TIME
   Link the two sentences with the conjunction given on the tape; change the verb in the dependent clause to the subjunctive.

   Example   (tape)   cuando . . .
                                  Vamos a salir. Llega el tren.
            (your response)   **Vamos a salir cuando llegue el tren.**

E.   ORAL EXERCISE: IMPERFECT SUBJUNCTIVE
Repeat each sentence substituting the verb in the dependent clause according
to the example.

    Example   (tape)   Quería que yo lo pagara. (entender)
          (your response)   **Quería que yo lo entendiera.**

F.   ORAL EXERCISE: IMPERFECT SUBJUNCTIVE
Answer the questions on the tape according to the drawings.

él   ella

    Example   (tape)   ¿Qué quería él?
          (your response)   **Él quería que fueran a
                                        la playa.**

la madre   Pepito

ellos   la profesora

la madre   Martita

¡Mi amigo está enfermo!

Juan

¡Los estudiantes no estudian!

la profesora

¿Hace sol?

Alicia

G. ORAL EXERCISE: *if* CLAUSES

Answer the questions on the tape according to the drawings.

Carlos

Example	(tape)	¿Qué jugaría Carlos si pudiera?
	(your response)	**Carlos jugaría al fútbol si pudiera.**

Juan

Carlota   Lupe

Lupe

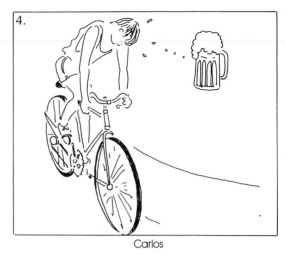

Carlos

Carlota

Pepe   Juanita   Ana

H. WRITTEN EXERCISE: *if* CLAUSES
    Write the *if* clauses you hear on the tape. Each clause will be given twice.
    Complete each sentence with an original conditional clause.

    Example (tape)   Si yo estuviera en un buen restaurante . . .
             (possible response)   **Si yo estuviera en un buen restaurante,
                                   pediría bistec, ensalada y vino.**

I. ORAL EXERCISE: PAST PERFECT SUBJUNCTIVE
    Repeat each sentence, changing the imperfect subjunctive verb in the depen-
    dent clause to the past perfect subjunctive.

    Example (tape)   Dudaba que yo lo hiciera.
             (your response)   **Dudaba que yo lo hubiera hecho.**

J.   WRITTEN EXERCISE: COMPREHENSION, **En el hotel**
You will hear a short paragraph which will be read twice. Write the answers
to the three questions that follow.

K.   DICTATION: **En el hotel**
Write the four sentences you hear on the tape. Each sentence is repeated
three times.

■ REPASO DE VOCABULARIO ACTIVO

Sustantivos

el **aire acondicionado**	la **información**
la **almohada**	la **llave**
el **ascensor**	la **piscina**
el **baño privado**	la **planta baja**
el **botones**	el **portero**
la **calefacción**	el **precio**
el (la) **camarero(a)**	la **propina**
la **cobija, manta**	el **recado**
la **criada**	la **recepción**
el **cuarto doble o de matrimonio**	el **recepcionista**
el **cuarto para uno**	el **recibo**
la **cuenta**	la **sábana**
la **habitación**	el **servicio de cuartos**
el **hotel**	la **tarjeta de crédito**
el **huésped**	el **vestíbulo**

Verbos

almorzar (ue)	**desayunar**
cenar	**quedarse**

Conjunciones

a menos que	**en caso de que**
antes de que	**hasta que**
con tal que	**para que**
cuando	**si**
después de que	**tan pronto como**

Números ordinales

primero(a)	**sexto(a)**
segundo(a)	**séptimo(a)**
tercero(a)	**octavo(a)**
cuarto(a)	**noveno(a)**
quinto(a)	**décimo(a)**

■ EJERCICIOS DE REPASO

I. El subjuntivo: después de conjunciones de finalidad, de condición y de tiempo

Conteste las preguntas según el modelo.

Modelo   ¿Vas al centro?
a menos que/mi amigo/llamarme
(Sí,) voy al centro a menos que mi amigo me llame.

1. ¿Vas al cine? a menos que/nuestra abuela/visitarnos
2. ¿Vas al restaurante? con tal que/yo/tener el dinero
3. ¿Llevas el paraguas? en caso de que/llover
4. ¿Para qué vas? para que/mi hermano/ver el centro
5. ¿Hasta cuándo te quedas? hasta que/el programa/terminar
6. ¿Cuándo te vistes? después de que/Manolito/despertarse
7. ¿Cuándo llamas el taxi? antes de que/nosotros/salir
8. ¿Cuándo vuelves? cuando/ser la medianoche
9. ¿Cuándo sales? tan pronto como/tú/no hacerme más preguntas

II. El imperfecto de subjuntivo

Conteste las preguntas según el modelo.

Modelo   ¿Qué querías? mi hermano/bañarse
Quería que mi hermano se bañara.

1. ¿Qué querías? mi hermano/cepillarse los dientes
2. ¿Qué esperabas? mis padres/no enojarse
3. ¿Qué temías? mis padres/preocuparse
4. ¿Qué dudabas? ellos/recibirlo
5. ¿De qué te alegrabas? ellos/poder venir

III. Cláusulas con si

Haga usted oraciones indicando la condición (si . . .) y lo que usted haría.

Modelo   hacer frío/quedarme en casa
Si hiciera frío, me quedaría en casa.

1. hacer calor/ir a la playa
2. yo tener tiempo/escribir una carta
3. mi novio(a) estar aquí/divertirme
4. yo ser médico(a)/ganar mucho dinero
5. yo poder/salir

IV. El pasado perfecto de subjuntivo

Conteste las preguntas según el modelo.

Modelo   ¿Qué sentías?
Paco/haber estado enfermo
Sentía que Paco hubiera estado enfermo.

1. ¿Qué sentías? Susana/no haber venido
2. ¿Qué negabas? ellos/haberlo hecho
3. ¿Qué era una lástima? nosotros/no haberlo visto
4. ¿Qué no creías? ellos/haberlo comido
5. ¿De qué no estabas seguro(a)? el niño/haberlo roto

V. Repaso general
A. Conteste en español en oraciones completas.

1. ¿Qué personas están en el hotel para ayudarte?
2. ¿Adónde vas para pedir la llave o información? ¿para esperar a tus amigos? ¿para subir de un piso a otro? ¿para nadar?
3. Si hace mucho frío, ¿qué necesitas en la habitación? ¿y en la cama?
4. ¿Qué querías que tus padres te compraran?
5. ¿Para qué querías que te compraran un coche?
6. ¿Adónde viajarías si tuvieras la oportunidad?
7. Si estuvieras en la ciudad de Nueva York, ¿qué harías?
8. Si tuvieras mucho dinero, ¿cómo lo gastarías?

B. Traduzca al español.

1. I will not wash the dishes until you (formal pl.) finish.
2. We are going to the airport as soon as he calls.
3. The airplane will arrive on time provided that the weather is good.
4. Were you (fam. sing.) looking for someone that had the schedule?
5. He asked her to wear the new coat.
6. They doubted that we would remember the flight number.
7. He was glad that we had invited him.
8. If he could, he would stay for two weeks.

VI. Repaso de verbos
Escriba oraciones cambiando el verbo a los tiempos indicados.
Use la forma **yo** del verbo y traduzca las oraciones al inglés.

quedarse en el hotel

1. presente
2. pretérito
3. imperfecto
4. futuro
5. condicional
6. presente perfecto
7. pasado perfecto
8. presente de subjuntivo **Sienten que** . . .
9. imperfecto de subjuntivo **Sentían que** . . .
10. presente perfecto de subjuntivo **Sienten que** . . .
11. pasado perfecto de subjuntivo **Sentían que** . . .

APPENDIX

SPANISH NAMES OF PUNCTUATION MARKS

colon	**dos puntos** (m)
comma	**coma** (f)
exclamation point	**signo de admiración** (¡!)
parenthesis	**paréntesis** (m)
period	**punto** (m)
punctuation	**puntuación** (f)
question mark	**signo de interrogación** (¿?)
semicolon	**punto y coma**

APPENDIX

DEFINITIONS OF GRAMMATICAL TERMS USED IN THE TEXT

adjective A word that limits, describes, or qualifies a noun or pronoun.

adjective dependent clause A clause that functions like an adjective in that it limits, describes, or qualifies a noun.

adverb A word that modifies a verb, adjective, or another adverb by expressing when, where, how, to what degree, or why.

adverbial dependent clause A clause that functions like an adverb in that it modifies the verb by expressing when, where, how, to what degree, or why the action takes place.

article A word, functioning as an adjective before a noun, that is used to limit or specify the noun (such as the definite article *the* in English) or is used when the referent is unspecified (such as the indefinite articles *a, an* in English).

clause A group of words that contains subject, verb, and qualifying words.

command A form of the verb that gives an order or directs with authority.

comparative A second degree of comparison in which a quality or attribute of one person or thing is expressed as being in a greater or lesser degree than that of another.

conditional A verb form expressing a potential, uncompleted action or state of being that takes place future to a past time reference and that is dependent on a condition or conditions.

conditional perfect A verb form expressing a potentially complete action or state of being that took place previous to a past time reference and that was dependent on a condition or conditions.

conjunction A word that connects words, phrases, or clauses. Coordinating conjunctions (such as *and, but, or*) connect expressions of equal importance. Subordinating conjunctions connect independent and dependent (subordinating) clauses.

demonstrative   An adjective or pronoun that points out a particular person or thing.

dependent clause   A subordinate clause that functions as a noun, adjective, or adverb and cannot stand alone.

direct object   A word that denotes the thing or person receiving the action from the verb and answers the question of *what?* or *whom?*

familiar   Describes a form of pronoun or verb used for the second person (*you*) when the style of address is informal or intimate.

formal   Describes a form of pronoun or verb used for the second person (*you*) when the style of address is courteous, conventional, or professional.

future tense   A verb form expressing action or state in time to come.

future perfect tense   A verb form expressing an action or state to be completed in relation to a specified time in the future.

gender   A classification of nouns and pronouns according to sex: masculine, feminine, or neuter in English (biologically based); masculine or feminine in Spanish (linguistically based).

gerund   A verb form (ending in *-ing* in English) expressing ongoing action or condition; used in the progressive tenses.

imperfect tense   A verb form expressing a continuous or repeated past action, a descriptive background in the past, a description of mental or emotional attitudes or characteristics in the past, or time in the past.

independent clause   A principal clause that states the main thought and can stand alone.

indicative   A mood of a verb used to express an act, state, or occurrence as fact.

indirect object   A word indicating the person or thing indirectly affected by the action of the verb (naming the person or thing to which something is given or directed or for which something is done).

infinitive   A simple form of the verb that expresses existence or action without reference to person, number, or tense.

interrogative   Any word that asks a question.

mood   The form a verb takes to denote the speaker's attitude toward the action or state expressed, indicating such action or state as fact (indicative), as supposal, wish, possibility, etc. (subjunctive), as a command, or as a condition.

noun   Any word (substantives) naming or denoting a person, thing, action, quality, etc.

noun dependent clause   A clause that functions like a noun and answers the question *what?*

neuter   A classification for things that are neither masculine nor feminine.

passive voice   A form of the verb indicating that the subject is acted upon and therefore is the receiver or object of the action.

past participle   A form of the verb having qualities of both verb and adjective and indicating a time or condition completed.

past perfect (pluperfect) tense   A verb form expressing action or state as completed before a stated or implied past time.

person   Refers to one of three classes of pronouns or verb forms indicating the subject as the speaker (*I, we*), the person spoken to (*you*), or the person or thing spoken of (*he, she, it, they*).

possessive   Any one of a class of words or constructions expressing possession or ownership.

preposition A relator word that connects a noun, pronoun, or noun phrase to another element of a sentence in terms of cause, time, space, etc.

present participle A form of the verb having qualities of both verb and adjective indicating a time or condition in progress.

present tense A verb form expressing an action as taking place now or as a state existing now, an action that is habitual, or an action or condition that is always true.

present perfect tense A verb form expressing action or state as completed at the time of speaking but without reference to a definite time in the past.

preterit tense A verb form expressing a single completed past action or a past action with a specific limitation of time (beginning and end).

progressive tense A verb form indicating development or continuity of an action.

pronoun A word used in place of or substitution for a noun.

reflexive A form of pronoun that refers back to the subject or doer of the action.

relative pronoun A word that introduces a dependent clause by establishing the relationship between that clause and an antecedent.

stem The part of a word to which endings (denoting person, number, tense, etc.) are added.

subject A word or group of words (generally nouns or pronouns) in a sentence about which something is stated.

subjunctive A mood of a verb used to express the speaker's attitude toward the action or state as subjective (supposal, wish, possibility, denial, disbelief, personal bias, command, etc.).

superlative The third degree of comparison in which a quality or attribute of a person or thing is expressed as being in the greatest or least degree.

tense The form of the verb indicating the time of an action or state of being.

verb A word that expresses an action or state of being.

voice A form of verb indicating whether the subject is performing the action (active) or is being acted upon (passive).

APPENDIX

VERBS

A. Conjugation of regular verbs

Infinitive

-ar	**-er**	**-ir**
hablar, *to speak*	comer, *to eat*	vivir, *to live*

Present Participle

hablando, *speaking*	comiendo, *eating*	viviendo, *living*

Past Participle

hablado, *spoken*	comido, *eaten*	vivido, *lived*

Indicative Mood

Present

I speak, do speak, am speaking, etc.	*I eat, do eat, am eating, etc.*	*I live, do live, am living, etc.*
hablo	como	vivo
hablas	comes	vives
habla	come	vive
hablamos	comemos	vivimos
habláis	coméis	vivís
hablan	comen	viven

Preterit

I spoke, did speak, etc.	*I ate, did eat, etc.*	*I lived, did live, etc.*
hablé	comí	viví
hablaste	comiste	viviste
habló	comió	vivió
hablamos	comimos	vivimos
hablasteis	comisteis	vivisteis
hablaron	comieron	vivieron

Imperfect

I was speaking, used to speak, spoke, etc.	*I was eating, used to eat, ate, etc.*	*I was living, used to live, lived, etc.*
hablaba	comía	vivía
hablabas	comías	vivías
hablaba	comía	vivía
hablábamos	comíamos	vivíamos
hablabais	comíais	vivíais
hablaban	comían	vivían

Future

I will speak, etc.	*I will eat, etc.*	*I will live, etc.*
hablaré	comeré	viviré
hablarás	comerás	vivirás
hablará	comerá	vivirá
hablaremos	comeremos	viviremos
hablaréis	comeréis	viviréis
hablarán	comerán	vivirán

Conditional

I would speak, etc.	*I would eat, etc.*	*I would live, etc.*
hablaría	comería	viviría
hablarías	comerías	vivirías
hablaría	comería	viviría
hablaríamos	comeríamos	viviríamos
hablaríais	comeríais	vivirías
hablarían	comerían	vivirían

Present Perfect

I have spoken, etc.	*I have eaten, etc.*	*I have lived, etc.*
he hablado	he comido	he vivido
has hablado	has comido	has vivido
ha hablado	ha comido	ha vivido
hemos hablado	hemos comido	hemos vivido
habéis hablado	habéis comido	habéis vivido
han hablado	han comido	han vivido

Past Perfect (Pluperfect)

I had spoken, etc.	*I had eaten, etc.*	*I had lived, etc.*
había hablado	había comido	había vivido
habías hablado	habías comido	habías vivido
había hablado	había comido	había vivido
habíamos hablado	habíamos comido	habíamos vivido
habíais hablado	habíais comido	habíais vivido
habían hablado	habían comido	habían vivido

Future Perfect

I will have spoken, etc.
habré hablado
habrás hablado
habrá hablado
habremos hablado
habréis hablado
habrán hablado

I will have eaten, etc.
habré comido
habrás comido
habrá comido
habremos comido
habréis comido
habrán comido

I will have lived, etc.
habré vivido
habrás vivido
habrá vivido
habremos vivido
habréis vivido
habrán vivido

Conditional Perfect

I would have spoken, etc.
habría hablado
habrías hablado
habría hablado
habríamos hablado
habríais hablado
habrían hablado

I would have eaten, etc.
habría comido
habrías comido
habría comido
habríamos comido
habríais comido
habrían comido

I would have lived, etc.
habría vivido
habrías vivido
habría vivido
habríamos vivido
habríais vivido
habrían vivido

Subjunctive Mood
Present Subjunctive

(that) I (may) speak, etc.
hable
hables
hable
hablemos
habléis
hablen

(that) I (may) eat, etc.
coma
comas
coma
comamos
comáis
coman

(that) I (may) live, etc.
viva
vivas
viva
vivamos
viváis
vivan

Imperfect Subjunctive

(that) I might speak, etc.
hablara
hablaras
hablara
habláramos
hablarais
hablaran

(that) I might eat, etc.
comiera
comieras
comiera
comiéramos
comierais
comieran

(that) I might live, etc.
viviera
vivieras
viviera
viviéramos
vivierais
vivieran

Present Perfect Subjunctive

(that) I (may) have spoken, etc.
haya hablado
hayas hablado
haya hablado
hayamos hablado
hayáis hablado
hayan hablado

(that) I (may) have eaten, etc.
haya comido
hayas comido
haya comido
hayamos comido
hayáis comido
hayan comido

(that) I (may) have lived, etc.
haya vivido
hayas vivido
haya vivido
hayamos vivido
hayáis vivido
hayan vivido

Past Perfect (Pluperfect) Subjunctive

(that) I might have spoken, etc.	*(that) I might have eaten, etc.*	*(that) I might have lived, etc.*
hubiera hablado	hubiera comido	hubiera vivido
hubieras hablado	hubieras comido	hubieras vivido
hubiera hablado	hubiera comido	hubiera vivido
hubiéramos hablado	hubiéramos comido	hubiéramos vivido
hubierais hablado	hubierais comido	hubierais vivido
hubieran hablado	hubieran comido	hubieran vivido

Command Forms

usted	hable	coma	viva
	no hable	no coma	no viva
ustedes	hablen	coman	vivan
	no hablen	no coman	no vivan
nosotros	hablemos	comamos	vivamos
	no hablemos	no comamos	no vivamos
tú	habla	come	vive
	no hables	no comas	no vivas
(vosotros)	[hablad]	[comed]	[vivid]
	[no habléis]	[no comáis]	[no viváis]

B. Stem-changing verbs

1. -ar and -er stem-changing verbs: e→ie and o→ue

pensar (ie)   *to think*

Present Indicative: pienso, piensas, piensa, pensamos, pensáis, piensan
Present Subjunctive: piense, pienses, piense, pensemos, penséis, piensen
Commands: piense (usted), piensen (ustedes), pensemos (nosotros), piensa (tú), no
pienses (tú), [pensad (vosotros), no penséis (vosotros)]

volver (ue)   *to return*

Present Indicative: vuelvo, vuelves, vuelve, volvemos, volvéis, vuelven
Present Subjunctive: vuelva, vuelvas, vuelva, volvamos, volváis, vuelvan
Commands: vuelva (usted), vuelvan (ustedes), volvamos (nosotros), vuelve (tú), no
vuelvas (tú), [volved (vosotros), no volváis (vosotros)]

Other verbs of this type are:

entender (ie)   *to understand*
querer (ie)   *to wish, want, love*
cerrar (ie)   *to close*
empezar (ie)   *to begin*
perder (ie)   *to lose*

negar (ie)   *to deny*
nevar (ie)   *to snow*
encender (ie)   *to turn on (light)*
sentarse (ie)   *to sit down*
despertarse (ie)   *to wake up*

poder (ue)   *to be able, can*
recordar (ue)   *to remember*
jugar (ue)   *to play*
encontrar (ue)   *to find*
contar (ue)   *to count, tell*
doler (ue)   *to hurt*

costar (ue)   *to cost*
llover (ue)   *to rain*
sonar (ue)   *to sound, ring*
acostarse (ue)   *to go to bed*
mostrar (ue)   *to show*
almorzar (ue)   *to have lunch*

2.   -ir stem-changing verbs: e→ie and o→ue, u

preferir (ie, i)   *to prefer*

Present Participle: prefiriendo
Present Indicative: prefiero, prefieres, prefiere, preferimos, preferís, prefieren
Preterit: preferí, preferiste, prefirió, preferimos, preferisteis, prefirieron
Present Subjunctive: prefiera, prefieras, prefiera, prefiramos, prefiráis, prefieran
Imperfect Subjunctive: prefiriera, prefirieras, prefiriera, prefiriéramos, prefirierais, prefi-
                              rieran
Commands: prefiera (usted), prefieran (ustedes), prefiramos (nosotros), prefiere (tú), no
                prefieras (tú), [preferid (vosotros), no prefiráis (vosotros)]

dormir (ue, u)   *to sleep*

Present Participle: durmiendo
Present Indicative: duermo, duermes, duerme, dormimos, dormís, duermen
Preterit: dormí, dormiste, durmió, dormimos, dormisteis, durmieron
Present Subjunctive: duerma, duermas, duerma, durmamos, durmáis, duerman
Imperfect Subjunctive: durmiera, durmieras, durmiera, durmiéramos, durmierais, dur-
                              mieran
Commands: duerma (usted), duerman (ustedes), durmamos (nosotros), duerme (tú), no
                duermas (tú), [dormid (vosotros), no durmáis (vosotros)]

Other verbs of this type are:

sentir (ie, i)   *to feel, regret*
divertirse (ie, i)   *to have a good time*
morir (ue, u)   *to die*

3.   ir stem-changing verbs: e→i, i

pedir (i,i)   *to ask for*

Present Participle: pidiendo
Present Indicative: pido, pides, pide, pedimos, pedís, piden
Preterit: pedí, pediste, pidió, pedimos, pedisteis, pidieron
Present Subjunctive: pida, pidas, pida, pidamos, pidáis, pidan
Imperfect Subjunctive: pidiera, pidieras, pidiera, pidiéramos, pidierais, pidieran
Commands: pida (usted), pidan (ustedes), pidamos (nosotros), pide (tú), no pidas (tú), [pe-
                did (vosotros), no pidáis (vosotros)]

Other verbs of this type are:

despedirse de (i, i)   *to say goodbye*
repetir (i, i)   *to repeat*
servir (i, i)   *to serve*
seguir (i, i)   *to follow*
vestirse (i, i)   *to get dressed*

C.   Verbs with orthographic changes

1.   c→qu

tocar   *to play (instrument)*

Preterit: toqué, tocaste, tocó, tocamos, tocasteis, tocaron
Present Subjunctive: toque, toques, toque, toquemos, toquéis, toquen
Commands: toque (usted), toquen (ustedes), toquemos (nosotros), toca (tú), no toques (tú),
               [tocad (vosotros), no toquéis (vosotros)]

Like **tocar** are **buscar**   *to look for* and **sacar**   *to take out*

2.   z→c

empezar (ie)   *to begin*

Preterit: empecé, empezaste, empezó, empezamos, empezasteis, empezaron
Present Subjunctive: empiece, empieces, empiece, empecemos, empecéis, empiecen
Commands: empiece (usted), empiecen (ustedes), empecemos (nosotros), empieza (tú),
               no empieces (tú) [empezad (vosotros), no empecéis (vosotros)]

Like **empezar** are **abrazar**   *to hug* and **cruzar**   *to cross.*

3.   g→gu

pagar   *to pay (for)*

Preterit: pagué, pagaste, pagó, pagamos, pagasteis, pagaron
Present Subjunctive: pague, pagues, pague, paguemos, paguéis, paguen
Commands: pague (usted), paguen (ustedes), paguemos (nosotros), paga (tú), no pagues
               (tú), [pagad (vosotros), no paguéis (vosotros)]

Like **pagar** are **llegar**   *to arrive;* **jugar (ue)**   *to play;* **negar (ie)**   *to deny;* **apagar**   *to turn off.*

4.   gu→g

seguir (i, i)   *to follow, continue*

Present Indicative: sigo, sigues, sigue, seguimos, seguís, siguen
Present Subjunctive: siga, sigas, siga, sigamos, sigáis, sigan

Commands: siga (usted), sigan (ustedes), sigamos (nosotros), sigue (tú), no sigas (tú), [seguid (vosotros), no sigáis (vosotros)]

5. g→j

recoger   *to pick up*

Present Indicative: recojo, recoges, recoge, recogemos, recogéis, recogen
Present Subjunctive: recoja, recojas, recoja, recojamos, recojáis, recojan
Commands: recoja (usted), recojan (ustedes), recojamos (nosotros), recoge (tú), no recojas (tú), [recoged vosotros), no recojáis (vosotros)]

6. i→y

leer   *to read*

Present Participle: leyendo
Preterit: leí, leíste, leyó, leímos, leísteis, leyeron

Like **leer** is **oír**   *to hear;* and in the present participle **traer**   *to bring:* **trayendo; ir**   *to go:* **yendo**.

D. Irregular Verbs

Only the tenses and commands that have irregular forms are given.

andar   *to walk, to go, to run (machinery)*

Preterit: anduve, anduviste, anduvo, anduvimos, anduvisteis, anduvieron
Imperfect Subjunctive: anduviera, anduvieras, anduviera, anduviéramos, anduvierais, anduvieran

conocer   *to know, be acquainted with*

Present Indicative: conozco, conoces, conoce, conocemos, conocéis, conocen
Present Subjunctive: conozca, conozcas, conozca, conozcamos, conozcáis, conozcan

dar   *to give*

Present Indicative: doy, das, da, damos, dais, dan
Preterit: di, diste, dio, dimos, disteis, dieron
Present Subjunctive: dé, des, dé, demos, deis, den
Imperfect Subjunctive: diera, dieras, diera, diéramos, dierais, dieran

decir   *to say, tell*

Present Participle: diciendo
Past Participle: dicho
Present Indicative: digo, dices, dice, decimos, decís, dicen
Preterit: dije, dijiste, dijo, dijimos, dijisteis, dijeron
Present Subjunctive: diga, digas, diga, digamos, digáis, digan
Imperfect Subjunctive: dijera, dijeras, dijera, dijéramos, dijerais, dijeran

Future: diré, dirás, dirá, diremos, diréis, dirán
Conditional: diría, dirías, diría, diríamos, diríais, dirían
Affirmative *tú* command: di

estar   *to be*

Present Indicative: estoy, estás, está, estamos, estáis, están
Preterit: estuve, estuviste, estuvo, estuvimos, estuvisteis, estuvieron
Present Subjunctive: esté, estés, esté, estemos, estéis, estén
Imperfect Subjunctive: estuviera, estuvieras, estuviera, estuviéramos, estuvierais, estuvieran

haber   *to have*

Present Indicative: he, has, ha, hemos, habéis, han
Preterit: hube, hubiste, hubo, hubimos, hubisteis, hubieron
Present Subjunctive: haya, hayas, haya, hayamos, hayáis, hayan
Imperfect Subjunctive: hubiera, hubieras, hubiera, hubiéramos, hubierais, hubieran
Future: habré, habrás, habrá, habremos, habréis, habrán
Conditional: habría, habrías, habría, habríamos, habríais, habrían

hacer   *to do, make*

Past Participle: hecho
Present Indicative: hago, haces, hace, hacemos, hacéis, hacen
Preterit: hice, hiciste, hizo, hicimos, hicisteis, hicieron
Present Subjunctive: haga, hagas, haga, hagamos, hagáis, hagan
Imperfect Subjunctive: hiciera, hicieras, hiciera, hiciéramos, hicierais, hicieran
Future: haré, harás, hará, haremos, haréis, harán
Conditional: haría, harías, haría, haríamos, haríais, harían
Affirmative *tú* command: haz

ir   *to go*

Present Participle: yendo
Past Participle: ido
Present Indicative: voy, vas, va, vamos, vais, van
Preterit: fui, fuiste: fue, fuimos, fuisteis, fueron
Imperfect: iba, ibas, iba, íbamos, ibais, iban
Present Subjunctive: vaya, vayas, vaya, vayamos, vayáis, vayan
Imperfect Subjunctive: fuera, fueras, fuera, fuéramos, fuerais, fueran
Affirmative *tú* command: ve
Affirmative *nosotros* command: vamos

oír   *to hear*

Present Participle: oyendo
Past Participle: oído
Present Indicative: oigo, oyes, oye, oímos, oís, oyen
Preterit: oí, oiste, oyó, oímos, oísteis, oyeron
Present Subjunctive: oiga, oigas, oiga, oigamos, oigáis, oigan
Imperfect Subjunctive: oyera, oyeras, oyera, oyéramos, oyerais, oyeran

poder   *to be able, can*

Present Participle: pudiendo
Present Indicative: puedo, puedes, puede, podemos, podéis, pueden
Preterit: pude, pudiste, pudo, pudimos, pudisteis, pudieron
Present Subjunctive: pueda, puedas, pueda, podamos, podáis, puedan
Imperfect Subjunctive: pudiera, pudieras, pudiera, pudiéramos, pudierais, pudieran
Future: podré, podrás, podrá, podremos, podréis, podrán
Conditional: podría, podrías, podría, podríamos, podríais, podrían

poner   *to put, place*

Past Participle: puesto
Present Indicative: pongo, pones, pone, ponemos, ponéis, ponen
Preterit: puse, pusiste, puso, pusimos, pusisteis, pusieron
Present Subjunctive: ponga, pongas, ponga, pongamos, pongáis, pongan
Imperfect Subjunctive: pusiera, pusieras, pusiera, pusiéramos, pusierais, pusieran
Future: pondré, pondrás, pondrá, pondremos, pondréis, pondrán
Conditional: pondría, pondrías, pondría, pondríamos, pondrías, pondrían
Affirmative *tú* command: pon

querer   *to wish, want*

Present Indicative: quiero, quieres, quiere, queremos, queréis, quieren
Preterit: quise, quisiste, quiso, quisimos, quisisteis, quisieron
Present Subjunctive: quiera, quieras, quiera, queramos, queráis, quieran
Imperfect Subjunctive: quisiera, quisieras, quisiera, quisiéramos, quisierais, quisieran
Future: querré, querrás, querrá, querremos, querréis, querrán
Conditional: querría, querrías, querría, querríamos, querríais, querrían

saber   *to know*

Present Indicative: sé, sabes, sabe, sabemos, sabéis, saben
Preterit: supe, supiste, supo, supimos, supisteis, supieron
Present Subjunctive: sepa, sepas, sepa, sepamos, sepáis, sepan
Imperfect Subjunctive: supiera, supieras, supiera, supiéramos, supierais, supieran
Future: sabré, sabrás, sabrá, sabremos, sabréis, sabrán
Conditional: sabría, sabrías, sabría, sabríamos, sabríais, sabrían

salir   *to go out, leave*

Present Indicative: salgo, sales, sale, salimos, salís, salen
Present Subjunctive: salga, salgas, salga, salgamos, salgáis, salgan
Future: saldré, saldrás, saldrá, saldremos, saldréis, saldrán
Conditional: saldría, saldrías, saldría, saldríamos, saldríais, saldrían
Affirmative *tú* command: sal

ser   *to be*

Present Indicative: soy, eres, es, somos, sois, son
Preterit: fui, fuiste, fue, fuimos, fuisteis, fueron
Imperfect: era, eras, era, éramos, erais, eran

Present Subjunctive: sea, seas, sea, seamos, seáis, sean
Imperfect Subjunctive: fuera, fueras, fuera, fuéramos, fuerais, fueran
Affirmative *tú* command: sé

tener   *to have*

Present Indicative: tengo, tienes, tiene, tenemos, tenéis, tienen
Preterit: tuve, tuviste, tuvo, tuvimos, tuvisteis, tuvieron
Present Subjunctive: tenga, tengas, tenga, tengamos, tengáis, tengan
Imperfect Subjunctive: tuviera, tuvieras, tuviera, tuviéramos, tuvierais, tuvieran
Future: tendré, tendrás, tendrá, tendremos, tendréis, tendrán
Conditional: tendría, tendrías, tendría, tendríamos, tendríais, tendrían
Affirmative *tú* command: ten

traducir   *to translate*

Present Indicative: traduzco, traduces, traduce, traducimos, traducís, traducen
Preterit: traduje, tradujiste, tradujo, tradujimos, tradujisteis, tradujeron
Present Subjunctive: traduzca, traduzcas, traduzca, traduzcamos, traduzcáis, traduzcan
Imperfect Subjunctive: tradujera, tradujeras, tradujera, tradujéramos, tradujerais, tradujeran

traer   *to bring*

Present Participle: trayendo
Past Participle: traído
Present Indicative: traigo, traes, trae, traemos, traéis, traen
Preterit: traje, trajiste, trajo, trajimos, trajisteis, trajeron
Present Subjunctive: traiga, traigas, traiga, traigamos, traigáis, traigan
Imperfect Subjunctive: trajera, trajeras, trajera, trajéramos, trajerais, trajeran

venir   *to come*

Present Participle: viniendo
Present Indicative: vengo, vienes, viene, venimos, venís, vienen
Preterit: vine, viniste, vino, vinimos, vinisteis, vinieron
Present Subjunctive: venga, vengas, venga, vengamos, vengáis, vengan
Imperfect Subjunctive: viniera, vinieras, viniera, viniéramos, vinierais, vinieran
Future: vendré, vendrás, vendrá, vendremos, vendréis, vendrán
Conditional: vendría, vendrías, vendría, vendríamos, vendríais, vendrían
Affirmative *tú* command: ven

ver   *to see*

Past Participle: visto
Present Indicative: veo, ves, ve, vemos, veis, ven
Preterit: vi, viste, vio, vimos, visteis, vieron
Imperfect: veía, veías, veía, veíamos, veíais, veían
Present Subjunctive: vea, veas, vea, veamos, veais, vean
Imperfect Subjunctive: viera, vieras, viera, viéramos, vierais, vieran

ANSWERS TO REVIEW EXERCISES

Ejercicios de repaso: capitulo uno

I. 1. ¿Cómo se llama usted? (¿Cómo te llamas?)
    2. ¿Cómo está usted? (¿Cómo estás?)
    3. Permítame presentar a (name).
    4. Gracias. 5. Mucho gusto. 6. Adiós.

II. A. 1. el lápiz 2. la pluma 3. el cuaderno 4. el papel 5. el ejercicio
       6. Abran el libro. 7. Cierre la puerta, por favor. 8. Repita la respuesta. 9.
       Estudien la lección 10. Escriba la palabra.
    B. 1. the assignment 2. the chalk 3. the desk 4. the chair 5. the window
       6. Answer the question. 7. Go to the blackboard. 8. Read aloud. 9. Sit
       down. 10. Translate the sentence.

III. 1. la mesa, una mesa 2. el profesor, un profesor 3. el libro, un libro 4. la lec-
     ción, una lección 5. la clase, una clase

IV. A. 1. El alumno es americano. 2. La señora Lunares es española. 3. Marta es in-
       teligente. 4. Andrés es un alumno superior.
    B. 1. Las profesoras son mexicanas. 2. Los estudiantes son peruanos. 3. Ana y
       Lupe son sentimentales. 4. Las clases son interesantes.

V. 1. Los libros no son interesantes. 2. El profesor no es ridículo. 3. La pregunta no
    es importante. 4. Andrés no es un alumno extraordinario.

VI. 1. ocho, diez, doce, catorce, diez y seis (dieciséis), diez y ocho, veinte, veinte y dos
       (veintidós), veinte y cuatro, veinte y seis.
    2. siete, nueve, once, trece, quince, diez y siete, diez y nueve, veinte y uno, veinte y
       tres, veinte y cinco, veinte y siete.
    3. martes, miércoles, jueves, viernes, sábado.

VII. A.   1. Es la una y cuarto (quince) de la tarde.
2. Son las nueve y media de la noche.   3. Son las cuatro menos veinte de la mañana.   4. Son las seis menos diez de la mañana.

B.   1. El programa es a las doce y cuarto (quince).
2. El drama es a las ocho.   3. El examen es a las once.   4. La excursión es a las siete menos cuarto.

Ejercicios de repaso: capitulo dos

I.   1. abuela   2. sobrino   3. prima   4. tío   5. nieta   6. novio

II.   1. Nosotros somos simpáticos.   2. Ella es abogada.   3. Tú eres bonita.   4. Ustedes son jóvenes.   5. Yo soy fuerte.   6. Vosotros sois americanos.

III.   1. Nosotros estamos en la playa.   2. Tú estás enfermo(a).   3. Yo estoy aburrido(a).   4. Las ventanas están abiertas.   5. Ella está triste.   6. Vosotros estáis cansados.

IV.   1. Ella es japonesa.   2. La casa es grande.   3. Yo estoy cansado(a).   4. Ellos son médicos.   5. Nosotros estamos muy mal.   6. Nosotros somos jóvenes.   7. Cecilia está aquí.   8. Tú eres rico(a).   9. El carro es viejo.   10. Ustedes están en la clase.

V.   1. Roberto y Pablo van a la escuela.   2. Nosotros vamos a las montañas.   3. Tú vas a la clase.   4. El señor Martínez va a Caracas.   5. Yo voy a Los Ángeles.   6. Vosotros vais a Sevilla.

VI.   A.   1. Yo soy inteligente, guapo(a), etc. . . .   2. Mi madre es bonita, alta, etc. . . .
3. El presidente es rico, viejo, etc. . . .   4. Mis amigos son simpáticos, jóvenes, etc. . . .   5. Estoy muy bien, gracias (enfermo) (cansado), etc. . . .   6. No, no estoy en la playa.   7. Sí, estamos en la universidad.   8. (Sí,) (No, no) voy al hospital.   9. (Sí,) (No, no) vamos al campo.   10. No, el profesor no va a la clase los domingos.

B.   1. (Yo) estoy cansado(a).   2. Los estudiantes (alumnos) no están aquí.   3. La abuela es vieja.   4. Los hermanos son altos.   5. La puerta está cerrada.   6. (Nosotros) somos americanos; (ella) es alemana.   7. (Él) no es médico.   8. (Ella) es la hija del profesor.   9. (Ella) es rica, inteligente y hermosa.   10. ¿Vas (tú) al campo?

Ejercicios de repaso: capitulo tres

I.   1. Mi abuela no bebe (compra) (necesita) cerveza.
2. ¿Vives (comes) (estudias) en el dormitorio?
3. Yo llego (trabajo) (camino) temprano por la mañana.
4. Los profesores abren (venden) (estudian) los libros.
5. Nosotros hablamos (aprendemos) (escribimos) mucho en la clase.

II.   1. ¿Qué bebe?   2. ¿Dónde vive?   3. ¿De dónde es?   4. ¿Cuándo trabaja?   5. ¿Adónde va?   6. ¿Cuántos carros necesita?   7. ¿Cómo te llamas?   8. ¿Cuál es tu clase favorita?

III.   1. treinta y tres   2. cuarenta y cuatro   3. cincuenta y cinco   4. sesenta y seis   5. setenta y siete   6. ochenta y ocho   7. noventa y nueve   8. cien

IV. A. 1. Como huevos, tocino, pan, etc. . . . 2. Como pollo, patatas, ensalada, etc.
. . . 3. Mi bebida favorita es la leche, etc. . . . 4. Mi postre favorito es el helado, etc. . . . 5. Mi fruta favorita es la naranja, etc. . . . 6. Estudio por la
noche, etc. . . . 7. Sí, aprendemos el español. 8. (Sí,) (No, no) escribimos todos los ejercicios. 9. Vivo en (*name of city*). 10. (Sí,) (No, no) llego a clase a
tiempo todos los días.

B. 1. (Yo) necesito crema y azúcar en mi café. 2. ¿Necesita la sopa sal y pimienta? 3. (Nosotros) bebemos vino todos los días. 4. ¿Venden (ustedes)
hielo? 5. (Nosotros) compramos frijoles, salchicha y sandía. 6. ¿Adónde vas
ahora? 7. ¿Por qué escribimos los ejercicios? 8. ¿Cuándo llegan (ellos)? 9.
¿Quién trabaja en la ciudad? 10. (Él) va a vivir aquí.

Ejercicios de repaso: capítulo cuatro

I. 1. Veo a mi amigo. Veo la casa. Veo a los muchachos.
2. Conozco a la señorita. Conozco al Señor Lorca. Conozco la ciudad de Nueva York.

II. 1. Yo traduzco (tú traduces) las preguntas. 2. Yo traigo (ella trae) el cuaderno.
3. Yo salgo (nosotros salimos) esta noche. 4. Yo hago (vosotros hacéis) errores.
5. Yo pongo (ustedes ponen) el azúcar en el té. 6. Yo veo (usted ve) al médico.
7. Yo doy (ellas dan) cincuenta pesos. 8. Yo conozco (nosotros conocemos) a Carmen. 9. Yo sé (tú sabes) cocinar.

III. 1. Carlos, ¿duermes en la clase? 2. Carlos, ¿pides una cerveza? 3. Carlos, ¿repites
la conversación? 4. Carlos, ¿juegas al béisbol? 5. Carlos, ¿prefieres descansar?
6. Carlos, ¿puedes salir ahora? 7. Carlos, ¿quieres cerrar la ventana? 8. Carlos,
¿vuelves temprano?

IV. 1. Yo vengo a la fiesta. 2. Nosotros venimos de la ciudad. 3. Yo digo la verdad.
4. Nosotros no decimos mentiras. 5. Yo tengo dolor de cabeza. 6. Nosotros tenemos dolor de estómago.

V. 1. Tengo hambre. 2. Tengo sed. 3. Tienen sueño. 4. Tiene miedo. 5. Tenemos calor. 6. Tenemos frío. 7. Tengo razón. 8. No tienes razón.

VI. A. 1. Las partes de la cara son: los ojos, la nariz, la boca, etc. . . . 2. Uso los bra-
zos, las piernas, etc. . . . 3. Salgo a las ocho y media, etc. . . . 4. Traigo galletas, etc. a la fiesta. 5. (Sí,) (No, no) duermo bien todas las noches. 6. Preferimos los profesores fáciles (difíciles). 7. (Sí) (No, no) vengo a clase a tiempo todos los días. 8. Tengo (*number*) años. 9. Tengo que trabajar, estudiar, etc.
10. Tengo ganas de ir a la playa, etc.

B. 1. (Yo) conozco a Roberto. 2. (Yo) sé nadar bien. 3. (Yo) pongo las plumas y
los lápices en el escritorio. 4. ¿Qué quieres (tú) hacer ahora? 5. (Yo) puedo
tocar el piano. 6. ¿Juegas (tú) al fútbol? 7. (Él) busca al niño; ve al niño; mira
al niño. 8. (Nosotros) tenemos ganas de ir a las montañas. 9. (Yo) tengo que
limpiar la casa hoy. 10. (Yo) tengo mucha hambre.

Ejercicios de repaso: capítulo cinco

I. 1. El niño está durmiendo la siesta. 2. Estoy leyendo la novela. 3. Ellos están escribiendo los ejercicios.   4. Estamos comiendo en el restaurante.   5. ¿Estás mirando la televisión?   6. ¿Están escuchando ustedes la radio?

II.   1. Yo trabajé.   2. Yo salí temprano.   3. Tú compraste un abrigo.   4. Tú comiste en el restaurante.   5. Ella llevó un vestido nuevo.   6. Ella leyó el menú.   7. Nosotros bailamos.   8. Nosotros bebimos vino.   9. Vosotros escuchasteis la música. 10. Vosotros abristeis los regalos.   11. Ellos manejaron.   12. Ellos volvieron a casa.

III.   1. Es la niña del señor Martínez.   2. Es el esposo de Elena.   3. Es la cartera de Felipe.   4. Es la bolsa de Carlota.

IV.   1. Es mi pluma. La pluma es mía.   2. Son sus joyas. Las joyas son suyas (de ella). 3. Son tus regalos. Los regalos son tuyos.   4. Es nuestro coche. El coche es nuestro.   5. Es vuestra casa. La casa es vuestra.   6. Es su radio. La radio es suya (de ellos).

V.   A.   1. Estoy escribiendo, etc.   2. Las mujeres llevan faldas, blusas, vestidos, etc. a un restaurante elegante.   3. Los hombres llevan trajes, camisas, corbatas, etc. a un restaurante elegante.   4. Voy a llevar dos suéteres, un abrigo, botas, etc. 5. Voy a llevar un traje de baño, un sombrero, etc.   6. La manzana es roja, la lechuga es verde y el maíz es amarillo.   7. (Sí,) (No, no) estudié mucho anoche.   8. (Sí, (No, no) comí toda la torta.   9. (Sí,) (No, no) bebimos toda la leche.   10. Mis libros de español están en la mesa, etc.   11. Los tres grupos más grandes de hispanoamericanos son los chicanos, los puertorriqueños y los cubanos.

B.   1. ¡(Yo) no estoy fumando!   2. (Nosotros) estamos repitiendo las oraciones. 3. (Ella) llevó la blusa roja ayer.   4. (Yo) llamé a las seis.   5. (Ellos) no entendieron la lección.   6. Mis padres van de compras mañana.   7. (Él) busca (está buscando) su abrigo y el mío.   8. Sus zapatos nuevos son muy caros.   9. (Ellos) compraron nuestra casa la semana pasada.   10. Sus amigos están aquí ahora.

Ejercicios de repaso: capítulo seis

I.   1. Ana, ¿durmió usted bien? Carlos y Felipe, ¿durmieron ustedes bien?   2. Ana, ¿prefirió usted el helado de fresa? Carlos y Felipe, ¿prefirieron ustedes el helado de fresa? 3. Ana, ¿pidió usted el arroz con pollo? Carlos y Felipe, ¿pidieron ustedes el arroz con pollo?   4. Ana, ¿repitió usted el poema? Carlos y Felipe, ¿repitieron ustedes el poema?

II.   1. Yo vine (usted vino) a clase temprano.   2. Yo no supe (ellos no supieron) la respuesta.   3. Ella no pudo (nosotros no pudimos) hacer el ejercicio.   4. Vosotros tuvisteis (tú tuviste) que salir.   5. Yo anduve (mi hermana anduvo) en motocicleta. 6. Nosotros fuimos (mis primos fueron) al museo.   7. Yo di (mis padres dieron) el dinero.   8. Carmen no estuvo (mis amigos no estuvieron) allí.   9. Nosotros quisimos (tú quisiste) volver a casa.

III.   1. junio, julio, agosto. Hace calor. Hace sol.   2. septiembre, octubre, noviembre. Hace fresco. Hace viento.   3. diciembre, enero, febrero. Hace frío. Nieva.

IV.   1. doscientos veinte y dos.   2. trescientos treinta y tres.   3. cuatrocientos cuarenta y cuatro.   4. quinientos cincuenta y cinco.   5. seiscientos sesenta y seis.   6. setecientos setenta y siete.   7. ochocientos ochenta y ocho.   8. novecientos noventa y nueve.   9. mil novecientos ochenta y seis.   10. mil ochocientos noventa y ocho.

V.   A.   1. Pedí bistec, en salada, etc.   2. Fui a las montañas, etc.   3. Estudié, comí, dormí, etc.   4. Puse los libros en el escritorio, etc.   5. Yo dije (los alumnos dijeron, etc.) que no hay examen hoy.   6. La fecha de la Navidad es el veinte y cinco de diciembre. La fecha del Año Nuevo es el primero de enero.   7. Veo taxis, autobuses, etc.   8. Puedo ir de compras en los almacenes, las tiendas, las joyerías, las librerías, etc.   9. Puedo visitar los museos, las catedrales, las iglesias, etc.   10. Los romanos y los moros contribuyeron más a la formación de la España moderna.   11. Madrid es la capital de España.   12. Francia está al norte de España, Portugal está al oeste, y el continente de África está al sur.

   B.   1. Los niños durmieron aquí toda la noche.   2. (Él) fue a Madrid y visitó el museo.   3. Mi madre puso las galletas en la mesa.   4. (Ellos) vinieron temprano y trajeron las bebidas.   5. (Él) espera (está esperando) un taxi.   6. ¿Piensan (ellos) visitar España?   7. ¿Qué tiempo hace en Venezuela?   8. ¿Cuál es la fecha?   9. ¿Hay una peluquería en el centro?   10. Mi reloj no anda bien.

VII.   1. a) El duerme en el sofá. b) El está durmiendo en el sofá. c) El durmió en el sofá.   2. a) El pide un favor. b) El está pidiendo un favor. c) El pidió un favor.   3. a) Yo hago los ejercicios. b) Yo estoy haciendo los ejercicios. c) Yo hice los ejercicios.   4. a) Yo digo la verdad. b) Yo estoy diciendo la verdad. c) Yo dije la verdad.

Ejercicios de repaso: capítulo siete

I.   1. Yo abrazaba a mi abuela.   2. Yo corría en el parque.   3. Tú amabas a tu perro.   4. Tú leías muchos libros.   5. El pedía galletas.   6. El andaba en bicicleta.   7. Nosotros queríamos jugar.   8. Nosotros visitábamos a nuestros tíos.   9. Vosotros salíais por la tarde.   10. Vosotros caminabais en la avenida.   11. Ustedes comían mucho helado.   12. Ustedes hablaban todo el día.

II.   1. El verano pasado fui a la playa.   2. Todos los sábados iba a la playa.   3. Una vez nadé en el lago.   4. Muchas veces nadaba en el lago.   5. Todos los días veía el programa.   6. Anoche vi el programa.   7. El año pasado hice el viaje.   8. Todos los veranos hacía el viaje.   9. La semana pasada llamé por teléfono.   10. Todos los domingos llamaba por teléfono.

III.   A.   1. Hace dos años que trabajo aquí.   2. Hace tres meses que juego al tenis.   3. Hace una semana que conozco a María.
   B.   1. Salí hace dos horas.   2. Limpié la casa hace tres días.   3. Fui al cine hace un mes.

IV.   1. Compré este vestido, ése y aquél.   2. Prefiero estas galletas, ésas y aquéllas.   3. Conozco a esta mujer, ésa y aquélla.   4. Abrí estos regalos, ésos y aquéllos.

V.   A.   1. Veo vacas, cerdos, caballos, gallinas, etc.   2. Los animales domésticos son los perros, los gatos, etc.   3. Veo árboles, hierba, flores, etc.   4. Veo desiertos, océanos, mares, lagos, ríos, valles, montañas, etc.   5.   Cuando era niño, jugaba, dormía, etc.   6.   Los estudiantes hablaban, comían, etc., cuando el profesor entró.   7.   Sí, este libro es mío. (No, este libro no es mío.)   8.   El Cid es el héroe de un famoso poema épico español.   9.   El compañero de Don Quijote de la Mancha se llama Sancho Panza.   10.   El personaje famoso de dos dramas españoles, y gran amante de las mujeres es Don Juan.

B.   1.   (Ella) era muy bonita.   2.   Era la medianoche.   3.   Las estrellas estaban en el cielo.   4.   (Yo) dormía cuando mi padre volvió.   5.   (Ellos) llegaron a las diez.   6.   Hace cinco meses que estudio el español.   7.   (Yo) comí hace una hora.   8.   Esto es fácil.   9.   Estas flores son bonitas.   10.   Estos caballos son nuestros; ése es de mi hermano.

VI.   1.   a) Soy estudiante. b) Fui estudiante. c) Era estudiante.   2.   a) Estoy en el desierto. b) Estuve en el desierto. c) Estaba en el desierto.   3.   a) Voy al lago. b) Fui al lago. c) Iba al lago.

Ejercicios de repaso: capitulo ocho

I.   1.   Juanita y Mario tendrán muchos hijos.   2.   Yo alquilaré una casa en Acapulco.   3.   Mi esposo(a) y yo pasaremos un año en Europa.   4.   Tú harás un viaje a Madrid.   5.   Vosotros volveréis a la universidad.   6.   Carlota irá a Italia.   7.   Alberto será millonario.   8.   Nosotros podremos ir a la luna.   9.   Ustedes trabajarán en Nueva York.

II.   1.   Yo compraría un Mercedes.   2.   Alicia daría el dinero a los pobres.   3.   Pepe pondría el dinero en el banco.   4.   Nosotros viajaríamos a la América del Sur.   5.   Mónica y Lupe saldrían de la universidad.   6.   Tú tendrías muchas vacaciones.   7.   Ustedes comerían en restaurantes muy caros.

III.   1.   No, no hay nadie en la bañera.   2.   No, no hay nada en la estufa.   3.   No, no tengo ninguna toalla limpia.   4.   No, yo nunca preparo la comida.   5.   No, yo no lavo los platos tampoco.

IV.   A.   1.   En mi casa hay: sala, comedor, cocina, dos alcobas, dos baños, etc.   2.   En la alcoba hay: cama, armario, espejo, alfombra, etc.   3.   En el baño hay: inodoro, bañera, lavabo, toallas, etc.   4.   En la mesa hay: cuchillos, cucharas, tenedores, platos, vasos, servilletas, etc.   5.   Este sábado dormiré mucho, trabajaré, iré al centro, etc.   6.   En Acapulco iría a la playa, bailaría en las discotecas, etc.   7.   Manejo rápidamente (lentamente).   8.   La ciudad de México es la capital de México.   9.   Antes de la llegada de los españoles, los mayas y los aztecas eran las dos civilizaciones de más importancia.   10.   Hernán Cortés conquistó a los aztecas en 1521.

B.   1.   (Yo) vendería el coche por $900.   2.   ¿Alquilarías (tú) esa casa?   3.   (Él) dijo que (ellos) saldrían el primero de abril.   4.   (Nosotros) pondremos la alfombra en la alcoba.   5.   (Yo) encenderé la luz.   6.   (Ellos) buscarán las gafas (los vasos).   7.   ¿Quién traerá la torta?   8.   (Yo) conozco a alguien que tiene un tocadiscos.   9.   Hay algo en mi sopa.   10.   (Él) probablemente llegará la semana que viene.

V.   1.   a. Tengo que esperar. b. Tuve que esperar. Tenía que esperar. d. Tendré que esperar. e. Tendría que esperar.   2.   a. Salgo a las cinco. b. Salí a las cinco. c. Salía a las cinco. d. Saldré a las cinco. e. Saldría a las cinco.

Ejercicios de repaso: capitulo nueve

I. A. 1. Antonio va a llevarme. 2. Antonio va a llevarnos. 3. Antonio va a llevarlos. 4. Antonio va a llevarlas. 5. Antonio va a llevarlos. 6. Antonio va a llevarlo. 7. Antonio va a llevarte.

B. 1. Sí, las perdí, 2. Sí, lo deposité. 3. Sí, los saqué. 4. Sí, la pagué. 5. Sí, las apagué.

II. 1. Ella nos escribe. 2. Ella te escribe. 3. Ella os escribe. 4. Ella le escribe. 5. Ella le escribe. 6. Ella acaba de escribirme. 7. Ella acaba de escribirles. 8. Ella acaba de escribirles. 9. Ella acaba de escribirte. 10. Ella acaba de escribirnos.

III. 1. Andrés me la mostró, 2. Andrés me los mostró. 3. Andrés nos lo mostró. 4. Andrés nos las mostró. 5. Voy a prestársela (a ella). 6. Voy a prestárselo (a ellos). 7. Voy a prestárselos (a ellas). 8. Voy a prestárselas (a él).

IV. 1. Le (te)(nos) gusta la sandía. 2. Me (le)(nos) gusta comer. 3. No les (no me)(no le) gustan las habichuelas. 4. ¿Les (os)(te) gustan los camarones?

V. A. 1. Escribo la dirección en el sobre. 2. Puedo comprar sellos, mandar paquetes, echar las cartas al correo, etc. 3. Puedo depositar el dinero, cobrar un cheque, cambiar dinero, etc. 4. Puedo encontrar máquinas de escribir, calculadoras, computadoras, etc. 5. Cuando empiezo un proyecto, (no) trato de terminarlo. 6. (Sí) (No, no) le presto mi libro de español. (o) (Sí,) (No, no) se lo presto. 7. Sí, alguien me escribió la semana pasada. (No, nadie me escribió.) 8. Me gusta cantar, bailar, jugar al fútbol, etc. 9. Sí, hay comidas que no me gustan. No me gusta(n) . . . 10. Diego Rivera es un famoso pintor mexicano de temas indio-revolucionarios. 11. Un ejemplo de la música mexicana es el mariachi; un ejemplo de arquitectura es el Museo de Antropología, un ejemplo del baile es el Ballet Folklórico.

B. 1. (Ella) no me conoce. 2. (Yo) los veo. 3. (Yo) estoy haciéndolo. 4. (Él) nos mandó el paquete. 5. (Yo) quiero dárselo (a ella). 6. (Él) me lo vendió. 7. (Yo) se lo leí (a ellos). 8. No nos gustan esas legumbres.

IV. 1. a. Le doy el regalo. b. Le di el regalo. c. Le daba el regalo. d. Le daré el regalo. e. Le daría el regalo. 2. a. Se lo traigo. b. Se lo traje. c. Se lo traía. d. Se lo traeré. e. Se lo traería.

Ejercicios de repaso: capitulo diez

I. 1. Mi compañero de cuarto se despierta. 2. Yo me levanto. 3. Tú te quitas los pijamas. 4. Vosotros os vestís. 5. Nosotros nos preocupamos por el examen. 6. Ana y Susana se enojan. 7. Yo me voy. 8. Yo acabo de bañarme. 9. Felipe acaba de secarse. 10. Tú acabas de lavarte la cara. 11. Nosotros acabamos de afeitarnos. 12. Ellos acaban de cepillarse los dientes. 13. Yo acabo de peinarme. 14. Pedro acaba de ponerse los calcetines.

II. A. 1. Quiero el bistec sin cebollas. 2. Carlos está delante de María. 3. Vamos a hablar después de comer. 4. El gato está encima del sofá. 5. Vivimos lejos de las montañas. 6. El perro duerme fuera de la casa.

B.   1. Trabajé para el Banco Nacional.   2. Trabajé para ir a México.   3. Salí para México a las cinco.   4. Estuve allí por diez días.   5. Compré la blusa para Lupe.   6. Pagué setecientos pesos por la blusa.

III. A.   1. Después de levantarme, me lavo, me visto, me peino, etc.   2. Para lavarme el pelo uso champú; para secarme el pelo uso una toalla o un secador de pelo; para peinarme uso un peine; para cepillarme los dientes uso un cepillo de dientes.   3. (Sí) (No, no) quiero casarme.   4. (Name) se sienta al lado, (name) se sienta detrás y (name) se sienta delante de mí.   5. Después de comer voy a estudiar, etc.; después de estudiar voy a mirar la televisión, etc.   6. (Sí) (No, no) limpiaría la casa por mi madre.   7. (Sí) (No, no) me gustaría ir a España contigo (con usted), con ellos y con él (ella).   8. Se puede estudiar en la biblioteca, etc.   9. Los países de la América Central son: Guatemala, Belice, Honduras, El Salvador, Nicaragua, Costa Rica y Panamá.   10. Son unidos por la lengua y la cultura españolas.   11. Los países de las Antillas de lengua española son: Cuba, Puerto Rico y la República Dominicana.   12. Puerto Rico es un "commonwealth."

B.   1. (Ellos) se enamoraron y se comprometieron.   2. (Nosotros) tenemos que acostarnos a las diez y media.   3. A las seis (yo) me levanto, me baño, me afeito y me visto.   4. ¿Dónde se vende pasta de dientes?   5. (Nosotros) debemos terminar el libro para mañana.   6. Caminamos por el bosque y por el río.   7. (Yo) necesito ir al banco por cheques de viajeros.   8. (Yo) voy a escuchar un disco en vez de mirar la televisión.   9. (El) vive cerca de mí.   10. (Yo) no quiero ir contigo.   11. ¿Es este regalo para nosotros? ¡No! Es para él.

IV.   1. a. Me despierto. b. Estoy despertándome. c. Me desperté. d. Me despertaba. e. Me despertaré. f. Me despertaría.   2. a. Se viste. b. Está vistiéndose. c. Se vistió. d. Se vestía. e. Se vestirá. f. Se vestiría.

Ejercicios de repaso: capítulo once

I.   1. Yo he caminado por la ciudad de Quito.   2. Nosotros hemos visitado la catedral.   3. Tú has tomado fotos de la plaza.   4. Inés ha ido al mercado público.   5. Vosotros habéis comprado muchas flores.   6. Mis amigos han escrito muchas tarjetas postales.   7. Usted ha viajado por los Andes.   8. Yo he subido las montañas.   9. Tú has visto la selva.   10. Ustedes han conocido el puerto de Guayaquil.   11. Yo he hecho muchas cosas interesantes.   12. Nosotros hemos vuelto a los Estados Unidos.

II.   1. El profesor lo había dicho.   2. Habíamos hecho la tarea.   3. Lupe y Cecilia habían escrito los ejercicios.   4. Había estudiado el vocabulario.   5. ¿Los habías terminado?   6. ¿Ustedes habían leído la lectura?

III.   1. Los hombres son tan inteligentes como las mujeres.   2. Roberto es tan alto como Miguel.   3. Lisa es tan simpática como Rosario.   4. Los Gutiérrez tienen tanto dinero como los Gómez.   5. Los Gutiérrez tienen tantos coches como los Gómez.   6. Los Gutiérrez tienen tanta ropa como los Gómez.

IV.   1. La clase de inglés es más difícil. La clase de matemáticas es la más difícil de las tres.   2. Mi hermano es más fuerte. Mi primo es el más fuerte de los tres.   3. El helado es mejor. La torta de chocolate es la mejor de las tres.

V. A. 1. Hay boletos de ida y vuelta, de primera y de segunda clase.   2. Se compran boletos en la taquilla y periódicos en el quiosco.   3. Las busco en el horario.   4. Puedo buscarlo en la guía telefónica o puedo llamar a la operadora.   5. Hoy yo he estudiado, he comido, etc.   6. (Sí) (No, no) hemos estudiado bastante (demasiado).   7. Sí, soy tan simpático(a) como mi profesor(a).   8. Soy menor (mayor) que mi profesor(a).   9. Era la civilización Inca.   10. El río principal se llama el Amazonas, y la cordillera principal se llama los Andes.   11. Buenos Aires es la capital de la Argentina; Bogotá es la capital de Colombia; Caracas es la capital de Venezuela.

B. 1. La novela "Don Quijote" fue escrita por Cervantes.   2. Los discos están rotos.   3. ¿Has dejado tus libros en el cuarto?   4. (Yo) he hecho la maleta.   5. (Él) ya ha marcado el número.   6. (Nosotros) no lo hemos terminado.   7. (Yo) estoy tan triste como él.   8. (Él) leyó tantas revistas como yo.   9. (Nosotros) trabajamos tanto como ellos.   10. (Él) es más pobre que yo.

VI. 1. Lo hago. I do (am doing) it.   2. Estoy haciéndolo. I am doing it.   3. Lo hice. I did it.   4. Lo hacía. I was doing (used to do) it.   5. Lo haré. I will do it.   6. Lo haría. I would do it.   7. Lo he hecho. I have done it.   8. Lo había hecho. I had done it.

Ejercicios de repaso: capítulo doce

I. 1. ¡Espere! ¡No espere!   2. ¡Úselo! ¡No lo use!   3. ¡Cómalo! ¡No lo coma!   4. ¡Vuelva! ¡No vuelva!   5. ¡Vaya! ¡No vaya!   6. ¡Escríbanme! ¡No me escriban!   7. ¡Tráiganmelo! ¡No me lo traigan!   8. ¡Díganmelo! ¡No me lo digan!   9. ¡Levántense! ¡No se levanten!   10. ¡Siéntense! ¡No se sienten!

II. 1. Vamos a bailar; bailemos; no bailemos.   2. Vamos a hacerlo; hagámoslo; no lo hagamos.   3. Vamos a venderlo; vendámoslo; no lo vendamos.   4. Vamos a acostarnos; acostémonos; no nos acostemos.

III. 1. canta; no cantes   2. déjalo; no lo dejes   3. duérmete; no te duermas   4. cásate; no te cases   5. hazlo; no lo hagas   6. dilo; no lo digas   7. sal; no salgas   8. ven; no vengas   9. vete; no te vayas   10. ponlo aquí; no lo pongas aquí

IV. A. 1. Revisa el aceite, etc.; llena el tanque; limpia el parabrisas; cambia la llanta, etc.   2. Lo contrario de hablar mucho es callarse; lo contrario de romper es arreglar; lo contrario de seguir es pararse.   3. Lo contrario de rápidamente es despacio (o lentamente); lo contrario de más tarde es ahora mismo.   4. Cuando el motor de mi coche no funciona digo "¡Caramba!" etc.; cuando hay una tragedia digo "lo siento mucho," etc.   5. Se llama la frontera.   6. Usamos un barco.   7. Miramos el semáforo.   8. Se llama la esquina.   9. Llamo al policía.   10. Se llama la Carretera Panamericana.

B. 1. Vaya a la derecha.   2. Doble a la izquierda en la esquina.   3. Siga recto (derecho) cuatro cuadras.   4. Esperen en la glorieta.   5. Repitan la dirección otra vez, por favor.   6. ¡No se estacionen allí!   7. ¡Date prisa!   8. ¡Ten cuidado!   9. ¡No te preocupes!   10. Salgamos (vamos a salir) ahora mismo.

V. A. 1. Vuelvo a tiempo. I am returning (return) on time.   2. Volví a tiempo. I returned on time.   3. Volvía a tiempo. I used to return (was returning) on time.   4. Volveré a tiempo. I will return on time.   5. Volvería a tiempo. I would return on time.   6.   He vuelto a tiempo. I have returned on time.   7. Había vuelto a tiempo. I had returned on time.

B.   1. ¡Vuelva! Return! 2. ¡Vuelvan! Return! 3. ¡Volvamos! (Vamos a volver.) Let's return.   4. ¡No vuelvas! Don't return!   5. ¡Vuelve! Return!

Ejercicios de repaso: capitulo trece

I. A.   1. No, quiero que Juan la llame.   2. No, prefiero que Lisa lo lleve.   3. No, recomiendo que ellos lo dejen.   4. No, insisto en que tú te duermas.   5. No, espero que tú te vayas.   6. No, siento que ellos estén aquí.   7. No, temo que ustedes lo pierdan.   8. No, dudo que ella lo sepa.   9. No, niego que él lo tenga.

B.   1. Es urgente que recuerden el número.   2. Es importante que espere el avión.   3. Es mejor que prepare la comida.   4. Es una lástima que lleguemos tarde.   5. Es posible que hagamos el viaje.   6. Es imposible que terminemos a tiempo.   7. No es verdad que tengan el dinero.

II.   1. Necesito un amigo que venda computadoras.   2. Quiero comprar una casa que esté cerca del centro.   3. Busco un profesor que no dé exámenes.   4. No tengo nada que te guste.   5. No hemos encontrado a nadie que pueda hacerlo.

III.   1. Temo que mi amigo no haya llegado.   2. No creo que tú hayas ido.   3. Es una lástima que nosotros no lo hayamos hecho.   4. Es posible que ellos hayan estado en el hotel.

IV. A.   1. Puedo hacer una reservación en el aeropuerto o en la agencia de viajes.   2. Debo facturarlo.   3. Debo mostrarlo en la aduana, al oficial.   4. El auxiliar de vuelo y la azafata están en el avión para ayudar a los pasajeros.   5. Deben abrocharse el cinturón.   6. Los pasajeros recogen el equipaje.   7. Los profesores quieren que los estudiantes estudien, hagan la tarea, vengan a clase, etc.   8. (Sí) (No, no) me alegro de que el semestre termine pronto.   9. Sí, conozco a alguien que ha viajado (No, no conozco a nadie que haya viajado) por todo el mundo.   10. Sí, dudo que esta universidad sea (No, no dudo que esta universidad es) la mejor de todas.

B.   1. (Yo) quiero que vengas conmigo.   2. (Nosotros) les pedimos que manejen más despacio.   3. (Yo) espero que (tú) no hayas gastado el dinero.   4. (Yo) temo (tengo miedo) que (ellos) se preocupen.   5. Es importante que (ellos) lo vean.   6. Es una lástima que (nosotros) no podamos ir al cine esta noche.   7. No creo que (él) estudie bastante.   8. (Yo) dudo que (él) haya recibido el regalo. ¿Conoce usted a alguien que tenga la dirección?   10. No, (yo) no conozco a nadie que la tenga.

V.   1. Vengo en avión. I am coming by plane.   2. Vine en avión. I came by plane.   3. Venía en avión. I was coming (used to come) by plane.   4. Vendré en avión. I will come by plane.   5. Vendría en avión. I would come by plane.   6. He venido en avión. I have come by plane.   7. Había venido en avión. I had come by plane.   8. Esperan que venga en avión. They hope that I come by plane.   9. Esperan que haya venido en avión. They hope that I have come by plane.

Ejercicios de repaso: capítulo catorce

I.   1. (Sí) voy al cine a menos que nuestra abuela nos visite.   2. (Sí) voy al restaurante con tal que yo tenga el dinero.   3. (Sí) llevo el paraguas en caso de que llueva. 4. Voy para que mi hermano vea el centro.   5. Me quedo hasta que el programa termine.   6. Me visto después de que Manolito se despierte.   7. Llamo al taxi antes de que nosotros salgamos.   8. Vuelvo cuando sea la medianoche.   9. Salgo tan pronto como tú no me hagas más preguntas.

II.   1. Quería que mi hermano se cepillara los dientes.   2. Esperaba que mis padres no se enojaran.   3. Temía que mis padres no se preocuparan.   4. Dudaba que ellos lo recibieran.   5. Me alegraba de que ellos pudieran venir.

III.   1. Si hiciera calor, iría a la playa.   2. Si (yo) tuviera tiempo, escribiría una carta. 3. Si mi novio(a) estuviera aquí, me divertiría.   4. Si (yo) fuera médico(a), ganaría mucho dinero.   5. Si (yo) pudiera, saldría.

IV.   1. Sentía que Susana no hubiera venido.   2. Negaba que ellos lo hubieran hecho. 3. Era una lástima que nosotros no lo hubiéramos visto.   4. No creía que ellos lo hubieran comido.   5. No estaba segura(a) de que el niño lo hubiera roto.

V.   A.   1. El recepcionista, el botones, la camarera, etc. están en el hotel para ayudarme.   2. Voy a la recepción; voy al vestíbulo; voy al ascensor; voy a la piscina.   3. Necesito calefacción en la habitación y una cobija en la cama. 4. Quería que mis padres me compraran un coche, etc.   5. Quería que me compraran un coche porque necesito un coche en la universidad, etc. 6. Viajaría a Europa, etc., si tuviera la oportunidad.   7. Si estuviera en la ciudad de Nueva York, iría al teatro, etc.   8. Si tuviera mucho dinero, lo gastaría en ropa, coches, etc.

B.   1. (Yo) no lavaré los platos hasta que (ustedes) terminen.   2. (Nosotros) vamos al aeropuerto tan pronto como (él) llame.   3. El avión llegará a tiempo con tal que haga buen tiempo.   4. ¿Buscabas a alguien que tuviera el horario?   5. (Él) le pidió que llevara el abrigo nuevo.   6. (Ellos) dudaban que (nosotros) recordáramos el número del vuelo.   7. (Él) se alegraba que (nosotros) lo hubiéramos invitado.   8. Si (él) pudiera, se quedaría por dos semanas.

VI.   1. Me quedo en el hotel. I am staying at the hotel.   2. Me quedé en el hotel. I stayed at the hotel.   3. Me quedaba en el hotel. I was staying (used to stay) at the hotel. 4. Me quedaré en el hotel. I will stay at the hotel.   5. Me quedaría en el hotel. I would stay at the hotel.   6. Me he quedado en el hotel. I have stayed at the hotel. 7. Me había quedado en el hotel. I had stayed at the hotel.   8. Sienten que me quede en el hotel. They are sorry that I am staying at the hotel.   9. Sentían que me quedara en el hotel. They were sorry that I stayed at the hotel.   10. Sienten que me haya quedado en el hotel. They are sorry that I have stayed at the hotel.   11. Sentían que me hubiera quedado en el hotel. They were sorry that I had stayed at the hotel.

RECIPES FROM THE SPANISH-SPEAKING WORLD

Gazpacho—*Spain*

Dip 4–6 medium tomatoes in boiling water 10 seconds. Rinse in cold water and peel off skins. Cut out cores, chop tomatoes coarsely to make 4 cups. Prepare 2 cups peeled, chopped cucumber, 1 cup cored, diced green pepper, 1/4 cup finely chopped sweet onion. Put 1/3 of tomatoes, onion, cucumber, and pepper in serving bowl. Mix remaining vegetables in blender with 2 cups tomato juice in two separate mixings. Add with one mixing:

1 slice white bread (crust removed)	1 1/2 tsp. salt
2 T. wine vinegar	1 tsp. Worcestershire sauce
2 T. olive oil	pepper
1 T. lemon juice	1 large clove garlic

Pour all the above over chopped vegetables in serving bowl and mix well. Cover and chill at least 5 hours. Serve with remaining vegetables and croutons.

Paella—*Spain*

2 1/2 c. long grain rice	1 lb. shrimp
5 c. chicken broth	1 lb. fish, clams, crab, or other seafood
pinch saffron	1 pkg frozen peas or 1 can peas
2 tsp. salt	2 pimientos, cut in strips
1 onion, chopped	1 chicken, cooked and deboned
1 large green pepper, cut in strips	1 pepperoni sausage, sliced

Cover bottom of Dutch oven with olive oil. Fry rice and onion slightly. Add liquid. Bring to a boil, add saffron and salt. Cover. Let simmer 15 minutes. Add meats and vegetables. Let simmer until all liquid is absorbed and everything is heated thoroughly. Season to taste.

Tacos—*Mexico*

Filling (for approximately 18 soft or crisp tortillas):

1 lb. lean ground beef
one large onion, chopped
1 can refried beans
1 can tomato sauce

1 tsp. chili powder or more to taste
1 tsp. salt
¼ tsp pepper

Brown meat and onions. Add remaining ingredients and let simmer 20 minutes. Serve on warm tortillas with "salsa picante" (taco sauce), grated cheese, diced tomatoes, and shredded lettuce.

Enchiladas—*Mexico*

30 (approximately) soft tortillas
1 lb. ground beef, browned and drained
5 medium onions (chop fine and pour boiling water over them through colander; cook in small amount fat)

6 hard boiled eggs, chopped
1½ lb. sharp cheese or Monterrey Jack cheese, grated
1 large (5¾ oz.) can black pitted olives, sliced

Prepare above ingredients ahead of time while sauce is cooking.

Sauce:
Cook ¼ cup corn meal with the following until thickened:

2 cloves garlic, crushed
2 T. salad oil
24 oz. (approximately) enchilada sauce

juice of olives
23 oz. (approximately) tomato sauce
1 can tomato soup

Dip tortillas in sauce—fill with 1 T. each ingredient. Fold over and secure with toothpick. Sprinkle grated cheese over all. Remaining sauce may be put on top, or served separately for those who desire more. Heat about 20 minutes at 350 degrees.

Arroz con pollo—*Cuba*

12 pieces chicken
⅓ c. olive oil
2 cloves garlic, crushed
1 green pepper, chopped
1 large onion, chopped
1 jar pimientos (small), chopped
1 can garbanzo beans, drained
1 can peas, drained

pinch saffron
2 tsp salt
¼ tsp. pepper
2 c. rice
8 oz. can tomato sauce
1½ c. chicken broth
1½ c. beer

Brown chicken in oil. Remove. Brown onion, garlic, and peppers. Return chicken to pot. Add remaining ingredients except rice, garbanzos, and peas. Simmer 30 min. Add rice and garbanzos. Cook until all liquid is absorbed. If more liquid is needed add beer or chicken broth. Add peas. Cook 5 minutes. Place on deep heated platter and decorate with pimiento strips, asparagus spears, and hard-boiled egg slices.

Frijoles puertorriqueños—*Puerto Rico*

Soak 4 cups pinto beans overnight. Cook beans about 2 hours in water (to cover) with salt (1 T.) and 3 cloves garlic until tender. Brown in skillet ½ to ¾ lb. minced bacon. Drain off drippings. Add a small piece of ham, minced. Then add 2 green peppers and 2 onions, minced. Cook until soft. Add 2 large cans tomatoes (28 oz. each) and 15 oz. can tomato sauce. Cook this sauce until it thickens. Add to beans; simmer 2 hours more.

Empandas de banana—*South America*

Dough:

1½ c. flour	1 tsp baking powder
1 egg	1 tsp. salt
4–5 T. milk	powdered sugar
2 T. olive oil	2 bananas, cut in thin slices

Mix first six ingredients until moist. Wrap in wax paper or plastic wrap and refrigerate at least 15 minutes. Dust rolling surface and rolling pin with flour. Break off a tablespoonful of dough. Roll the dough into a circular shape. Place 2–3 slices of banana on dough. Fold over and pinch shut with water on finger tips. (Dough may also be rolled out half at a time and cut with a cup to form circles.) Fry in oil on both sides until lightly browned. Remove and place on paper towels. Dust with powdered sugar.

Flan—*Spain*

Caramel sauce:

Melt ½ cup sugar in heavy pan over low heat, shaking pan as sugar melts. Heat until melted to a golden brown syrup. Pour into a 1-½ quart baking dish. Let cool.

Custard:

3 eggs	2 cups milk, scalded
⅓ cup sugar	½ tsp. vanilla
¼ tsp. salt	

Heat oven to 350 degrees. Beat eggs, sugar and salt slightly to mix. Stir in scalded milk. Add vanilla. Pour into baking dish. Set in pan and pour in hot water to depth of 1 inch. Bake 45–50 minutes or until knife inserted 1″ from edge comes out clean. Let cool. Chill in refrigerator. Unmold before serving.

VOCABULARY

■ SPANISH-ENGLISH

The numbers refer to the lessons in which words in the active vocabulary are first introduced.

A

a at, to, 2; **a bordo** on board; **a la vez** at the same time; **a menos que** unless, 14; **a tiempo** on time, 3; **a través de** throughout; **a veces** at times, 8

abierto open, 2

abogada *f* lawyer, 2

abogado *m* lawyer, 2

abrazar to hug, 4

abrigo *m* coat, 5

abril April, 6

abrir to open, 3

abrocharse to fasten, 13

abuela *f* grandmother, 2

abuelo *m* grandfather, 2

aburrido bored, 2

a.C. (antes de Cristo) B.C.

acabar de to have just, 9

accidente *m* accident, 12

aceite *m* oil, 12

aceituna *f* olive

acento *m* accent

acentuación *f* accents, stress

aceptar to accept

acera *f* sidewalk

acercarse to approach

acompañado accompanied

acostarse (ue) to go to bed, 10

acostumbrado usual, customary

actividad *f* activity

además de besides

adiós goodbye, 1

admirar to admire

¿adónde? to where?, 3

adornar to adorn, decorate

aduana *f* customs, 13

aéreo: correo aéreo *m* airmail, 9; **línea aérea** *f* airline, 13

aeropuerto *m* airport, 13

afeitarse to shave, 10

aficionado fond

agencia *f* agency, 13; **agencia de viajes** *f* travel agency, 13

agosto August, 6

agrícola agricultural

agua *f* water, 3

aguacate *m* avocado

ahora now, 3; **ahora mismo** right now, 12

aire *m* air; **aire acondicionado** *m* air conditioning, 14

al on, upon, 10; **al lado de** beside, 10

ala *f* wing

alcoba *f* bedroom, 8

alegrarse to be happy, glad, 13

alegre happy

alemán German, 2

alfabeto *m* alphabet

alfombra *f* carpet, rug, 8

algo something, 8

407

alguien someone, somebody, 8
alguno someone (pron.), some (adj.), 8
allí there, 2
almacén m department store, 6
almendra f almond
almohada f pillow, 14
almorzar (ue) to have lunch, 14
almuerzo m lunch, 3
alojamiento m lodging
alquilar to rent, 8
alto tall, high, 2; stop; **en voz alta** aloud, 1
altura f height, altitude
alumna f student, 1
alumno m student, 1
amante m, f lover
amar to love, 4
amarillo yellow, 5
ambiente m atmosphere
americano m American, 2
amiga f friend, 2
amigo m friend, 2
andar to walk, to go, run (machinery), 6
andino Andean
anillo m ring
animal m animal, 7
año m year, 6; **el año pasado** last year, 5; **el año que viene** next year, 8; **tener . . . años** to be . . . years old, 5
anoche last night, 5
antes de before, 10; **antes de que** before (conj.), 14
antitético antithetical
antiguo ancient
antropología f anthropology
anunciar to announce
anuncio m announcement
apagar to turn off, 8
aparecer to appear
aprender to learn, 3
apropiado appropriate
aproximarse to approach
aquel m that, 7; **aquellos** m those, 7

aquella f that, 7; **aquellas** f those, 7
aquí here, 2
araña f spider, 7
árbol m tree, 7
arena f sand, 7
arete m earring
armario m bureau, closet, 8
arqueología f archeology
arquitectónico architectural
arreglar to fix, 12
arrox m rice, 3
arte m art
artesanía f artifact
artículo m article
asado roasted; roast m
ascensor m elevator, 14
así so, 1; thus
asiento m seat, 13
aspecto m aspect
ataque m attack; **ataque cardíaco** m heart attack
atendido attended to, cared for
aún yet, still, even
aunque although
austero austere
auto m car, 2
autobús m bus, 6
autor m author
auxiliar de vuelo m steward, 13
avance m advance
avenida f avenue, 6
aventura f adventure
avión m airplane, 13
aviso m notice, notification
¡ay! oh!
ayer yesterday, 5
ayudar to help, 13
azafata f stewardess, 13
azúcar m sugar, 3
azul blue, 5

B

bahía f bay
bailar to dance, 4

baile m dance
bajar to go down, get off, 8
bajo short, low, 2; under; **planta baja** f main floor, 14
balcón m balcony ◆
banana f banana, 3
banco m bank, bench, 6
bañarse to bathe, take a bath, 10
bañera f bathtub, 8
baño m bath, bathroom, 8; **traje de baño** m bathing suit, 6
barato cheap, 5
barco m boat, ship, 7
barril m barrel
basar to base
básquetbol m basketball
bastante enough, quite, 11
basura f trash
bata f robe
batalla f battle
beber to drink, 3
bebida drink, beverage, 3
béisbol m baseball
belleza f beauty
bello beautiful
beneficiarse to benefit
besar to kiss, 4
biblioteca f library, 6
bicicleta bicycle, 6
bien well, fine, 1
bienvenido welcome, 14
bistec m steak, 3
blanco white, 5
bluejeans m jeans, 5
blusa f blouse, 5
boca f mouth, 4
boletero (a) m, f ticket agent, 9
boleto m ticket, 11; **boleto de ida y vuelta** round-trip ticket, 11
bolsa f purse, bag, 5
bomba f bomb
bonito pretty, 2
bordo: a bordo on board
bosque m forest, woods, 7
botas f boots, 5
botella f bottle

botones *m* bellboy, 14
brazo *m* arm, 4
brisa *f* breeze
buceo *m* diving (skin or scuba)
bueno good, 2
bulto *m* bulk, package
burro *m* donkey, 7
buscar to look for, 4
buzón *m* mailbox, 9

C

caballería *f* chivalry
caballo *m* horse, 7
cabeza *f* head, 4
cacahuete *m* peanut
cacao *m* cocoa
cada each
cadena *f* chain
café *m* coffee, 3
calabaza *f* squash
calcetines *m* socks, 5
calculadora *f* calculator, 9
calefacción *f* heating, 14
calendario *m* calendar
calidad *f* quality
caliente hot, 3
calor *m* heat, 4; **hacer calor** to
  be hot (weather), 6; **tener ca-**
  lor to be hot (persons), 4
callar(se) to be quiet, 12
calle *f* street, 6
calzoncillos *m* underpants
cama *f* bed, 8
camarera *f* waitress, 14
camarero *m* waiter, 14
camarón *m* shrimp, 3
cambiar to change, 9
cambio *m* change, 9
caminar to walk, 3
camino *m* road, 12
camión *m* truck, 12
camisa *f* shirt, 5
camiseta *f* undershirt
campamento *m* camping
campana *f* bell

campeón *m* champion
campesino(a) *m, f* peasant
campo *m* country, field, 2
cancelar to cancel
canción *f* song
cancha *f* court; **cancha de tenis**
  f tennis court
cansado tired, 2
cantar to sing, 4
capacidad *f* capacity
capilla *f* chapel
cara *f* face, 4
¡caramba! my goodness!, 12
caricatura *f* cartoon, 11
cariño *m* affection
carne *f* meat, 3
carnicería *f* butcher shop
caro expensive, 5
carta *f* letter, card, 9; menu
cartera *f* wallet, 5
carretera *f* highway, 12
carro *m* car, 2
casa *f* house, 2; **casa de correos**
  f post office, 9
casarse (con) to get married, 10
casi almost
caso *m* case; **en caso de que** in
  case, 13
castillo *m* castle
catedral *f* cathedral, 6
catorce fourteen, 1
caudillo *m* political boss
cautivar to captivate
cebolla *f* onion, 3
ceder to yield
cena *f* super, dinner, 3
cenar to dine, have dinner (supper), 14
centavo *m* cent
centro *m* center, downtown, 6;
  centro comercial *m* shopping
  center
cepillar(se) to brush, 10
cepillo *m* brush, 10; **cepillo de**
  dientes *m* toothbrush, 10
cerca de near, 10
cerdo *m* pig, 7

cero zero, 1
cerveza *f* beer, 3
cerrar (ie) to close, 4; **cerrado**
  closed, 2
certificado certified
cielo *m* sky, 7
cien(to) one hundred, 3
cigarro *m* cigar
cine *m* movie theater, movies, 6
cinco five, 1
cincuenta fifty, 3
cinturón *m* belt, seatbelt, 13
ciudad *f* city, 2
ciudadano *m* citizen
claro clear; **¡claro!** of course
clase *f* class, 1
clasificado classified
cláusula *f* clause
clima *m* climate
cobarde *m* coward
cobija *m* blanket, 14
cobrar to cash, 9
cocina *f* kitchen, 8
cocinar to cook, 4
coche *m* car, 2
collar *m* necklace
color *m* color
combinar to combine
comedor *m* dining room, 8
comer to eat, 3
comida *f* meal, food, 3
como as, 11; like, 10; **¿cómo?**
  how?, 1; **¡cómo no!** of course!
cómodo comfortable
compañero *m* companion; **com-**
  pañero(a) de cuarto *m, f* roommate, 10
compañía *f* company
comparar to compare
competencia *f* competition
complejo complex
complemento *m* object (of an
  action)
comprar to buy, 3
compras: ir de compras to go
  shopping, 5
comprendido included

comprometer(se) to get engaged, 10

comprometido engaged

compuesto composed

computadora f computer, 9

común common

con with, 10; con permiso excuse me, 1; con tal que provided that, 14

concierto m concert

condensado condensed

conducto: por conducto de through

conductor m driver

conjugación f conjugation

conjugar to conjugate

conmigo with me, 10

conocer to know, to be acquainted with (persons, places), 4

conocimiento m knowledge

conquistar to conquer

consejo m advice

conservar to conserve, to keep

consonante f consonant

constituir to constitute

construir to construct

contar (ue) to count

contemplar to contemplate

contemporáneo contemporary

contento happy, content, 2

contestar to answer, 9

contigo with you (fam.), 10

continuar to continue

contra against

contrario contrary, opposite

contribuir to contribute

conversar to converse

convertir (ie, i) to convert

corazón m heart

corbata f tie, 5

cordillera f mountain range

correo m mail, 9; correo aéreo m airmail, 9

correr to run, 4

corrida de toros f bullfight

cortar(se) to cut (oneself), 10

cortina f curtain, 8

corto short, 5

cosa f thing, 5

costa f coast

costar (ue) to cost, 5

costumbre f custom

crear to create

crecer to grow

crédito m credit; tarjeta de crédito f credit card, 14

creer to believe, 13

crema f cream, 3; crema de afeitar f shaving cream, 10

criada f maid, 14

criollo m creole

Cristo Christ

cruce m crossing

cruzar to cross, 12

cuaderno m notebook, 1

cuadra f block, 12

cualquier any

¿cuál? which (one)?, 3; ¿cuáles? which (ones)?, 3

cuando when, 3

¿cuándo? when?, 3

¿cuánto? how much?, 3; ¿cuántos? how many?, 3

cuarenta forty, 3

cuarto m room, 8; fourth, 14; quarter, 1

cuatro four, 1

cuatrocientos four hundred, 6

cubierto covered

cubrir to cover

cuchara f spoon, 8

cucharada f spoonful

cuchillo m knife, 8

cuenta f bill, 14; por cuenta de responsibility of

cuerpo m body, 4

cuidado m care; tener cuidado to be careful, 12

cuidar to take care of

culebra f snake, 7

cultura f culture

cumpleaños m birthday, 6

curso m course

curva f curve

CH

chaqueta f jacket, 5

champú m shampoo, 10

charlar to talk

cheque m check, 9; cheque de viajero f traveler's check, 9

chica f girl, 2

chicle m gum

chico m boy, 2

chimenea f chimney, fireplace

chino Chinese, 2

chuleta f: chuleta de cerdo f pork chop, 3

churro m Spanish-style donut

D

danza f dance

dar to give, 4; dar de comer to feed; darse prisa to hurry up, 12

d. C. (después de Cristo) A.D.

de of, from, about, 2; de nada you are welcome, 1

debajo (de) beneath, under, 10

deber to owe, must, should, ought, 4

débil weak, 2

debilitar to weaken

decadencia f decline

décimo tenth, 4

decir to say, tell, 4

declarar to declare

dedicar to dedicate

dedo m finger, 4

dejar to leave behind, allow, let, 11

delante (de) in front (of), ahead, 10

delgado slender, 2

delicioso delicious

demás rest, remainder

demasiado too, too much, 11

denso thick

dentro (de) inside, 10

dependienta *f* saleswoman, clerk

dependiente *m* salesman, clerk

deporte *m* sport

depositar to deposit, 9

derecha *f* right (direction), 12

derecho *m* law; right; **derecho** (adv.) straight ahead, 12

desarrollo *m* development

desayunar to have breakfast, 14

desayuno *m* breakfast, 3

descansar to rest, 4

descubrir to discover

descuento *m* discount

desde from

desear to desire, to wish, to want

desembarcar to disembark

deseo *m* desire

desierto *m* desert, 7

desigual unequal

despacio slowly, 12

despedirse (i, i) to say good-bye, 13

despertarse (ie) to wake up, 10

después (de) after, 10; **después de que** after, 14

destruir to destroy

desván *m* attic

determinado definite

detrás(de) behind, 10

día *m* day, 1; **buenos días** good morning, 1; **hoy día** nowadays; **todo el día** all day, 3; **todos los días** everyday, 3

diariamente daily

diario daily (adj.); newspaper (noun) *m*

dibujar to draw

dibujo *m* drawing

diciembre December, 6

dictador *m* dictator

dictadura *f* dictatorship

dicho said, 11

diente *m* tooth, 4

diez ten, 1

difícil difficult, 2

digestivo digestive

dinero *m* money, 6

Dios *m* God; **¡Dios mío!** My God!

diptongo *m* diphthong

dirección *f* address, direction, 9

directo direct

disco *m* phonograph record, 8

discutir to discuss

distinto different

divertirse (ie, i) to have a good time, 10

doblar to turn, 12

doble: cuarto doble *m* double room, 14

doce twelve, 1

documento *m* document, paper, 13

dólar *m* dollar

dolor *m* pain, ache, 4

dominar to dominate

domingo *m* Sunday, 1

don title of respect for men

¿dónde? where? 3; **¿de dónde?** from where? 3; **¿adónde?** to where? 3

doña title of respect for women

dormir (ue, u) to sleep, 4; **dormirse** to fall asleep, to go to sleep, 10

dormitorio *m* dormitory, 10

dos two, 1

doscientos two hundred, 6

ducha *f* shower, 8

dudar to doubt, 13

dulces *m* sweets, candy

durante during

durazno *m* peach, 3

E

e and (before *i, hi*)

echar to throw; **echar al correo** to mail, 9

edad *f* age

edificio *m* building, 6

ejemplo *m* example

ejercicio *m* exercise, 1

él *m* he (subject), 2; him (obj. of prep.), 10

el the, 1

elegir to elect, choose

ella *f* she (subject), 2; her (obj. of prep.), 10

ellas *f* they (subject), 2; them (obj. of prep.), 10

ellos *m* they (subject), 2; them (obj. of prep.), 10

embarazada pregnant

empezar (ie) to begin, 9

empleado *m* employee

en in, on, at, 10; **en caso de que** in case, 14; **en punto** sharp (time); **en resumen** in short, in summary; **en seguida** right away; **en vez de** instead of, 10

enamorado in love, 10

enamorar(se) to fall in love, 10

encantador enchanting

encanto *m* enchantment

encender (ie) to turn on (lights), 8

encima (de) on top of, 10

encinta pregnant

encontrar (ue) to find, 9

enchiladas *f* regional dish from Mexico

enero January, 6

enfermo sick, 2

enfrente de in front of, facing

enojarse to get angry, 10

enorme enormous

ensalada *f* salad, 3

enseñanza *f* learning

entender (ie) to understand, 4

entonces then

entrada *f* entrance

entrar (en) to enter, to go in, 6

entre between, among, 10

entusiasmo *m* enthusiasm

época *f* era

equipaje *m*   luggage, 11
equipo *m*   team, equipment
esa *f*   that, 7; **esas** *f*   those, 7
escalera *f*   stairs, 8
esconder   to hide
escondido   hidden
escribir   to write, 3; **escribir a máquina**   to type, 9
escrito   written, 11
escritorio *m*   desk, 1
escuchar   to listen (to), 4
escuela *f*   school, 2
escultura *f*   sculpture
ese *m*   that, 7; **esos**   those, 7
eso *neuter*   that, 7
espacioso   spacious
espalda *f*   back, 4
español   Spanish (adj.), 2; Spaniard (noun) *m*, 2
espectáculo *m*   spectacle
espejo *m*   mirror, 8
esperar   to wait, hope (for), 6
espíritu *m*   spirit
esposa *f*   wife, 2
esposo *m*   husband, 2
esquina *f*   corner, 12
esta *f*   this, 7; **estas** *f*   these, 7
estabilidad *f*   stability
establecer   to establish
estación *f*   station, 11; season, 6; **estación de ferrocarril** *f*   railroad station, 11; **estación de servicio** *f*   service station, 12
estacionarse   to park, 12
estado *m*   state; **estado civil**   marital status
estar   to be, 2; **estar enamorado de**   to be in love with, 10
estatua *f*   statue
este *m*   this, 7; **estos** *m*   these, 7
este *m*   east
estilo *m*   style
esto *neuter*   this, 7
estómago *m*   stomach, 4
estratégico   strategic
estrecho *m*   strait

estrella *f*   star, 7
estudiante *m, f*   student, 1
estudiar   to study, 3
estufa *f*   stove, 8
étnico   ethnic
evocar   to evoke
examen *m*   examination, test
existir   to exist
experiencia *f*   experience
explorador *m*   explorer
explorar   to explore
extender (ie)   to extend
extenso   extensive, vast

F

faceta *f*   facet
fácil   easy, 2
fácilmente   easily, 8
facturar   to check, 13
falda *f*   skirt, 5
faltar   to lack, to need, 9
fama *f*   fame
familia *f*   family, 2
famoso   famous
fascinar   to fascinate
favor: por favor   please, 1
febrero   February, 6
fecha *f*   date, 6
felicitaciones *f*   congratulations
feliz   merry, happy, 6
feo   ugly, 2
ferrocarril *m*   railroad, 11
fiel   faithful
fiesta *f*   party
fin *m*   end; **fin de semana** *m*   weekend 8; **por fin**   finally
firma *f*   signature, 9
firmar   to sign, 9
flaco   skinny, 2
flan *m*   custard
flauta *f*   flute
flor *f*   flower, 7
florido   flowery
fondo musical   background music
formalidad *f*   formality

formar   to form
formular   to formulate
fortaleza *f*   fortress
fracturar   to break
francés   French (adj.), 2; Frenchman *m*, 2
frase *f*   phrase
frecuente   frequent, 8
frecuentemente   frequently, 8
fregadero *m*   sink (kitchen), 8
fresa *f*   strawberry, 3
fresco   cool, fresh, 6; **hacer fresco**   to be cool (weather), 6
frescura *f*   freshness
frijol *m*   bean, 3
frío *m*   cold, 3; **hacer frío**   to be cold (weather), 6; **tener frío**   to be cold (person), 4
frito   fried
frívolo   frivolous
frontera *f*   border, 12
fruta *f*   fruit, 3
fuera (de)   outside, 10
fuerte   strong, 2
fumar   to smoke, 4
funcionar   to work (machinery), 12
fútbol *m*   football, soccer

G

gafas *f*   glasses, 5; **gafas de sol** *f*   sunglasses, 5
galleta *f*   cookie, 3
gallina *f*   chicken, 7
ganado *m*   cattle, livestock
ganar   to earn, win, 9
ganas: tener ganas de   to feel like, 4
garaje *m*   garage, 8
garantizado   guaranteed
garganta *f*   throat, 4
gasolina *f*   gasoline, 12
gastar   to spend (money), 9
gato *m*   cat, 7
gaucho *m*   Argentine cowboy

generación f generation
general general, 8
generalmente generally, 8
gente f people, 6
gerundio m gerund
gimnasia f gymnastics
glorieta f traffic circle, 12
gobierno m government
gordo fat, 2
gozar to enjoy
gracias thanks, 1
gracioso funny, entertaining
grado m degree
gran great
grande large, big, 2
grandeza f greatness
gratis free
gris grey, 5
grupo m group
guacamole m regional avocado salad from Mexico
guantes m gloves
guapo handsome, 2
guía m,f guide; **guía telefónica** f phone book, 11
guión story line
guisante m pea, 3
guitarra f guitar
gustar to like, to be pleasing, 9
gusto m pleasure, taste; **mucho gusto** pleased to meet you, 1

H
haber (auxiliary verb) to have
habitación f room, 14
habitante m inhabitant
habichuelas f green beans
hablar to speak, 3
hacer to do, make, 4; **hacer buen (mal) tiempo** to be good (bad) weather, 6; **hacer calor** to be hot, 6; **hacer campamento** to camp; **hacer fresco** to be cool, 6; **hacer frío** to be cold, 6; **hacer sol**

to be sunny, 6; **hacer viento** to be windy, 6
hacienda f farm, ranch, 7
hambre f hunger, 4; **tener hambre** to be hungry, 4
hasta until; **hasta luego** see you later, 1; **hasta mañana** see you tomorrow, 1; **hasta que** until (conj.), 14
hay there is, there are, 6
hecho done, 11
helado m ice cream, 3
herencia f heritage
hermana f sister, 2
hermano m brother, 2
hermoso beautiful, 2
hidalgo m nobleman
hielo m ice, 3
hierba f grass, 7
hija f daughter, 2
hijo m son, 2
hogar m home, 8
hola hello, hi, 1
hombre m man, 2; **hombre de negocios** m business man, 2
hombro m shoulder, 4
hora f hour, time, 1
horario m schedule, 11
hotel m hotel, 14
hoy today, 3; **hoy día** nowadays
huésped guest, 14
huevo m egg, 3

I
ibérico Iberian
ida y vuelta round trip, 11
identidad f identity
identificar to identify
iglesia f church, 6
igualar to equal
igualdad f equality
ilustre illustrious
imágen f image
imaginar to imagine
impaciente impatient, 11;

ponerse impaciente to become impatient, 11
impedir (i, i) impede, prohibit
imperio m empire
impermeable m raincoat, 5
importancia f importance
importante important, 13
imposible impossible, 13
impresionante impressive
impresionar to impress
improbable improbable, 13
increíble incredible
indeciso indecisive
indeterminado indefinite
indicar to indicate
indicativo indicative
indígena indigenous, Indian
indio m Indian
indirecto indirect
inestabilidad f instability
influencia f influence
influir to influence
información f information, 14
ingeniería f engineering
inglés English, 2
iniciar to initiate
inmenso immense
inodoro m toilet, 8
insecto m insect, 7
insistir to insist
instrucción direction, instruction
íntegro integral
inteligente intelligent, 2
interfón m intercom
interior: ropa interior f underclothing, 5
intrínseco intrinsic
invasor m invader
invierno m winter, 6
invitar to invite, 9
ir to go, 2; **irse** to go away, 10; **ir de compras** to go shopping, 5
irrespetuoso disrespectful
isla f island, 7
izquierda f left, 12

J

jabón *m* soap, 8
jamón *m* ham, 3
japonés Japanese, 2
jardín *m* garden, 8
jarra *f* pitcher
jefe *m* head, boss
joven young, 2
joyas *f* jewelry, 5
joyería *f* jewelry shop, 6
jueves *m* Thursday, 1
jugar (ue) to play (game), 4
jugo *m* juice, 3
julio July, 6
junio June, 6
junto together
juventud *f* youth

K

kilo *m* kilogram (2.20 lbs.)
kilómetro *m* kilometer (0.62 mile)

L

la *f* the, 1; you (sing), her, it (dir. obj.), 9
labio *m* lip, 4
lado *m* side, edge; **al lado de** beside, 10
ladrillo *m* brick
lago *m* lake, 7
lámpara *f* lamp, 8
langosta *f* lobster, 3
lápiz *m* pencil, 1
largo long, 5
las *f* the (pl.) 1; you (pl.), them (dir. obj.), 9
lástima *f* pity, shame, 13
lavabo *m* sink, 8
lavarse to wash oneself, 10
le to him, to her, to you (ind. obj.), 9
lección *f* lesson, 1
lectura *f* reading
leche *f* milk, 3
lechería *f* dairy
lechuga *f* lettuce, 3

leer to read, 4
legumbre *f* vegetable, 3
legendario legendary
lejos (de) far (from), 10
lengua *f* tongue, language, 4
lentamente slowly, 8
lento slow, 8
les to them, to you (ind. obj.), 9
levantarse to get up, 10
libertad *f* freedom, liberty
librería *f* bookstore, 6
libro *m* book, 1
líder *m* leader
ligero light
limitado por surrounded, bordered by
limón *m* lemon
limpiar to clean, 4
limpio clean, 5
lindo pretty
línea *f* line; **línea aérea** *f* airline, 13
lío: ¡qué lío! what a mess!, 12
litro *m* liter (0.26 gallons)
lo *m* you (sing.), him, it (dir. obj.), 9; **lo demás** the rest, remainder; **lo que** that which, what, 3
loco crazy
los *m* the (pl.), 2; you (pl.), them (dir. obj.), 9
lucha *f* fight, struggle
luego: hasta luego see you later, 1
lugar *m* place, 13
lujo *m* luxury
lujoso luxurious
luna *f* moon, 7; **luna de miel** honeymoon
lunes *m* Monday, 1
luz *f* light, 8

LL

llamada *f* call, 11, **llamada de cobro revertido** *f* collect, 11; **llamada de larga distancia** *f* long-distance, 11

llamar to call, knock, 4; **llamarse** to be called, named
llanta *f* tire, 12
llave *f* key, 14
llegada *f* arrival, 11
llegar to arrive, 3
llenar to fill, 12
llevar to carry, wear, take, 5
llover (ue) to rain; **llueve** it's raining, 6
lluvia *f* rain, 6

M

machismo *m* manliness
madera *f* wood
madre *f* mother, 2
magnífico magnificent, terrific
maíz *m* corn, 3
majestuoso majestic
mal bad, badly, 2
maleta *f* suitcase, 11; **hacer la maleta** to pack, 11
malo bad, 2
mandar to send, command, order, 9
mandato *m* command
manejar to drive, 4
manera *f* way
manifestar to manifest
maniquí *m* manequin
mano *f* hand, 4
manta *f* blanket, 14
mantener to maintain
mantequilla *f* butter, 3
manzana *f* apple, 3; block, 12
mañana *f* morning, 1; tomorrow (adv.) 3; **por la mañana** in the morning, 1
mapa *m* map
máquina *f* machine; **máquina de afeitar** *f* electric shaver, 10; **máquina de escribir** *f* typewriter, 9
mar *m* sea, 7
maravilla *f* marvel
maravilloso marvelous

marca *f* brand
marcar to dial, 11; to mark
mariachi *m* Mexican musician
mariscos *m* seafood, 3
marítimo maritime, marine
martes *m* Tuesday, 1
marzo March, 6
más more, 11; plus
mayo May, 6
mayor older, 11; major; **el mayor** the oldest, 11
mayoría *f* majority
me me, to me, 9; myself, 10
mediano medium
medianoche *f* midnight, 1
medias *f* stockings, 5
médica *f* doctor, 2
médico *m* doctor, 2
medio middle, half, 1; average
mediodía *m* noon, 1
mejor better, 11; **el mejor** the best, 11
mencionar to mention
menor younger, 11; **el menor** the youngest, 11
menos less, 11; minus; **a menos que** unless, 14; **por lo menos** at least
mentira *f* lie, 4
menú *m* menu
mercado *m* market, 3
mermelada *f* jam, preserves, 3
mes *m* month, 6
mesa *f* table, 1
meseta *f* plateau
mestizo of mixed Indian and Spanish ancestry
metro *m* metro, 6
mezcla *f* mixture
mezquita *f* mosque
mi my, 5
mí me (obj. of prep.), 10
miedo *m* fear, 4; **tener miedo** to be afraid, 4
miel *f* honey; **luna de miel** *f* honeymoon
miembro *m* member

mientras while
miércoles *m* Wednesday, 1
mil thousand, 6
milla *f* mile
millón *m* million, 6
mío mine, of mine, 5
mirar to look (at), 4
mismo same; **ahora mismo** right now, 12; **hoy mismo** this very day
misterioso mysterious
moda *f* fashion
moneda *f* coin, money, currency
monstruo *m* monster
montaña *f* mountain, 2
montañoso mountainous
morado purple, 5
moreno dark, brunette, 2
moro *m* Moor
morir (ue, u) to die, 6
mosaico *m* mosaic
mosca *f* fly, 7
mosquito *m* mosquito, 7
mostrar (ue) to show, 9
motocicleta *f* motorcycle, 6
mozo *m* young man
muchacha *f* girl, 2
muchacho *m* boy, 2
mucho much, a lot, 3; **muchos** many, 1
mudar(se) to move
muebles furniture, 8
muerte *f* death
muerto dead, 11
mujer *f* woman, 2; **mujer de negocios** *f* business woman, 2
mundo world, 13; **todo el mundo** *m* everybody
museo *m* museum, 6
muy very, 1

N

nada nothing, not anything, 8; **de nada** you are welcome, 1
nadar to swim, 4
nadie no one, nobody, 8

naranja *f* orange, 3
nariz *f* nose, 4
narrar to narrate
natación *f* swimming
natal native
navaja *f* razor, 10
Navidad *f* Christmas, 6
necesario necessary, 13
necesitar to need, 3
negar (ie) to deny, 13
negocios: hombre de negocios *m* business man, 2
negro black, 5
nevar (ie) to snow; **nieva** it's snowing, 6
ni . . . ni neither . . . nor, 8
nieta *f* granddaughter, 2
nieto *m* grandson, 2
nieve *f* snow, 6
niña *f* girl, 2
ninguno not one, none, (pron.), 8; not one, not any (adj.), 8
niño *m* boy, 2
noche *f* night, 1; **buenas noches** good evening, night, 1; **esta noche** tonight, 3; **por la noche** in the evening, 3
nombre *m* name
norte *m* north
nos us, to us, 9; ourselves, 10
nosotros we, 2; us (obj. of prep.) 10
notar to note, to notice
noticia *f* news, 11
novecientos nine hundred, 6
noveno ninth, 14
noventa ninety, 3
novia *f* girlfriend, sweetheart, 2
noviembre November, 6
novio *m* boyfriend, sweetheart, 2
nube *f* cloud, 7
nuestro our, 5
nueve nine, 1
nuevamente again
nuevo new, 2
número *m* number, 1
nunca never, 8

O

o or, 8
o . . . o either . . . or, 8
obra f work
observador m observer
obtener to obtain, get
occidente m west
océano m ocean, 7
ochenta eighty, 3
ocho eight, 1
ochocientos eight hundred, 6
octavo eighth, 14
octubre October, 6
ocupado busy, occupied, 11
ocupar to occupy
oeste m west
oficial official (adj. or m
  noun), 13
oficina f office
ofrecer to offer
oír to hear, 4
ojo m eye, 4
olvidar to forget
once eleven, 1
operador(a) m, f operator, 11
oportunidad f opportunity
oración f sentence, 1
oreja f ear, 4
organizar to organize
orgullo m pride
oriental eastern
orilla f edge, shore
os you, to you (fam. pl.), 9; yourselves, 10
otoño m autumn, 6
otro other, another, 5; **otra vez**
  again, 12
oveja sheep, 7

P

padre m father, 2
padres m parents, 2
padrino m godfather
paella f regional dish from Spain
pagar to pay (for), 9
país m country, 11

paisaje m landscape
pájaro m bird, 7
palabra f word, 1
palmera f palm tree
pampa f plain
pan m bread, 3
panadería f breadshop, bakery
pantalones m pants, 5
papel m paper, 1; **papel
  higiénico** toilet paper, 10
paquete m package, 9
para for, by, in order to, 10; **para
  que** so that, in order that, 14
parabrisas m windshield, 12
parada f stop (bus, train)
paraguas m umbrella, 5
paraíso m paradise
parar(se) to stop, 12
pardo brown, 5
parecer to seem, 9
pared f wall
pariente m relative, 2
parque m park, 6
parte f part; **por todas partes**
  everywhere
participar to participate
participio m participle
pasado m past
pasajero m passenger, 13
pasaporte m passport, 13
pasar to pass, spend (time), happen, 7
pasatiempo m pastime
pascuas Christmas, Easter, 6
pasear to walk, stroll
paseo m ride; **paseos a caballo**
  horseback rides
paso m step, pass
pasta: pasta de dientes toothpaste, 10
pastel m pastry, pie, 3
pastelería f bakery
pastilla f pill
patata f potato, 3
patria f fatherland
peatón m pedestrian

pecho m chest, breast, 4
pedir (i, i) to ask (for), 4
peinarse to comb (hair), 10
peine m comb, 10
película f film, 6
peligro m danger
peligroso dangerous
pelo m hair, 4
peluquería f hairdressers, beauty
  shop, 6
pensar (ie) to think, intend, 6
pensamiento m thought
peor worse, 11
pequeño small, little, 2
pera f pear, 3
perder (ie) to lose, 9
perdón pardon me, excuse me, 1
perfectamente perfectly, 8
perfecto perfect, 8
periódico m newspaper, 11
periodista m newspaper reporter
perla f pearl
permiso m pardon; **con permiso** excuse me, 1
permitir to allow, to let; **permítame presentar a . . .** allow
  me to introduce . . ., 1
pero but
perro m dog, 7
persona f person, 6
personaje m character
personal personal, 8
personalidad f personality
personalmente personally, 8
pescado m fish, 3
pescar to fish
peseta f monetary unit of Spain
peso m monetary unit of Mexico,
  Argentina, Colombia, Uruguay,
  and Philippines
pez m fish
picante spicy
pico m peak
pie m foot, 4
pierna f leg, 4
pieza f piece, article

pijama *m* pajama
piloto *m* pilot, 13
pimienta *f* pepper, 3
pino *m* pine
pintar to paint, 4
pintoresco picturesque
pintura *f* painting
piña *f* pineapple, 3
pirámide *f* pyramid
piscina *f* pool, 14
piso *m* floor, story, 8
pizarra *f* blackboard, 1
placer *m* pleasure
planta *f* plant; **planta baja** *f* main floor, 14
plata *f* silver
platillo *m* prepared dish
plato *m* plate, dish, 8
playa *f* beach, 2
plaza *f* square
pluma *f* pen, 1; feather
población *f* population
pobreza *f* poverty
pobre poor, 2
poco little (quantity), 3
poder (ue) to be able, can, 4; power *m*
policía *m* policeman, 12
pollo *m* chicken, 3
poner to put, place, 4; **ponerse** to put on, 10; **ponerse impaciente** to become impatient, 11
por for, by, through, along, around, down, by way of, because of, on account of, on behalf of, in exchange for, per, 10; **por conducto de** through; **por cuenta de** responsibility of; **por favor** please, 1; **por fin** finally; **por lo menos** at least; **por supuesto** of course; **¿por qué?** why, 3; **porque** because, 3
portero *m* doorman
posibilidad *f* possibility

posible possible, 8
posiblemente possibly, 8
postre *m* dessert, 3
practicar to practice
precio *m* price, 14
precolombino pre-Columbian
preferir (ie, i) to prefer, 4
pregunta *f* question, 1
preguntar to ask (question), 9
prenda *f* garment
preocuparse to worry, 10
preparar to prepare, 8
preparativo *m* preparation
presentar to present, introduce, 1
prestar to lend, 9
prima *f* cousin, 2
primavera *f* spring, 6
primero first, 11
primo *m* cousin, 2
privado private, 14
privilegio *m* privilege
probable probable, 8
probablemente probably, 8
problema *m* problem
producir to produce
profesional professional, 8
profesionalmente professionally, 8
profesor *m* professor, teacher, 1
profesora *f* professor, teacher, 1
profundo profound, deep
progresista progressive
progresivo progressive
pronombre *m* pronoun
pronto soon, quickly, right away, 12; **hasta pronto** see you soon
propietario *m* owner
propio own
propina *f* tip, 14
próspero prosperous, 6
protagonista *m* main character
próximo next
psicológico psychological
pueblo *m* village, town, 6

puente *m* bridge, 12
puerto *m* port
puerta *f* door, 1
pues well
puesta del sol *f* sunset
puesto put, placed, 11
pulsera *f* bracelet
punto *m* point; **en punto** sharp (time)

Q
que that, who, which, 3; than, 7
¡qué! what!, what a . . .!; **¡Qué barbaridad!** How awful!, 12
¿qué? what?, 3; **¿qué tal?** How are you?, 1
quedarse to stay, remain, 14
querer (ie) to wish, want, desire, love, 4
querido dear
queso *m* cheese, 3
¿quién(es)? who?, 3
quince fifteen, 1
quinientos five hundred, 6
quinto fifth, 14
quiosco *m* newsstand, 11
quitar to take away; **quitarse** to take off, 10

R
raíz *f* root, stem
rápidamente rapidly, 8
rápido rapid, fast, 8
rascacielos *m* skyscraper, 6
rato *m* a short time
raza *f* race
razón *f* reason; **tener razón** to be right, 5; **no tener razón** to be wrong, 5
rebasar to pass
rebelde *m* rebel (noun); rebellious (adj.)
recado *m* message, 14
recepción *f* front desk, 14
recepcionista *m, f* receptionist, desk clerk, 14

recibir   to receive, 9
recibo *m*   receipt, 14
reciente   recent, 8
recientemente   recently, 8
recoger   to pick up, 13
recomendar   to recommend
reconocer   to recognize
recordar (ue)   to remember, 6; re-mind
recto   straight ahead, 12
reflejar   to reflect
refrigerador *m*   refrigerator, 8
regalo *m*   gift, present, 5
régimen *m*   regime
registrado   registered
regular   regular, fair, 1
reloj *m*   clock, watch, 5
remoto   remote
renacimiento *m*   renaissance
repasar   to review
repaso *m*   review
repetir (i, i)   to repeat, 4
requisito *m*   requirement
reservación *f*   reservation, 13
resfriado *m*   cold, 4; **tener res-friado**   to have a cold
residencia *f*   residence; **residencia estudiantil**   dormitory, 10
respuesta *f*   reply, answer, 1
restaurante *m*   restaurant, 6
resumen *m*   summary, resume
retirar(se)   to withdraw
reunir   to gather, meet
revelar   to reveal
revisar   to check, 12
revista *f*   magazine, 11
rey *m*   king
rico   rich, 2; delicious
rincón   corner
río *m*   river, 7
riqueza *f*   wealth
ritmo *m*   rhythm
robo *m*   robbery
rojo   red, 5
romper   to break, tear, 11
ropa *f*   clothing, 5; **ropa interior**   underclothing, 5

rosado   rosé, pink, 5
roto   broken, torn, 11
rubio   blonde, 2
ruido *m*   noise
ruina *f*   ruin
ruso   Russian, 2
ruta *f*   route

S

sábado *m*   Saturday, 1
sábana *f*   sheet, 14
saber   to know (how to), 4
sabor *m*   flavor, taste
sacar   to take out, 9
sabroso   tasty
sal *f*   salt, 3
sala *f*   living room, 8; **sala de espera** *f*   waiting room, 13; **sala de reclamación de equipajes** *f*   baggage claim room, 13
salchicha *f*   sausage, 3
salida *f*   exit, departure, 11
salir (de)   to leave, go out of, 4
saludo *m*   greeting
sandía *f*   watermelon, 3
sarape *m*   blanket, shawl
se   himself, herself, yourself, themselves, yourselves, 10
secador *m*   dryer; **secador de pelo** *m*   hair dryer, 10
secar(se)   to dry, 10
seco   dry
secretaria *f*   secretary
secundaria   secondary (school)
sed *f*   thirst, 4; **tener sed**   to be thirsty, 4
seguir (i, i)   to follow, continue, 12
según   according to
segundo   second, 11
seguro   sure, certain, 13
seis   six, 1
seiscientos   six hundred, 6
sello *m*   stamp, 9
selva *f*   jungle, 7
semáforo *m*   traffic street light, 12
semana *f*   week, 1; **la semana pa-**

sada *f*   last week, 5; **la semana que viene** *f*   next week, 8; **el fin de semana** *m*   weekend, 8
sencillo   simple
sensibilidad *f*   sensitivity
sentarse (ie)   to sit down, 10
sentido *m*   feeling
sentir (ie, i)   to regret, feel sorry, 13
señor *m*   man, gentleman, sir, Mr., 1
señora *f*   ma'am, lady, Mrs., 1
señorita *f*   lady, Miss, 1
septiembre   September, 6
séptimo   seventh, 14
ser   to be, 2
serie *f*   series
serio   serious
servicio *m*   service, 14; restroom, 11
servilleta *f*   napkin, 8
servir (i, i)   to serve
sesenta   sixty, 3
setecientos   seven hundred, 6
setenta   seventy, 3
sexo *m*   sex
sexto   sixth, 14
si   if, 14
sí   yes, 1
siempre   always, 8
sierra *f*   mountain range
siete   seven, 1
siglo *m*   century
siguiente   following
silla *f*   chair, 1
sillón *m*   (easy) chair, 8
simpático   nice, 2
sin   without, 10; **sin embargo**   nevertheless
singularidad *f*   singularity, difference
síntesis *f*   synthesis
sistema *m*   system
sitio *m*   site
situado   situated
sobre *m*   envelope, 9; about; **sobre todo**   above all

sobrina *f* niece, 2
sobrino *m* nephew, 2
¡socorro! help!, 12
sofá *m* sofa, 8
sol *m* sun, 7; **hacer sol** to be sunny, 6
solamente only
solicitar to solicit, get, obtain
solidificar to solidify
solo alone
sólo only
sombrero *m* hat, 5
son *m* beat (music), sound
sonar (ue) to ring, sound
sonrisa *f* smile
sopa *f* soup, 3
sorprendido surprised
sostén *m* bra
sótano *m* basement, 8
su his, her, your, its, their, 5
subir (a) to climb, go up, get on, 8
sublevación *f* uprising
sucio dirty, 5
sudoeste *m* southwest
sueño *m* dream; **tener sueño** to be sleepy, 4
suerte *f* luck; **tener suerte** to be lucky
suéter *m* sweater, 5
sufrir to suffer
sujeto *m* subject
suplicar to beg, ask
supuesto: por supuesto of course
sur *m* south
surtido *m* assortment
sustantivo *m* noun
sustituir to substitute
suyo his, hers, its, theirs, yours, 5

T
tal such, like; **con tal que** provided that, 13; **¿qué tal?** how are you?, 1; **tal vez** perhaps
talla *f* size
también also, too, 8
tampoco neither, not either, 8

tan so, as, 11; **tan pronto como** as soon as, 14
tanque *m* tank, 12
tanto so much, as much, 11; **tantos** so many, as many, 11
taquilla *f* ticket window, 11
tarde *f* afternoon, 1; late, 3; **buenas tardes** good afternoon, 1; **más tarde** later, 3; **por la tarde** in the afternoon, 3
tarea *f* task, homework, assignment, 1
tarifa *f* price list, fare
tarjeta *f* card; **tarjeta de crédito** *f* credit card, 14; **tarjeta postal** *f* postcard, 9
taxi *m* taxi, 6
taza *f* cup, 8
té *m* tea, 3
te you, to you, 9; yourself, 10
teatro *m* theater, 6
telefonear to telephone, 11
teléfono *m* telephone, 9; **teléfono público** *m* public telephone, 11
temer to fear, 13
templado mild, temperate
templo *m* temple
temprano early, 3
tenedor *m* fork, 8
tener to have, 4; **tener . . . años** to be . . . years old, 4; **tener cuidado** to be careful, 12; **tener ganas de** to feel like, 4; **tener que** to have to, 4; **tener razón** to be right, 4; **tener resfriado** to have a cold; **tener sueño** to be sleepy, 4; **tener suerte** to be lucky
tercero third, 14
terminar to finish, 9
término *m* end
terraza *f* terrace
terrestre by land
tesoro *m* treasure
testigo *m* witness
ti you (obj. of prep.), 10

tía *f* aunt, 2
tiempo *m* time, 8; weather, 6; tense (verb); **a tiempo** on time, 3
tienda *f* store, shop, 6
tierra *f* land, earth, 7
tigre *m* tiger
tío *m* uncle, 2
tipo *m* type
típico typical
tiza *f* chalk, 1
toalla *f* towel, 8
tocadiscos *m* record player, 8
tocar to touch, to play (instrument), 4
tocino *m* bacon, 3
todavía yet, still
todo all, 3; **todo el día** all day, 3; **toda la noche** all night, 3; **todos los días** everyday, 3
tomar to take, drink, eat, 3
tomate *m* tomato, 3
tonto dumb, stupid, silly, 2
tope *m* speed bump
toro *m* bull; **corrida de toros** *f* bullfight
torta *f* cake, 3
tortilla *f* flat cornmeal pancake (Mexico); omelet (Spain)
trabajar to work, 3
traducir to translate, 4
traer to bring, 4
tráfico *m* traffic, 12
traje *m* suit, 5; **traje de baño** *m* bathing suit, 5
tranquilidad *f* tranquility
tránsito *m* traffic
tratar de to try to, 9
trece thirteen, 1
treinta thirty, 3
tren *m* train, 11; **tren expreso** *m* express train, 11
tres three, 1
trescientos three hundred, 6
trigo *m* wheat
triste sad, 2
tú you, 2

tu your, 5
tuyo yours, of yours, 5

U

último last, ultimate
un a, an, 1; **una** a, an, one, 1;
  uno one, 1
único unique, only
unido united
universidad f university, 2
urgente urgent
usar to use, 4
usted you, 2; **ustedes** you
  (pl.), 2
uva f grape, 3

V

vaca f cow, 7
valiente brave
valor m value
valer to be worth
valle m valley, 7
vaquero m cowboy
variado varied
variedad f variety
vario various
vasallo m vassal
vaso m glass, 8
vecino m neighbor
veinte twenty, 1
vela f candle, sail

vendedor(a) m, f vendor
vender to sell, 3
venir to come, 4
venta f sale
ventana f window, 1
ventanilla f cashier's window, 9
ver to see, 4; **a ver** let's see
verano m summer, 6
verdad f truth, 4; really
verde green, 5
vestíbulo m lobby, 14
vestido m dress, 5
vestirse (i, i) to dress, to get
  dressed, 10
vez f time, occasion; **a la vez** at
  the same time; **a veces** at
  times, sometimes, 8; **cada vez**
  each time; **en vez de** instead
  of, 10; **muchas veces** often, 7;
  otra vez again, 12; **tal vez**
  perhaps; **una vez** once, 7
vía f route, way
viajar to travel, 7
viaje m trip, 7; **hacer un viaje**
  to take a trip, 7
viajero m traveler, 9
vida f life
vidrio m glass
viejo old, 2
viento m wind, 6; **hacer**
  viento to be windy, 6

viernes m Friday, 1
vino m wine, 3
visitante m visitor, 5
visitar to visit, 6
vista f view
visto seen, 11
vivir to live, 3
vivo bright
vocabulario m vocabulary
vocal f vowel
volcán m volcano
volar (ue) to fly, 13
volver (ue) to return, 4
vosotros you (fam pl), 2
voz f voice; **en voz alta**
  aloud, 1
vuelo m flight, 13
vuelta: ida y vuelta round
  trip, 11
vuelto returned, 11
vuestro your, 5

Y

y and, 1; plus
ya already, 11; **ya que** since
yo I, 2

Z

zapato m shoe, 5

■ ENGLISH-SPANISH

A

a un, una, 1
able, to be poder (ue), 4
about de, 2; sobre
above encima de, 10
accent acento m
accept aceptar
accident accidente m, 12
accompanied acompañado
according to según

ache dolor m, 4
acquire adquirir
activity actividad f
A.D. d. C. (después de Cristo)
address dirección f, 9
admire admirar
adorn adornar
advance avance m
adventure aventura f
advice consejo m

affection cariño m
afraid, to be temer, 13; tener
  miedo, 4
after después de, 10; después de
  que, 14
afternoon tarde f, 1; **good after-**
  noon buenas tardes, 1; **in the**
  afternoon por la tarde, 3
again otra vez, 12
against contra

age   edad *f*

agency   agencia *f*

agricultural   agrícola

air   aire *m*; **air conditioning**   aire acondicionado *m*, 14

airline   línea aérea *f*, 13

airmail   correo aéreo *m*, 9

airplane   avión *m*, 13

airport   aeropuerto *m*, 13

all   todo(s), 3

allow   dejar, permitir, 1

almond   almendra *f*

almost   casi

alone   solo

along   por, 10

already   ya

aloud   alto; en voz alta, 1

alphabet   alfabeto *m*

also   también, 8

although   aunque

altitude   altura *f*

always   siempre, 8

American   americano, 2

among   entre, 10

ancient   antiguo

and   y, 1; e (before *i*, *hi*)

Andean   andino

angry, to get   enojarse, 10

animal   animal *m*, 7

announce   anunciar

announcement   anuncio *m*

another   otro, 5

answer   contestar, 9; respuesta *f*, 1

anthropology   antropología *f*

antithetical   antitético

any   cualquier

appear   aparecer

apple   manzana *f*,3

approach   aproximarse, acercarse

appropriate   apropiado

April   abril, 4

arm   brazo *m*, 4

around   por, 10

archeology   arqueología *f*

architectural   arquitectónico

arrival   llegada *f*, 11

arrive   llegar, 3

art   arte *m*

article   artículo *m*

artifact   artesanía *f*

as   como, tan, 11; **as if**   como si; **as much (many) as**   tanto(s) como, 11; **as soon as**   tan pronto como, 14

ask   preguntar, 9; **to ask for**   pedir (i, i), 4

aspect   aspecto *m*

assignment   tarea *f*,1

assortment   surtido *m*

at   a, en 2; **at least**   por lo menos; **at the same time**   a la vez

atmosphere   ambiente *m*

attic   desván *m*

August   agosto, 6

aunt   tía *f*, 2

austere   austero

author   autor, *m*

autumn   otoño *m*, 6

avenue   avenida *f*, 6

average   medio

avocado   aguacate *m*

awful: how awful   ¡qué barbaridad!, 12

B

back   espalda *f*, 4

background   fondo *m*

bacon   tocino *m*, 3

bad   malo, 2

badly   mal, 2

bag   bolsa *f*, 5

baggage   equipaje, 13; **baggage claim room**   sala de reclamación de equipaje *f*,   13

bakery   panadería *f*; pastelería *f*

balcony   balcón *m*

banana   banana *f*, 3

bank   banco *m*, 6

barrel   barril *m*

baseball   béisbol *m*

based   basado

basement   sótano *m*, 8

basketball   básquetbol *m*

bath   baño *m*, 8; **to take a bath**   bañarse, 10

bathing suit   traje de baño *m*, 5

bathroom   baño *m*, 8

bathtub   bañera *f*, 8

battle   batalla *f*

bay   bahía *f*

B.C.   a. C. (antes de Cristo)

be   ser, estar, 2

beach   playa *f*, 2

bean   frijol *m*, 3

beat   (music) son *m*

beautiful   hermoso, 2; bello

beauty   belleza *f*; **beauty shop**   peluquería *f*, 6

because   porque, 3; **because of**   por, 10; debido a

bed   cama *f*, 8

bedroom   alcoba *f*, 8

beer   cerveza *f*, 3

before   antes de, 10; antes de que, 14

beg   suplicar

begin   empezar (ie), 9

behind   detrás de, 10

believe   creer, 13

bell   campana *f*

bellboy   botones *m*, 14

bench   banco *m*, 4

beneath   debajo de, 10

benefit   beneficiar

beside   al lado de, 10

besides   además de

best   el mejor, 11

better   mejor, 11

between   entre, 10

beverage   bebida *f*, 3

bicycle   bicicleta *f*, 6

big   grande, 2

bill   cuenta *f*, 14

bird   pájaro *m*, 7

birthday   cumpleaños *m*, 6

black negro, 5
blackboard pizarra f, 1
blanket cobija f, 14
block cuadra f, 12; manzana f, 12
blonde rubio, 2
blouse blusa f, 5
blue azul, 5
boat barco m, 7
body cuerpo m, 4
bomb bomba f
book libro m, 1
bookstore librería f, 6
boots botas f, 5
border frontera f, 12
bored aburrido, 2
boss jefe m
bottle botella f
boy chico m, 2; muchacho m, 2
boyfriend novio m, 2
bra sostén m
bracelet pulsera f
brand marca f, 10
brave valiente
bread pan m, 3; **bread shop** panadería f
break romper, 11; fracturar
breakfast desayuno m, 3; **to have breakfast** desayunar, 14
breast pecho m, 4
breeze brisa f
brick ladrillo m
bridge puente m, 12
bright vivo
bring traer, 4
broken roto, 11
brother hermano m, 2
brown pardo, 5
brunette moreno, 2
brush cepillar(se), 10; cepillo m, 10
building edificio m, 6
bulk bulto m
bull toro m; **bullfight** corrida de toros f
bureau armario m, 8

bus autobús m, 6
business man hombre de negocios m, 2
business woman mujer de negocios f, 2
busy ocupado
but pero
butter mantequilla f, 3
buy comprar, 3
by por, 10; para, 10; **by way of** por

C

cake torta f, 3
call llamar, 4; llamada f, 11; **collect call** llamada de cobro revertido f, 11; **long-distance call** llamada de larga distancia f, 11
calculator calculadora f, 9
calendar calendario m
camp hacer campamento
camping campamento m
cancel cancelar
candle vela f
capacity capacidad f
captivate cautivar
car coche m, 2; carro m, 2; auto m, 2
card tarjeta f; **credit card** tarjeta de crédito f, 14
care cuidado m; **to be careful** tener cuidado, 12
carpet alfrombra f, 8
carry llevar, 5
cartoon caricatura f, 11
case caso m; **in case** en caso de que, 14
cash cobrar, 9
castle castillo m
cat gato m, 7
cathedral catedral f, 6
cattle ganado m
cent centavo m
center centro m, 6
century siglo m

certain seguro, 13
certified certificado
chain cadena f
chair silla f, 1; **easy chair** sillón m, 8
chalk tiza f, 1
champion campeón m
change cambiar, 9; cambio m, 9
chapel capilla f
character personaje m
charge card tarejeta de crédito f
cheap barato, 5
check facturar, 13; revisar, 12; cheque m, 9; **traveler's check** cheque de viajero m, 9
cheese queso m, 3
chest pecho m, 4
chicken pollo m, 3; gallina f, 7
child niño m, 2; niña f, 2
chimney chimenea f
Chinese chino, 2
chivalry caballería f
choose elegir
Christ Cristo
Christmas Navidad f, 6; Pascuas f, 6
church iglesia f, 6
city ciudad f, 2
cigar cigarro m
class clase f, 1
classified clasificado
clause cláusula f
clean limpiar, 4; limpio, 5
clear claro
clerk dependiente(a) m, f
climate clima m
climb subir, 8
clock reloj m, 5
close cerrar (ie), 4; **closed** cerrado, 4
closet armario m, 8
clothing ropa f, 5
cloud nube f, 7
coast costa f
coat abrigo m, 5
cocoa cacao m

coffee café *m*, 3
coin moneda *f*
cold frío, 3; resfriado *m*, 4; **to be cold** (*persons*) tener frío, 4; **to be cold** (*weather*) hacer frío, 6; **to have a cold** tener un resfriado
color color *m*
comb peinarse, 10; peine *m*, 10
combine combinar
come venir, 4
comfortable cómodo
command mandar, 9; mandato *m*
common común
communicate comunicar
companion compañero *m*
company compañía *f*
compare comparar
competition competencia *f*
complex complejo
composed compuesto
computer computadora *f*, 9
concert concierto *m*
condensed condensado
congratulations felicitaciones *f*
conjugate conjugar
conjugation conjugación *f*
conquer conquistar
conserve conservar
consonant consonante *f*
construct construir
contemplate contemplar
contemporary contemporáneo
continue seguir (i, i), 12; continuar
contribute contribuir
converse conversar
convert convertir (ie, i)
cook cocinar, 4
cookie galleta *f*, 3
cool fresco, 6; **to be cool** (*weather*) hacer fresco, 6
corn maíz *m*, 3
corner equina *f*, 12; rincón
cost costar (ue), 5

count contar (ue)
country campo *m*, 2; país *m*, 11
course curso *m*; **of course** claro, 12
cousin primo *m*, 2; prima *f*, 2
covered cubierto
cover cubrir
cow vaca *f*, 7
coward cobarde *m*
cowboy gaucho *m* (*Argentina*); vaquero *m*
crazy loco
cream crema *f*, 3
create crear
credit card tarjeta de crédito *f*, 14
creole criollo *m*
cross cruzar, 12
crossing (*railroad*) cruce *m*
culture cultura *f*
cup taza *f*, 8
curtain cortina *f*, 8
curve curva *f*
custard flan *m*
custom costumbre *f*
customs aduana *f*, 13
cut cortar(se), 10

D

daily diario, diariamente
dance bailar, 4; baile *m*, danza *f*
danger peligro *m*
dangerous peligroso
date fecha *f*, 6; cita *f*
daughter hija *f*, 2
day día *m*, 1; **all day** todo el día, 3; **everyday** todos los días, 3
dead muerto, 11
dear querido
death muerte *f*
December diciembre, 6
declare declarar
decline decadencia *f*
dedicate dedicar
deep profundo

definite determinado
degree grado *m*
delicious rico, delicioso; riquísimo
deny negar (ie), 13
department store almacén *m*, 6
departure salida *f*, 11
deposit depositar, 9
desert desierto *m*, 7
desire querer (ie), 4; desear; deseo *m*
desk escritorio *m*, 1; **desk clerk** recepcionista *m, f*, 14; **front desk** recepción *f*, 14
dessert postre *m*, 3
destroy destruir
development desarrollo *m*
dial marcar, 11
dictator dictador *m*
dictatorship dictadura *f*
die morir (ue, u), 7
died muerto, 11
different distinto
difficult difícil, 2
digestive digestivo
dine cenar, 14
dining room comedor *m*, 8
dinner, to have cenar; cena *f*, 14
diphthong diptongo *m*
direction instrucción *f*
dirty sucio, 5
discount descuento *m*
discover descubrir
discuss discutir
disembark desembarcar
dish platillo *m*; plato *m*, 8
disrespectful irrespetuoso
diving (*skin or scuba*) buceo *m*
do hacer, 4
doctor médico *m*, 2; médica *f*, 2
document documento *m*, 13
dog perro *m*, 7
dollar dólar *m*
dominate dominar
done hecho, 11
donkey burro *m*, 7

door puerta *f*, 1
doorman portero *m*, 14
dormitory dormitorio *m*; residencia estudiantil *f*, 10
double doble, 14
doubt dudar, 13
down por, 10
downtown centro *m*, 6
draw dibujar
drawing dibujo *m*
dream sueño *m*
dress vestido *m*, 5; **to get dressed** vestirse (i, i), 10
drink beber, 3; tomar, 3; bebida *f*, 3
drive manejar, 4
driver operador *m*, conductor *m*
dry secar(se), 10; seco
dumb tonto, 2
during durante

E

each cada
ear oreja *f*, 4
early temprano, 3
earn ganar, 9
earring arete *m*
earth tierra *f*, 7
easily fácilmente, 8
Easter Pascuas *f*
eastern oriental
easy fácil, 2
east este *m*
eat comer, 3; tomar, 3
edge orilla *f*
egg huevo *m*, 3
eight ocho, 1
eighteen diez y ocho, 1
eighth octavo, 14
eighty ochenta, 3
either . . . or o . . . o, 8
electric eléctrico; **electric shaver** máquina de afeitar *f*, 10
elevator ascensor *m*, 14
eleven once, 1
empire imperio *m*
employee empleado *m*

enchanting encantador
enchantment encanto
end fin *m*; término *m*
engaged comprometido, 10
engineering ingeniería *f*
English inglés, 2
enjoy gozar
enormous enorme
enough bastante, 11
enter entrar (en), 6
enthusiasm entusiasmo *m*
entrance entrada *f*
envelope sobre *m*, 9
environment ambiente *m*
equal igualar
equality igualdad *f*
equipment equipo *m*
era época *f*
establish establecer
ethnic étnico
even aún
evening noche *f*, 13; **good evening** buenas noches, 1
every todo(s), 3; **everyday** todos los días, 3; **everywhere** por todas partes
evoke evocar
exam examen *m*
example ejemplo *m*
exchange cambio, 9
excuse me perdón, 1; con permiso, 1
exercise ejercicio *m*, 1
exist existir
exit salida *f*, 11
expensive caro, 5
experience experiencia *f*
explore explorar
explorer explorador *m*
extend extender (ie)
extensive extenso
eye ojo *m*, 4

F

face cara *f*, 4
facet faceta *f*

fair (*neither good nor bad*) regular, 1
faithful fiel
fall: to fall in love enamorar(se), 10
fame fama *f*
family familia *f*, 2
famous famoso
far lejos, 10
fare tarifa *f*
farm hacienda *f*, 7
fascinate fascinar
fashion moda *f*
fast rápido, 8
fasten abrocharse, 13
fat gordo, 2
father padre *m*, 2
fatherland patria *f*
fear miedo *m*, 4; temer, 13; tener miedo, 4
feather pluma *f*
February febrero, 6
feed dar de comer
feel sentir (ie, i), 13; **to feel like** tener ganas de, 4
feeling sentido *m*
field campo *m*, 2
fifteen quince, 1
fifth quinto, 14
fifty cincuenta, 3
fight lucha *f*
fill llenar, 12
film película *f*, 6
finally por fin
find encontrar (ue), 9
fine bien, 2
finger dedo *m*, 4
finish terminar, 9
first primero, 11
fish pescar; pescado *m*, 3; pez *m*
five cinco, 1
fix arreglar
flavor sabor *m*
flight vuelo *m*, 13
floor piso *m*, 8; **main floor** planta baja *f*, 14
florid florido

flower   flor *f*, 7
flute   flauta *f*
fly   volar (ue), 13; mosca *f*, 7
follow   seguir (i, i), 12
following   siguiente
fond   aficionado
food   comida *f*, 3
foot   pie *m*, 4
football   fútbol *m*
for   por, 10; para, 10
forest   bosque *m*, 7
forget   olvidar
fork   tenedor *m*, 8
form   formar
formality   formalidad *f*
formulate   formular
fortress   fortaleza *f*
forty   cuarenta, 3
four   cuatro, 1
fourteen   catorce, 1
fourth   cuarto, 14
free   gratis
freedom   libertad *f*
French   francés, 2
frequent   frecuente, 8
frequently   frecuentemente, 8
fresh   fresco, 4; frescura *f*
Friday   viernes *m*, 1
fried   frito
friend   amigo(a) *m, f*, 2; compañero(a) *m, f*
frivolous   frívolo
from   de, 2; desde
fruit   fruta *f*, 3
funny   gracioso
furniture   muebles *m*, 8

G

garage   garaje *m*, 8
garden   jardín *m*, 8
garment   prenda *f*
gasoline   gasolina *f*,12
general   general, 8
generally   generalmente, 9
generation   generación *f*
German   alemán, 2
gerund   gerundio *m*

get (*receive*)   obtener; recibir, 9; **get dressed**   vestirse, 10; **get angry**   enojarse, 10; **get engaged**   comprometerse, 10; **get married**   casarse, 10; **get** (*obtain*)   obtener, solicitar; **get off**   bajar, 8; **get on**   subir, 8; **get up**   levantarse, 10
gift   regalo *m*, 5
girl   chica *f*, 2; muchacha *f*
girlfriend   novia *f*, 2
give   dar, 4
glad, to be   alegrarse, 13
glass (*drinking*)   vaso *m*, 8; vidrio *m*
glasses   gafas *f*,5
gloves   guantes *m*
go   ir, 2; **to go away**   irse, 10; **to go shopping**   ir de compras, 5; **to go up**   subir, 8; **to go down**   bajar, 8; **to go out**   salir, 4; **to go to bed**   acostarse (ue), 10; **to go to sleep**   dormirse, 10
God   Dios
godfather   padrino *m*
good   bueno, 2; **my goodness**   caramba, 12
goodbye   adiós, 1; **to say goodbye**   despedirse, 13
government   gobierno *m*
granddaughter   nieta *f*, 2
grandfather   abuelo *m*, 2
grandmother   abuela *f*,2
grandson   nieto *m*, 2
grape   uva *f*, 3
grass   hierba *f*, 7
great   grande, 2; gran
greatness   grandeza *f*
green   verde, 5; **green beans**   habichuelas *f*, 3
greeting   saludo
grey   gris, 5
group   grupo *m*
grow   crecer
guaranteed   garantizado
guest   huésped *m*, 14
guide   guía *m, f*

guitar   guitarra *f*
gum   chicle *m*
gymnastics   gimnasia *f*

H

hair   pelo *m*, 4
hairdresser's   peluquería *f*, 6
hairdryer   secador de pelo *m*, 10
half   medio, 1
ham   jamón *m*, 3
hand   mano *f*, 4
handsome   guapo, 2
happen   pasar, 7
happy   contento, 2; alegre; **to be happy**   alegrarse, 13
hard   difícil, 2
hat   sombrero *m*, 5
have   tener, 4; haber, 11; **to have a good time**   divertirse (ie, i), 10; **to have just**   acabar de, 9; **to have to**   tener que, 4
he   él, 2
head   cabeza *f*, 4
hear   oír, 4
heart   corazón *m*; **heart attack**   ataque cardíaco *m*
heat   calor *m*
heating   calefacción *f*, 14
height   altura *f*
hello   hola, 1
help   ayudar, 13
hen   gallina *f*, 7
her   su (poss.), 5; ella (obj. of prep.), 10; la (dir. obj.), 9; le (ind. obj.), 9
here   aquí, 2
heritage   herencia *f*
hers   suyo (de ella), 5
herself   se, 10
hi!   ¡hola!, 1
hidden   escondido
hide   esconder
high   alto, 2; **high school**   escuela secundaria *f*
highway   carretera *f*, 12
him   lo (dir. obj.), 9; él (obj. of prep.), 10; le (ind. obj.), 9

himself se, 10
his su, 5; suyo (de él), 5
home hogar *m*, 8
honey miel *f*; **honeymoon** luna
  de miel *f*
hope esperar, 13
horse caballo *m*, 7
hot caliente, 3; **to be hot** (*per-*
  sons) tener calor, 4; **to be hot**
  (*weather*) hacer calor, 6
hotel hotel *m*, 14
hour hora *f*, 4
house casa *f*, 2
how ¿cómo?, 1; **how are you?**
  ¿qué tal?, 1; ¿cómo está?, 1
how many ¿cuántos?, 3
how much ¿cuánto?, 3
hundred cien, 3
hug abrazar, 4
hunger hambre *m*, 4; **to be hun-**
  gry tener hambre, 4
hurry darse prisa, 12
husband esposo *m*, 2

I
I yo, 2
Iberian ibérico
ice hielo *m*, 3
ice cream helado *m*, 3
identify identificar
identity identidad *f*
if si, 14
illustrious ilustre
image imagen *f*
imagine imaginar
immense immenso
impatient impaciente; **to be-**
  come impatient ponerse impaciente, 11
impede impedir (i, i)
importance importancia *f*
important importante, 13
impossible imposible, 13
impress impresionar
impressive impresionante
improbable improbable, 13

in en, 10; **in case** en caso de
  que, 14; **in exchange for** por,
  10; **in front of** delante de, 10;
  enfrente de, 10; **in order that**
  para que, 14; **in order to**
  para, 10
included comprendido
incredible increíble
indecisive indeciso
indefinite indefinido
Indian indio, indígena
indicate indicar
indicative indicativo
indigenous indígena
influence influencia *f*; influir
information información *f*, 14
inhabitant habitante *m*
initiate iniciar
insect insecto *m*, 7
inside dentro de, 10
insist insistir
instability inestabilidad *f*
instead of en vez de, 10
integral íntegro
intelligent inteligente, 2
intend pensar, 6
intercom interfón *m*
intrinsic intrínseco
introduce presentar, 1
invader invasor *m*
invite invitar 9
island isla *f*, 7

J
jacket chaqueta *f*, 5
jam mermelada *f*, 3
January enero, 6
Japanese japonés, 2
jeans bluejeans *m*, 5
jewelry joyas *f*, 5; **jewelry**
  shop joyería *f*, 6
juice jugo *m*, 3
July julio, 6
June junio, 6
jungle selva *f*, 7

K
keep conservar
key llave *f*, 14
kilogram kilo *m*, kilogramo *m*
  (2.20 lbs.)
kilometer kilómetro *m* (0.62
  mile)
king rey *m*
kiss besar, 4
kitchen cocina *f*, 8
knife cuchillo *m*, 8
knock llamar
know (*facts, skills*) saber, 4; (*per*
  sons, places) conocer, 4
knowledge conocimiento *m*

L
lack faltar, 9
lady señora *f*, 1; señorita *f*, 1
lake lago *m*, 7
lamp lámpara *f*, 8
land tierra *f*, 7; terrestre (adj.)
landscape paisaje *m*
language lengua *f*
large grande, 2
last último; **last week** la semana pasada, 5
last night anoche, 5
late tarde, 3; **later** más tarde, 3
law derecho *m*
lawyer abogado *m*, 2; abogada
  f, 2
leader líder *m*
learn aprender, 3
learning enseñanza *f*
leave salir, 4; dejar (*leave be-*
  hind), 11
left izquierda, 12
leg pierna *f*, 4
legendary legendario
lend prestar, 9
less menos, 11
lesson lección *f*, 1
let dejar, 11
letter carta *f*, 9
lettuce lechuga *f*, 3

library biblioteca *f*, 6
lie mentira *f*, 4
life vida *f*
light luz *f*, 8; ligero
like gustar, 9; querer (ie), 5; como, 10
line línea *f*, 11
lip labio *m*, 4
listen escuchar, 4
liter litro *m* (0.26 gallons)
little pequeño (*size*), 2; poco (*quantity*), 3
live vivir, 3
living room sala *f*, 8
lobby vestíbulo *m*, 14
lobster langosta *f*, 3
lodging alojamiento *m*
long largo, 5
look at mirar, 4
look for buscar, 4
lose perder (ie), 9
love amar, 4; querer, 4; **to be in love with** estar enamorado de, 10
lover amante *m, f*
low bajo, 2
luck suerte *f*; **to be lucky** tener suerte
luggage equipaje *m*, 11
lunch almuerzo *m*, 3; **to have lunch** almorzar (ue), 14
luxurious lujoso
luxury lujo *m*

M

ma'am señora, 1
made hecho, 11
magazine revista *f*, 11
majestic majestuoso
magnificent magnífico
maid criada *f*, 14
mail correo *m*, 9; echar al correo, 9
mailbox buzón *m*, 9
maintain mantener

major mayor
majority mayoría *f*
make hacer, 4
man hombre *m*, 2
manifest manifestar (ie)
mannequin maniquí *m*
many muchos, 1; **so many** tantos, 11
map mapa *m*
March marzo, 6
market mercado *m*, 3
marry casarse (con), 10
marvel maravilla *f*
marvelous maravilloso
May mayo, 6
me mí (obj. of prep.), 10; me (dir. obj. or ind. obj.), 9
meal comida *f*, 3
meat carne *f*, 3
medium mediano
meet reunir; conocer, 4
mention mencionar
menu menú *m*; carta *f*
merry feliz, 6
mess lío *m*, 12
message recado *m*, 14
metro metro *m*, 6
middle medio
midnight medianoche *f*, 1
mild templado (*climate*)
mile milla *f*
milk leche *f*, 3
million millón *m*, 6
mine mío, 5
minus menos
mirror espejo *m*, 8
miss señorita *f*,1
mixture mezcla *f*
Monday lunes *m*, 1
money dinero *m*, 6; moneda *f*
monster monstruo *m*
month mes *m*, 6
moon luna *f*, 7
Moor moro *m*
more más, 11
morning mañana *f*, 3; **good**

morning buenos días, 1; **in the morning** por la mañana, 3
mosaic mosaico *m*
mosque mezquita *f*
mosquito mosquito *m*, 7
mother madre *f*, 2
motorcycle motocicleta *f*, 6
mountain montaña *f*, 2; **mountain range** sierra *f*, cordillera *f*
mountainous montañoso
mouth boca *f*, 4
movies cine *m*, 6
movie theater cine *m*, 6
Mr. señor, 1
Mrs. señora, 1
much mucho, 3; **so much** tanto, 11
museum museo *m*, 6
must deber, 4
my mi, 5
myself me, 10
mysterious misterioso

N

name nombre *m*
napkin servilleta *f*, 8
narrate narrar
native natal
near cerca de, 10
necessary necesario, 13
need necesitar, 3; faltar, 9
neighbor vecino *m*
neither tampoco, 8
neither . . . nor ni . . . ni, 8
necklace collar
nephew sobrino, 2
never nunca, 8
nevertheless sin embargo
new nuevo, 2
news noticia *f*, 11
newspaper periódico *m*, 11
newsstand quiosco *m*, 11
next proximo; **next week** la semana que viene, 8; **next year** el año que viene, 8
nice simpático, 2

niece sobrina *f*, 2
night noche *f*, 3; **all night** toda la noche, 3; **in the evening** por la noche, 3
nine nueve, 1
nineteen diez y nueve, 1
ninety noventa, 3
ninth noveno, 14
nobleman hidalgo *m*
nobody nadie, 8
noise ruido *m*
none ninguno, 8
noon mediodía *m*, 1
no one nadie, 8; ninguno, 8
north norte *m*
nose nariz *f*, 4
note notar
notebook cuaderno *m*, 1
nothing nada, 8
notice notar
notification aviso *m*
noun sustantivo *m*
November noviembre, 6
now ahora, 3
nowadays hoy día
number número *m*

O
object complemento *m*
observer observador *m*
obtain obtener
occupied ocupado
occupy ocupar
ocean océano *m*, 7
October octubre, 6
of de, 2; **of course** claro, por supuesto, ¿cómo no?
offer ofrecer
office oficina *f*
official oficial (noun and adj.), 13
often muchas veces, 7
oh! ¡ay!
oil aceite *m*, 12
old viejo, 2
older mayor, 11

oldest el mayor, 11
olive aceituna *f*
on en, 10; **on top of** encima de, 10
once una vez, 7
one uno, 1
onion cebolla *f*, 3
only único, sólo, solamente
open abierto, 2, abrir, 3
operator operador (a) *m*, *f*, 11
opportunity oportunidad *f*
opposite contrario
or o, 8; **either . . . or** o . . . o, 8
orange naranja *f*, 3
organize organizar
other otro, 5
otherwise de lo contrario
ought deber, 4
our nuestro, 5; **ours** nuestro, 5
ourselves nos, 10
outside fuera de, 10
overcoat abrigo *m*, 5
owe deber, 4
own propio
owner propietario *m*

P
pack hacer la maleta, 11
package paquete *m*, 9; bulto *m*
pain dolor *m*, 4
paint pintar, 4
painting pintura *f*
pajamas pijamas *f*
palm tree palmera *f*
pants pantalones *m*, 5
paper papel *m*, 1
pardon me perdón, 1; con permiso, 1
parents padres *m*,2
park parque *m*, 6; estacionarse, 12
part parte *f*
participle participio *m*
participate participar
party fiesta *f*
pass rebasar; pasar, 7; paso *m*

passenger pasajero *m*, 13
passport pasaporte *m*, 13
pastime pasatiempo *m*
past pasado *m*
pastry pastel *m*, 3
pay (for) pagar, 9
peach durazno *m*, 3
peak pico
peanut cacahuete *m*
pear pera *f*, 3
pearl perla *f*
peas guisantes *m*, 3
peasant campesino *m*
pedestrian peatón *m*
pen pluma *f*, 1
pencil lápiz , 1
people gente *f*, 6; personas *f*, 6
pepper pimienta *f*, 3
per por, 10
perfect perfecto, 8
perfectly perfectamente, 8
perhaps tal vez
person persona *f*, 6
personal personal, 8
personality personalidad *f*
personally personalmente, 8
phrase frase *f*
pick up recoger, 13
picturesque pintoresco
pie pastel *m*, 3
piece pieza *f*
pig cerdo *m*, 7
pill pastilla *f*
pillow almohada *f*, 14
pilot piloto *m*, 13
pine pino *m*
pineapple piña *f*, 3
pink rosado, 5
pitcher jarra *f*
pity lástima *f*, 13
place poner, 4; lugar *m*, 13; sitio *m*
placed puesto, 11
plain pampa *f*
plant planta *f*
plate plato *m*, 8

plateau   meseta f
play (*game*)   jugar (ue), 4; (*instrument*)   tocar, 4
please   por favor, 1
pleasure   placer m, gusto m
plus   más
point   punto m
policeman   policía m, f, 12
pool   piscina f, 14
poor   pobre, 2
population   población f
pork: pork chop   chuleta de cerdo f, 3
port   puerto m
possibility   posibilidad f
possible   posible, 8
possibly   posiblemente, 8
postcard   tarjeta postal f, 9
post office   casa de correos f, 9
potato   patata f, 3
poverty   pobreza f
power   poder m
practice   practicar
pre-Columbian   precolombino
prefer   preferir (ie, i), 4
pregnant   embarazada, encinta
prepare   preparar, 8
present   presentar, 1
preserves   mermelada f, 3
pretty   bonito, 2; lindo
price   precio m, 14
pride   orgullo m
private   privado, 14
privilege   privilegio m
probable   probable, 8
probably   probablemente, 8
problem   problema m
produce   producir
professional   profesional, 8
professionally   profesionalmente, 8
professor   profesor m, 1; profesora f, 2
profound   profundo
progressive   progresivo, progresista

pronoun   pronombre m
prosperous   próspero
provided that   con tal que, 14
psychological   psicológico
purple   morado, 5
purse   bolsa f, 5
put   poner, 4; **to put on** ponerse, 10
pyramid   pirámide f

Q

quality   calidad f
quarter   cuarto, 1
question   pregunta f, 1
quickly   pronto
quiet: to be quiet   callarse, 12
quite   bastante

R

race   raza f
railroad   ferrocarril m, 11
rain   lluvia f, 6; llover (ue); **it's raining**   llueve, 6
raincoat   impermeable m, 5
ranch   hacienda f, 7
rapid   rápido, 8
rapidly   rápidamente, 8
razor   navaja f
read   leer, 4
reading   lectura f
really   verdad f
reason   razón f
rebellious   rebelde m
receipt   recibo m, 14
receive   recibir, 9
recent   reciente, 8
recently   recientemente, 8
recognize   reconocer
recommend   recomendar
record (*phonograph*)   disco m, 8
record player   tocadiscos m, 8
red   rojo, 5
reflect   reflejar
refrigerator   refrigerador m, 8
regime   régimen m

registered   registrado
regret   sentir (ie, i), 13
relative   pariente m, f, 2
remain   quedarse, 14
remainder   demás
remember   recordar (ue), 6
remote   remoto
rent   alquilar, 8
renaissance   renacimiento m
repeat   repetir (i, i), 4
reply   respuesta, 1
reporter (*newspaper*)   periodista m
requirement   requisito m
reservation   reservación f, 13
rest   descansar, 4
restaurant   restaurante m, 6
restroom   servicio m, 11
return   volver (ue), 4
returned   vuelto, 11
reveal   revelar
review   repaso m; repasar
rhythm   ritmo m
rice   arroz m, 3
rich   rico, 2
ride   paseo m
right (*direction*)   derecha f, 12; (*legal*)   derecho m; **to be right**   tener razón, 4; **right away**   pronto, 12; **right now**   ahora mismo, 12
ring   sonar (ue); anillo m
rise   levantarse, 10
river   río m, 7
road   camino m, 12
roast   asado m; **roasted**   asado
robe   bata f
room   cuarto m, 8; habitación f, 14
roommate   compañero(a) de cuarto m, f, 10
root   raíz f
rosé   rosado
route   ruta f, vía f
rug   alfombra f, 8
ruin   ruina f

run correr, 4; (*machinery*) andar, 6; (*machinery*) funcionar, 12
Russian ruso, 2

S

sad triste, 2
said dicho, 11
sail vela *f*
salad ensalada *f*, 3
sale venta *f*
salesman dependiente *m*
saleswoman dependienta *f*
salt sal *f*, 3
same igual
sand arena *f*, 7
Saturday sábado, 1
sausage salchicha *f*, 3
say decir, 4
schedule horario *m*, 11
school escuela *f*, 2
sculpture escultura *f*
sea mar *m*, 7
seafood marisco *m*, 3
season estación *f*, 6
seat asiento *m*, 13
seatbelt cinturón *m*, 13
second segundo, 11
secondary (*school*) secundaria
secretary secretaria *f*
see ver, 4; **let's see** a ver; **see you later** hasta luego, 1; **see you tomorrow** hasta mañana, 1
seem parecer, 9
seen visto, 11
sell vender, 3
send mandar, 9
sensitivity sensibilidad *f*
sentence oración *f*, 1
September septiembre, 6
series serie *f*
serious serio
serve servir (i, i)
service servicio *m*, 14
service station estación de servicio *f*, 12

seven siete, 1
seventeen diez y siete, 1
seventh séptimo, 14
seventy setenta, 3
sex sexo *m*
shame lástima *f*, 13
shampoo champú *m*, 10
sharp (*time*) en punto
shave afeitarse, 10
shaving cream crema de afeitar *f*, 10
she ella, 2
sheep oveja *f*, 7
sheet sábana *f*, 14
shirt camisa *f*, 5
shoe zapato *m*, 5
shopping, to go ir de compras, 5; **shopping center** centro comercial *m*
short (*height*) bajo, 2; (*length*) corto, 5; **in short** en resumen
should deber, 4
shoulder hombro *m*, 4
show mostrar (ue), 9
shower ducha *f*, 8
shrimp camarón *m*, 3
sick enfermo, 2
side lado *m*
sidewalk acera *f*
sign firmar, 9
signature firma *f*, 9
silly tonto, 2
silver plata *f*
since ya que
sing cantar, 4
singularity singularidad *f*
sink lavabo *m*, 8; fregadero *m*, 8
sir señor *m*, 1
sister hermana *f*, 2
sit down sentarse (ie), 10
site sitio *m*
situated situado
six seis, 1
sixteen diez y seis, 1
sixth sexto, 14
sixty sesenta, 3

size talla *f*
skinny flaco, 2
skirt falda *f*, 5
sky cielo *m*, 7
skyscraper rascacielos *m*, 6
sleep dormir (ue, u), 4; **to go to sleep** dormirse, 10; sueño *m*, 4; **to be sleepy** tener sueño, 4
slender delgado, 2
slow lento, 8
slowly lentamente, 8; despacio, 12
small pequeño, 2
smile sonrisa *f*
smoke fumar, 4
snake culebra *f*, 7
snow navar (ie); nieve *f*, 6; **it's snowing** nieva, 6
so así, 1; **so that** para que, 14
soap jabón *m*, 8
socks calcetines *m*, 5
sofa sofá *m*, 7
solicit solicitar
solidify solidificar
some alguno, 8
someone alguien, 8
something algo, 8
sometimes a veces, 8
son hijo *m*, 2
song canción *f*
soon pronto
sorry, to be sentir (ie, i), 13
sound sonar (ue); son *m*
soup sopa *f*, 3
south sur *m*
southwest sudoeste *m*
spacious espacioso
Spaniard español *m*, 2
Spanish español, 2
speak hablar, 3
spectacle espectáculo *m*
speed bump tope *m*
spend (*money*) gastar, 9; (*time*) pasar, 7
spicy picante
spider araña *f*, 7

spirit espíritu *m*
spoon cuchara *f*, 8
spoonful cucharada *f*
sport deporte *m*
spring primavera *f*, 6
square plaza *f*
squash calabaza *f*
stability estabilidad *f*
stairs escalera *f*, 8
stamp sello *m*, 9
star estrella *f*, 7
state estado *m*
station estacion *f*, 11; **railroad station** estación de ferrocarril *f*, 11
statue estatua *f*
stay quedarse, 14
steak bistec *m*, 3
step paso *m*
steward auxiliar de vuelo *m*, 13
stewardess azafata *f*, 13
still todavía
stockings medias *f*, 5
stomach estómago *m*, 4
stop alto; parar, 12
store tienda *f*, 6
stove estufa *f*, 8
straight ahead recto, 12; derecho, 12
strait estrecho *m*
strategic estratégico
strawberry fresa *f*, 3
street calle *f*, 6
strong fuerte, 2
student estudiante *m, f*, 1; alumno *m*, alumna *f*, 1
study estudiar, 3; estudio *m*
style estilo *m*
subject sujeto *m*
substitute sustituir
such así
suffer sufrir
sugar azúcar *m*, 3
suit traje *m*, 5
suitcase maleta *f*, 11
summary resumen *m*

summer verano *m*, 6
sun sol *m*, 6; **to be sunny** hacer sol, 6
Sunday domingo *m*, 1
sunglasses gafas de sol *f*, 5
sunset puesta del sol *f*
supper cena *f*, 3
sure seguro, 13
surprised sorprendido
surrounded limitado por
sweater suéter *m*, 5
sweets dulces *m*
swim nadar, 4
swimming natación *f*
synthesis síntesis *f*
system sistema *m*

T

table mesa *f*, 1
take llevar (*carry*), 5; tomar, 3; **to take away** quitar; **to take a bath** bañarse, 10; **to take off** quitarse, 10; **to take out** sacar, 9; **to take care of** cuidar
talk charlar, hablar, 3
tall alto, 2
tank tanque *m*, 12
taste gusto *m*; sabor *m*
tasty sabroso
taxi taxi *m*, 6
tea té *m*, 3
teacher profesor *m*, profesora *f*, 1
team equipo *m*
telephone teléfono *m*, 11; telefonear, 11; **telephone book** guía telefónica *f*, 11; **public telephone** teléfono público *m*, 11
tell decir, 4
teller cajero(a) *m, f*, 9
temperate templado
temple templo *m*
ten diez, 1
tennis tenis *m*; **tennis court** cancha de tenis *f*

tense (*verb*) tiempo *m*
tenth décimo, 14
terrific magnífico
than que, 11
thanks gracias, 1
that ese *m*, 7; esa *f*, 7; eso (*neuter*), 7; aquel *m*, 7; aquella *f*, 7; que, 3; **that which** lo que, 3
the el, la, los, las, 1
theater teatro *m*, 6
their su(s), 5
theirs suyo, 5
them las, los (dir. obj.), 9; les (ind. obj.), 9; ellos, ellas (obj. of prep.), 10
themselves se, 10
then entonces
there allí, 2
there is (are) hay, 6
these estos *m*, 7; estas *f*, 7
they ellos *m*, 2; ellas *f*, 2
thick denso
thing cosa, 5
think pensar (ie), 6; creer, 13
third tercero, 14
thirst sed *f*, 5; **to be thirsty** tener sed, 4
thirteen trece, 1
thirty treinta, 3
this este *m*, 7; esta *f*, 7; esto (*neuter*), 7
those esos *m*, 7; esas *f*, 7; aquellos *m*, 7; aquellas *f*, 7
thousand mil, 6
three tres, 1
throat garganta *f*, 4
through por, 10
throughout através de
throw echar, 9
Thursday jueves *m*, 1
ticket boleto *m*, 11; **round-trip ticket** boleto de ida y vuelta, 11; **ticket window** taquilla *f*, 11
tie corbata *f*, 5
tiger tigre *m*

time hora *f*, 1; tiempo *m*, 7; vez *f*; **each time** cada vez; **on time** a tiempo, 3; **short time** rato *m*

tip propina *f*, 14

tire llanta *f*, 12

tired cansado, 2

to a, 2

today hoy, 3

together juntos

toilet inodoro *m*, 8; **toilet paper** papel higiénico *m*, 10

told dicho, 11

tomato tomate *m*, 3

tomorrow mañana, 3

tongue lengua *f*, 4

tonight esta noche, 3

too también, 8; demasiado, 11; **too much** demasiado, 11

tooth diente *m*, 4

toothbrush cepillo de dientes *m*, 10

toothpaste pasta de dientes *f*, 10

torn roto, 10

touch tocar, 4

toward para, 11

towel toalla *f*, 8

town pueblo *m*, 6

traffic tránsito *m*, tráfico, 12; **traffic circle** glorieta *f*, 12; **traffic light** semáforo *m*, 12

train tren *m*, 11

translate traducir, 4

tranquility tranquilidad *f*

trash basura *f*

travel viajar, 7; **travel agency** agencia de viajes *f*, 13; **traveler's check** cheque de viajero *m*, 9

traveler viajero *m*, 9

treasure tesoro *m*

tree árbol *m*, 7

trip viaje *m*, 7; **to take a trip** hacer un viaje, 7

truck camión *m*, 12

truth verdad *f*, 4

try to tratar de, 9

Tuesday martes *m*, 1

turn doblar, 12; **turn off** apagar, 8; **turn on** encender (ie), 8

twelve doce, 1

twenty veinte, 1

two dos, 1

type tipo *m*; escribir a máquina, 9

typewriter máquina de escribir *f*, 9

typical típico

U

ugly feo, 2

umbrella paraguas *m*, 5

uncle tío *m*, 2

under debajo de, 10; bajo

underpants calzoncillos *m*

undershirt camiseta *f*

understand entender (ie), 4

underwear ropa interior *f*, 5

unequal desigual

unique único

united unido

university universidad *f*, 2

unless a menos que, 14

until hasta, 14; hasta que, 14; **until later (see you later)** hasta luego, 1

upon al, 10

uprising sublevación *f*

urgent urgente

us nos (dir. obj. or ind. obj.), 9, nosotros (obj. of prep.), 10

use usar, 4

usual acostumbrado

V

valley valle *m*, 7

value valor *m*

varied variado

variety variedad *f*

various vario

vassal vasallo *m*

vast extenso

vegetable legumbre *f*, 3

vendor vendedor(a) *m*, *f*

very muy, 1

view vista *f*

village pueblo *m*, 6

visit visitar, 6

visitor visitante *m*, *f*

vocabulary vocabulario *m*

voice voz *f*

volcano volcán *m*

vowel vocal *f*

W

wait esperar, 6

waiting room sala de espera *f*, 13

waiter camarero *m*, 14

waitress camarera *f*, 14

wake up despertarse (ie), 10

walk caminar, 3; andar, 6; pasear

wall pared *f*

wallet cartera *f*, 5

want querer (ie), 4; desear

wash lavarse, 10; lavar, 8

watch reloj *m*, 5; (*look at*) mirar, 4

water el agua *f*, 3

watermelon sandía *f*, 3

way manera *f*

we nosotros(as), 2

weak débil, 2

weaken debilitar

wealth riqueza *f*

wear llevar, 5

weather tiempo *m*, 6

Wednesday miércoles *m*, 1

week semana *f*, 1; **weekend** fin de semana *m*, 8; **last week** la semana pasada, 5; **next week** la semana que viene, 8

welcome bienvenido, 14; **you are welcome** de nada, 1;

well bien, 1; pues

west oeste *m*, occidente *m*

what ¿qué?, 3; **what a . . .** ¡qué . . .!, lo que, 3

wheat trigo *m*

when   cuando, 3; ¿cuándo?, 3
where   ¿dónde?, 3; **to where**
   ¿adónde?, 3; **from where**   ¿de
   dónde?, 3
which   ¿cuál(es)?, 3; que, 3
while   mientras
white   blanco, 5
who   ¿quién(es)?, 3; que, 3
whom   ¿a quién(es)?, 3
why   ¿por qué?, 3
wife   esposa f, 2
win   ganar, 9
wind   viento m, 6; **to be windy**
   hacer viento, 6
window   ventana f, 1; **cashier's**
   window   ventanilla f, 9
windshield   parabrisas m, 12
wine   vino m, 3
wing   ala f
winter   invierno m, 6
wish   querer (ie), 4; desear
with   con, 10; **with me**   conmigo, 10; **with you**   contigo, 10
withdraw   retirarse

without   sin, 10
witness   testigo m
woman   mujer f, 2
wood   madera f
woods   bosque m, 7
word   palabra f, 1
work   trabajar, 3; (*machinery*) andar, 6; (*machinery*) funcionar,
   12; obra f
world   mundo m, 13
worry   preocuparse, 10
worse   peor, 11
worst   el peor, 11
worth   valer
write   escribir, 3
written   escrito, 11
wrong, to be   no tener razón, 4

Y

year   año m, 4; **last year** el año
   pasado m, 5; **next year**   el año
   que viene m, 8; **to be . . . years**
   old   tener . . . años, 4
yellow   amarillo, 5

yes   sí, 1
yesterday   ayer, 5
yet   todavía, aún
yield   ceder
you   tú (fam.), 2; usted (formal),
   2; vosotros (fam. pl.), 2; ustedes
   (formal pl.), 2; ti (obj. of prep.),
   10; te (dir. obj.), 9; lo, la, los, las
   (dir. obj.), 9; le, les (indir. obj.),
   9; os (fam. pl.), 9
young   joven, 2
younger   menor, 11
youngest   el menor, 11
youth   juventud f
your   tu (fam.), 5; su (formal), 5;
   vuestro (fam. pl.), 5
yours   tuyo (fam.), 5; suyo (formal), 5; vuestro (fam. pl.), 5
yourself   te (fam.), 9; se (formal), 10
yourselves   se, 10

Z

zero   cero, 1

PHOTO CREDITS

Chapter 8

Page 189: Stuart Cohen. Page 191: Sarah Putnam/The Picture Cube. Page 194: Paul Almasy. Page 195: Peter Menzel. Page 199: David Kupferschmid. Page 201: Beryl Goldberg.

Chapter 9

Page 216: Peter Menzel. Page 128: Peter Menzel. Page 220: Carl Frank/Photo Researchers. Page 223: Gervas Blakely.

Chapter 10

Page 245: Peter Menzel. Page 247: Abbas/Magnum. Page 251: Rebbot/Sygma. Page 253: Euguene Gordon/Photo Researchers. Page 254: Fritz Henee/Photo Researchers.

Chapter 11

Page 271: Beryl Goldberg. Page 275: Bernard Pierre Wolff/Photo Researchers. Page 280: George Holton/Photo Researchers. Page 281: Stuart Cohen. Page 283: Davis Pratt/Photo Researchers.

Chapter 12

Page 302: Peter Menzel. Page 305: Peter Menzel. Page 306: Peter Menzel. page 311: Georg Gerster/Photo Researchers.

Chapter 13

Page 328: Stuart Cohen. Page 333: Owen Franken. Page 334: Owen Franken. Page 338: Fritz Henee/Photo Researchers. Page 354: Stuart Cohen. Page 357: Peter Menzel. Page 364: Tom Carter/Jeroboam.

Color Insert

C-1   George Holton/Photo Researchers.
C-2   Ronny Jaques/Photo Researchers.
C-3   Porter Field-Chickering/Photo Researchers.
C-4   Susan McCartney/Photo Researchers.
C-5   Ronny Jaques/Photo Researchers.
C-6   Ned Haines/Photo Researchers.
C-6A   Lucy Perron/Photo Researchers.
C-7   Stuart Cohen.
C-8   Peter Menzel.
C-9   Vautier-Decool.
C-10   Christian Delbert/The Picture Cube.
C-11   D. Donne Bryant.
C-12   Chuck O'Rear/West Light.
C-12A   Peter Menzel.

INDEX

INDEX